THE
GLUTEN-FREE
BREAD
MACHINE
COOKBOOK

175

Recipes
for Splendid Breads
and Delicious Dishes to
Make with Them

Jane Bonacci & Shannon Kinsella

HARVARD
COMMON
PRESS

Quarto is the authority on a wide range of topics.

Quarto educates, entertains and enriches the lives of our readers—enthusiasts and lovers of hands-on living.

www.QuartoKnows.com

First published in the United States of America in 2017 by
The Harvard Common Press, an imprint of
Quarto Publishing Group USA Inc.
100 Cummings Center
Suite 406-L
Beverly, Massachusetts 01915-6101
Telephone: (978) 282-9590
Fax: (978) 283-2742
QuartoKnows.com
Visit our blogs at QuartoKnows.com

21 20 19 18 17   1 2 3 4 5

ISBN: 978-1-55832-796-2

Library of Congress Cataloging-in-Publication Data

Bonacci, Jane, author. | Kinsella, Shannon, author.
The gluten-free bread machine cookbook : 175 recipes for splendid breads and delicious dishes to make with them / Jane Bonacci and Shannon Kinsella.

ISBN 9781558327962 (paperback)
1. Gluten-free diet--Recipes. 2. Cooking (Bread) 3. Automatic
   bread machines.
RM237.86 .B66 2017
641.5/639311--dc23
2016031329

Design and Page Layout: Megan Jones Design
Cover Image: Glenn Scott Photography

Printed in China

We have written this book as food professionals, sharing with you the way we live our lives and the food we make for our families. We are not medical professionals. Both of us have multiple food sensitivities in our homes that required us to create gluten-free households. Any suggestions we make about gluten-free eating are based on our own personal experience and are not intended as medical directives. If you need more information about celiac disease or non-celiac gluten sensitivity, please consult your doctor or other health-care provider.

This book does not provide medical advice. Its content and suggestions do not substitute for consultation with a physician. Medical and nutritional science changes rapidly, individuals have different sensitivity levels, and information contained in this book might not be current when read. Neither the publisher nor the authors are liable for any loss, injury, or damage arising from information in this book, including loss or injury arising from typographical or mechanical errors.

To my husband James for his never-ending love, patience, and support. To Mimi, who first taught me to love baking and knowing when to carefully measure ingredients and when I can just add a pinch here and there. To my angel parents, brother, grandparents, and friends—I miss you all.

—JANE BONACCI

This book is dedicated to my daughters, Riley and Olivia, who amaze and inspire me every day. I am blessed by their unconditional love and sense of adventure in a very challenging food world.

—SHANNON KINSELLA

Contents

RECIPES

Preface

BY SHANNON KINSELLA

While I am not diagnosed with celiac disease, I have experienced autoimmune issues from a very young age. Before it was fashionable to be gluten free and long before I trained to become a chef, I was following a gluten-free diet. Twenty-five years ago, store-bought options were very few and far between, as were offerings at bakeries. Restaurants didn't understand the complexity of what it meant to be gluten free or how to make proper substitutions. Often it seemed as if my only option was to stop eating bread.

I have baked and cooked all of my life, long before I pursued my dream of going to culinary school. I started baking as a teenager, making the standard chocolate chip cookies, snickerdoodles, and my grandmother's molasses cookies. Next up, quick breads. In these pages, you will see quite a few of my family favorites adapted to be gluten free.

One of my daughters follows a nut-free diet, while the other follows a yeast-free diet—and both must avoid gluten and dairy. Trying to create great-tasting recipes with so many dietary restrictions has been a welcome challenge, but a challenge nonetheless. My daughter recently asked me, "How come these recipes are all coming out so well now? In the beginning, they were terrible." She was right. It has been a steep learning curve, but I hope the results will have even those without dietary challenges cooking from this book. These safe-to-eat old favorites, as well as a host of new flavors, will be enjoyed in my house for years to come—and I hope in yours, too.

Preface

BY JANE BONACCI

When I was little, I would wake up every morning to the aroma of buttered toast and coffee, my mother's favorite way to start the day. As I grew up, my own mornings usually began with buttered toast or a bagel with cream cheese. Then I was diagnosed with gluten intolerance, and with one directive from my doctor, my morning routine was gone and I gave up gluten for good.

I had to learn how to bake all over again. It was like going from graduate school back to kindergarten. The learning curve was very challenging. I had to find out what ingredients I would need to make up for the gluten that I could no longer consume. Flours, starches, emulsifiers, hydrocolloids . . . the list seemed endless and impossible to decipher. But within a month I was having moderate success. Over the past few years, I have become a confident baker again, making beautiful desserts that everyone loves, whether they need to avoid gluten or not.

Making gluten-free bread remained a challenge. After a string of failures, it was easy to see why so many people end up throwing in the towel and settle for store-bought gluten-free breads, spending a fortune for a tiny loaf that often is not much better than cardboard. Without gluten to provide structure, you are left with a pile of batterlike dough and no idea what went wrong. So, when Shannon and I began work on this book, we started from scratch, reading everything we could find about gluten-free baking. Why were breads so difficult? What could we do to have them turn out consistently delicious, with the right texture and structure?

We tried a slew of different ingredient combinations before finding the right formula for our flour blends. We played with all kinds of flours to discover how their flavors blended together to provide variety and interest. Then we got to work on creating recipes that would be easy for you to replicate in your own home using a bread machine.

From classic sandwich breads and family favorites to new and exciting combinations, this book is a collection of recipes we hope you love as much as we do. We are delighted to have the heavenly aroma of baking breads wafting through the house again—and know you will, too. Thank you for joining us on this journey.

Introduction

MAKING GREAT GLUTEN-FREE BREADS

GOING GLUTEN FREE

There are three primary reasons people adopt a gluten-free diet: celiac disease, gluten intolerance, and personal choice.

Celiac disease is a chronic digestive condition in which a person's body perceives gluten as an allergic compound and responds with chronic inflammation. The condition damages the villi (tiny fingerlike tissues in the intestinal tract that aid in digestion). If a person with celiac disease ingests even the smallest amount of gluten, he or she can experience symptoms such as bloating, cramping, skin rashes, or difficulty breathing. In some cases, it can be life threatening or hospitalization could be required. When making food for someone with celiac disease, it is best to assume that even the slightest contact will cause a severe reaction. Use the strictest practices to keep your kitchen and food prep areas spotless. Cross-contamination from cooking utensils, equipment, and surfaces is enough for many people to get sick.

Gluten intolerance, also known as non-celiac gluten sensitivity, is a condition in which the body has difficulty processing gluten, thus making the person feel ill. While not as serious as celiac disease, it can severely impact a person's well-being and quality of life. Ingesting gluten can cause headaches, brain fog, exhaustion, joint pain, bloating, or diarrhea. There is a wide range of sensitivities, and knowing where you fall on that scale can help you know what your actual limitation is. This is where being tested can be invaluable: Some people can eat small amounts of wheat products, while others can't even have something that was touched by a gluten-containing ingredient.

Bread products in America have been enhanced with vitamins and minerals for decades, so if you are no longer consuming them, you should consult your health care provider about taking supplements to make up for this lost source of nutrients. In addition, because of inflammation in the gastrointestinal tract, many people with celiac disease and gluten intolerance can suffer from malabsorption. This means that you can follow a perfectly sensible diet, but your body is incapable of absorbing iron, vitamins, and other nutrients. If you are on a gluten-free diet, you should be tested regularly to make sure you are getting the nutrients your body needs.

The recent trend of people making the personal choice to eat gluten free—because they believe it is healthier or because they think it will help them lose weight—is problematic for people with real gluten issues, because they may not be taken seriously. If a person is simply cutting out breads, pastas, cereals, and fried foods while increasing vegetables and other healthy foods, he or she may lose weight, but we can tell you from personal experience that we can eat our weight in gluten-free rice and potatoes, which are not always low in calories. In addition, many gluten-free processed foods contain extra sugars to boost flavor, increasing their caloric count.

Following a gluten-free diet is very challenging, because wheat and other gluten-containing ingredients are added to a wide variety of foods. However, in the last ten to fifteen years, with an increasing awareness of gluten sensitivity, the gluten-free food industry is booming, with new products hitting supermarket shelves every day. This makes it much easier than it used to be, but it is still difficult. In addition to avoiding gluten in your foods, you have to figure out how to replace the function it provides in baked goods. But we'll get to that in a minute.

What Is Gluten?

Gluten is the general term for two different proteins, gliadin and glutenin, found in the endosperm of wheat, rye, and barley. Strands of these proteins, when kneaded to develop them, are what produce the structure and chewiness in breads. Gluten also helps breads rise by capturing the gases released by yeast and chemical leaveners.

Just because a label says "No Wheat" doesn't mean it is gluten free, because it may contain rye, barley, or one of the many hidden-source ingredients, as you will see in the following sections. You really have to become a gluten sleuth, but new labeling laws are helping us quickly determine whether a product is safe.

PRIMARY SOURCES OF GLUTEN

- Wheat
- Rye
- Barley
- Oats*

* Oats do not naturally contain gluten, but they can be contaminated with gluten products during either growing or processing. Some people need to avoid oats entirely if they are highly sensitive to gluten.

OTHER NAMES FOR WHEAT

- Common wheat
- Durum wheat
- Hard red winter wheat
- Soft winter wheat
- Sprouted wheat
- Wheatberries
- Wheat bran
- Wheat germ or wheat germ oil
- Wheatgrass
- Wheat protein isolate
- Wheat sprouts
- Wheat starch

TYPES OF WHEAT FLOURS

- All-purpose flour
- Bread flour
- Bromated flour
- Cake flour
- Durum
- Einkorn
- Enriched flour
- Farina
- Graham flour
- High-gluten flour
- High-protein flour
- Instant pastry flour
- Kamut
- Maida
- Phosphated flour
- Self-rising flour
- Semolina
- Soft wheat flour
- Spelt
- Triticale
- Triticum
- Unbleached white/wheat flours
- Whole-wheat flour
- Winter wheat flour

Where Does Gluten Hide?

The following is a partial list of foods and products that often contain gluten. In some cases there are gluten-free versions (like soy sauce), but you are advised to read all labels carefully before consuming any product, even if it has been safe in the past, as manufacturers can change ingredients at any time.

- Artificial flavoring, natural flavoring
- Beer
- Blue cheese
- Bread and bread crumbs
- Brown rice syrup (if it contains barley malt)
- Bulgur
- Cereals
- Coated foods
- Food colorings
- Couscous
- Crackers or cracker meal
- Dextrin
- Emmer
- Extracts
- Farro
- Fillers
- Flours (see "Types of Wheat Flours" above)
- Foods fried in the same oil as gluten-full foods
- Food starch* (gelatinized starch, modified wheat starch, modified wheat food starch)
- Fu
- Gluten (wheat gluten, vital gluten, vital wheat gluten, fu)
- Grain alcohol (beer, ale, rye, scotch, bourbon, grain vodka)
- Hoisin sauce
- Homeopathic remedies
- Hydrolyzed wheat protein
- Malt, malt extract, barley malt, or malt flavor
- Matzo (also spelled matzoh, matzah, or matza)
- Monosodium glutamate (MSG)
- Noodles
- Pasta
- Ponzu sauce
- Preservatives
- Salad dressings
- Sauces
- Seitan (also known as "wheat meat")
- Soba noodles
- Soups
- Soy sauce and other sauces made with soy
- Spices (if they contain anticaking ingredients)
- Starches* made from wheat, rye, barley, or oats
- Surimi
- Tabbouleh
- Tamari sauce
- Teriyaki sauce
- Textured vegetable protein
- Vegetable gum (when made from oats)
- Vegetable protein

The word "starch" in a product's ingredient list typically means cornstarch. Any starch made from other sources should be designated, such as wheat starch.

A GLUTEN-FREE HOME AND LIFESTYLE

Getting a diagnosis of gluten intolerance or celiac disease is challenging. Your entire life is going to change, and many foods you have always enjoyed are no longer allowed in your diet. You have to figure out what you can safely eat and how to prepare your own gluten-free foods. You've heard that gluten lurks in many processed foods and ingredients, but which ones?

The first thing you have to do is clear out your kitchen. When you start reading food labels, you'll be shocked at how many items contain gluten. You will find yourself giving away the food in your pantry to friends and family, and then restocking with foods that are safe to eat.

Depending on the severity of the gluten sensitivity, some families have to keep an entirely gluten-free kitchen. Others can get by with designating specific areas of the kitchen and pantry for gluten-free use.

If You Need to Create an Entirely Gluten-Free Home

If you or your child has been diagnosed with severe gluten intolerance or celiac disease, you will have to maintain an entirely gluten-free house. Some people (children in particular) are so sensitive that just touching packaged foods with gluten in them can cause a reaction that requires hospitalization. This can be a life-threatening condition.

The logical place to start cleaning is your kitchen. Start at the top and work your way down. Discard or give away any foods that contain gluten. Empty the cabinets and wipe down all of the surfaces, including the top of the refrigerator and any other high surfaces. Thoroughly wash the containers of food you will be keeping to remove traces of residual flour. Put your remaining foods back in the cupboards and get started on the counters and equipment.

Most appliances can be adequately cleaned (don't forget the interior of your refrigerator), but your toaster and toaster oven are two that should be replaced. There are just too many places for gluten and flour dust to hide for them to be safe to use. You can donate them to a local charity or give them to a friend. Once you are done cleaning, throw away all your sponges, brushes, and any cleaning equipment that can harbor residual flour particles.

You also will need to get rid of all your wooden utensils and cutting boards. Flour is sneaky and gets down into the crevices of anything wooden or porous. It is safest to start over with a fresh set. Even though plastic cutting boards can be washed, because you've broken the surface when cutting, you should replace those as well.

Creating an entirely gluten-free kitchen can be an expensive task. Try to turn this into a fun activity, looking forward to having new equipment to use. Consider getting new silicone spoons and spatulas, which can add a pop of color to your kitchen and brighten up your day. It's like having a brand-new kitchen, and it will be sparkling clean!

If You Are Designating Specific Areas for Gluten-Free Use

If you are going to be cooking gluten free occasionally for visiting friends and family, or if only one person in your household follows a gluten-free diet, you can dedicate a cupboard or two and a specific area of your counters to do all of your work with gluten-free ingredients. Designating a single area will make it much easier for you and your gluten-free family members to know where their food is. If you have little ones, putting a strip of brightly colored duct tape on their containers of food can help them know which ones are theirs. This will keep them safe if they are looking for snacks when you are not around to supervise.

In this kind of dual-kitchen situation, you won't have to give away your toaster, but you will need to buy a new one that is just for toasting gluten-free breads. Keep it near the cupboards containing the gluten-free foods and ingredients, some distance from your "regular" toaster, so someone doesn't use it by mistake for wheat breads. Having the gluten-free toaster in a different color really helps. You can set up a cute pitcher and keep your gluten-free-specific mixing spoons and spatulas there, too. Collecting all the gluten-free items in one area will make it much easier for you.

You can use your bread machine to make both gluten-free and regular kinds of breads, but you need to thoroughly clean the inside and exterior as well as the bread pan and beater paddle in between. If you make bread often, it may be less work to purchase a separate bread pan and paddle that you keep just for gluten-free breads. You still have to clean the machine completely, but at least you'll know the pan and paddle are ready whenever you are. Just be sure you don't use the same sponges or cloths to wash the gluten-free equipment.

IS A GLUTEN-FREE LIFESTYLE A DIET TO LOSE WEIGHT?

There has been a lot of talk about people going gluten free as a way to lose weight. If you remove pasta, breads, and breaded and fried foods from your diet and eat more fruits and vegetables instead, then yes, you will likely lose weight. Those are healthier food choices. But if you simply replace the gluten-containing foods you were eating with gluten-free versions, it may result in weight gain. Following a gluten-free diet is a lifestyle, not a weight-loss plan. The processed gluten-free foods available in supermarkets often have chemicals and sometimes extra sugar to compensate for the lack of wheat flavor. They are full of calories, many with few nutrients.

When you make your own gluten-free foods from scratch, you have complete control over what goes into each recipe and can choose the best ingredients for your family's health. Increasing your intake of naturally gluten-free foods, especially fruits, vegetables, and proteins, will help offset the carb-heavy tendency of many processed gluten-free substitutions.

HOW TO MAKE GLUTEN-FREE BREAD IN A MACHINE

Bread machines were originally designed to make wheat-flour breads with gluten. Gluten needs to be worked or kneaded to develop the proteins and give structure to the bread. The multiple kneading stages are called knock-downs or punch-downs in traditional bread recipes. You would normally do this by hand, but the machine has been programmed to do it for you.

Gluten-free breads have no gluten to develop, so they do not require the typical multiple kneading and rising stages. And since we use other ingredients to mimic the actions of gluten, the loaves are much more delicate. Gluten-free doughs need a minimum of mixing and only one rise cycle. If you knock them down and knead for a second time (or more), you will likely end up with denser, shorter loaves.

Newer machines have a gluten-free setting, but beware: Not all gluten-free settings are created equal. Two of our machines with gluten-free settings have similar single-knead, rise, and bake cycles, but another machine has two kneading cycles with a rise in between. For the latter machine, using the gluten-free setting yields loaves that are an inch shorter than the ones from the other two machines. Finding out what a specific machine's gluten-free functions are will help you choose which model to purchase. Or you might decide to work with the one you already have.

If you are working with an older model bread machine that does not have a gluten-free setting, you can still make good gluten-free bread. You will get the best results with the fewest kneading stages and a single long rise before baking. You may be able to use alternative settings and/or program your machine to eliminate the second kneading cycle. Look at your machine's user manual. Most of them have a chart or timetable that tells you how long each program lasts and outlines the different stages that are included. It will help you figure out which cycle will work best for making good gluten-free bread.

In some machines, the quick or rapid bread cycle may have a single rise, which is useful for gluten-free baking. For other machines, you might need to program which cycles you want to use. Another option is to use the dough cycle for mixing and rising, then press stop and select the bake only cycle to finish the loaf. Ideally, your bread machine will have three cycles in these time ranges:

Mix/Knead: 20 to 25 minutes
Rise: 50 to 70 minutes
Bake: 70 to 80 minutes

As you can tell, there is some wiggle room within each cycle, and the timing will depend on the model you own. Because we cannot anticipate all situations and equipment, you should do a couple of test runs to figure out what works best and then use those results to guide you in making future breads.

SHINE SOME LIGHT

Keep a flashlight by the bread machine: You can use it to check on the progress of the bread without opening the lid!

If you have tried to make a recipe and aren't getting good results, you can also use your machine to mix the dough, transfer it to a loaf pan, let it rise, and then finish by baking it in the oven. See "How to Convert Recipes for Baking in the Oven" (page 19).

TIPS FOR SUCCESSFUL GLUTEN-FREE BREAD-MACHINE BAKING

If you are new to gluten-free bread baking, forget your expectations of what doughs and batters look like and how they behave. Although kneading the dough to develop the gluten might have been your favorite part of bread baking, it's no longer relevant. And forming a sticky "batter" is much different from making a kneaded dough. But once you get the hang of what the batter is supposed to look like—and learn to resist the urge to add more flour!—you'll be making beautiful baked goods again.

Measuring your ingredients accurately is very important. We recommend you buy a kitchen scale, digital thermometer, and glass liquid measuring cups (see Resources, page 376). All of these will help you get consistently great results. When measuring liquids, place the cup on the counter and bend down so it is at eye level. This way you can see exactly when you are at the right amount.

Set the bread pan on the counter with the paddle inserted before adding the liquids and then the dry ingredients. This eliminates the possibility of getting any liquid on the electrical components of the machine.

Blend your dry and liquid ingredients separately. In one bowl, whisk the dry components together to make sure the leaveners, gums, and seasonings are evenly distributed. In a separate

---

DISTILLED WATER

If possible, use distilled water when making gluten-free breads. While helpful for all loaves, this is especially important when using a sourdough starter. The chlorine and other additives in regular tap water can interfere with the leavening action and cause your breads to be shorter and denser.

---

bowl, blend the liquids, and especially beat the eggs, to help the machine with the mixing.

Gluten-free doughs are very heavy and sticky. If you put the dry ingredients in the pan first, the motor will have to work much harder to mix them. Putting the liquids on the bottom of the pan helps slowly incorporate the dry ingredients, easing strain on the machine's motor.

Most bread machines have a single beater blade and are not as efficient as machines with two paddles. During the mixing process, you will need to help it incorporate the dry ingredients. We always find some flour tucked into the corners of the pan and underneath the mixed dough. It takes a quick hand with the rubber spatula to sneak a peek under the dough when the blade is mixing, but with practice you will be able to do this with ease.

Follow the recipes in this book exactly as they are written the first time or two, until you get to know the minor adjustments that may be needed in your kitchen. A little too much liquid will make the top of the bread sink; too much flour will give you a dense, short bread. Some doughs are thicker than others due to the type of flour used.

You are welcome to remove the beater paddle once the kneading cycle is done, but we have found that doing so with many of the sandwich-style breads results in loaves that are shorter and heavier than when the paddle is left in place. Yes, you wind up with a hole in the middle, but the bread usually turns out better, and you can use the inside slices to make half sandwiches or toast. It is totally up to you.

The optimal internal temperature at which most of our breads are done is 206°F to 210°F (97°C to 99°C). This guarantees that the center is fully cooked and you won't get a gummy texture. The use of a reliable instant-read thermometer is critical for this step.

If your bread hasn't reached the correct internal temperature at the end of the bake cycle, hit stop to cancel the current setting and then press bake or bake only to add additional baking time. Then monitor the bread closely, because it can get to full temperature quite quickly—often within 5 to 10 minutes.

Always slide the bread out of the pan within a minute or two of taking it out of the machine. It needs to cool in the air to let the steam escape so you don't wind up with a soggy loaf. If needed, remove the paddle with a pair of tongs (it will be very hot) before the loaf cools too much. Once the loaf is cool, it becomes much more difficult to pry the bread away from the paddle.

Letting a loaf cool on its side or upside down on a wire rack gives the internal structure time to stabilize, so the loaf is less likely to collapse on the top.

Using a sharp serrated knife to slice the bread will also help keep the loaf from collapsing. If you have any issues cutting slices, try placing the loaf on its side and slicing from there.

If you know you will not eat the entire loaf before it starts to go stale, slice the bread and wrap pairs of slices tightly with plastic wrap. Stack the pairs of slices and wrap those with more plastic wrap before freezing them. This makes it very easy to pull out a couple of slices as needed.

USEFUL EQUIPMENT BEYOND THE BREAD MACHINE

The following list describes some pieces of equipment that we used while developing the recipes in this book and that may help you in your bread-baking adventures.

Kitchen Scale: We recommend a scale that weighs ingredients up to at least 11 pounds (about 5 kg), gives readings in both ounces/pounds and grams/kilograms, and has a tare function to zero out weights. If it has an on/off switch, that will save your battery life. Make sure that it is big enough so that you can see the display while you have a bowl sitting on it.

DON'T DELAY!

Avoid using the machine's delay feature when making gluten-free breads. These doughs work best when they are mixed and baked immediately. If you let them sit, you risk having them turn into a glue-like substance that is very difficult for the machine to mix.

Measuring Cups: We prefer to use glass Pyrex measuring cups for liquids because of their durability and low cost. We use a 2-cup (0.5 liter) and a 4-cup (1 liter) to measure the wet ingredients, and the spouts make pouring those ingredients into the bread pan a snap. If you prefer not to weigh your dry ingredients, use a high-quality set of metal measuring cups with straight sides so you can scoop flour into the cup and use a straight edge to scrape excess off the top. This will give you the most accurate measurement other than weighing.

Measuring Spoons: Buy two sets of high-quality metal measuring spoons—one for the dry ingredients and another for the wet. This will save you from washing and drying between uses. Metal spoons are a great investment as they are sturdy, don't bend, and will last for decades.

Mixing Bowls: They can be glass or stainless steel, but any lighter-weight bowls are easier to work with. A 4-quart (4 liter) bowl will hold all the dry ingredients for a loaf of bread with enough room to easily whisk them together. An 8-quart (8 liter) bowl will hold a large batch of the flour blends with room to whisk them. A small prep bowl or ramekin—about ½ cup (120 ml)—is ideal for the yeast.

Whisks: A 9-inch (23 cm) whisk is perfect for the wet ingredients, and a 12-inch (30 cm) or larger whisk will make quick work of blending the dry ingredients or flour blends.

Silicone Spatulas: We use these sturdy, flexible spatulas to transfer all the liquids and dry ingredients into the bread pan, and then to move the dry ingredients toward the center of

WEIGHT VS. VOLUME

It is extremely important to accurately measure certain ingredients in gluten-free baking—especially flours and starches. Each person scoops and fills cups of flour differently. To eliminate discrepancies, use a kitchen scale to weigh the ingredients for the most accurate results. A scale is not very expensive (see page 16), and if you are baking a lot of gluten-free treats, it will more than pay for itself by giving you consistent results. Once you get used to using it, weighing all of your baking and cooking ingredients will become second nature.

the pan while the machine mixes the dough. Silicone will not scratch your bread pan. The spatulas that are all one piece work best, as there is no risk of the handle coming off when you fold the ingredients into some of the denser doughs. Having several on hand will save you from having to wash them constantly, and if you get the heat-safe variety, you can use them for almost any kitchen task.

Crosshatch Wire Cooling Racks: These will hold your loaves as they cool, ensuring the movement of air around the entire loaf for the quickest cooling. The crosshatch pattern prevents the impressions you would get on your loaves from racks with single rows of bars. Get stainless-steel racks and dry them in a warm oven after washing to reduce rusting.

Long-Handled Tongs: These long, thin tongs (sometimes sold as "kitchen tweezers") make it easy to remove the beater paddle from the bottom of the baked loaf while the bread is still hot. We recommend 7-inch (18 cm) tongs to keep your hands away from the hot paddle as you wiggle it to release it from the bread. Tongs also come in handy for tasks like pushing down/piercing the dough bubble that is sometimes created during the kneading cycle. You can easily find them online.

Pot Holders: Heavy-duty, washable pot holders are essential for removing the hot bread pan from the machine, turning the bread out of the pan, and moving the hot loaf around.

Portable Timer: Having a timer that you can set and hang around your neck is a convenient way to keep track of when the bread is done so you can get it out of the machine before it overcooks or begins to steam in the pan. A timer that can keep track of multiple dishes will also help on busy cooking days. The timers from ThermoWorks are excellent quality.

Instant-Read Thermometer: The best way to know when bread is done is to take the temperature in the center of the loaf. You will get much more consistent results than if you go by baking time alone. It is a worthwhile investment to buy an instant-read thermometer that registers the temperature quickly and accurately, like the Thermapen from ThermoWorks. You can use it for everything from breads to grilled foods, and even candy making.

Serrated Bread Knife: This may seem like a no-brainer, but a sharp serrated knife makes a huge difference when cutting breads, especially soft breads with a hard crust. The teeth allow greater pressure to be exerted on the bread, and it is generally thinner than a straight-edged blade, so you can cut slender slices without pressing down and compressing the loaf. Always use a sawing action for the best results. A double-serrated bread knife stays sharp longer and cuts very cleanly, leaving you with fewer crumbs to clean up.

Large Food-Safe Plastic Bins: These are by far the best way to store your flour blends. Cambro makes a line of very sturdy, long-wearing containers that are often used in professional kitchens. A 6-quart (6 liter) container will hold enough of the flour blends to make about four loaves at a time and is easy to refill. The tight-sealing lid allows you to vigorously shake the mixture to blend it before each use.

Small and Medium Storage Containers: Get these for ingredients you use all the time, such as yeast and xanthan gum. They're great for storage, and it's much easier to measure the ingredients out of a container than a bag. Make sure you label each container to avoid confusion.

Large Food-Safe Plastic Bags: You definitely need to have bags on hand to store your cooled bread. The All-Purpose Bread Bags from King Arthur Flour are reasonably priced and come in packs of 100, though you have to supply your own twist ties. One-gallon (4 liter) resealable bags also work; just be sure to press out all the air.

Large Rubber Bands: We've found that the easiest way to keep opened bags of flours and starches closed is to fold down the top and secure them with sturdy rubber bands.

HOW TO CONVERT RECIPES FOR BAKING IN THE OVEN

If you prefer to bake your breads in the oven instead of letting the machine complete the whole cycle, it is easy to convert.

Once the dough has been mixed and kneaded by the bread machine (making sure you let the machine mix until the dough is smooth), press the stop button and turn off the machine. Remove the bread pan from the machine and scoop the dough into a baking pan of your choice. If you are making a traditionally shaped loaf, we recommend using the pan specifically designed for gluten-free bread sold by King Arthur Flour (see Resources, page 376). This 9 x 4 x 4-inch (23 x 10 x 10 cm) pan will give your breads more support as they rise in the oven, helping them cook fully and evenly.

Once the dough is transferred to an oiled bread pan, use wet fingers to gently smooth the top of the dough. Cover the pan with a sheet of plastic wrap coated with flourless nonstick cooking spray, sprayed side down. Set the pan in a warm, draft-free area and let it rest and rise for about 1 hour. You want the dough to rise to the top edge of the pan, or just slightly above, but no higher. Preheat your oven to 350°F (180°C).

When the dough has risen, remove the plastic wrap and slip the pan into the hot oven. Bake until the loaf reaches 206°F to 210°F (97°C to 99°C) in the center on an instant-read thermometer. The timing will vary depending on the recipe, types of flours used, density of the dough, and your oven. Look for a golden color on the top and for the bread to start to pull away from the sides of the pan. Leave it in the oven until it is fully baked so you don't wind up with a gummy interior.

Remove the bread from the oven, turn it out of the pan, and let it cool on its side or upright on a wire rack until thoroughly cooled, at least an hour or two, before slicing.

WHAT TO DO WITH "FAILURES"

When you start to bake gluten-free bread, failures are inevitable. Don't let them stop you. We've all shed our share of tears, but we kept going and can now stand proudly with our gluten-free baked goods in hand. And we know you will do that, too. So, what can you do with the loaves that just don't turn out right? Here are some ideas:

- If bread is undercooked or too moist in the center, cut it into slices and double-toast it: Start on a light setting to evaporate some of the moisture. Toast again at a slightly higher setting to finish drying it out and give it the golden color and crispy exterior we crave.

- If you have hamburger buns that are too moist in the center, cut them in half and toast the cut sides.

- If a loaf is dry and falling apart, cut or break it into chunks, toast them, and turn them into bread crumbs in your food processor.

- If you have too much bread, cut it into cubes and turn it into stuffing or croutons. The cubes can be frozen for future use.

- Leftover bread can also be made into crostini and used as a base for delicious appetizers.

TIPS FOR HIGH-ALTITUDE BAKING

Baking at any location higher than 3,000 feet (900 m) above sea level is considered high-altitude baking. Two primary changes take place when baking in these conditions. First, liquids evaporate faster. Second, due to the lower air pressure, the gases in baked goods expand more quickly, making them rise higher and faster. The higher your altitude, the more dramatic the differences in your results. And don't forget, each location and type of machine differs, so some adjustments will likely be needed no matter where you live.

Baking at high altitude is complex, even for regular wheat breads. But when you add the challenges of gluten-free baking, it is going to take more testing for you to find the right combination of adjustments for your specific location and equipment. Be patient, and you will figure them out. Luckily, we have some quick adjustments you can try to alleviate some of your frustrations.

Several of our testers live at high altitudes and were able to get very good results with a few adjustments to the recipes. Here are some of their hints:

- Remember, the tops of most gluten-free loaves are flat; do not expect them to rise into a dome.
- If your breads are not browning well, you can brush the top of the dough (before the rise cycle) with a little melted butter.
- You do not need as much yeast or baking powder, because they are both more efficient at high altitudes. Try reducing the yeast by ¼ to ½ teaspoon and the baking powder by ¼ teaspoon. If the bread still rises too high, reduce the baking powder by another ¼ teaspoon next time. Keep making adjustments until you find the right combination.
- To get a slower, more even rise, add more salt, which retards the action of the yeast. Start by increasing the salt by ¼ teaspoon and go up from there as needed.
- Reduce the sugar by about 1 tablespoon, which will slow the rising.
- Add ¼ teaspoon lecithin to help stabilize the structure of the bread, making it less likely to collapse.
- Flour is much drier at higher altitudes, and will absorb more liquid. You will likely need to add a little more water as the flour is mixing and kneading. Start with 1 tablespoon additional water and go up from there as needed.
- If the dough is rising too quickly, you can stop the machine during the rising cycle and switch to bake only to reduce the rising time.
- You may find that your breads bake faster, so keep an eye on the internal temperature with a good-quality instant-read thermometer.

If you live higher than 4,000 to 5,000 feet (1200 to 1500 m) above sea level, there may be additional adjustments needed. Each increase of 1,000 to 1,500 feet (300 to 450 m) calls for extra changes in your recipes.

We are not high-altitude experts and have gathered most of this information from our testers and the Internet. For the most comprehensive information on how to adjust recipes for high-altitude baking, consult the Colorado State University Extension Resource Center. For more resources, see page 376.

FREQUENTLY ASKED QUESTIONS

Weights and Measures

Why do I have to weigh the flours and other dry ingredients?

When you are working with gluten-free flours, it is extremely important to weigh them. Each ingredient in a flour blend is a different weight. If you were to line up a cup of each one side by side and weigh them, you would be shocked at the variance. Gluten-free flours are also more sensitive to changes in humidity, so the weight can change from day to day. And then there is the issue of how compactly you fill your measuring cups—even a small modification is enough to make a big difference in your baked goods. The most accurate way to guarantee consistent results is to weigh your dry ingredients.

Why don't I have to weigh smaller amounts?

The primary dry ingredients are the ones that need the most careful measuring for consistent results, and weighing is by far the most accurate method. For the smaller amounts, it is easier to use measuring spoons or small measuring cups. A slight difference one way or the other will make little to no difference in the smaller measures.

Why do my measurement weights differ from what the recipe says?

When you use cups and spoons to measure dry ingredients, there is a lot of room for variation. Whether the ingredients are packed or sifted or fluffed before scooping and whether you scrape the top level, and even using different brands—all of these factors can make a big difference. If you are getting good results, keep doing what you're doing, because it is working!

WEIGHING FLOUR

Turn on your kitchen scale and set it for grams (g/kg). Set the empty bowl on the scale and press the Tare/Zero button to cancel out the weight of the bowl. Scoop the well-shaken flour blend into the bowl until it reaches the weight called for in the recipe. Transfer the weighed flour to another mixing bowl. Repeat with the other weighed dry ingredients.

How do I know my scale is weighing correctly?

Kitchen scales are calibrated at the factory, but the settings may get changed during shipping. You can buy a 100 gram weight online and use it to calibrate your own scale. If you place the weight on your scale and it registers 99 grams instead of 100, then you know to increase your amounts by 1 gram (on your scale) to compensate for the difference.

Why does my scale sometimes bounce back and forth between two numbers?

Don't get frustrated or think your scale isn't working. If your ingredients are somewhere between the two weights, it will let you know by alternating on the display. Use a small spoon to take a little out or to add a touch more, until the correct number shows.

Do I have to be absolutely exact in my weight measurements?

The short answer is no. However, the more accurate you are, the more consistent your results will be.

The weight of the dry milk I am using is different from the weights listed in the recipes. Which is right?

They both are. The differences in the way a liquid is dried and the particles pulverized can cause a variety of weights in something that would appear to be the same regardless of brand. It isn't unusual to measure ¼ cup of three different brands of milk powder and find that there are three different weights. And if you use a different kind of dried milk (nut, soy, coconut, etc.), it can vary even more. The good news is that it isn't a problem. Because the milk powders would be dissolved in a liquid for use in an ordinary situation, technically they are actually part of the liquid measurements, so the weight isn't as important as the volume of the liquids in the ratio of liquid to dry. We incorporate them with the dry ingredients in these recipes to reduce a step and to make it easier on the machine.

Gluten-Free Flour

What is the best way to store gluten-free flour?

Because gluten-free flours tend to have no preservatives and often have more natural oils in them, you will extend their shelf life if you keep them in the refrigerator or freezer. You should always smell your ingredients before using; if they have an "off" odor, do not use them. You don't want that flavor in your baked goods.

How long will gluten-free flours last?

This depends on how you store them, how long they were in the grocery store before you purchased them, and their manufacturer. It is always best to check on each manufacturer's website for the best estimation of shelf life.

I would prefer to use the Whole-Grain Flour Blend in place of the Light Flour Blend in some recipes. Is that okay?

Yes, either blend can be used in these recipes. We recommend you make each recipe as written first to know the texture and results you are looking for. Then making adjustments will be easier for you to anticipate.

I bake gluten free only occasionally. Do I have to use your flour blends?

All of our recipes were developed and tested using our blends, but a number of commercial blends are good alternatives. Namaste Foods' Perfect Flour Blend, King Arthur Flour's Gluten-Free Multi-Purpose Flour, Bob's Red Mill Gluten-Free 1-to-1 Baking Flour, and Authentic Foods' GF Classical Blend will all work in these recipes. Because blends differ in composition, you may have to adjust certain recipes with additional water or flour. A blend without gums will work most closely to our flour blends, but if your store-bought blend already contains xanthan or guar gum, add half the amount of the gum called for in the recipe. If the recipe calls for psyllium, add it exactly as written. If your bread seems crumbly, add a little more gum or psyllium the next time.

Do gluten-free flours measure and act the same as wheat flours?

Gluten-free flours and starches are much lighter and more finely ground than wheat flours. They tend to compact when sitting and can separate. This is why we recommend you vigorously shake or whisk the flour blend before measuring. Gluten-free flours are also more hygroscopic, meaning they tend to absorb more moisture from the air than wheat does. This is why weighing your ingredients is much more accurate than measuring them by the cup—the scale will take into account the extra moisture in the flours so you don't have to adjust the liquids. Be careful when you are opening or closing the containers of flours and starches, because gluten-free products tend to send powdery clouds into the air. They are easy to wipe up but can make your kitchen floors feel slick.

Yeast

Why do you use both yeast and baking powder in most of the recipes?

Gluten-free flours need all the help they can get to rise and bake into beautiful breads that you and your family will love. Using the quicker chemical reaction of the baking powder to get things started and then having the yeast do its magic gives us the best results.

Why do some recipes call for active dry yeast and others use instant yeast? Can I use a different yeast from what is called for in the recipe?

The gluten-free cycle on most bread machines takes about 2 hours 45 minutes and is designed to give yeast time to rise. The quick bread/cake cycles take about 1 hour less. Instant yeast activates much more quickly and lets you take advantage of the quicker bake time when using one of the faster cycles. While the sandwich breads and any breads that use the gluten-free cycle work well with active dry yeast, you can also substitute instant yeast without making any other changes.

What if I already have yeast? Do I have to buy new yeast for these recipes?

You do not have to buy new yeast, but if you have had yours for a long time, it may not be as efficient. If you will be making a lot of bread regularly, you can save money by buying yeast in bulk. Whole Foods Market and King Arthur Flour both sell 1-pound (454 g) packages. These larger packages are also a lot easier to measure from, making them a double win!

Other Ingredients

Why do you call for granulated cane sugar? Can't I use any sugar?

You can, but unless it is clearly marked as cane sugar on the container, most sugar sold in the United States is beet sugar. Because sugar beets grow beneath the ground, it is virtually impossible to completely remove all the bits of soil and impurities from the sugar during processing. As minuscule as they are, they can affect the outcome of your baked goods. If you have been making a recipe for years and suddenly one day it doesn't turn out, it may be that you used a different sugar.

I use margarine in my baking—will that work in these recipes?

Yes, but because margarine contains more water than butter, you may need to reduce the water or milk in the recipe slightly. For the best flavor, we recommend grass-fed or pastured butter.

Why do you use so many eggs in the recipes?

Gluten-free flours contain very little protein, not nearly as much as wheat flours. In order to get the structure needed for the bread to perform at its best, using beaten eggs helps guarantee that each loaf will rise high and not collapse.

For eggs, you can use commercial egg replacers, such as Ener-G. Another option is to make a flax or chia slurry. The ratio is simple: 1 tablespoon ground flaxseed or chia seeds to 3 tablespoons (45 ml) warm water for each egg being replaced. Place the seeds in a bowl, add the water, and whisk until fully incorporated. Then set the bowl aside and let it rest for 10 to 15 minutes. While it sits, the flax or chia will absorb the water and create a gel-like consistency very similar to a beaten raw egg.

Remember that egg replacers do not contain any fat, whereas each egg yolk has about 1½ teaspoons of fat in it. For the best mouthfeel and results when using egg replacers, increase whatever fat is called for in the recipe (butter, oil, and the like) by 1 teaspoon for each egg called for. You may need to add a little more flour to adjust, but you will like the resulting loaves a lot better.

Do I need to use distilled water in every recipe?

Distilled water is very important when making sourdough recipes because the chlorine and other additives can react with the starter and cause havoc. For the rest of the recipes you can use tap water (as long as it tastes good) or bottled water, but we recommend distilled water because then you won't have the faint flavor of chlorine in your finished breads.

Do I have to use the same vinegar called for in the recipe? Can I use a different one I have in my pantry?

Most vinegars are fairly similar, like apple cider, sherry, and wine vinegars. But some are milder than others (such as champagne

vinegar), and your recipe may benefit from an extra ½ teaspoon to keep the yeast happy.

Why do you call for ascorbic acid as an optional ingredient?

Yeast loves an acidic environment to grow. Adding the ascorbic acid (also known as citric acid) helps the yeast and also increases the shelf life of the breads. Use the powdered variety (available at Whole Foods Market, health markets, or from LorAnn—see Resources, page 376) for the easiest way to add it.

Why do some recipes call for xanthan gum and others for psyllium husk flakes or powder? How would I substitute psyllium for xanthan if I am avoiding gums?

Psyllium husk flakes or powder gives breads the wonderful chewiness we look for in artisan-style loaves. Sandwich breads are typically softer with less chew, so we use xanthan gum for those. If you avoid or are sensitive to gums, you can substitute psyllium for the xanthan in a two-to-one ratio. If the recipe calls for

STORING XANTHAN & PSYLLIUM

Store xanthan gum in the freezer for the longest shelf life. Use ¼ teaspoon xanthan gum per 120 g (4¼ oz or 1 cup) flour. You can use twice the amount of psyllium husk flakes or powder for the xanthan in any recipe, but note that it tends to give you a slightly chewier texture. If you want to experiment with whole psyllium husks (rather than the flakes or powder), be aware that you will likely get different results.

1 teaspoon xanthan, substitute 2 teaspoons psyllium.

I am baking bread for people who are vegan and dairy free. How do I make substitutions for their diet requirements?

For a dairy-free or vegan version of any recipe, replace milk with another liquid, such as unsweetened coconut milk, soy milk, rice milk, hemp milk, almond milk, or water. Use DariFree Original (made from potatoes) or soy milk powder (such as Better Than Milk Soy Original) in place of the milk powder. If a recipe calls for buttermilk powder, substitute DariFree Original powder, increase the flour blend by 1 teaspoon, and add an extra teaspoon of vinegar or lemon juice. Use Earth Balance Vegan Buttery Sticks or your favorite nondairy butter substitute in place of the butter.

Equipment

If I use my bread machine for both regular and gluten-free baking, what do I have to do to make sure it is safe for my friends with celiac disease?

By far the safest solution is to keep two completely separate machines. But if that is not an option, thoroughly clean the pan and paddle and wipe out the entire interior. Pay careful attention to the nooks and crannies for any hidden flour dust, especially the inside of the lid. For more detailed information, see page 13.

Do I always have to use two bowls to measure the dry ingredients?

Once you are comfortable using the scale, you can add all your ingredients to the same bowl using the Tare/Zero function after each

USING A STAND MIXER

If you don't don't have a bread machine or don't want to use it for mixing the dough, you can use any heavy-duty stand mixer instead. Just make sure you use the beater paddle—*not* the dough hook.

addition. This zeroes out the weight of the ingredients already in the bowl. If you choose this method of measuring, add each ingredient in its own area of the bowl so you can easily remove some if you go over on the weight. Keep a small spoon handy for returning overages to the original packages.

I checked the length of the baking cycle on my bread machine and it is not as long as you recommend. Should I be worried?

Brands and models of bread machines vary and are programmed differently. Hopefully, they will be close to what you need. We give you the ideal range of temperature in each recipe to know when your bread is fully baked; if your machine stops baking before the bread is done, start the bake only cycle and add time, watching the temperature. Make a note of how much extra time you needed and use that as a guideline for future breads. If the bread reaches the ideal temperature range before the cycle is finished, press stop and pull out the pan. A few tries and you should know how your machine performs and any adjustments you may need to make regularly. If your machine has the option to program unique settings, once you have figured out the right amount of time for mixing/kneading, rising, and baking, you can program that in for a fully customized cycle perfect for your equipment.

What is the best way to store my baked breads?

It is preferable to store your thoroughly cooled loaves of bread, wrapped in plastic or in a plastic bag, at room temperature for up to two to three days. Refrigerating them tends to dry them out. If you decide to refrigerate them right away, make sure they are totally cooled and double-wrap the unsliced loaves. For longer storage, slice the bread, wrap pairs of slices in plastic wrap, reassemble the loaf, and place it in a resealable plastic bag or airtight container. Freeze for up to three months.

Procedure

When I am making sourdough breads, why do I always seem to have to make adjustments to the dough, adding a little more water or flour?

The ratio of liquid to flour in a sourdough starter can vary depending on how recently you fed it, the percentage of water to flour that you use, and even the weather. Sourdough is an art (see page 173), and one where you will need to trust your instincts more than with the other breads. If you are making adjustments and your breads are turning out, then you know exactly what consistency the dough should be while mixing. Bravo!

After the bread was done baking I noticed some flour on the bottom of the loaf. Where did that come from?

There were probably some unmixed dry ingredients hidden under the dough that didn't get incorporated during mixing. Next time be sure to lift the dough with the spatula as you are scraping the pan and stir in any extra flour caught in the corners of the pan. After a little practice, you will get good at lifting it quickly before the paddle circles around again. You can also pause the machine while you do the scraping, giving you more time and no chance of hitting the moving paddle.

My machine finished baking, but the loaf hasn't reached the right temperature. What do I do?

Sometimes your dough will have extra liquid that needs to bake off, or a specific machine's bake cycle is shorter than the dough needs. In this case, press the stop button to cancel the cycle (some require you to unplug the machine; read your manual for specifics), and set it to the bake only cycle. Depending on your machine, this may be a predetermined amount of time (like ten-minute intervals) or up to an hour. This additional baking step should take only a few minutes, so don't wander too far. Check the bread's internal temperature every couple

WET VS. DRY

If the dough looks too wet as it is mixing, you can sprinkle a teaspoon or two of the flour blend over the top and let the machine mix it in. When in doubt, moister is better than drier. It is easier to toast moister slices than to salvage bread that is too dry.

of minutes until it is in the right range (206°F to 210°F/97°C to 99°C).

Why do I have to leave the breads upside down while cooling?

Without the structure of gluten to support them, gluten-free breads have a tendency to sink in the center. You can reduce this risk by leaving the breads upside down or on their sides while on the cooling racks. If a recipe specifically calls for cooling the bread on its side, it is because the bread is delicate enough that the weight of the loaf would reduce the overall height if it is left upside down.

HOW TO USE THIS BOOK

You may have noticed that nearly all our recipes are for 1½-pound (680 g) loaves. Why? We chose this size because all bread machines have a 1½-pound (680 g) option, and bigger loaves have a tendency to collapse without gluten for support. We would rather you make slightly smaller loaves that turn out beautifully!

Always make the recipes exactly as written the first time. This is especially important in gluten-free baking, where the ratio of liquids to dry ingredients and weights and measures are critical. Following the recipes we've developed and tested gives you the best chance for success. It will also give you an idea what the dough is supposed to look like, since each bread is a little different. Then, depending on how it turned out, the next time you make it you will recognize whether it is too wet or too dry and can make adjustments accordingly.

Note that the age of your ingredients, the weather, and the type of bread machine you own can all affect the outcome of your baking. You will likely need to make small adjustments each time you make a recipe. Keep an eye on the dough as it is mixing and add small amounts of water or flour blend as needed to get the texture you desire. The more you use your machine, the better your breads will turn out.

We suggest you start with the Simple Sandwich Bread recipe on page 38. It has a very detailed description of every step of the process. This is designed to give you all the information you need to learn how to make gluten-free bread using a bread machine, what to look for, how to make adjustments if needed, and how to judge when the bread is done. The other recipes in the book have less detailed methods, but you can always refer to this first recipe if you need a refresher or more information.

All about Flours

AND OUR TWO MASTER FLOUR BLENDS

One of the biggest challenges of learning to bake gluten-free bread is understanding the role of the different ingredients in flour blends. A combination of ingredients is needed to mimic the behavior and qualities of wheat flour. There is no single gluten-free flour that can do everything that wheat does.

But before you panic, think about this: There are different types of wheat with varying percentages of proteins. In order for you to go to the grocery store and pick up that package of all-purpose flour, someone had to combine different types of wheat flours to create a blend that works for most applications. When you make your own flour blend, you are essentially doing the same thing!

Quite a few gluten-free all-purpose flour blends are available in supermarkets; our favorites include products from Authentic Foods, Bob's Red Mill, King Arthur Flour, and Namaste Foods (see Resources, page 376). If you are cooking and baking gluten free only occasionally, commercial blends are a wonderful way to be able to quickly, easily, and safely prepare foods for everyone at your table. To maintain their optimal freshness, we recommend you store them in the freezer.

In some cases you can substitute a gluten-free flour blend in recipes calling for wheat flour. But keep in mind that not all blends are created equal. In addition to gluten-free flours, a blend needs starches and gums or psyllium to give structure to your baked goods. The starches are nearly always included, but it is not a given that the blend you buy will contain gums. If it doesn't, you will likely need to add some, or use psyllium if preferred. If you are using a commercial blend that contains xanthan gum, reduce the amount called for in the recipe by half. Yeast breads require more structure than other gluten-free baked goods to support the rise, and you want to be sure you have enough. Additional eggs will help increase the protein percentage that also helps give strength and support to the breads as they bake.

Before we share our own flour blends, let's take a look at some of the different ingredients often used in gluten-free baking.

COMMONLY USED GLUTEN-FREE FLOURS

Amaranth Flour: Amaranth, an ancient grain used by the Aztecs, has a lovely, slightly nutty flavor that enhances many gluten-free baked goods. It aids in browning, but because of its high moisture content, using too much can leave you with a gummy center. It is best used in recipes with less liquid. Use it in combination with other flours to add a slightly sweet flavor.

Buckwheat Flour: Despite its name, buckwheat is a gluten-free plant unrelated to wheat—buckwheat is in fact related to rhubarb. It comes in light and dark varieties, and the light version is the most flexible for gluten-free baking. Traditionally used in pancakes, waffles, and muffins, it has a distinct flavor that can sometimes be interpreted as sour, which makes it a wonderful addition to gluten-free versions of pumpernickel and rye breads.

Corn Flour, Cornmeal, and Masa Harina: These are all made from dried corn, and the primary difference is the coarseness of the grind. Corn flour is the finest grind and adds wonderful flavor to a wide variety of baked goods. Cornmeal comes in coarse, medium, and fine grinds and is commonly used to make cornbread. You can replace a portion of the cornmeal with corn flour when making cornbread for a smoother, less crumbly texture. Be sure to look for gluten-free versions, as some brands are processed in facilities that also produce wheat products. Masa harina is made from dried corn kernels that have been treated in a lime and water solution. It is the flour used to make tortillas and tamales, and is a wonderful thickener for soups, chili, and stews.

Legume Flours: These flours are ground from beans, lentils, peas, and peanuts. The most prevalent flours are fava bean, garbanzo, garfava (made from a blend of garbanzo and fava bean flours), pea, soy, and white bean. White bean flour is the most subtle of them all and can be used in sweet baked goods where other bean flours would be overpowering.

Millet Flour: Ground from a tiny seed that is very high in protein, vitamins, and minerals, millet flour is a good choice to add to your gluten-free baked goods. Millet is believed to be the oldest grain, a staple in the diets of people from Africa, Asia, and India. It has a beautiful pale yellow color and adds a light, sweet flavor. Millet flour can add a somewhat crumbly texture to gluten-free baked goods, making it a great ingredient in streusel toppings for the breads.

Nut Flours or Meals: The two most common nut flours are made from almonds and hazelnuts. Their natural oils give baked goods a luscious texture and both add lovely flavors. They are best used with a flour blend and should not make up more than about 25 percent of the total flour in any recipe. Because of their high fat content, always store these flours in your freezer and bring to room temperature before measuring.

Quinoa Flour: Quinoa is another ancient grain that originated thousands of years ago in the Andes of South America. It is used as a whole grain and is also ground into flour or pressed into cereal flakes. It adds protein and helps keep your breads fresher longer, making it a popular addition to recipes.

Rice Flours: These are the most popular gluten-free flours and the backbone of the majority of flour blends, including ours. There are three versions: white rice, brown rice, and sweet rice. White rice flour has the most neutral flavor and therefore is a natural choice for delicately flavored desserts, breads, and muffins. Brown rice flour includes the bran coating, making it higher in fiber and a slightly healthier option. It is heavier than white flour and is best blended with other flours and starches. Sweet rice flour, also known as mochiko, is made from short-grain rice with a high starch content; it helps keep breads and baked goods from being crumbly. Contrary to its name, it does not have an appreciably sweet flavor.

The biggest complaint about rice flours is their tendency to be gritty. That is why we recommend using the superfine ground rice flours from Authentic Foods (see Resources, page 376).

Sorghum Flour: Another of our favorites, sorghum is probably the closest in flavor to wheat. It is a wonderful gluten-free flour that works in a myriad of recipes. It has a pale tan color that deepens when it is baked. Along with rice flour, sorghum is perfect to have on hand when a recipe calls for 1 or 2 tablespoons of flour or when you need to dust proteins with flour before cooking.

Teff Flour: Native to Africa, teff is the world's smallest cereal grain. Because it is so small, the entire seed, including its husk, is ground into flour, making it a very nutritious choice. It has a unique flavor that is best when used as a small percentage of a mixed flour blend.

STARCHES

The primary function of starches in gluten-free baking is to lighten the texture. Gluten-free flour blends often use a combination of two or more to take advantage of their different properties.

Arrowroot starch (also called arrowroot, arrowroot flour, or arrowroot powder) is an option for those who cannot have potatoes or nightshades in their diets, and it may also help those who cannot have corn. Arrowroot has a neutral flavor, making it a good choice for subtly flavored baked goods.

Potato flour is made from whole potatoes that are dried and ground into a powder. It is highly absorbent. You can use it as a thickener or as an ingredient in some baked goods, but it may add weight or bulk to your final products. There are a few situations where using a little potato flour is a good thing—such as potato rolls or breads—but it should always be a small percentage of the dry ingredients. Because it contains the entire vegetable, potato flour should *never* be confused with potato starch. If you accidentally use potato flour in lieu of potato starch, you will wind up with leaden, gummy bricks instead of light and fluffy baked goods!

Potato starch, along with tapioca (see page 32), is the foundation starch in many gluten-free flour blends (including ours). Made from only the starchy proteins of potatoes, it is very different from potato flour—the two are *not* interchangeable. Potato starch is much lighter and powdery, has virtually no flavor, and adds a fluffy texture to your baked goods. It is often used in a blend to help lighten it and balance the weight of the flours. It is a good option for those who cannot eat corn.

Tapioca flour (or tapioca starch) is made from the starch extracted from the South American cassava plant. It has a slightly sweet flavor. Tapioca flour, used in conjunction with other gluten-free flours, has a variety of uses in baking. It helps with browning but can make foods dry and tough, so it is often used along with potato starch.

GUMS AND EMULSIFIERS

The two primary gums used in gluten-free baking are xanthan and guar. These gums are emulsifiers or hydrocolloids, substances that form a gel in the presence of water and act as a liaison between two elements that naturally repel each other (such as water and oil), helping them stabilize and stay blended. For example, you will see xanthan gum listed as an ingredient in many commercial salad dressings.

Our recipes call for small amounts of xanthan gum. Do not be put off by its cost—one bag will last you a long time. Store it in a small jar next to your flour blend. It's easier to measure a teaspoon or two out of a jar.

The reason we use xanthan gum in our recipes is because guar gum is known to cause gastric distress in some people. Others have issues with xanthan. If you are following a gluten-free diet but still have digestive issues, try leaving out the gums. Some people cannot tolerate even small amounts.

CLEANING UP XANTHAN

If you spill any xanthan, do not get it wet. Instead, sweep it up with a brush. When mixed with water, xanthan gum becomes extremely slippery. Here's a fun experiment to do with kids: Have them put some on their hands and then try to wash it off with just water. Hilarity ensues.

Instead, try psyllium husk flakes or powder—an excellent alternative. It adds a wonderful chewy texture, which is why we use it in our recipes for pretzels and pizza crusts. Replace the xanthan called for in the recipe with twice as much psyllium husk powder or flakes. If you have trouble finding psyllium in the baking aisle at the store, try looking in the health section, as it is often sold as a digestive aid.

WHERE TO BUY INGREDIENTS

We made an effort to use ingredients that are readily available in major American grocery store chains or easily ordered online. If you will be doing a lot of baking, you should do cost comparisons for the primary ingredients you will need. Sometimes a local source is less expensive, but online retailers often offer discounts for buying in bulk. See page 376 for our product recommendations.

FLOUR BLENDS

The starting point for all gluten-free baking is your flour blend. It has to contain the right mix of flours and starches to mimic as closely as possible the function of gluten, which gives cakes, cookies, and breads enough structure to support the lift from yeast and other leaveners.

Some gluten-free cookbooks offer many flour blends—each one a little different—and it seems that every recipe you want to make requires a different blend. This is complicated and requires you to store a huge variety of flours.

We have developed just two flour blends to cover virtually all of your gluten-free baking projects. The Light Flour Blend is designed to create delicate-flavored breads that children will love and to showcase any added flours, fruits, herbs, spices, and the like. The Whole-Grain Flour Blend has more protein and fiber for a healthier option and is best suited for breads with bolder flavors and those benefiting from extra structure. Keeping a container of each blend readily available lets you be more spontaneous in your baking, able to whip up a loaf for sandwiches, gifts for friends, or sweets for parties.

The recipes in this book may call for a specific flour blend, but this is more of a recommendation—you can use either blend in any recipe. In addition, you can use either blend when making other gluten-free baked goods like cakes and cookies, thickening gravies, or dusting proteins before cooking. They are both all-purpose blends.

We left gums out of our base flour blends so we can add the exact amount needed for each recipe. And for those who cannot tolerate gums, psyllium or other alternatives can be substituted more easily. Many people with gluten issues also have difficulty with dairy, so leaving milk powder out of our base blends was another requirement. When you see milk powder in a recipe, it is there for a specific reason, usually for flavor and to increase the protein. Unless you cannot have dairy, try the recipes as they are written. There are a number of alternatives if you need to make substitutions. For ideas, see our recommendations on page 25.

CHANGING BATCH SIZE

Both of our flour blends are easy to increase or decrease to meet your needs. If you bake regularly, double or triple the amounts listed—just be sure to whisk after each addition and then shake the container thoroughly to combine. When using metric weights, it is simple to scale recipes!

LIGHT FLOUR BLEND

YIELD: 800 G (1.8 LB OR ABOUT 6 CUPS), ENOUGH TO MAKE MORE THAN 2 LOAVES

280 g (9.9 oz or 2 cups plus 2 tablespoons) sweet rice flour (*not* white rice flour)

280 g (9.9 oz or 2 cups plus 4¾ teaspoons) brown or white rice flour (preferably from Authentic Foods—see Resources, page 376)

120 g (4.2 oz or 1 cup plus 4¾ teaspoons) tapioca flour/starch

120 g (4.2 oz or ½ cup plus 3 tablespoons plus 2¼ teaspoons) potato starch (*not* potato flour)

WHOLE-GRAIN FLOUR BLEND

YIELD: 800 G (1.8 LB OR ABOUT 6⅔ CUPS), ENOUGH TO MAKE MORE THAN 2 LOAVES

200 g (7.1 oz or 1½ cups plus ¾ teaspoon) sweet rice flour (*not* white rice flour)

200 g (7.1 oz or 1¾ cups plus ¼ teaspoon) millet flour

160 g (5.6 oz or 1⅓ cups plus 2½ teaspoons) sorghum flour or brown rice flour (preferably from Authentic Foods—see Resources, page 376)

120 g (4.2 oz or 1 cup plus 4¾ teaspoons) tapioca flour

120 g (4.2 oz or ½ cup plus 3 tablespoons plus 2¼ teaspoons) potato starch (*not* potato flour)

INSTRUCTIONS FOR MIXING EITHER FLOUR BLEND

1. Whisk the ingredients together in a large food-safe plastic bin (see page 18). Secure the lid on the container and shake vigorously to distribute all the ingredients evenly.

2. Gluten-free flours tend to settle and sometimes separate while sitting, so always shake the container well before measuring for each baking project.

PANTRY INGREDIENTS

In addition to the base flour blend ingredients listed in this chapter, there are some others that you may want to keep in your pantry, refrigerator, or freezer so you can make breads easily without a trip to the grocery store. They will be called for in many of our recipes.

Apple cider vinegar, champagne vinegar, and ume plum vinegar (all interchangeable)

Baking powder (preferably Rumford brand, which is gluten free)

Buttermilk powder (or nondairy equivalent plus 1 teaspoon vinegar; see Resources, page 376)

Flaxseed meal (also called ground flaxseed)

Gluten-free oats and oat flour (see note on page 31)

Kosher salt or fine sea salt

Large eggs or egg replacer (such as Ener-G or a flax slurry—see page 24)

Milk powder (or a nondairy equivalent; see Resources, page 376)

Olive and vegetable oil

Ascorbic Acid (see Resources, page 376)

Basic Sandwich BREADS

This chapter is likely the one you will start with, and we recommend that you begin with our Simple Sandwich Bread (page 38). It has the most detailed instructions to guide you as you learn to make gluten-free breads.

Unlike traditional bread doughs, gluten-free doughs are loose—more like a heavy, sticky cake batter. They do not come together into a nice ball that is easy to recognize, so it may take a couple of tries to understand what you are looking for as the machine mixes the ingredients. We have included visual clues that will help you learn what each dough should look like as it is mixing. The remaining recipes in the book have shorter methods, but you can always refer to this first recipe for details and guidance with any of the breads in the book.

In this chapter, we have created recipes for the most popular breads that people like to use to make sandwiches with, from the mildest, most similar to Wonder Bread to a delightful mock rye bread that you will love with pastrami and Swiss cheese. These moist, tender breads do not crumble apart like many store-bought gluten-free breads and do not require toasting to enjoy.

If you are a white bread fan, you will love the Tender Buttermilk Bread, Traditional Egg Bread, and Golden Millet Bread. These are the closest to regular sandwich bread, with a similar delicate texture and flavor. If you miss wheat bread, you may be surprised at how close our Almost Wheat Sandwich Bread gets to it. While we cannot mimic the actual flavor of wheat, the flaxseed meal definitely gives us the chewy texture we are looking for and makes for a very satisfying loaf.

The multi-grain and oat breads add extra texture, flavor, and protein, making them a little heavier, with a chewier bite. They hold up very well to piles of sliced meats and cheeses. They can also be lightly toasted and used to dip into soup, stew, or chili.

The rye and pumpernickel breads are fascinating, because of course we cannot use rye flour. So how do we get that characteristic deep color, slight sourness, and distinctive "rye" flavor? A combination of interesting ingredients form a bread that is remarkably close to the rye breads we remember with fondness. Molasses and espresso powder help with the color and each adds a component of the complex flavor. But the most unique ingredient is ground caraway seeds. We have come to associate the flavor of caraway with rye breads, and adding the ground-up seeds (in addition to whole seeds, if you like them) yields a surprisingly similar aroma and flavor. It had us making a special trip to the deli just to grab some sliced pastrami and corned beef!

Welcome back to the world of sandwiches, toast, and enjoying bread again!

SIMPLE SANDWICH BREAD

MAKES 1 (1½-POUND/680 G) LOAF

This recipe will give you a good baseline for all the breads you make from this book. The method is very detailed to give you as much information as possible to make delicious gluten-free bread loaves. Turn back to this recipe any time you need help. Each kitchen is a unique environment, with humidity levels that can change with weather fluctuations. And each brand of bread machine works differently and may have unique requirements. The more loaves you bake, the better you will be able to anticipate what works for your kitchen and machine. Make notes of any adjustments as you go along so you can repeat them with other recipes if needed.

DRY INGREDIENTS

21 g (0.7 oz or 2 tablespoons) active dry yeast

360 g (12.7 oz or 3 cups) Light Flour Blend (page 34)

48 g (1.7 oz or ¼ cup) granulated cane sugar

1 tablespoon baking powder

2 teaspoons xanthan gum

1 teaspoon kosher salt

⅛ teaspoon ascorbic acid, optional

WET INGREDIENTS

270 ml (1 cup plus 2 tablespoons) 1% milk or water, heated to 80°F (27°C)

60 ml (¼ cup) olive oil

2 teaspoons apple cider vinegar

3 large eggs, at room temperature (see opposite)

1. Set the bread pan on the counter and insert the beater paddle(s). Unless otherwise directed by your machine's manufacturer, add the liquids first, then the dry ingredients, and finally the yeast.

2. Measure the yeast into a small bowl and set aside. Shake or whisk the flour blend vigorously before measuring. Weigh the flour blend and transfer it to a large bowl. Add the sugar, baking powder, xanthan gum, salt, and ascorbic acid (if using) to the bowl with the flour. Whisk the dry ingredients until evenly blended. Set the bowl beside the yeast and bread pan.

3. In a 2-cup (0.5 liter) glass measuring cup, combine the warm milk or water, olive oil, and vinegar.

4. When the eggs are warm, crack them into a 4-cup (1 liter) glass measuring cup and whisk lightly to blend. While whisking, add the olive oil mixture. Whisk until combined, then carefully pour the liquids into the bread pan.

5. Add the dry ingredients to the bread pan on top of the wet ingredients (they will float). Use a rubber spatula to completely cover the liquids with the dry ingredients. Make a shallow well in the center of the flour mixture with the spatula. Pour the yeast into the well (this will help keep the yeast and liquids separate until they are mixed together by the machine).

6. Place the bread pan in the machine, settle it in the center, and lock it in place. Close the lid and select:

   Gluten-free cycle (see page 14 if your machine does not have this setting)
   Loaf size: 1½ pounds/750 g
   Medium crust
   Start

BRINGING INGREDIENTS TO ROOM TEMPERATURE

EGGS: Fill a bowl with hot tap water and submerge the eggs (in their shells). Let the eggs sit for about ten minutes to safely bring them to room temperature.

MILK: If your milk (or water) is cold, pour it into a heatproof measuring cup and microwave for about thirty seconds. Even if it is a little too warm, it will cool by the time all of the ingredients are assembled.

---

7. About 3 minutes after the machine has started mixing/kneading, open the lid and use a spatula to scrape the sides of the pan, avoiding the moving paddle, and push any excess flour into the center. Check once or twice more, scraping the edges, corners, and under the dough and pushing any remaining unmixed dry ingredients into the center.

8. Don't be surprised when the dough looks more like a really thick pancake batter than a traditional bread dough. The correct consistency will look slightly dull on the surface but not dry, and it will tend to clump around the paddle (for a single paddle machine), creating a lump in the center. Due to the fluctuations in the weather and humidity in your kitchen, you may need to add a little more flour blend if the dough looks too moist (shiny) or a little more warm water if it appears dry or if your machine is laboring to mix it. You can make adjustments up to about halfway through the mix/knead cycle.

9. Once the kneading is done, do not lift the lid or touch the dough until the bread is done. Although some books recommend removing the beater paddle at this point to eliminate the hole in the bottom of the loaf, resist the temptation (unless specifically given the option in the recipe). Your loaf will not rise as high as it should if you remove the paddle. There is also no need to smooth the top; it will even out as it bakes.

10. As it bakes, the loaf will rise to within about ½ inch (1 cm) of the top of the pan, rounded in the center. Then it will settle back, flattening out and filling in the corners. At the end of the bake cycle, lift the lid and check the temperature. The bread is done when it reaches 206°F to 210°F (97°C to 99°C) on an instant-read thermometer inserted in its center. Depending on your machine, this may occur during or after the baking cycle has ended. Other doneness cues are that the loaf will pull away from the sides of the pan and have a beautiful golden-brown top (for the lighter-colored loaves), and the aroma of baked bread will fill the room—but the best indicator is internal temperature. If it hasn't reached the correct temperature, switch to the bake cycle and leave the loaf in the machine with the lid closed until it does. Gluten-free sandwich loaves made in a bread machine will not have a rounded top like wheat breads. Your goal is to wind up with a flat, even top. If it sinks in the center, there was probably too much liquid; cut the milk or water back by about 1 tablespoon next time.

ADDING BAKING TIME

To add baking time once the gluten-free cycle is done, hit cancel or stop. Select the bake only cycle and start. Set a timer for the additional time you need, but don't walk away—the loaves usually need just a little boost to get them to the correct internal temperature, which may take only a few minutes. Keep your thermometer ready and test often.

11. Using pot holders, remove the bread pan from the machine and set it on its side on a wire cooling rack. Leave the bread in the pan for 3 minutes, then turn it upside down on the cooling rack and the loaf should slip out of the pan. If it sticks, use a thin flexible plastic spatula or spreader to release the edges of the bread. Remove the paddle if it is embedded in the bottom of the loaf. Long-handled tongs are a good tool for this task.

12. Leave the bread upside down or on its side and cool it completely—at least 2 hours—before slicing. Leaving it upside down helps reduce sinking in the center. The longer resting period gives the loaf time to fully finish baking and firm up as it cools. The loaf may have a slightly gummy texture if you cut it too soon. If this happens, double-toast the slices (see page 19).

13. Store the bread in a resealable plastic bag or airtight container on the counter for up to 3 days. For longer storage, cut into even slices, double-wrap tightly in plastic, place in a resealable plastic bag, and freeze for up to 3 months.

REMOVING THE PADDLE

Use long-handled tongs or kitchen tweezers to peel back small pieces of the bottom crust, exposing the embedded paddle. Once the round part is completely unobstructed, find the "arm" of the paddle and follow it, pulling back the crust covering it. Insert one prong of the tongs into the center of the paddle, pinch the tongs together tightly, and gently wiggle them until the paddle releases and you can pull it out. As you pull, twist your wrist, tipping the paddle up to slip the arm out. Be careful, because the paddle will be very hot.

TENDER BUTTERMILK BREAD

MAKES 1 (1½-POUND/680 G) LOAF

This is a beautiful cream-colored bread, as close to white bread as we can get. It's soft, with a mild tangy flavor from the buttermilk. You will love this toasted with butter or for a PB&J, and there is nothing better for grilled cheese sandwiches.

DRY INGREDIENTS

21 g (0.7 oz or 2 tablespoons) active dry yeast

360 g (12.7 oz or 3 cups) Light Flour Blend (page 34)

58 g (2 oz or ½ cup) buttermilk powder

39 g (1.4 oz or 3 tablespoons) granulated cane sugar

1 tablespoon baking powder

2 teaspoons xanthan gum

2 teaspoons kosher or fine salt

⅛ teaspoon ascorbic acid, optional

WET INGREDIENTS

56 g (2 oz or 4 tablespoons/½ stick) unsalted butter, melted and slightly cooled

3 large eggs, at room temperature (see page 39), beaten

270 ml (1 cup plus 2 tablespoons) water, warmed to 80°F (27°C)

1 teaspoon apple cider vinegar

1. Set the bread pan on the counter and insert the beater paddle(s). Unless otherwise directed by your machine's manufacturer, add the liquids first, then the dry ingredients, and finally the yeast.

2. Measure the yeast into a small bowl and set aside. Combine the remaining dry ingredients in a large mixing bowl, whisking until thoroughly combined.

3. In a 4-cup (1 liter) glass measuring cup, whisk the wet ingredients together and pour into the bread pan. Use a spatula to spread the dry ingredients over the wet ingredients. Make a shallow well in the center and pour in the yeast.

4. Place the bread pan in the machine, settle it in the center, and lock it in place. Close the lid and select:

   Gluten-free cycle (see page 14 if your machine does not have this setting)
   Loaf size: 1½ pounds/750 g
   Medium crust
   Start

5. About 3 minutes after the machine has started mixing/kneading, open the lid and use the spatula to scrape the sides of the pan, avoiding the moving paddle, and push any flour that has accumulated around the edges or under the dough into the center. Check again once or twice during kneading, scraping any loose flour into the center. The dough will look like a very sticky pancake batter with a slightly dull surface. If the dough looks too wet or too dry, add a little flour blend or tiny amounts of warm water. Once the mixing/kneading is done, leave the lid closed during the rise and bake cycles.

6. At the end of the bake cycle, lift the lid and check the temperature. When the center of the bread reaches 206°F to 210°F (97°C to 99°C) on an instant-read thermometer, it is done. Remove the bread pan from the machine and set it on its side on a wire cooling rack. Leave the bread in the pan for a couple of minutes, then turn the pan upside down and slide the loaf onto the wire rack. Remove the paddle if it is embedded in the bottom of the loaf. Cool the loaf upside down on the wire rack for at least 2 hours before slicing.

7. Store the bread in a resealable plastic bag or airtight container on the counter for up to 3 days. For longer storage, cut into even slices, double-wrap tightly in plastic, place in a resealable plastic bag, and freeze for up to 3 months.

TRADITIONAL EGG BREAD

MAKES 1 (1½-POUND/680 G) LOAF

Eggs add lushness to this gluten-free bread, and the simplicity of the other ingredients lets the eggs shine in this loaf. Having a rich, decadent bread is a real treat for special occasions and holidays. This dough can also be used to make a gluten-free version of Dinner Rolls (page 98), and if you still have some left after a couple of days, you can use it for truly amazing French toast.

DRY INGREDIENTS

21 g (0.7 oz or 2 tablespoons) active dry yeast

270 g (9.5 oz or 2¼ cups) Light Flour Blend (page 34)

150 g (5.3 oz or 1¼ cups) millet flour

¼ cup milk powder (22 g/0.8 oz) or DariFree (40 g/1.4 oz)

26 g (0.9 oz or 2 tablespoons) granulated cane sugar

2½ teaspoons baking powder

1 teaspoon xanthan gum

½ teaspoon kosher or fine sea salt

⅛ teaspoon ascorbic acid, optional

WET INGREDIENTS

20 g (0.7 oz or 1 tablespoon) honey or agave nectar

180 ml (¾ cup) water, warmed to 80°F (27°C)

3 large eggs, at room temperature (see page 39), beaten

85 g (3 oz or 6 tablespoons/¾ stick) salted butter, melted and slightly cooled

2 teaspoons apple cider vinegar

1. Set the bread pan on the counter and insert the beater paddle(s). Unless otherwise directed by your machine's manufacturer, add the liquids first, then the dry ingredients, and finally the yeast.

2. Measure the yeast into a small bowl and set aside. Combine the remaining dry ingredients in a large mixing bowl, whisking until thoroughly combined. Set the bowl beside the yeast and bread pan.

3. Whisk the honey and water together in a 4-cup (1 liter) glass measuring cup. Add the remaining wet ingredients and whisk again. Pour into the bread pan. Add the dry ingredients over the top of the liquids, spreading them out with a spatula to completely cover the liquids. Make a shallow well in the center and pour in the yeast.

4. Place the bread pan in the machine, settle it in the center, and lock it in place. Close the lid and select:

   Gluten-free cycle (see page 14 if your machine does not have this setting)
   Loaf size: 1½ pounds/750 g
   Medium crust
   Start

5. About 3 minutes into the mixing process, open the lid and use the spatula to scrape down the sides of the pan, avoiding the paddle. Push any flour that has accumulated around the edges and under the dough into the center. Check again once or twice during kneading, scraping the edges, corners, and under the dough. If the dough looks too wet or too dry, add a little flour blend or tiny amounts of warm water. Once the mixing/kneading is done, leave the lid closed during the rise and bake cycles.

6. At the end of the bake cycle, lift the lid and check the temperature. When the bread reaches 206°F to 210°F (97°C to 99°C) on an instant-read thermometer inserted in the center, it is done. Remove the pan from the machine and set it on its side on a wire cooling rack. Leave the bread in the pan for a couple of minutes, then turn the pan upside down and slide the loaf onto the wire rack. Carefully remove the paddle if it is embedded in the bottom of the loaf. Let the bread cool, upside down, for at least 2 hours before slicing.

7. Store the bread in a resealable plastic bag or airtight container on the counter for up to 3 days. For longer storage, cut into even slices, double-wrap tightly in plastic, place in a resealable plastic bag, and freeze for up to 3 months.

PAIN DE MIE

MAKES 1 (1½-POUND/680 G) LOAF • DAIRY FREE

This is the everyday bread you find in supermarkets all over France. The French use it for tartines, or what we would call open-faced sandwiches. Try it as an afternoon snack, toasted and spread with Nutella. For those who are dairy free, this is a wonderful bread you and your family will love.

DRY INGREDIENTS

1 tablespoon instant yeast

367.5 g (13 oz or 3 cups plus 3 tablespoons) Light Flour Blend (page 34) or Whole-Grain Flour Blend (page 34)

1½ teaspoons kosher or fine sea salt

39 g (1.4 oz or 3 tablespoons) granulated cane sugar

1½ teaspoons xanthan gum

WET INGREDIENTS

4 large eggs, at room temperature (see page 39), beaten

240 ml (1 cup) unsweetened soy, rice, or coconut milk, warmed to about 80°F (27°C)

56 g (2 oz or 4 tablespoons/½ stick) nondairy butter substitute, melted and slightly cooled

2 teaspoons apple cider vinegar

1. Set the bread pan on the counter and insert the beater paddle(s). Unless otherwise directed by your machine's manufacturer, add the liquids first, then the dry ingredients, and finally the yeast.

2. Measure the yeast into a small bowl and set aside. In a large mixing bowl, whisk the remaining dry ingredients together. Set aside.

3. In a 4-cup glass measuring cup, whisk the wet ingredients together and pour into the bread pan. Use a spatula to spread the dry ingredients over the wet ingredients. Make a shallow well in the center and pour in the yeast.

4. Place the bread pan in the machine, settle it in the center, and lock it in place. Close the lid and select:

   Gluten-free cycle (see page 14 if your machine does not have this setting)
   Loaf size: 1½ pounds/750 g
   Medium crust
   Start

5. After the first kneading cycle, scrape the sides and bottom of the pan with the spatula to make sure all the dry ingredients are incorporated.

6. At the end of the bake cycle, lift the lid and check the temperature. The bread is done when it registers 206°F to 210°F (97°C to 99°C) on an instant-read thermometer inserted in the center of the loaf. Remove the pan from the machine and place it on its side on a wire rack. Leave the bread in the pan for a couple of minutes, then turn the pan upside down and slide the loaf onto the wire rack. Carefully remove the paddle if it is embedded in the bottom of the loaf. Let the bread cool upside down for at least 2 hours before slicing.

7. This bread is best eaten the day it is made. If you have any left the next day, toast it. For longer storage, cut into even slices, double-wrap tightly in plastic, place in a resealable plastic bag, and freeze for up to 3 months.

BRIOCHE LOAF

MAKES 1 (1½-POUND/680 G) LOAF

Chef Nicole Plue generously shared this recipe for the brioche they serve at Cyrus restaurant in Healdsburg, California. With Chef Plue's help, we were able to adapt the recipe to a gluten-free bread that is close to the rich, buttery loaves famous in France.

This is the perfect bread to serve before dinner, as they do in restaurants. It also makes the most heavenly French toast—you can add a sprinkle of cinnamon to the beaten egg mixture for a little more pop. A favorite after-school treat in the Midwest is a sugar sandwich. Spread slices of this bread with butter, sprinkle with sugar, and fold in half. It will tide your kids over until dinner and definitely put a smile on their faces!

Thanks to the higher percentage of butter, the dough looks very wet when it is mixing, but resist the urge to add more flour. Part of the reason it has such a delicate crumb is the moisture. But the added moisture also makes the dough very heavy, so if the motor starts to labor, ease the burden by lifting the dough away from the paddle, allowing it to move freely. The resulting loaf is light and airy, the tallest one we've gotten, incredibly tender and absolutely intoxicating.

DRY INGREDIENTS

2 teaspoons active dry yeast

480 g (17 oz or 4 cups) Light Flour Blend (page 34)

63 g (2.2 oz or ⅓ cup) granulated cane sugar

¼ cup milk powder (22 g/0.8 oz) or DariFree (40 g/1.4 oz)

2½ teaspoons kosher or fine sea salt

1 teaspoon baking powder

1 teaspoon xanthan gum

½ teaspoon dough enhancer

⅛ teaspoon ascorbic acid, optional

WET INGREDIENTS

170 g (6 oz or 12 tablespoons/1½ sticks) unsalted European-style butter, melted and slightly cooled

4 large eggs, at room temperature (see page 39), beaten

160 ml (⅔ cup) 1% milk or water, warmed to about 80°F (27°C)

2 teaspoons apple cider vinegar

1. Set the bread pan on the counter and insert the beater paddle(s). Unless otherwise directed by your machine's manufacturer, add the liquids first, then the dry ingredients, and finally the yeast.

2. Measure the yeast into a small bowl and set aside. In a large mixing bowl, whisk the remaining dry ingredients together.

3. In a 4-cup (1 liter) glass measuring cup, whisk the wet ingredients together and pour into the bread pan. Use a spatula to spread the dry ingredients over the wet ingredients. Make a shallow well in the center and pour in the yeast.

4. Place the bread pan in the machine, settle it in the center, and lock it in place. Close the lid and select:

   Gluten-free cycle (see page 14 if your machine does not have this setting)
   Loaf size: 1½ pounds/750 g
   Medium crust
   Start

5. About 3 minutes into the mixing process, open the lid and use a spatula to scrape down the sides of the pan and under the dough as needed. Push any flour that has accumulated into the center. Check again once or twice during kneading, scraping the edges, corners, and under the dough. This dough is heavier and stickier than others, so listen as the machine mixes/kneads. If you hear it laboring, use your spatula to move the dough in the pan, pulling it away from the paddle if it is clumping around it, to ease the stress on the motor. Stay close to the machine until it is done kneading in case the dough needs to be adjusted. Once the mixing/kneading is done, leave the lid closed during the rise and bake cycles.

6. At the end of the bake cycle, lift the lid and check the temperature. When the bread reaches 206°F to 210°F (97°C to 99°C) on an instant-read thermometer inserted in the center, it is done. Remove the pan from the machine and set it on its side on a wire cooling rack. Leave the bread in the pan for a couple of minutes, then turn the pan upside down and slide the loaf onto the wire rack. Carefully remove the paddle if it is embedded in the bottom of the loaf. Set the bread back on its side and cool for at least 2 hours before slicing.

7. Store the bread in a resealable plastic bag or airtight container on the counter for up to 2 days. For longer storage, cut into even slices, double-wrap tightly in plastic, place in a resealable plastic bag, and freeze for up to 3 months.

POTATO BREAD

MAKES 1 (1½-POUND/680 G) LOAF • DAIRY-FREE OPTION

This bread is like Wonder Bread on steroids. It's denser, with a more savory flavor; pliable, yet sturdy enough to stand up to chicken and other sandwich salads. The potato adds nutrients and helps keep the bread moist longer. This dough is another great option to use to make Dinner Rolls (page 98). If you use Yukon Gold potatoes, the bread will have a slight golden hue.

DRY INGREDIENTS

1 tablespoon instant yeast

300 g (10.6 oz or 2½ cups) Light Flour Blend (page 34) or Whole-Grain Flour Blend (page 34)

82 g (2.9 oz or ½ cup) potato starch (*not* potato flour)

½ cup DariFree (69 g/2.4 oz) or milk powder (44 g/1.6 oz)

26 g (0.9 oz or 2 tablespoons) sugar

2 teaspoons tapioca flour/starch

2 teaspoons psyllium husk flakes or powder

2 teaspoons kosher or fine sea salt

⅛ teaspoon ascorbic acid, optional

WET INGREDIENTS

300 ml (1¼ cups) water, warmed to about 80°F (27°C)

2 large eggs, at room temperature (see page 39), beaten

2 teaspoons apple cider vinegar

28 g (1 oz or 2 tablespoons/¼ stick) nondairy butter substitute, melted and slightly cooled

170 g (6 oz or 1½ cups) riced or mashed cooked and peeled potatoes

1. Set the bread pan on the counter and insert the beater paddle(s). Unless otherwise directed by your machine's manufacturer, add the liquids first, then the dry ingredients, and finally the yeast.

2. Measure the yeast into a small bowl and set aside. In a large mixing bowl, whisk the remaining dry ingredients together.

3. Whisk the water, eggs, vinegar, and butter in a 4-cup (1 liter) glass measuring cup until smooth. Pour into the bread pan. Add the potatoes. Use a spatula to spread the dry ingredients over the wet ingredients. Make a shallow well in the center and pour in the yeast.

4. Place the bread pan in the machine, settle it in the center, and lock it in place. Close the lid and select:

   Gluten-free cycle (see page 14 if your machine does not have this setting)
   Loaf size: 1½ pounds/750 g
   Medium crust
   Start

5. After the first kneading cycle, scrape the sides and bottom of the pan with a spatula to make sure all the dry ingredients are incorporated.

6. At the end of the bake cycle, lift the lid and check the temperature. The bread is done when it registers 206°F to 210°F (97°C to 99°C) on an instant-read thermometer inserted in the center of the loaf. Remove the pan from the machine and place it on its side on a wire rack. Leave the bread in the pan for a couple of minutes, then turn the pan upside down and slide the loaf onto the wire rack. Carefully remove the paddle if it is embedded in the bottom of the loaf. Let the bread cool upside down for at least 2 hours before slicing.

7. Store the bread in a resealable plastic bag or airtight container on the counter for up to 3 days. For longer storage, cut into even slices, double-wrap tightly in plastic, place in a resealable plastic bag, and freeze for up to 3 months.

"THANKSGIVING" SANDWICH BREAD

MAKES 1 (1½-POUND/680 G) LOAF   ◆   DAIRY-FREE OPTION

The combination of herbs in poultry seasoning creates the perfect bread for sandwiches made with leftover Thanksgiving turkey. Whether you slather it with cranberry sauce, add a touch of leftover gravy, or tuck a little dressing on top of the turkey, this bread will enhance the flavors and make everything taste fresh and original. You can also cut this bread into cubes and bake them to make croutons for your holiday stuffing or dressing—perfect for layering flavors!

DRY INGREDIENTS

21 g (0.7 oz or 2 tablespoons) active dry yeast

240 g (8.5 oz or 2 cups) Light Flour Blend (page 34)

120 g (4.2 oz or 1 cup) sorghum flour

½ cup milk powder (44 g/1.6 oz) or DariFree (69 g/2.4 oz)

26 g (0.9 oz or 2 tablespoons) granulated cane sugar

14 g (0.5 oz or 2 tablespoons) flaxseed meal or ground flaxseed

2 tablespoons gluten-free oats

2 teaspoons baking powder

2 teaspoons xanthan gum

1½ teaspoons kosher or fine sea salt

1½ teaspoons dried poultry seasoning

¾ teaspoon onion powder

⅛ teaspoon ascorbic acid, optional

WET INGREDIENTS

2 large eggs, at room temperature (see page 39), beaten

315 ml (1¼ cups plus 1 tablespoon) water, heated to about 80°F (27°C)

60 ml (¼ cup) olive oil

2 teaspoons apple cider vinegar

A LITTLE LIFT

If you want lighter loaves or more lift, use sparkling water instead of regular water. It helps the other leaveners, adding a little extra rise to your breads.

1. Set the bread pan on the counter and insert the beater paddle(s). Unless otherwise directed by your machine's manufacturer, add the liquids first, then the dry ingredients, and finally the yeast.

2. Measure the yeast into a small bowl and set aside. In a large mixing bowl, whisk the remaining dry ingredients together.

3. In a 4-cup (1 liter) glass measuring cup, whisk the wet ingredients together and pour into the bread pan. Use a spatula to spread the dry ingredients over the wet ingredients, covering completely. Make a shallow well in the center and pour in the yeast.

4. Place the bread pan in the machine, settle it in the center, and lock it in place. Close the lid and select:

   Gluten-free cycle (see page 14 if your machine does not have this setting)
   Loaf size: 1½ pounds/750 g
   Medium crust
   Start

5. About 3 minutes into the mixing process, open the lid and use a spatula to scrape down the sides of the pan, avoiding the paddle. Push any flour that has accumulated around the edges and under the dough into the center. Check again once or twice during kneading, scraping the edges and corners. If the dough/batter looks too wet or too dry, add a little flour blend or tiny amounts of warm water. Close the lid and do not open it during the rise and bake cycles.

6. At the end of the bake cycle, lift the lid and check the temperature. When the bread reaches 206°F to 210°F (97°C to 99°C) on an instant-read thermometer inserted into the center, it is done. Remove the bread pan from the machine and set it on its side on a wire cooling rack. Leave the bread in the pan for a couple of minutes, then turn the pan upside down and slide the loaf onto the wire rack. Carefully remove the paddle if it is embedded in the bottom of the loaf. Place the bread back on its side and cool for at least 2 hours before slicing.

7. Store the bread in a resealable plastic bag or airtight container on the counter for up to 3 days. For longer storage, cut into even slices, double-wrap tightly in plastic, place in a resealable plastic bag, and freeze for up to 3 months.

HERBED SANDWICH BREAD

MAKES 1 (1½-POUND/680 G) LOAF ◆ DAIRY-FREE OPTION

Herb breads are wonderful for sandwiches and also make the best croutons! The beauty of this recipe is that you have control over the balance of flavors. If you like one herb more than the others, add more of it. If you don't like one of them, leave it out. It is completely up to you.

DRY INGREDIENTS

21 g (0.7 oz or 2 tablespoons) active dry yeast

360 g (12.7 oz or 3 cups) Light Flour Blend (page 34)

48 g (1.7 oz or ¼ cup) granulated cane sugar

1 tablespoon baking powder

2 teaspoons xanthan gum

2 teaspoons kosher salt

1 teaspoon dried dill weed

1 teaspoon dried oregano

1 teaspoon dried basil

1 teaspoon dried thyme

1 teaspoon onion powder

⅛ teaspoon ascorbic acid, optional

WET INGREDIENTS

3 large eggs, at room temperature (see page 39), beaten

270 ml (1 cup plus 2 tablespoons) 1% milk or water, warmed to about 80°F (27°C)

60 ml (¼ cup) olive oil

2 teaspoons apple cider vinegar

1. Set the bread pan on the counter and insert the beater paddle(s). Unless otherwise directed by your machine's manufacturer, add the liquids first, then the dry ingredients, and finally the yeast.

2. Measure the yeast into a small bowl and set aside. In a large mixing bowl, whisk the remaining dry ingredients together.

3. In a 4-cup (1 liter) glass measuring cup, whisk the wet ingredients together and pour into the bread pan. Use a spatula to spread the dry ingredients over the wet ingredients, covering completely. Make a shallow well in the center and pour in the yeast.

4. Place the bread pan in the machine, settle it in the center, and lock it in place. Close the lid and select:

   Gluten-free cycle (see page 14 if your machine does not have this setting)
   Loaf size: 1½ pounds/750 g
   Medium crust
   Start

5. About 3 minutes after the machine has started mixing/kneading, open the lid and use a spatula to scrape the sides of the pan, avoiding the paddle, and push any loose flour into the center of the pan. Check again once or twice during the knead cycle, scraping any loose flour into the dough. If the dough/batter looks too wet or too dry, add a little flour blend or tiny amounts of warm water. Once the mix/knead cycle is done, leave the lid closed during the rise and bake cycles.

6. At the end of the bake cycle, lift the lid and check the temperature. When the bread reaches 206°F to 210°F (97°C to 99°C) on an instant-read thermometer inserted in the center, it is done. Remove the bread pan from the machine and set it on its side on a wire cooling rack. Leave the bread in the pan for a couple of minutes, then turn the pan upside down and slide the loaf onto the wire rack. Carefully remove the paddle if it is embedded in the bottom of the loaf. Cool the loaf upside down for at least 2 hours before slicing.

7. Store the bread in a resealable plastic bag or airtight container on the counter for up to 3 days. For longer storage, cut into even slices, double-wrap tightly in plastic, place in a resealable plastic bag, and freeze for up to 3 months.

ALMOST WHEAT SANDWICH BREAD

MAKES 1 (1½-POUND/680 G) LOAF   •   DAIRY-FREE OPTION

While no gluten-free flour can mimic the flavor of wheat breads exactly, this bread comes pretty close. Loaded with extra flavor from the sorghum flour and texture from the flaxseed meal, this bread might fool you if you close your eyes! The flax adds soluble and insoluble fiber to your diet as well as heart-healthy omega-3 essential fatty acids.

DRY INGREDIENTS

21 g (0.7 oz or 2 tablespoons) active dry yeast

240 g (8.5 oz or 2 cups) Light Flour Blend (page 34)

110 g (3.9 oz or 1 cup) sorghum flour

½ cup milk powder (44 g/1.6 oz) or DariFree (69 g/2.4 oz)

26 g (0.9 oz or ¼ cup) flaxseed meal or ground flaxseed

39 g (1.4 oz or 3 tablespoons) granulated cane sugar

2 teaspoons baking powder

2 teaspoons xanthan gum

1½ teaspoons kosher or fine sea salt

⅛ teaspoon ascorbic acid, optional

WET INGREDIENTS

3 large eggs, at room temperature (see page 39), beaten

270 ml (1 cup plus 2 tablespoons) water, heated to about 80°F (27°C)

45 ml (3 tablespoons) olive oil

2 teaspoons apple cider vinegar

1. Set the bread pan on the counter and insert the beater paddle(s). Unless otherwise directed by your machine's manufacturer, add the liquids first, then the dry ingredients, and finally the yeast.

2. Measure the yeast into a small bowl and set aside. In a large mixing bowl, whisk the remaining dry ingredients together.

3. In a 4-cup (1 liter) glass measuring cup, whisk the wet ingredients together and pour into the bread pan. Use a spatula to spread the dry ingredients over the wet ingredients, covering completely. Make a shallow well in the center and pour in the yeast.

4. Place the bread pan in the machine, settle it in the center, and lock it in place. Close the lid and select:

   Gluten-free cycle (see page 14 if your machine does not have this setting)
   Loaf size: 1½ pounds/750 g
   Medium crust
   Start

5. About 3 minutes after the machine has started mixing/kneading, open the lid and use a spatula to scrape the sides of the pan. Push any flour that has accumulated around the edges and under the dough into the center. Check again once or twice during kneading, scraping any loose flour into the dough, avoiding the paddle. The dough will look like a very sticky pancake batter with a slightly dull surface. If the dough looks too wet or too dry, add a little flour blend or tiny amounts of warm water. Once the mix/knead cycle is done, leave the lid closed during the rise and bake cycles.

6. At the end of the bake cycle, lift the lid and check the temperature. When the bread reaches 206°F to 210°F (97°C to 99°C) on an instant-read thermometer inserted in the center, it is done. Remove the bread pan from the machine and set it on its side on a wire cooling rack. Leave the bread in the pan for a couple of minutes, then turn the pan upside down and slide the loaf onto the wire rack. Remove the paddle if it is embedded in the bottom of the loaf. Cool the loaf upside down on the wire rack for at least 2 hours before slicing.

7. Store the bread in a resealable plastic bag or airtight container on the counter for up to 3 days. For longer storage, cut into even slices, double-wrap tightly in plastic, place in a resealable plastic bag, and freeze for up to 3 months.

EASY SORGHUM SANDWICH BREAD

MAKES 1 (1½-POUND/680 G) LOAF • DAIRY-FREE OPTION

Sorghum is one of the world's most widely grown cereal crops. In the United States, its original popularity and use was to make the molasses-like sweetener called sorghum syrup. With the rise in gluten intolerance and subsequent need for alternative flours, there has been a resurgence in the demand for sorghum flour. People are discovering its delicate, slightly sweet flavor, and pastry chefs are adding it to their baked goods, both regular and gluten free. Sorghum's protein and fiber content help the structure of breads, giving the loaves more strength and helping them bake a little higher and lighter.

DRY INGREDIENTS

21 g (0.7 oz or 2 tablespoons) active dry yeast

240 g (8.5 oz or 2 cups) Light Flour Blend (page 34)

110 g (3.9 oz or 1 cup) sorghum flour

48 g (1.7 oz or ¼ cup) granulated cane sugar

¼ cup milk powder (22 g/0.8 oz) or DariFree (40 g/1.4 oz)

2 teaspoons xanthan gum

2 teaspoons baking powder

1 teaspoon kosher salt

⅛ teaspoon ascorbic acid, optional

WET INGREDIENTS

3 large eggs, at room temperature (see page 39), beaten

240 ml (1 cup) water, heated to about 80°F (27°C)

60 ml (¼ cup) olive oil

2 teaspoons apple cider vinegar

1. Set the bread pan on the counter and insert the beater paddle(s). Unless otherwise directed by your machine's manufacturer, add the liquids first, then the dry ingredients, and finally the yeast.

2. Measure the yeast into a small bowl and set aside. In a large mixing bowl, whisk the remaining dry ingredients together.

3. In a 4-cup (1 liter) glass measuring cup, whisk the wet ingredients together and pour into the bread pan. Use a spatula to spread the dry ingredients over the wet ingredients, covering completely. Make a shallow well in the center and pour in the yeast.

4. Place the bread pan in the machine, settle it in the center, and lock it in place. Close the lid and select:

    Gluten-free cycle (see page 14 if your machine does not have this setting)
    Loaf size: 1½ pounds/750 g
    Medium crust
    Start

5. About 3 minutes into the mixing process, open the lid and use a spatula to scrape down the sides of the pan, avoiding the paddle. Push any flour that has accumulated around the edges and under the dough into the center. Check again once or twice during kneading, scraping the edges, corners, and under the dough. If the dough looks too wet or too dry, add a little flour blend or tiny amounts of warm water. Once the mix/knead cycle is done, leave the lid closed during the rise and bake cycles.

6. At the end of the bake cycle, lift the lid and check the temperature. When the bread reaches 206°F to 210°F (97°C to 99°C) on an instant-read thermometer inserted in the center, it is done. Remove the pan from the machine and set it on its side on a wire cooling rack. Leave the bread in the pan for a couple of minutes, then turn the pan upside down and slide the loaf onto the wire rack. Carefully remove the paddle if it is embedded in the bottom of the loaf. Let the bread cool for at least 2 hours before slicing.

7. Store the bread in a resealable plastic bag or airtight container on the counter for up to 3 days. For longer storage, cut into even slices, double-wrap tightly in plastic, place in a resealable plastic bag, and freeze for up to 3 months.

SORGHUM-OAT BUTTERMILK BREAD

MAKES 1 (1½-POUND/680 G) LOAF

With the addition of the sorghum and oat flours, this loaf is closer in flavor to a wheat bread than many gluten-free breads. The buttermilk gives it an almost "white bread" texture. This bread is tender and soft with a hint of oats you will love.

DRY INGREDIENTS

4 teaspoons active dry yeast

165 g (5.8 oz or 1½ cups) sorghum flour

120 g (4.2 oz or 1 cup) Light Flour Blend (page 34)

63 g (2.2 oz or ½ cup) gluten-free oat flour

58 g (2 oz or ½ cup) buttermilk powder

39 g (1.4 oz or 3 tablespoons) granulated cane sugar

2 teaspoons xanthan gum

2 teaspoons kosher or fine sea salt

1½ teaspoons baking powder

½ teaspoon baking soda

⅛ teaspoon ascorbic acid, optional

WET INGREDIENTS

2 teaspoons honey

270 ml (1 cup plus 2 tablespoons) water, warmed to 80°F (27°C)

3 large eggs, at room temperature (see page 39), beaten

60 ml (¼ cup) olive oil

1 teaspoon apple cider vinegar

1. Set the bread pan on the counter and insert the beater paddle(s). Unless otherwise directed by your machine's manufacturer, add the liquids first, then the dry ingredients, and finally the yeast.

2. Measure the yeast into a small bowl and set aside. In a large mixing bowl, whisk the remaining dry ingredients together.

3. Whisk the honey and water together in a 4-cup (1 liter) glass measuring cup to dissolve the honey. Add the remaining wet ingredients and whisk again. Pour into the bread pan. Use a spatula to spread the dry ingredients over the wet ingredients, covering completely. Make a shallow well in the center and pour in the yeast.

4. Place the bread pan in the machine, settle it in the center, and lock it in place. Close the lid and select:

   Gluten-free cycle (see page 14 if your machine does not have this setting)
   Loaf size: 1½ pounds/750 g
   Medium crust
   Start

5. About 3 minutes after the machine has started mixing/kneading, open the lid and use a spatula to scrape the sides of the pan, avoiding the paddle, and push any loose flour into the center of the pan. Check again once or twice during kneading, scraping the edges, corners, and under the dough. If the dough looks too wet or too dry, add a little flour blend or tiny amounts of warm water. Once the mix/knead cycle is done, leave the lid closed during the rise and bake cycles.

6. At the end of the bake cycle, lift the lid and check the temperature. When the bread reaches 206°F to 210°F (97°C to 99°C) on an instant-read thermometer inserted in the center, it is done. Remove the bread pan from the machine and set it on its side on a wire cooling rack. Leave the bread in the pan for a couple of minutes, then turn the pan upside down and slide the loaf onto the wire rack. Carefully remove the paddle if it is embedded in the bottom of the loaf. Let the bread cool upside down for at least 2 hours before slicing.

7. Store the bread in a resealable plastic bag or airtight container on the counter for up to 3 days. For longer storage, cut into even slices, double-wrap tightly in plastic, place in a resealable bag, and freeze for up to 3 months.

OAT BREAD

MAKES 1 (1½-POUND/680 G) LOAF ◆ DAIRY FREE

This bread will remind you of a bowl of oatmeal—but without the brown sugar and milk. Gluten free and dairy free, it is a delicious option for those with multiple allergies. It is a wonderful base for cold cuts (gluten free, of course), tuna, and chicken salad sandwiches.

DRY INGREDIENTS

21 g (0.7 oz or 2 tablespoons) active dry yeast

240 g (8.5 oz or 2 cups) Light Flour Blend (page 34)

125 g (4.4 oz or 1 cup) gluten-free oat flour

21 g (0.7 oz or ¼ cup) gluten-free oats or oatmeal

48 g (1.7 oz or ¼ cup) granulated cane sugar

18 g (0.6 oz or 4 teaspoons) baking powder

2 teaspoons xanthan gum

1¼ teaspoons kosher or fine sea salt

⅛ teaspoon ascorbic acid, optional

WET INGREDIENTS

3 large eggs, at room temperature (see page 39), beaten

270 ml (1 cup plus 2 tablespoons) water, warmed to about 80°F (27°C)

60 ml (¼ cup) olive oil

2 teaspoons apple cider vinegar

TOPPING

Water, for brushing

Gluten-free oats, for sprinkling

1. Set the bread pan on the counter and insert the beater paddle(s). Unless otherwise directed by your machine's manufacturer, add the liquids first, then the dry ingredients, and finally the yeast.

2. Measure the yeast into a small bowl and set aside. In a large mixing bowl, whisk the remaining dry ingredients together.

3. In a 4-cup (1 liter) glass measuring cup, whisk the wet ingredients together and pour into the bread pan. Use a spatula to spread the dry ingredients over the wet ingredients, covering completely. Make a shallow well in the center and pour in the yeast.

4. Place the bread pan in the machine, settle it in the center, and lock it in place. Close the lid and select:

   Gluten-free cycle (see page 14 if your machine does not have this setting)
   Loaf size: 1½ pounds/750 g
   Medium crust
   Start

5. About 3 minutes into the mixing process, open the lid and use a spatula to scrape down the sides of the pan, avoiding the paddle. Push any flour that has accumulated around the edges into the center. Check again once or twice during kneading, scraping the edges, corners, and under the dough. If the dough looks too wet or too dry, add a little flour blend or tiny amounts of warm water. When the mix/knead cycle is done, brush the top of the loaf with a little water and sprinkle with oats, then close the lid and leave it closed during the rise and bake cycles.

6. At the end of the bake cycle, lift the lid and check the temperature. When the bread reaches 206°F to 210°F (97°C to 99°C) on an instant-read thermometer inserted in the center, it is done. Remove the pan from the machine and set it on its side on a wire cooling rack. Leave the bread in the pan for a couple of minutes, then turn the pan upside down and slide the loaf onto the wire rack. Carefully remove the paddle if it is embedded in the bottom of the loaf. Let the bread cool for at least 2 hours before slicing.

7. Store the bread in a resealable plastic bag or airtight container on the counter for up to 3 days. For longer storage, cut into even slices, double-wrap tightly in plastic, place in a resealable plastic bag, and freeze for up to 3 months.

HONEY OAT BREAD

MAKES 1 (1½-POUND/680 G) LOAF • DAIRY-FREE OPTION

This delicious bread has a hint of oat flavor and a touch of sweetness from the honey. It makes great cold-cut sandwiches. And there is nothing better for making French toast or Monte Cristo sandwiches.

DRY INGREDIENTS

21 g (0.7 oz or 2 tablespoons) active dry yeast

1 tablespoon active dry yeast

240 g (8.5 oz or 2 cups) Light Flour Blend (page 34)

125 g (4.4 oz or 1 cup) gluten-free oat flour (see Note)

¼ cup milk powder (22 g/0.8 oz) or DariFree (40 g/1.4 oz)

26 g (0.9 oz or 2 tablespoons) granulated cane sugar

2 teaspoons xanthan gum

2 teaspoons baking powder

2 teaspoons kosher or fine sea salt

⅛ teaspoon ascorbic acid, optional

WET INGREDIENTS

85 g (3 oz or ¼ cup) honey

240 ml (1 cup) water, warmed to 80°F (27°C)

3 large eggs, at room temperature (see page 39), beaten

60 ml (¼ cup) olive oil

2 teaspoons apple cider vinegar

TOPPING

Milk or water, for brushing

Gluten-free oats, for sprinkling

NOTE: Add an additional tablespoon of oat flour on rainy or very humid days, or as needed.

1. Set the bread pan on the counter and insert the beater paddle(s). Unless otherwise directed by your machine's manufacturer, add the liquids first, then the dry ingredients, and finally the yeast.

2. Measure the yeast into a small bowl and set aside. In a large mixing bowl, whisk the remaining dry ingredients together.

3. Whisk the honey and water together in a 4-cup (1 liter) glass measuring cup to dissolve the honey. Add the remaining wet ingredients and whisk again. Pour into the bread pan. Use a spatula to spread the dry ingredients over the wet ingredients, covering completely. Make a shallow well in the center and pour in the yeast.

4. Place the bread pan in the machine, settle it in the center, and lock it in place. Close the lid and select:

    Gluten-free cycle (see page 14 if your machine does not have this setting)
    Loaf size: 1½ pounds/750 g
    Medium crust
    Start

5. About 3 minutes into the mixing process, open the lid and use a spatula to scrape down the sides of the pan and under the dough, avoiding the paddle. Push any flour that has accumulated into the center. Check again once or twice during kneading, scraping the edges, corners, and under the dough. If the dough looks too wet or too dry, add a little flour blend or tiny amounts of warm water.

6. When the mixing and kneading is done, gently brush the top of the bread with a little milk or water and sprinkle oats over it. Close the lid and do not open it during the rise and bake cycles.

7. At the end of the bake cycle, lift the lid and check the temperature. When the bread reaches 206°F to 210°F (97°C to 99°C) on an instant-read thermometer inserted in the center, it is done. Remove the bread pan from the machine and set it on its side on a wire cooling rack. Leave the bread in the pan for a couple of minutes, then turn the pan upside down and slide the loaf onto the wire rack. Carefully remove the paddle if it is embedded in the bottom of the loaf. Let the loaf cool upside down for at least 2 hours before slicing.

8. Store the bread in a resealable plastic bag or airtight container on the counter for up to 3 days. For longer storage, cut into even slices, double-wrap tightly in plastic, place in a resealable plastic bag, and freeze for up to 3 months.

WALNUT OAT BREAD

MAKES 1 (1½-POUND/680 G) LOAF   •   DAIRY FREE

Walnuts and oats have complementary flavors that go together beautifully. Enjoy this bread as part of a heart-healthy breakfast or snack. Spread with light cream cheese, this is a great alternative to a bagel.

DRY INGREDIENTS

21 g (0.7 oz or 2 tablespoons) active dry yeast

240 g (8.5 oz or 2 cups) Light Flour Blend (page 34)

125 g (4.4 oz or 1 cup) gluten-free oat flour

60 g (2.1 oz or ½ cup) chopped walnuts

48 g (1.7 oz or ¼ cup) granulated cane sugar

18 g (0.6 oz or 4 teaspoons) baking powder

2 teaspoons xanthan gum

1¼ teaspoons kosher or fine sea salt

⅛ teaspoon ascorbic acid, optional

WET INGREDIENTS

3 large eggs, at room temperature (see page 39), beaten

255 ml (1 cup plus 1 tablespoon) water, warmed to about 80°F (27°C)

60 ml (¼ cup) olive oil

2 teaspoons apple cider vinegar

TOPPING

Water, for brushing

Gluten-free oats, for sprinkling

1. Set the bread pan on the counter and insert the beater paddle(s). Unless otherwise directed by your machine's manufacturer, add the liquids first, then the dry ingredients, and finally the yeast.

2. Measure the yeast into a small bowl and set aside. In a large mixing bowl, whisk the remaining dry ingredients together.

3. In a 4-cup (1 liter) glass measuring cup, whisk the wet ingredients together and pour into the bread pan. Use a spatula to spread the dry ingredients over the wet ingredients, covering completely. Make a shallow well in the center and pour in the yeast.

4. Place the bread pan in the machine, settle it in the center, and lock it in place. Close the lid and select:

   Gluten-free cycle (see page 14 if your machine does not have this setting)
   Loaf size: 1½ pounds/750 g
   Medium crust
   Start

5. About 3 minutes into the mixing process, open the lid and use a spatula to scrape down the sides of the pan, avoiding the paddle. Push any flour that has accumulated around the edges and under the dough into the center. Check again once or twice during kneading, scraping the edges, corners, and under the dough. If the dough looks too wet or too dry, add a little flour blend or tiny amounts of warm water.

6. Once the mix/knead cycle is done, gently brush the top of the dough with a little water and sprinkle with oats. Gently press the oats into the dough to help them stick. Leave the lid closed and do not open it during the rise and bake cycles.

7. At the end of the bake cycle, lift the lid and check the temperature. When the bread reaches 206°F to 210°F (97°C to 99°C) on an instant-read thermometer inserted in the center, it is done. Remove the pan from the machine and set it on its side on a wire cooling rack. Turn the pan upside down and slide the loaf onto the wire rack. Carefully remove the paddle if it is embedded in the bottom of the loaf. Cool the bread on its side for at least 2 hours before slicing.

8. Store the bread in a resealable plastic bag or airtight container on the counter for up to 3 days. For longer storage, cut into even slices, double-wrap tightly in plastic, place in a resealable plastic bag, and freeze for up to 3 months.

GOLDEN MILLET BREAD

This is a lovely golden-hued bread, tender and mild flavored. Enjoy it toasted with homemade butter, made into French toast, as a sandwich, or even as bread crumbs. Millet is an ancient grain, common in many areas of the world.

DRY INGREDIENTS

4 teaspoons active dry yeast

120 g (4.2 oz or 1 cup) Light Flour Blend (page 34)

177 g (6.2 oz or 1½ cups) millet flour

60 g (2.1 oz or ½ cup) sorghum flour

58 g (2 oz or ½ cup) buttermilk powder

48 g (1.7 oz or ¼ cup) granulated cane sugar

2 teaspoons xanthan gum

2 teaspoons kosher or fine sea salt

1½ teaspoons baking powder

⅛ teaspoon ascorbic acid, optional

WET INGREDIENTS

3 large eggs, at room temperature (see page 39), beaten

240 ml (1 cup) water, warmed to 80°F (27°C)

60 ml (¼ cup) olive oil

1 teaspoon apple cider vinegar

1. Set the bread pan on the counter and insert the beater paddle(s). Unless otherwise directed by your machine's manufacturer, add the liquids first, then the dry ingredients, and finally the yeast.

2. Measure the yeast into a small bowl and set aside. In a large mixing bowl, whisk the remaining dry ingredients together.

3. In a 4-cup (1 liter) glass measuring cup, whisk the wet ingredients together and pour into the bread pan. Use a spatula to spread the dry ingredients over the wet ingredients, covering completely. Make a shallow well in the center and pour in the yeast.

4. Place the bread pan in the machine, settle it in the center, and lock it in place. Close the lid and select:

Gluten-free cycle (see page 14 if your machine does not have this setting)
Loaf size: 1½ pounds/750 g
Medium crust
Start

5. About 3 minutes after the machine has started mixing/kneading, open the lid and use a spatula to scrape the sides of the pan, avoiding the paddle, and push any loose flour into the center of the pan. Check again once or twice during the knead cycle, scraping the sides, corners, and under the dough. If the dough looks too wet or too dry, add a little flour blend or tiny amounts of warm water. Once the mix/knead cycle is done, leave the lid closed during the rise and bake cycles.

6. At the end of the bake cycle, lift the lid and check the temperature. When the bread reaches 206°F to 210°F (97°C to 99°C) on an instant-read thermometer inserted in the center, it is done. Remove the pan from the machine and set it on its side on a wire cooling rack. Leave the bread in the pan for a couple of minutes, then turn the pan upside down and slide the loaf onto the wire rack. Carefully remove the paddle if it is embedded in the bottom of the loaf. Cool the loaf upside down for at least 2 hours before slicing.

7. Store the bread in a resealable plastic bag or airtight container on the counter for up to 3 days. For longer storage, cut into even slices, double-wrap tightly in plastic, place in a resealable plastic bag, and freeze for up to 3 months.

HOMEMADE CULTURED BUTTER

MAKES 1½ TO 2 CUPS (360 TO 480 G)

Whisk 3 cups (720 ml) heavy cream and 3 tablespoons (45 ml) buttermilk or yogurt in a bowl and leave at room temperature, covered with a clean kitchen towel or cheesecloth, for at least 24 hours to create an active culture.

Set a double layer of clean cheesecloth in a bowl. Fill another bowl with ice cubes and water.

Pour the cultured cream into a food processor or a mixer fitted with the whisk attachment, and process or beat until it separates into clumps of solids and liquid (curds and whey), 1 to 2 minutes. Pour this into the bowl with the cheesecloth. Gather the ends of the cheesecloth and twist them together to form a ball. Gently squeeze the ball, forcing out the excess whey. Dipping the cheesecloth ball into the ice water occasionally will make this process easier. When most of the liquid has been extracted and the butter starts to coat your hands, secure the top of the cheesecloth with a rubber band or twist tie and leave it in a strainer set over a bowl to finish draining.

If desired, you can knead in some salt (start with 1 teaspoon and add more to taste). Then transfer the butter to a container and store in the refrigerator or freezer.

BUCKWHEAT SANDWICH BREAD

MAKES 1 (1½-POUND/680 G) LOAF • DAIRY-FREE OPTION

While most of us think of pancakes when we hear "buckwheat," it is a versatile flour that adds flavor, nutrients, and fiber to baked goods. Despite the inclusion of "wheat" in the name, buckwheat is a ground fruit seed that is naturally gluten free.

DRY INGREDIENTS

21 g (0.7 oz or 2 tablespoons) active dry yeast

240 g (8.5 oz or 2 cups) Light Flour Blend (page 34)

138 g (4.9 oz or 1 cup) buckwheat flour

½ cup milk powder (44 g/1.6 oz) or DariFree (69 g/2.4 oz)

26 g (0.9 oz or ¼ cup) flaxseed meal or ground flaxseed

1 tablespoon baking powder

2 teaspoons xanthan gum

1½ teaspoons kosher or fine sea salt

⅛ teaspoon ascorbic acid, optional

WET INGREDIENTS

80 g (2.8 oz or ¼ cup) pure maple syrup, at room temperature

270 ml (1 cup plus 2 tablespoons) water, heated to about 80°F (27°C)

3 large eggs, at room temperature (see page 39), beaten

45 ml (3 tablespoons) olive oil

2 teaspoons apple cider vinegar

1. Set the bread pan on the counter and insert the beater paddle(s). Unless otherwise directed by your machine's manufacturer, add the liquids first, then the dry ingredients, and finally the yeast.

2. Measure the yeast into a small bowl and set aside. In a large mixing bowl, whisk the remaining dry ingredients together.

3. Whisk the maple syrup and water together in a 4-cup (1 liter) glass measuring cup to dissolve the syrup. Add the remaining wet ingredients and whisk again. Pour into the bread pan. Use a spatula to spread the dry ingredients over the wet ingredients, covering completely. Make a shallow well in the center and pour in the yeast.

4. Place the bread pan in the machine, settle it in the center, and lock it in place. Close the lid and select:

    Gluten-free cycle (see page 14 if your machine does not have this setting)
    Loaf size: 1½ pounds/750 g
    Medium crust
    Start

5. About 3 minutes into the mixing process, open the lid and use a spatula to scrape down the sides of the pan, avoiding the paddle. Push any flour that has accumulated around the edges and under the dough into the center. Check again once or twice during kneading, scraping the edges, corners, and under the dough. If the dough looks too wet or too dry, add a little flour blend or tiny amounts of warm water. Once the mix/knead cycle is done, leave the lid closed during the rise and bake cycles.

6. At the end of the bake cycle, lift the lid and check the temperature. When the bread reaches 206°F to 210°F (97°C to 99°C) on an instant-read thermometer inserted in the center, it is done. Remove the pan from the machine and set it on its side on a wire cooling rack. Leave the bread in the pan for a couple of minutes, then turn the pan upside down and slide the loaf onto the wire rack. Carefully remove the paddle if it is embedded in the bottom of the loaf. Cool the loaf upside down for at least 2 hours before slicing.

7. Store the bread in a resealable plastic bag or airtight container on the counter for up to 3 days. For longer storage, cut into even slices, double-wrap tightly in plastic, place in a resealable plastic bag, and freeze for up to months.

LIGHT "RYE" BREAD

MAKES ONE (1½-POUND/680 G) LOAF • DAIRY-FREE OPTION

Light rye bread is what many call "deli" rye, the go-to choice for pastrami and corned beef sandwiches. Honey replaces the molasses you'd find in a dark rye, and there's no espresso powder or cocoa powder. This loaf has a milder flavor that may be more appealing to people who are not crazy about rye breads. Spread it with French mustard and pile high with pastrami, and you've got your own gluten-free deli sandwich.

DRY INGREDIENTS

21 g (0.7 oz or 2 tablespoons) active dry yeast

240 g (8.5 oz or 2 cups) Light Flour Blend (page 34)

155 g (5.5 oz or 1 cup plus 2 tablespoons) buckwheat flour

¼ cup milk powder (22 g/0.8 oz) or DariFree (40 g/1.4 oz)

30 g (1.1 oz or 2 tablespoons firmly packed) brown sugar

2 tablespoons caraway seeds or 1 teaspoon caraway powder (see Resources, page 376), optional

14 g (0.5 oz or 2 tablespoons) flaxseed meal or ground flaxseed (double this amount if not using caraway seeds)

1 tablespoon baking powder

2 teaspoons xanthan gum

2 teaspoons dried minced onions or shallots

1½ teaspoons gluten-free rye flavoring (see opposite), optional

1 teaspoon kosher salt

½ teaspoon dried dill weed

⅛ teaspoon ascorbic acid, optional

WET INGREDIENTS

60 g (2 oz or 3 tablespoons) honey

255 ml (1 cup) plus 1 tablespoon water, heated to about 80°F (27°C)

3 large eggs, at room temperature (see page 39), beaten

45 ml (3 tablespoons) olive oil

2 teaspoons apple cider vinegar

1 teaspoon finely grated orange zest, optional

1. Set the bread pan on the counter and insert the beater paddle(s). Unless otherwise directed by your machine's manufacturer, add the liquids first, then the dry ingredients, and finally the yeast.

2. Measure the yeast into a small bowl and set aside. In a large mixing bowl, whisk the remaining dry ingredients together.

3. Whisk the honey and water together in a 4-cup (1 liter) glass measuring cup to dissolve the honey. Add the remaining wet ingredients and whisk again. Pour into the bread pan. Use a spatula to spread the dry ingredients over the wet ingredients, covering completely. Make a shallow well in the center and pour in the yeast.

4. Place the bread pan in the machine, settle it in the center, and lock it in place. Close the lid and select:

   Gluten-free cycle (see page 14 if your machine does not have this setting)
   Loaf size: 1½ pounds/750 g
   Medium crust
   Start

   > **NOTE:** Gluten-free rye flavoring is available online from Authentic Foods (see Resources, page 376).

5. About 3 minutes into the mixing process, open the lid and use a spatula to scrape down the sides of the pan, avoiding the paddle. Push any flour that has accumulated around the edges and under the dough into the center. Check again once or twice during kneading, scraping the edges, corners, and under the dough. If the dough looks too wet or too dry, add a little flour blend or tiny amounts of warm water. Once the mix/knead cycle is done, leave the lid closed during the rise and bake cycles.

6. At the end of the bake cycle, lift the lid and check the temperature. When the bread reaches 206°F to 210°F (97°C to 99°C) on an instant-read thermometer inserted in the center, it is done. Remove the pan from the machine and set it on its side on a wire cooling rack. Leave the bread in the pan for a couple of minutes, then turn the pan upside down and slide the loaf onto the wire rack. Carefully remove the paddle if it is embedded in the bottom of the loaf. Let the bread cool upside down for at least 2 hours before slicing.

7. Store the bread in a resealable plastic bag or airtight container on the counter for up to 3 days. For longer storage, cut into even slices, double-wrap tightly in plastic, place in a resealable bag, and freeze for up to 3 months.

DARK "RYE" BREAD

MAKES 1 (1½-POUND/680 G) LOAF • DAIRY FREE

Just like many breads made with rye flour, this loaf has a denser texture than other sandwich breads, as well as a deep, rich flavor. What makes it dark is the addition of molasses, cocoa, and espresso powder. Along with the other ingredients (especially the caraway), they create a bread that is surprisingly close to rye. As with any dark dough or batter, it will be a little more difficult to tell by sight when the loaf is done, so checking the temperature is important. Gluten-free breads actually bake up lighter than traditional rye and wheat breads, giving you all of the flavor and a moist crumb. You may even find you like them better.

DRY INGREDIENTS

21 g (0.7 oz or 2 tablespoons) active dry yeast

240 g (8.5 oz or 2 cups) Light Flour Blend (page 34)

138 g (4.9 oz or 1 cup) buckwheat flour

15 g (0.5 oz or 2 tablespoons) unsweetened cocoa powder

28 g (1 oz or 2 tablespoons firmly packed) brown sugar

2 tablespoons caraway seeds or 1 teaspoon caraway powder (see Resources, page 376), optional

14 g (0.5 oz or 2 tablespoons) flaxseed meal or ground flaxseed (double this amount if not using caraway seeds)

1 tablespoon baking powder

2 teaspoons xanthan gum

2 teaspoons instant espresso powder or instant coffee

⅛ teaspoon ascorbic acid, optional

2 teaspoons dried minced onions or shallots

1½ teaspoons gluten-free rye flavor (see Note, page 73), optional

1 teaspoon kosher salt

½ teaspoon dried dill weed

WET INGREDIENTS

60 g (2.1 oz or 3 tablespoons) molasses (*not* blackstrap)

255 ml (1 cup plus 1 tablespoon) water, heated to about 80°F (27°C)

3 large eggs, at room temperature (see page 39), beaten

45 ml (3 tablespoons) olive oil

2 teaspoons apple cider vinegar

1 teaspoon finely grated orange zest, optional

1. Set the bread pan on the counter and insert the beater paddle(s). Unless otherwise directed by your machine's manufacturer, add the liquids first, then the dry ingredients, and finally the yeast.

2. Measure the yeast into a small bowl and set aside. In a large mixing bowl, whisk the remaining dry ingredients together.

3. Whisk the molasses and water together in a 4-cup (1 liter) glass measuring cup to dissolve the molasses. Add the remaining wet ingredients and whisk again. Pour into the bread pan. Use a spatula to spread the dry ingredients over the wet ingredients, covering completely. Make a shallow well in the center and pour in the yeast.

4. Place the bread pan in the machine, settle it in the center, and lock it in place. Close the lid and select:

   Gluten-free cycle (see page 14 if your machine does not have this setting)
   Loaf size: 1½ pounds/750 g
   Medium crust
   Start

5. About 3 minutes into the mixing process, open the lid and use a spatula to scrape down the sides of the pan, avoiding the paddle. Push any flour that has accumulated around the edges or under the dough into the center. Check again once or twice during kneading, scraping the edges, corners, and under the dough. If the dough looks too wet or too dry, add a little flour blend or tiny amounts of warm water. Once the mix/knead cycle is done, leave the lid closed during the rise and bake cycles.

6. At the end of the bake cycle, lift the lid and check the temperature. When the bread reaches 206°F to 210°F (97°C to 99°C) on an instant-read thermometer inserted into the center, it is done. Remove the pan from the machine and set it on its side on a wire cooling rack. Leave the bread in the pan for a couple of minutes, then turn the pan upside down and slide the loaf onto the wire rack. Carefully remove the paddle if it is embedded in the bottom of the loaf. Let the bread cool upside down for at least 2 hours before slicing.

7. Store the bread in a resealable plastic bag or airtight container on the counter for up to 3 days. For longer storage, cut into even slices, double-wrap tightly in plastic, place in a resealable plastic bag, and freeze for up to 3 months.

RUSSIAN "RYE" BREAD

MAKES 1 (1½-POUND/680 G) LOAF   •   DAIRY FREE

Dark, heavy rye breads were first made in Northern Europe. When immigrants came to the United States, they incorporated easily found local ingredients, including wheat flour. This Russian-inspired "rye" bread mirrors a traditional loaf with its dense, dark color and slightly sour flavor. This recipe uses molasses, caraway seeds, rye flavoring, and buckwheat to create that earthy, slightly sweet tangy flavor.

DRY INGREDIENTS

21 g (0.7 oz or 2 tablespoons) active dry yeast

240 g (8.5 oz or 2 cups) Light Flour Blend (page 34)

120 g (4.2 oz or 1 cup) buckwheat flour

28 g (1 oz or ¼ cup) flaxseed meal or ground flaxseed

45 g (1.6 oz or 3 tablespoons firmly packed) brown sugar

2 tablespoons sorghum flour

1 teaspoon caraway powder (see Resources, page 376)

1 tablespoon baking powder

2 teaspoons xanthan gum

2 teaspoons instant espresso powder or instant coffee granules

2 teaspoons dried minced onions or shallots

1½ teaspoons gluten-free rye flavor (see Note, page 73), optional

1 teaspoon kosher or fine sea salt

½ teaspoon dried dill weed

⅛ teaspoon ascorbic acid, optional

WET INGREDIENTS

60 g (2.1 oz or 3 tablespoons) molasses (*not* blackstrap)

255 ml (1 cup plus 1 tablespoon) water, heated to about 80°F (27°C)

3 large eggs, at room temperature (see page 39), beaten

45 ml (3 tablespoons) olive oil

2 teaspoons apple cider vinegar

1. Set the bread pan on the counter and insert the beater paddle(s). Unless otherwise directed by your machine's manufacturer, add the liquids first, then the dry ingredients, and finally the yeast.

2. Measure the yeast into a small bowl and set aside. In a large mixing bowl, whisk the remaining dry ingredients together.

3. Whisk the molasses and water together in a 4-cup (1 liter) glass measuring cup to dissolve the molasses. Add the remaining wet ingredients and whisk again. Pour into the bread pan. Use a spatula to spread the dry ingredients over the wet ingredients, covering completely. Make a shallow well in the center and pour in the yeast.

4. Place the bread pan in the machine, settle it in the center, and lock it in place. Close the lid and select:

   Gluten-free cycle (see page 14 if your machine does not have this setting)
   Loaf size: 1½ pounds/750 g
   Medium crust
   Start

5. About 3 minutes after the machine has started mixing/kneading, open the lid and use a spatula to scrape the sides of the pan. Push any flour that has accumulated around the edges and under the dough into the center. Check again once or twice during kneading, scraping any loose flour into the center, avoiding the paddle. If the dough looks too wet or too dry, add a little flour blend or tiny amounts of warm water. Once the mix/knead cycle is done, leave the lid closed during the rise and bake cycles.

6. At the end of the bake cycle, lift the lid and check the temperature. When the bread reaches 206°F to 210°F (97°C to 99°C) on an instant-read thermometer inserted into the center, it is done. Remove the bread pan from the machine and set it on its side on a wire cooling rack. Leave the bread in the pan for a couple of minutes, then turn the pan upside down and slide the loaf onto the wire rack. Remove the paddle if it is embedded in the bottom of the loaf. Let the bread cool upside down for at least 2 hours before slicing.

7. Store the bread in a resealable plastic bag or airtight container on the counter for up to 3 days. For longer storage, cut into even slices, double-wrap tightly in plastic, place in a resealable plastic bag, and freeze for up to 3 months.

RICH PUMPERNICKEL BREAD

MAKES 1 (1½-POUND) LOAF • DAIRY-FREE OPTION

Traditional pumpernickel bread was baked in stages and then steamed for up to 24 hours, which created its distinctive color and caramelized flavor. American bakers added wheat to the European recipe, which contained rye meal only. It seems fitting to remove the wheat again and significantly reduce the cooking time to create a wonderful loaf of dark bread. In traditional bread baking, the combination of rye flours and caraway has become synonymous. That's a good thing for gluten-free baking, because caraway powder gives this bread a rye-like flavor without the crunchy seeds.

DRY INGREDIENTS

21 g (0.7 oz or 2 tablespoons) active dry yeast

150 g (5.3 oz or 1¼ cups) Light Flour Blend (page 34)

229 g (8 oz or 1¾ cups) buckwheat flour

26 g (1 oz or 2 tablespoons firmly packed) brown sugar

21 g (0.7 oz or 3 tablespoons) flaxseed meal or ground flaxseed

2 teaspoons unsweetened cocoa powder

2 teaspoons baking powder

2 teaspoons xanthan gum

1 teaspoon kosher or fine sea salt

1 teaspoon onion powder

½ teaspoon caraway powder

⅛ teaspoon ascorbic acid, optional

WET INGREDIENTS

60 g (2.1 oz or 3 tablespoons) molasses (*not* blackstrap)

240 ml (1 cup) 1% milk or water, warmed to about 80°F (27°C)

3 large eggs, at room temperature (see page 39), beaten

60 ml (¼ cup) olive oil

2 teaspoons apple cider vinegar

1. Set the bread pan on the counter and insert the beater paddle(s). Unless otherwise directed by your machine's manufacturer, add the liquids first, then the dry ingredients, and finally the yeast.

2. Measure the yeast into a small bowl and set aside. In a large mixing bowl, whisk the remaining dry ingredients together.

3. Whisk the molasses and water together in a 4-cup (1 liter) glass measuring cup to dissolve the molasses. Add the remaining wet ingredients and whisk again. Pour into the bread pan. Use a spatula to spread the dry ingredients over the wet ingredients, covering completely. Make a shallow well in the center and pour in the yeast.

4. Place the bread pan in the machine, settle it in the center, and lock it in place. Close the lid and select:

   Gluten-free cycle (see page 14 if your machine does not have this setting)
   Loaf size: 1½ pounds/750 g
   Medium crust
   Start

5. About 3 minutes into the mixing process, open the lid and use a spatula to scrape down the sides of the pan, avoiding the paddle. Push any flour that has accumulated around the edges and under the dough into the center. Check again once or twice during kneading, scraping the edges, corners, and under the dough. If the dough looks too wet or too dry, add a little flour blend or tiny amounts of warm water. Once the mix/knead cycle is done, leave the lid closed during the rise and bake cycles.

6. At the end of the bake cycle, lift the lid and check the temperature. When the bread reaches 206°F to 210°F (97°C to 99°C) on an instant-read thermometer inserted into the center, it is done. Remove the pan from the machine and set it on its side on a wire cooling rack. Leave the bread in the pan for a couple of minutes, then turn the pan upside down and slide the loaf onto the wire rack. Carefully remove the paddle if it is embedded in the bottom of the loaf. Let the bread cool upside down for at least 2 hours before slicing.

7. Store the bread in a resealable plastic bag or airtight container on the counter for up to 3 days. For longer storage, cut into even slices, double-wrap tightly in plastic, place in a resealable plastic bag, and freeze for up to 3 months.

DELECTABLE BROWN BREAD

Brown bread might not be the first thing you think of when you are making sandwiches, but this one is great with any number of fillings: tuna salad, grilled cheese, ham with grainy mustard, turkey with cranberry sauce. It is also the perfect accompaniment to a hearty bowl of soup on cold days. It is a substantial bread, so one sandwich will fill you up when you are famished.

DRY INGREDIENTS

21 g (0.7 oz or 2 tablespoons) active dry yeast

137 g (4.8 oz or 1¼ cups) sorghum flour

120 g (4.2 oz or 1 cup) Light Flour Blend (page 34)

120 g (4.2 oz or 1 cup) millet flour

32 g (1.1 oz or ⅓ cup) flaxseed meal or ground flaxseed

45 g (1.6 oz or 3 tablespoons firmly packed) brown sugar

1 tablespoon baking powder

2 teaspoons xanthan gum

1 teaspoon kosher salt

⅛ teaspoon ascorbic acid, optional

WET INGREDIENTS

40 g (1.4 oz or 2 tablespoons) molasses (*not* blackstrap)

320 ml (1⅓ cups) buttermilk, warmed to about 80°F (27°C)

3 large eggs, at room temperature (see page 39), beaten

60 ml (¼ cup) olive oil

1 teaspoon cider vinegar

> **NOTE:** If you do not have buttermilk on hand, you can use buttermilk powder instead. Add 5 tablespoons (36 g) of the powder to the dry ingredients and 1¼ cups (300 ml) warm water to the wet ingredients.

1. Set the bread pan on the counter and insert the beater paddle(s). Unless otherwise directed by your machine's manufacturer, add the liquids first, then the dry ingredients, and finally the yeast.

2. Measure the yeast into a small bowl and set aside. In a large mixing bowl, whisk the remaining dry ingredients together.

3. Whisk the molasses and buttermilk together in a 4-cup (1 liter) glass measuring cup to dissolve the molasses. Add the remaining wet ingredients and whisk again. Pour into the bread pan. Use a spatula to spread the dry ingredients over the wet ingredients, covering completely. Make a shallow well in the center and pour in the yeast.

4. Place the bread pan in the machine, settle it in the center, and lock it in place. Close the lid and select:

   Gluten-free cycle (see page 14 if your machine does not have this setting)
   Loaf size: 1½ pounds/750 g
   Medium crust
   Start

5. About 3 minutes into the mixing process, open the lid and use a spatula to scrape down the sides of the pan, avoiding the paddle. Push any flour that has accumulated around the edges and under the dough into the center. Check again once or twice during kneading, scraping the edges, corners, and under the dough. If the dough looks too wet or too dry, add a little flour blend or tiny amounts of warm water. Once the mix/knead cycle is done, leave the lid closed during the rise and bake cycles.

6. At the end of the bake cycle, lift the lid and check the temperature. When the bread reaches 206°F to 210°F (97°C to 99°C) on an instant-read thermometer inserted in the center, it is done. Remove the pan from the machine and set it on its side on a wire cooling rack. Leave the bread in the pan for a couple of minutes, then turn the pan upside down and slide the loaf onto the wire rack. Carefully remove the paddle if it is embedded in the bottom of the loaf. Let the bread cool upside down for at least 2 hours before slicing.

7. Store the bread in a resealable plastic bag or airtight container on the counter for up to 3 days. For longer storage, cut into even slices, double-wrap tightly in plastic, place in a resealable plastic bag, and freeze for up to 3 months.

CALIFORNIA BROWN BREAD

MAKES 1 (1½-POUND/680 G) LOAF ◆ DAIRY-FREE OPTION

Inspired by the traditional Boston brown bread, this lighter version has a touch of sweetness and a hint of corn flavor. Fantastic for sandwiches, smeared with luscious soft French cheese, or served alongside a hearty bowl of chowder, this bread is a real winner.

DRY INGREDIENTS

1 tablespoon active dry yeast

240 g (8.5 oz or 2 cups) Light Flour Blend (page 34)

90 g (3.2 oz or ¾ cup) sorghum flour

¼ cup milk powder (22 g/0.8 oz) or DariFree (40 g/1.4 oz)

30 g (1.1 oz or ¼ cup) corn flour or masa harina

26 g (0.9 oz or 2 tablespoons) granulated cane sugar

1 tablespoon baking powder

2 teaspoons xanthan gum

1½ teaspoons kosher or fine sea salt

75 g (2.6 oz or ½ cup) dried currants or golden raisins, optional

⅛ teaspoon ascorbic acid, optional

WET INGREDIENTS

170 g (6 oz or ½ cup) molasses (*not* blackstrap)

255 ml (1 cup plus 1 tablespoon) water, heated to about 80°F (27°C)

2 large eggs, at room temperature (see page 39), beaten

60 ml (¼ cup) olive oil

2 teaspoons apple cider vinegar

1. Set the bread pan on the counter and insert the beater paddle(s). Unless otherwise directed by your machine's manufacturer, add the liquids first, then the dry ingredients, and finally the yeast.

2. Measure the yeast into a small bowl and set aside. Whisk the remaining dry ingredients— *except* the currants—together in a large mixing bowl. Stir in the currants, if using.

3. In a 4-cup (1 liter) glass measuring cup, whisk the molasses and warm water to dissolve the molasses. Whisk in the remaining wet ingredients and pour into the bread pan. Use a spatula to spread the dry ingredients over the wet ingredients, covering completely. Make a shallow well in the center and pour in the yeast.

4. Place the bread pan in the machine, settle it in the center, and lock it in place. Close the lid and select:

   Gluten-free cycle (see page 14 if your machine does not have this setting)
   Loaf size: 1½ pounds/750 g
   Medium crust
   Start

5. About 3 minutes after the machine has started mixing/kneading, open the lid and use a spatula to scrape the sides of the pan, avoiding the paddle. Push any loose flour into the center of the pan. Check again once or twice during the knead cycle, scraping the sides, corners, and under the dough. If the dough looks too wet or too dry, add a little flour blend or tiny amounts of warm water. Once the mix/knead cycle is done, leave the lid closed during the rise and bake cycles.

6. At the end of the bake cycle, lift the lid and check the temperature. When the bread reaches 206°F to 210°F (97°C to 99°C) on an instant-read thermometer inserted in the center, it is done. Remove the bread pan from the machine and set it on its side on a wire cooling rack. Leave the bread in the pan for a couple of minutes, then turn the pan upside down and slide the loaf onto the wire rack. Carefully remove the paddle if it is embedded in the bottom of the loaf. Let the bread cool upside down for at least 2 hours before slicing.

7. Store the bread in a resealable plastic bag or airtight container on the counter for up to 3 days. For longer storage, cut into even slices, double-wrap tightly in plastic, place in a resealable plastic bag, and freeze for up to 3 months.

PALEO BREAD

MAKES 1 (1½-POUND/680 G) LOAF • DAIRY FREE

Paleo has been a popular approach to healthy eating for a few years now. A shift to eliminating processed foods that are at odds with our health (grains, legumes, and dairy) is the basic principle. Flaxseed meal and coconut flour provide the structure and nutty flavor for this bread. But unlike many paleo breads, this one is nut free.

DRY INGREDIENTS

1 tablespoon active dry yeast

132 g (4.7 oz or 1 cup) arrowroot

128 g (4.5 oz or 1 cup) tapioca flour

90 g (3.2 oz or ⅔ cup) coconut sugar

36 g (1.3 oz or ⅓ cup) coconut flour

1 teaspoon kosher or fine sea salt

1½ teaspoons baking soda

¼ teaspoon cream of tartar

84 g (3 oz or ¾ cup) flaxseed meal or ground flaxseed

142 g (5 oz or 1 cup) sunflower seeds, ground to the consistency of sand in a food processor

WET INGREDIENTS

240 ml (1 cup) water, warmed to about 80°F (27°C)

2 large eggs, at room temperature (see page 39), beaten

73 g (2.6 oz or ⅓ cup) coconut oil, melted and slightly cooled

2 teaspoons apple cider vinegar

NOTE: Paleo bread does not use baking powder because it often contains cornstarch or potato starch. We use baking soda and cream of tartar.

1. Set the bread pan on the counter and insert the beater paddle(s). Unless otherwise directed by your machine's manufacturer, add the liquids first, then the dry ingredients, and finally the yeast.

2. Measure the yeast into a small bowl and set aside. In a large mixing bowl, whisk the remaining dry ingredients together.

3. In a 4-cup (1 liter) glass measuring cup, whisk the wet ingredients together. Scrape the mixture into the bread pan. Use a spatula to spread the dry ingredients over the wet ingredients. Make a shallow well in the center and pour in the yeast.

4. Place the bread pan in the machine, settle it in the center, and lock it in place. Close the lid and select:

   Gluten-free cycle (see page 14 if your machine does not have this setting)
   Loaf size: 1½ pounds/750 g
   Medium crust
   Start

5. After the first kneading cycle, scrape the sides and bottom of the pan with the spatula to make sure all the dry ingredients are incorporated. Once the mix/knead cycle is done, leave the lid closed during the rise and bake cycles.

6. At the end of the bake cycle, lift the lid and check the temperature. When the bread registers 206°F to 210°F (97°C to 99°C) on an instant-read thermometer inserted in the center, it is done. Remove the pan from the machine and set it on its side on a wire rack. Leave the bread in the pan for a couple of minutes, then turn the pan upside down and slide the loaf onto the wire rack. Carefully remove the paddle if it is embedded in the bottom of the loaf. Let the bread cool on its side for at least 2 hours before slicing.

7. Store the bread in a resealable plastic bag or airtight container on the counter for up to 3 days. For longer storage, cut into even slices, double-wrap tightly in plastic, place in a resealable plastic bag, and freeze for up to 3 months.

MULTI-GRAIN BREAD

MAKES 1 (1½-POUND/680 G) LOAF

Blending a variety of whole-grain flours adds flavor, color, and texture. Sorghum, millet, and amaranth are combined with flaxseed meal for a rich and delicious loaf sure to please anyone who loves wheat bread. While it doesn't have the same flavor as wheat, this bread will be very satisfying for all.

DRY INGREDIENTS

21 g (0.7 oz or 2 tablespoons) active dry yeast

120 g (4.2 oz or 1 cup) Light Flour Blend (page 34)

110 g (3.9 oz or 1 cup) sorghum flour

58 g (2 oz or ½ cup) buttermilk powder

60 g (2.1 oz or ½ cup) millet flour

60 g (2.1 oz or ¼ cup) amaranth flour

48 g (1.7 oz or ¼ cup) granulated cane sugar

26 g (0.9 oz or ¼ cup) flaxseed meal or ground flaxseed

1 tablespoon baking powder

2 teaspoons xanthan gum

2 teaspoons kosher or fine sea salt

⅛ teaspoon ascorbic acid, optional

WET INGREDIENTS

20 g (0.7 oz or 1 tablespoon) honey

255 ml (1 cup plus 1 tablespoon) water, warmed to 80°F (27°C)

3 large eggs, at room temperature (see page 39), beaten

60 ml (¼ cup) olive oil

1 teaspoon apple cider vinegar

1. Set the bread pan on the counter and insert the beater paddle(s). Unless otherwise directed by your machine's manufacturer, add the liquids first, then the dry ingredients, and finally the yeast.

2. Measure the yeast into a small bowl and set aside. In a large mixing bowl, whisk the remaining dry ingredients together.

3. In a 4-cup (1 liter) glass measuring cup, whisk the honey and water together to dissolve the honey. Add the remaining wet ingredients and whisk again. Pour into the bread pan. Use a spatula to spread the dry ingredients over the wet ingredients, covering completely. Make a shallow well in the center and pour in the yeast.

4. Place the bread pan in the machine, settle it in the center, and lock it in place. Close the lid and select:

   Gluten-free cycle (see page 14 if your machine does not have this setting)
   Loaf size: 1½ pounds/750 g
   Medium crust
   Start

5. About 3 minutes into the mixing process, open the lid and use a spatula to scrape down the sides of the pan, avoiding the paddle. Push any flour that has accumulated around the edges and under the dough into the center. Check again once or twice during kneading, scraping the edges, corners, and under the dough. If the dough looks too wet or too dry, add a little flour blend or tiny amounts of warm water. Once the mixing is done, close the lid and do not open it during the rise and bake cycles.

6. At the end of the bake cycle, lift the lid and check the temperature. When the bread reaches 206°F to 210°F (97°C to 99°C) on an instant-read thermometer inserted in the center, it is done. Remove the bread pan from the machine and set it on its side on a wire cooling rack. Leave the bread in the pan for a couple of minutes, then turn the pan upside down and slide the loaf onto the wire rack. Carefully remove the paddle if it is embedded in the bottom of the loaf. Let the bread cool upside down for at least 2 hours before slicing.

7. Store the bread in a resealable plastic bag or airtight container on the counter for up to 3 days. For longer storage, cut into even slices, double-wrap tightly in plastic, place in a resealable plastic bag, and freeze for up to 3 months.

VARIATION

Multi-Grain Pecan Bread
Follow the instructions for Multi-Grain Bread, but in step 2, add 1 cup (110 g) chopped pecans to the dry ingredients and toss well. Proceed with the recipe.

Shaped Breads, Rolls,

AND MORE

Bagels, dinner rolls, pretzels—these are all things we miss with a gluten-free lifestyle. The same goes for baguettes and holiday breads such as stollen and babka. Well, all these and more are possible with the bread machine. The machine does the work of mixing and kneading, then you turn out the dough, shape it, let it rise, and bake.

The key to these shaped breads is to remember that they are softer and stickier than a regular dough, so it is best to work with slightly damp or oiled hands. The surface you work on should be lightly coated with nonstick cooking spray or gluten-free flour. Be careful with the flour, though: too much will make the bread tough. And try not to over-handle the dough.

These doughs are delicate, so many of the recipes call for special pans to support the

ADD SOME OIL

Wet or oiled hands will help you glide over the super sticky dough and smooth out the tops of gluten-free breads.

dough as it rises and bakes. Hamburger buns need 4-inch (10 cm) cake rings, and there's a special pan for hot dog buns and another for baguettes. Muffin tins are great for rolls. Loaf pans work for stollen if you don't care about the traditional folded-over look. You can also leave some breads in the machine to finish, as we do with the Chocolate Cherry Stollen.

AMAZING SEEDED BAGELS

MAKES 8 BAGELS ◆ DAIRY FREE

You can top your bagels with one of your favorite seeds or a combination of them. The topping given here is a variation on an everything bagel topping, minus the onion. Bagels are a perfect alternative to English muffins for eggs Benedict or mini toaster pizzas.

DRY INGREDIENTS

1 tablespoon instant yeast

240 g (8.5 oz or 2 cups) Light Flour Blend (page 34) or Whole-Grain Flour Blend (page 34)

70 g (2.5 oz or ½ cup) teff flour

59 g (2.1 oz or ½ cup) millet flour

42.5 g (1.5 oz or ⅓ cup) tapioca starch

14 g (0.5 oz or 2 tablespoons) flaxseed meal or ground flaxseed

1 teaspoon kosher salt

¾ teaspoon xanthan gum or psyllium husk flakes or powder

½ teaspoon dough enhancer

WET INGREDIENTS

40 g (1.4 oz or 2 tablespoons) honey

240 ml (1 cup) water, warmed to about 80°F (27°C)

1 large egg, at room temperature (see page 39), beaten

30 ml (2 tablespoons) vegetable oil

2 teaspoons cider vinegar

BAKING SODA WASH

¼ teaspoon baking soda

240 ml (1 cup) warm water

TOPPING

2 tablespoons poppy seeds

16 g (0.6 oz or 2 tablespoons) white sesame seeds

1 tablespoon sunflower seeds

1 tablespoon flaxseed meal or ground flaxseed

1 teaspoon kosher salt

1. Line a baking sheet with parchment.

2. Set the bread pan on the counter and insert the beater paddle(s). Unless otherwise directed by your machine's manufacturer, add the liquids first, then the dry ingredients, and finally the yeast.

3. Measure the yeast into a small bowl and set aside. In a large mixing bowl, whisk the remaining dry ingredients together.

4. In a 2-cup (0.5 liter) glass measuring cup, whisk the honey and water together to dissolve the honey. Add the remaining wet ingredients and whisk again. Pour into the bread pan. Use a spatula to spread the dry ingredients over the wet ingredients. Make a shallow well in the center and pour in the yeast.

5. Place the bread pan in the machine, settle it in the center, and lock it in place. Close the lid and select:
Dough cycle
Loaf size: 1½ pounds/750 g
Start

6. After the first knead cycle, scrape the sides and bottom of the pan with a spatula to make sure all the dry ingredients are incorporated. Once the cycle is complete, remove the dough from the bread pan and divide it into eight pieces on a lightly oiled surface.

7. In a 2-cup (0.5 liter) glass measuring cup, whisk the baking soda into the warm water until the soda is dissolved.

8. Roll each piece of dough into a 6-inch (15 cm) log. Form each into a circle, pinching the ends to seal. Place them on the baking sheet. Brush with the baking soda wash.

9. Stir all the topping ingredients together and sprinkle over the bagels. Press lightly to help the seeds adhere to the dough. Cover with a sheet of oiled plastic wrap, oiled side down, and let rise for 1 hour. They will not double in size, but they will puff up.

10. While the bagels rise, preheat the oven to 400°F (200°C).

11. Bake the bagels until they are golden brown, 25 to 30 minutes.

12. Store the bagels in a resealable plastic bag or airtight container on the counter for up to 2 days. For longer storage, double-wrap tightly in plastic, place in a resealable plastic bag, and freeze for up to 3 months.

BRIOCHE HAMBURGER AND HOT DOG BUNS

MAKES 8 HAMBURGER OR 10 HOT DOG BUNS • DAIRY-FREE OPTION

When you are having a summertime barbecue, there is nothing your kids want more than good old-fashioned burgers and hot dogs. You can buy gluten-free buns, but they are often dry and crumbly. Making your own from scratch, with the help of your bread machine, gives you delectable rolls with very little effort. Your family will love them. These buns are delicious with hamburgers, patty melts, hot dogs, grilled sausages, lobster rolls, chili dogs, tuna salad—even open-faced sandwiches. If you have any left over, they make outstanding French toast!

DRY INGREDIENTS

21 g (0.7 oz or 2 tablespoons) active dry yeast

360 g (12.7 oz or 3 cups) Light Flour Blend (page 34)

1 tablespoon baking powder

1 tablespoon psyllium husk flakes or powder

2 teaspoons kosher or fine sea salt

2 teaspoons granulated cane sugar

½ teaspoon dough enhancer

WET INGREDIENTS

2 teaspoons honey

270 ml (1 cup plus 2 tablespoons) 1% milk or water, warmed to about 80°F (27°C)

56 g (2 oz or 4 tablespoons/½ stick) salted butter or nondairy butter substitute, melted and slightly cooled

3 large eggs, at room temperature (see page 39), beaten

2 teaspoons champagne vinegar

EGG WASH

1 large egg

1 tablespoon water

TOPPING (OPTIONAL)

2 teaspoons sesame seeds or poppy seeds

1. Prepare the pans:

   For hamburger buns
   Line two baking sheets with parchment, place four English muffin rings on each sheet, and coat the insides thoroughly with nonstick cooking spray or brush with oil.

   For hot dog buns
   Generously coat a hot dog bun pan with nonstick cooking spray or brush with oil, making sure all the inside surfaces are coated.

2. Set the bread pan on the counter and insert the beater paddle(s). Unless otherwise directed by your machine's manufacturer, add the liquids first, then the dry ingredients, and finally the yeast.

3. Measure the yeast into a small bowl and set aside. In a large mixing bowl, whisk the remaining dry ingredients together.

4. In a 4-cup (1 liter) glass measuring cup, whisk the honey and milk together to dissolve the honey. Add the remaining wet ingredients and whisk again. Pour into the bread pan. Use a spatula to spread the dry ingredients over the wet ingredients. Make a shallow well in the center and pour in the yeast.

5. Place the bread pan in the machine, settle it in the center, and lock it in place. Close the lid and select:

   Dough cycle
   Loaf size: 1½ pounds/750 g
   Start

6. Let the machine mix and knead until all of the dry ingredients have been incorporated, using a rubber spatula to move any flour caught in the corners or under the dough to the center so the paddle can mix it in. Do this a few times to be sure everything is incorporated. Let the machine mix and knead for about 5 minutes, until the

---

PANS FOR PERFECTION

There are specially designed hamburger bun pans, but they can be expensive. Instead, you can use eight 4-inch (10 cm) round cake pans or English muffin rings to help support the delicate dough and bake it into perfect rounds. The rings and pans are available in kitchen stores and online.

A specialty pan is the easiest way to make hot dog buns. The one we use is from USA Pan and is sold by King Arthur Flour (see Resources, page 376). It has ten slots.

---

dough is smooth and has no lumps, then hit stop to cancel the cycle and turn off the machine. Remove the pan.

7. Shape the dough:

   For hamburger buns
   a. Divide the dough into eight equal pieces.

   b. Oil your hands and pat each piece into a 3-inch (7.5 cm) flattened disk.

   c. Set the disks into the rings. It's okay if they don't reach all the way to the edges.

   For hot dog buns
   a. Divide the dough into ten equal pieces.

   b. Oil your hands and form each piece into a cigar shape and set into the slots.

   c. Then use your fingers to stretch them slightly (if needed) to fill the length of each slot, pinching the sides a little to help keep them even. Smooth the tops. As the buns rise, they will expand and their sides will touch—this will help support them and keep them tender.

8. Lay an oiled sheet of plastic wrap, oiled side down, over the buns. Let the dough rest for about 45 minutes, until it has risen and is puffy. The dough will not double in size, but it will expand. Depending on the size they started as and the heat in your kitchen, some of the buns may rise slightly above the pan edges.

9. While the buns are rising, set the racks in the upper third and lower third of the oven for hamburger buns or in the center for hot dog buns and preheat to 325°F (170°C).

10. Make an egg wash by beating the egg and water together in a small bowl.

11. When the buns have risen, brush the tops very gently with the egg wash and sprinkle with sesame seeds or poppy seeds if you like.

12. Bake until the buns have risen and are beginning to get rounded tops, 12 to 15 minutes.

    For hamburger buns
    Carefully remove the baking rings, using a knife to release them if needed. Rotate the baking sheets and return them to the oven, swapping top and bottom.

    For hot dog buns
    Rotate the pan front to back.

13. Continue baking until the tops are golden brown, another 10 to 15 minutes. If the buns are browning too quickly, tent them loosely with a sheet of aluminum foil. They are done when the temperature on an instant-read thermometer inserted in the center registers about 210°F (99°C). Insert the probe through the side of one bun to check.

14. *For hamburger buns*, carefully transfer them to a wire cooling rack with a spatula. *For hot dog buns*, leave them in their pan; place the pan on a wire rack to cool for about 10 minutes, then lift them out and place directly on a wire rack. Let the buns cool for at least 30 minutes before serving, then use a serrated knife to slice them horizontally nearly all the way through.

15. Store the buns in a resealable plastic bag or airtight container on the counter for 1 day or in the refrigerator for up to 3 days. For longer storage, double-wrap tightly in plastic, place in a resealable plastic bag, and freeze for up to 3 months.

PRETZEL ROLLS

MAKES 6 REGULAR-SIZE ROLLS OR 12 SMALL ROLLS • DAIRY FREE

Have you wistfully watched others order pretzel rolls, disappointed that you can't enjoy them too? Your frustrations are over. These rolls have the unique chewiness of pretzels, the crunchy bite of coarse salt, and all of the delicious flavor you've been dreaming of. Make some today and you will be amazed how good they are! Pretzels made with regular wheat dough take a bath in a boiling alkaline solution, traditionally made with lye or, in the home kitchen, baking soda. The chemical reaction gives pretzels their dark, glossy crust and characteristic chewy texture. Because gluten-free doughs are so delicate, it is better to brush on the soda solution rather than risk having them collapse and become dense and gummy. They will not get as dark, but they will get close to the color and flavor you are looking for. You can use any coarse salt on the outside of the formed dough, but using actual pretzel salt is a lot of fun—and because you need so little, not that expensive.

DRY INGREDIENTS

21 g (0.7 oz or 2 tablespoons) active dry yeast

360 g (12.7 oz or 3 cups) Light Flour Blend (page 34) or Whole-Grain Flour Blend (page 34)

96 g (3.4 oz or ¾ cup) cornstarch, potato starch (*not* potato flour), or arrowroot

2½ teaspoons kosher or fine sea salt

2 teaspoons psyllium husk flakes or powder

¾ teaspoon baking powder

⅛ teaspoon ascorbic acid, optional

WET INGREDIENTS

1 teaspoon honey

300 ml (1¼ cups) water, warmed to about 80°F (27°C)

2 large egg whites, at room temperature

2 teaspoons apple cider vinegar

BAKING SODA WASH

240 ml (1 cup) water

¼ teaspoon baking soda

TOPPING

1 large egg yolk

2 teaspoons water

Pretzel salt or coarse flaked salt, such as Maldon

1. Line a baking sheet with parchment and lightly brush it with oil. Lightly oil a muffin pan (either a 6-cup jumbo pan or a 12-cup regular pan).

2. Set the bread pan on the counter and insert the beater paddle(s). Unless otherwise directed by your machine's manufacturer, add the liquids first, then the dry ingredients, and finally the yeast.

3. Measure the yeast into a small bowl and set aside. In a large mixing bowl, whisk the remaining dry ingredients together.

4. In a 4-cup (1 liter) glass measuring cup, whisk the honey and water together to dissolve the honey. Add the remaining wet ingredients and whisk again. Pour into the bread pan. Use a spatula to spread the dry ingredients over the wet ingredients. Make a shallow well in the center and pour in the yeast.

5. Place the bread pan in the machine, settle it in the center, and lock it in place. Close the lid and select:

   Dough cycle
   Loaf size: 1½ pounds/750 g
   Start

6. Let the machine mix and knead the dough until all the dry ingredients have been incorporated, using a rubber spatula to move any flour caught in the corners or under the dough to the center so the paddle can mix it in. Do this a few times to be sure everything is incorporated. Let the machine mix and knead for about 5 minutes, until the dough is smooth and has no lumps. Hit stop to cancel the cycle and turn off the machine.

7. Remove the pan from the machine. Scoop the dough onto the baking sheet. Lightly brush the top of the dough with a little oil. Use your hands to flatten the dough into a disk. For larger rolls, divide the dough into six equal pieces. For smaller rolls, divide the dough into twelve equal pieces.

8. Using lightly oiled hands, roll each piece into a ball and put them in the muffin pan cups. Cover with an oiled sheet of plastic wrap, oiled side down, and set in a warm area of your kitchen to rise for about 1½ hours. They will not double in size, but they will expand and puff up.

9. While the rolls are rising, place a rack in the center of the oven and preheat to 350°F (180°C).

10. When the rolls are almost done rising, combine the water and baking soda in a saucepan. Bring to a boil over medium-high heat, stirring occasionally to dissolve the baking soda; remove from the heat.

11. Beat the egg yolk and water together in a small bowl. The egg wash will help the salt adhere to the dough and deepen the browning in the oven.

> ### CREATE WARMTH TO REST
>
> If you are baking in the cooler months when your kitchen is chilly, you can heat your oven to its lowest setting and then turn it off. Use this space for resting your dough; the warmth will encourage the yeast to grow and you will get higher, lighter rolls.

12. Use a pastry brush to gently brush the top of each ball of dough thoroughly with the baking soda wash. Let sit for 1 minute, then brush the entire top with the beaten egg. Sprinkle each roll with salt. Use a sharp serrated knife to cut an X in the top of each roll. This helps them rise higher.

13. Bake until deep brown and an instant-read thermometer inserted in the center registers 210°F (99°C) or higher. Larger rolls will take 50 to 60 minutes. For smaller rolls, start checking at about 35 minutes or when the rolls are golden brown.

14. Let the rolls rest in the pan for about 2 minutes, then transfer to a wire rack to cool—this will let the steam escape and keep the rolls crunchy on the outside. Make sure they cool for at least 20 minutes to let them finish setting up inside before serving.

15. These rolls taste best on the day they are made, but if you make them a day ahead, you can refresh and recrisp them by heating for a few minutes in the oven before serving.

VARIATIONS

Pretzel Sticks

Pinch off pieces of dough about the size of a walnut. Oil your hands and roll each ball into a 7-inch (18 cm) log. Set on a lightly oiled baking sheet and cover with an oiled piece of plastic wrap, oiled side down. Let them rise at room temperature for 1 hour. Brush the tops with the baking soda wash, wait 1 minute, then brush with the egg wash. Sprinkle liberally with pretzel salt. Bake until golden brown, crispy, and baked through, 20 to 25 minutes. Break one open, and if it is still gummy inside, return the rest to the oven. When done, let them firm up on the baking sheet for 2 minutes, then gently transfer them to a wire rack. Unlike most gluten-free breads, these are great eaten straight out of the oven—just don't burn your fingers!

Pretzel Bites

Prepare Pretzel Stick logs. Cut each one into 1-inch (2.5 cm) pieces and scatter them on the baking sheet. Cover, let rise, brush with the baking soda solution, sprinkle with salt, and bake as directed.

Pretzels

Pinch off larger pieces of dough, about the size of a golf ball. Oil your hands and roll each piece into a 10-inch (25 cm) log. Set each log on an oiled baking sheet and form it into a U. Bring the left end about halfway up the opposite side and pinch to secure it. Now bring the right end up to the opposite side and pinch. Cover with an oiled sheet of plastic wrap, oiled side down, and let rise for about 1½ hours. Brush with the baking soda wash, wait 1 minute, then brush with the egg wash. Sprinkle liberally with pretzel salt. Bake until golden brown, crispy, and baked through, 25 to 30 minutes. Break one open, and if it is still gummy inside, return the rest to the oven to finish baking. Let rest on the sheet for 2 minutes, then gently transfer to a wire rack to cool. Bring out the mustard and enjoy!

DINNER ROLLS

MAKES 12 ROLLS • DAIRY-FREE OPTION

Dinner rolls are an important part of most holiday meals and often the only time people make bread from scratch. Instead of having to politely decline the rolls as they are passed around the table, you can eat as many of these gluten-free rolls as you want. Their texture is a cross between a yeast roll and a biscuit, tender and soft and a perfect accompaniment to dinner. Serve alongside a bowl of steaming hot soup or use them for ham or turkey sandwiches on a buffet. These are definitely best on the day they are baked, but you can make and form the dough into rolls the night before, cover them, and let them rise slowly in the refrigerator. This will not only make it easier for you on the big day, but it also develops a richer flavor.

DRY INGREDIENTS

31.5 g (1.1 oz or 2½ tablespoons) active dry yeast

360 g (12.7 oz or 3 cups) Light Flour Blend (page 34)

64 g (2.3 oz or ½ cup) cornstarch, potato starch (*not* potato flour), or arrowroot

26 g (0.9 oz or 2 tablespoons) granulated cane sugar

1 teaspoon baking powder

1 teaspoon xanthan gum

1 teaspoon kosher or fine sea salt

⅛ teaspoon ascorbic acid, optional

WET INGREDIENTS

40 g (1.4 oz or 2 tablespoons) honey or agave nectar

160 ml (⅔ cup) water, warmed to about 80°F (27°C)

3 large eggs, at room temperature (see page 39), beaten

85 g (3 oz or 6 tablespoons/¾ stick) unsalted butter or nondairy butter substitute, melted and slightly cooled

2 teaspoons apple cider vinegar

TOPPING (OPTIONAL)

Melted salted butter or nondairy butter substitute, plain or with minced garlic added

Sesame seeds, poppy seeds, coarse salt, chopped fresh rosemary or other herbs, flaxseed, sunflower seeds, or finely grated cheese

1. Thoroughly coat a 12-cup muffin pan and a baking sheet with nonstick cooking spray.

2. Set the bread pan on the counter and insert the beater paddle(s). Unless otherwise directed by your machine's manufacturer, add the liquids first, then the dry ingredients, and finally the yeast.

3. Measure the yeast into a small bowl and set aside. In a large mixing bowl, whisk the remaining dry ingredients together.

4. In a 2-cup (0.5 liter) glass measuring cup, whisk the honey and water together to dissolve the honey. Add the remaining wet ingredients and whisk again. Pour into the bread pan. Use a spatula to spread the dry ingredients over the wet ingredients, covering completely. Make a shallow well in the center and pour in the yeast.

5. Place the bread pan in the machine, settle it in the center, and lock it in place. Close the lid and select:
   Dough cycle
   Loaf size: 1½ pounds/750 g
   Start

6. About 3 minutes into the mixing process, open the lid and use a spatula to scrape down the sides of the pan, pushing any flour that has accumulated around the edges and under the dough into the center. Let the machine mix the dough until it is smooth and has no lumps, about 5 minutes, scraping the pan a few times. This dough will appear quite wet, so unless there are obvious puddles of liquid, avoid adding any extra flour even if you think it needs it. Press the stop button to cancel the cycle, turn off the machine, and remove the pan.

7. Scoop the dough onto the oiled baking sheet. Sprinkle the top of the dough with a little more oil. Press the dough into an 8 x 12-inch (20 x 30 cm) rectangle, starting in the center and pressing the dough outward. If your hands start to stick, add more oil.

8. Shape the dough:

   For regular dinner rolls
   a. Use an oiled bench scraper or knife to divide the dough into 12 equal pieces.

   b. Roll each one into a ball and drop into the center of the oiled muffin cups.

   For cloverleaf rolls
   a. Use an oiled bench scraper or knife to divide the dough into 36 equal pieces.

   b. Roll each into a ball and drop 3 balls into each of the 12 oiled muffin cups, setting them next to each other in a triangle design. These will rise into the classic shamrock shape.

9. Cover the muffin pan with a sheet of oiled plastic wrap, oiled side down, and set in a warm, draft-free area to rise for about 2 hours. Gluten-free dough doesn't rise as high as wheat dough, but the rolls will increase in size and puff up as the yeast and baking powder work together.

10. About 30 minutes before the rolls finish rising, set an oven rack in the center of the oven and preheat to 350°F (180°C).

11. If you like, gently brush the tops of the rolls with melted butter and sprinkle with your choice of toppings.

12. Bake until the rolls are golden brown and an instant-read thermometer registers about 210°F (99°C) when inserted in the center, 20 to 24 minutes, rotating the pan halfway through. Let the rolls sit in the pan for about 2 minutes, then transfer to a wire rack and cool for at least 15 minutes before serving.

13. While these rolls are best eaten on the day they are baked, you can store leftovers in a resealable plastic bag or airtight container on the counter for a day, or in the refrigerator for up to 3 days. Reheat gently in a warm oven. For longer storage, double-wrap tightly in plastic, place in a resealable plastic bag, and freeze for up to 3 months.

SOFT BREAD STICKS

MAKES 8 BREAD STICKS ◆ DAIRY-FREE OPTION

Soft bread sticks are a delightful indulgence. Great with fresh butter (page 69) or dipped into pizza sauce (page 203), these are a little like sticks of focaccia. Puffy and soft when they first come out of the oven, they tend to become more chewy as they sit. You can add more herbs to both the dough and for sprinkling on the tops if you want, and a coarse salt like Maldon adds a nice crunch. Serve them with a plate of cheese and some charcuterie and you have the perfect party platter. All that is missing is a glass of wine and laughter shared with good friends!

DRY INGREDIENTS

1 tablespoon active dry yeast

240 g (8.5 oz or 2 cups) Light Flour Blend (page 34) or Whole-Grain Flour Blend (page 34)

64 g (2.3 oz or ½ cup) cornstarch, potato starch (*not* potato flour), or arrowroot

¼ cup milk powder (22 g/0.8 oz) or DariFree (40 g/1.4 oz)

1 tablespoon granulated cane sugar

2 teaspoons xanthan gum

1 teaspoon baking powder

1 teaspoon kosher or fine sea salt

⅛ teaspoon ascorbic acid, optional

WET INGREDIENTS

120 ml (½ cup) water, warmed to about 80°F (27°C)

2 large egg whites, at room temperature

30 ml (2 tablespoons) vegetable or olive oil

2 teaspoons apple cider vinegar

TOPPINGS

Melted unsalted butter or nondairy butter substitute

Coarse sea salt, such as Maldon

Dried oregano or other herbs, optional

1. Line a baking sheet with parchment and brush lightly with vegetable oil.

2. Set the bread pan on the counter and insert the beater paddle(s). Unless otherwise directed by your machine's manufacturer, add the liquids first, then the dry ingredients, and finally the yeast.

3. Measure the yeast into a small bowl and set aside. In a large mixing bowl, whisk the remaining dry ingredients together.

4. In a 2-cup (0.5 liter) glass measuring cup, whisk the wet ingredients together and pour into the bread pan. Use a spatula to spread the dry ingredients over the wet ingredients. Make a shallow well in the center and pour in the yeast.

5. Place the bread pan in the machine, settle it in the center, and lock it in place. Close the lid and select:

   Dough cycle
   Loaf size: 1 pound/500 g (if available)
   or 1½ pounds/750 g
   Start

6. While the machine is mixing and kneading the ingredients, open the lid and use a spatula to scrape down the sides of the pan, pushing any flour that has accumulated around the edges and under the dough into the center. Let the machine mix the dough until it is smooth and has no lumps, about 5 minutes, scraping the sides, corners, and under the dough occasionally. Press the stop button to cancel the cycle, turn off the machine, and remove the pan.

7. Scoop the dough out of the bread pan and onto the baking sheet. Oil your hands and press the dough out into an 8 x 12-inch (20 x 30 cm) rectangle.

8. Oil a bench scraper or knife and cut the dough into eight 6 x 2-inch (15 x 5 cm) "sticks." Leave them next to each other to give them support as they rise. Cover with an oiled sheet of plastic wrap, oiled side down, and set the pan aside to rest and let the dough rise for 1 hour. It will not double, but it will get puffy.

9. While the dough is rising, preheat the oven to 350°F (180°C).

10. Brush the tops with the melted butter, sprinkle with salt, and add a little oregano if you want. Bake until puffed and golden brown and an instant-read thermometer inserted in the center registers 210°F (99°C), 30 to 35 minutes, rotating the pan halfway through.

11. Let cool on the pan for a couple of minutes before carefully using the parchment to transfer the bread sticks to a wire rack. Slip the parchment out from underneath and discard. Cool for at least 15 minutes before pulling apart. Serve warm or at room temperature.

12. These are best eaten the day they are baked, but you can store them in an airtight container or resealable plastic bag in the refrigerator for up to 2 days. Reheat in a low oven if desired. Freezing is not recommended.

CRISPY, CHEWY BREAD STICKS

MAKES ABOUT 32 BREAD STICKS   •   DAIRY-FREE OPTION

When these bread sticks come out of the oven, they are well browned and crunchy, with a slightly chewy center. The longer they sit, the chewier they become, and they are absolutely addictive both ways. Leave them plain or add one or more toppings. Try serving several different toppings to add interest. If you are including them on a buffet, stand them upright in a glass for a more attractive presentation. Make more than you think you will need because they tend to disappear quickly!

DRY INGREDIENTS

21 g (0.7 oz or 2 tablespoons) active dry yeast

300 g (10.6 oz or 2½ cups) Light Flour Blend (page 34)

96 g (3.4 oz or ¾ cup) cornstarch, potato starch (*not* potato flour), or arrowroot

¼ cup milk powder (22 g/0.8 oz) or DariFree (40 g/1.4 oz)

1 tablespoon granulated cane sugar

2 teaspoons kosher or fine sea salt

2 teaspoons psyllium husk flakes or powder

⅛ teaspoon ascorbic acid, optional

WET INGREDIENTS

240 ml (1 cup) water, warmed to about 80°F (27°C)

3 large egg whites, at room temperature

15 ml (1 tablespoon) vegetable or olive oil

2 teaspoons champagne vinegar or cider vinegar

SHAPING

30 ml (2 tablespoons) vegetable or olive oil

TOPPINGS (OPTIONAL)

Melted butter or nondairy butter substitute, milk, olive oil or flavored oil, or beaten egg whites

Coarse sea or pretzel salt, powdered or grated cheese, fresh herbs, sesame seeds, poppy seeds, sunflower seeds

1. Set the bread pan on the counter and insert the beater paddle(s). Unless otherwise directed by your machine's manufacturer, add the liquids first, then the dry ingredients, and finally the yeast.

2. Measure the yeast into a small bowl and set aside. In a large mixing bowl, whisk the remaining dry ingredients together.

3. Whisk the wet ingredients together in a 2-cup (0.5 liter) measuring cup and pour into the bread pan. Use a spatula to spread the dry ingredients over the wet ingredients. Make a shallow well in the center and pour in the yeast.

4. Place the bread pan in the machine, settle it in the center, and lock it in place. Close the lid and select:

   Dough cycle
   Loaf size: 1½ pounds/750 g
   Start

5. While the machine is mixing and kneading the ingredients, open the lid and use a spatula to scrape down the sides of the pan as needed, pushing any flour that has accumulated around the edges, corners, and under the dough into the center to be blended. This dough is drier than other breads, which makes it heavier and harder for the paddle to blend. The dough tends to be pushed out to the edges of the pan, no longer being blended or kneaded. Use a spatula to lift the dough onto the paddle repeatedly to get as much mixing done as possible. Let the machine mix the dough until it is smooth and has no lumps, 4 to 5 minutes. Press the stop button to cancel the cycle, turn off the machine, and remove the bread pan.

6. For shaping the dough, pour the oil into a large mixing bowl. Use a spatula to scoop the dough into the bowl. Fold the oiled parts of the dough up and over the top, creating a disk of dough that is oiled on all sides.

7. Set the racks in the upper and lower thirds of the oven and preheat to 400°F (200°C). Line two baking sheets with parchment paper.

8. Divide the dough in half, then divide in half again, and continue halving until you have 32 equal pieces. Working with oiled hands, roll each piece of dough into a slender log by setting it on a very lightly oiled work surface. Using the palms of both hands and starting in the center, gently roll the dough back and forth while moving your hands out to the ends to elongate it into a 10-inch (25 cm) rope. Transfer to the lined baking sheets and continue with the remaining dough, placing 16 pieces on each baking sheet. Leave a little room between each one to allow for some expansion while they bake and to get crispy edges.

VARIATIONS

Add about ½ cup (10 to 20 g) finely chopped fresh herbs of your choice, such as rosemary, parsley, oregano, chives, or thyme, to the dry ingredients before mixing the dough.

For a cheesy, spiral version, sprinkle the top of each 10-inch (25 cm) rope with cheese powder (see Resources, page 376), then roll your hands in opposite directions to create a spiral effect and lengthen the ropes to 12 inches (30 cm). Bake as directed.

You can also take these in a totally different direction and make them sweet! Add 1 teaspoon pure vanilla extract or paste to the wet ingredients during mixing. Then sprinkle with cinnamon-sugar before popping into the oven. For the holidays, add a touch of ground nutmeg and ginger to the dry ingredients before mixing for a gingerbread flavor.

9. Leave the bread sticks plain or brush them with a little butter, milk, or beaten egg white and then sprinkle with your choice of topping. For chewier bread sticks, let them rest uncovered for 10 to 15 minutes to rise slightly.

10. Place the sheets in the oven and bake for about 10 minutes, then rotate the pans. This will give you the most even browning. Bake until golden brown and firm to the touch, another 10 to 15 minutes. The darker they are, the crunchier they will be. Use the parchment to transfer the bread sticks to a wire rack, then slide the parchment out. They will finish crisping as they cool.

11. While these are definitely best and crunchiest on the day they are baked, you can store them in an airtight container on the counter for a couple of days (the longer they sit, the chewier they become). Freezing is not recommended.

CHEESY SOFT BREAD STICKS WITH GARLIC AND HERBS

MAKES 12 BREAD STICKS

Bread and cheese is a combination that has been served together for centuries. Whether picnicking at the beach, having lunch in a garden in Paris, or sharing fondue with friends, bread and cheese is an integral part of our lives—or it was until we couldn't have gluten anymore. These bread sticks give us both in one bite. They are a snap to throw together, so we can have them any time we want. Combine the ingredients, add them to the bread machine, and let it do the work. The only thing that takes time is letting the dough rise. The hard part is waiting for them to cool!

DRY INGREDIENTS

1½ tablespoons active dry yeast

360 g (12.7 oz or 3 cups) Light Flour Blend (page 34) or Whole-Grain Flour Blend (page 34)

64 g (2.3 oz or ½ cup) cornstarch, potato starch (*not* potato flour), or arrowroot

63 g (2.2 oz or ¾ cup) cheddar cheese powder, such as Cabot (see Resources, page 376)

2 teaspoons xanthan gum

2 teaspoons kosher or fine sea salt

2 teaspoons garlic powder

1 teaspoon baking powder

⅛ teaspoon ascorbic acid, optional

WET INGREDIENTS

1 teaspoon honey

300 ml (1¼ cups) water, warmed to about 80°F (27°C)

1 egg white, at room temperature

15 ml (1 tablespoon) vegetable or olive oil

2 teaspoons apple cider vinegar

TOPPING

20 g (0.7 or ¼ cup) shredded Parmesan, Asiago, or other aged cheese

2 tablespoons minced fresh basil

2 teaspoons garlic powder

42–55 g (1.5–2 oz or 3–4 tablespoons) unsalted butter, melted

1. Line a baking sheet with parchment. Brush lightly with oil.

2. Set the bread pan on the counter and insert the beater paddle(s). Unless otherwise directed by your machine's manufacturer, add the liquids first, then the dry ingredients, and finally the yeast.

3. Measure the yeast into a small bowl and set aside. In a large mixing bowl, whisk the remaining dry ingredients together.

4. In a 2-cup (0.5 liter) glass measuring cup, whisk the honey and water together to dissolve the honey. Add the remaining wet ingredients and whisk again. Pour into the bread pan. Use a spatula to spread the dry ingredients over the wet ingredients, covering completely. Make a shallow well in the center and pour in the yeast.

5. Place the bread pan in the machine, settle it in the center, and lock it in place. Close the lid and select:
   Dough cycle
   Loaf size: 1½ pounds/750 g
   Start

6. While the machine is mixing and kneading the ingredients, open the lid and use a spatula to scrape down the sides of the pan as needed, pushing any flour that has accumulated around the edges and under the dough into the center. Let the machine mix the dough until it is smooth and has no lumps, about 5 minutes. Press the stop button to cancel the cycle, turn off the machine, and remove the pan.

7. Scrape the dough (it will be very soft and sticky) onto the baking sheet. Using oiled hands, press the dough into a 12-inch (30 cm) square—work from the center out, pressing to flatten and spread the dough. Square the edges. Use an oiled bench scraper or knife to cut the dough into 12 equal slices.

8. Mix the shredded Parmesan, minced basil, and garlic powder together in a bowl.

9. Gently brush the tops of the bread sticks with the melted butter and sprinkle with the cheesy topping. Cover loosely with a sheet of plastic wrap and set aside to rise in a warm place for 1 hour.

10. While the bread sticks rise, preheat the oven to 400°F (200°C).

11. Remove the plastic wrap and bake until puffed and golden brown and an instant-read thermometer inserted in the center registers 212°F (100°C), 30 to 35 minutes, rotating the baking sheet halfway through.

12. Use the parchment to transfer the bread sticks to a wire rack, then slide the parchment out. Cool for at least 15 minutes. Serve warm or at room temperature.

13. These are best eaten the day they are baked, but you can store them in an airtight container or resealable plastic bag in the refrigerator for up to 2 days. Reheat in a low oven if desired. Freezing is not recommended.

CINNAMON ROLLS

MAKES 10 ROLLS ◆ DAIRY FREE

Baking cinnamon rolls makes your house smell like a special occasion, but mixing the dough in the bread machine is so easy you'll make these all the time. The bread machine creates a light, malleable dough that is easy to shape into a rectangle. The dough is soft enough to press with your lightly oiled hands, but you can use a lightly oiled rolling pin if desired. You can bake the rolls in a 9-inch (23 cm) round cake pan or use a cast-iron skillet, which bakes them very evenly.

DRY INGREDIENTS

1 tablespoon active dry yeast

300 g (10.6 oz or 2½ cups) Light Flour Blend (page 34) or Whole-Grain Flour Blend (page 34)

70 g (2.5 oz or ½ cup) potato starch (*not* potato flour)

40 g (1.4 oz or ¼ cup) DariFree

26 g (0.9 oz or 2 tablespoons) granulated cane sugar

1 tablespoon psyllium husk flakes or powder

2 teaspoons baking powder

½ teaspoon kosher or fine sea salt

½ teaspoon dough enhancer

WET INGREDIENTS

300 ml (1¼ cups) unsweetened coconut milk

1 tablespoon freshly squeezed lemon juice

42 g (1.5 oz or 3 tablespoons) nondairy butter substitute, melted and slightly cooled

FILLING

30 g (1 oz or 2 tablespoons firmly packed) brown sugar

26 g (0.9 oz or 2 tablespoons) granulated cane sugar

1 teaspoon ground cinnamon

1 tablespoon nondairy butter substitute, melted

GLAZE

90 g (3.2 oz or ¾ cup) confectioners' sugar

1 tablespoon nondairy butter substitute, melted

1 teaspoon pure vanilla extract

1 to 2 tablespoons hot water

1. Preheat the oven to 425°F (220°C). Coat a muffin tin, a 9-inch (23 cm) round cake pan, or an 8-inch (20 cm) cast-iron skillet with nonstick flourless cooking spray.

2. Insert the beater paddle(s) into the bread pan. Unless otherwise directed by your machine's manufacturer, add the liquids, dry ingredients, and then the yeast.

3. Measure the yeast into a small bowl and set aside. In a large mixing bowl, whisk the remaining dry ingredients together.

4. In a 4-cup (1 liter) glass measuring cup, whisk the wet ingredients together and pour into the bread pan. Use a spatula to spread the dry ingredients over the wet ingredients. Make a shallow well in the center and pour in the yeast.

5. Place the bread pan in the machine and lock it in place. Close the lid and select:

   Dough cycle
   Loaf size: 1½ pounds/750 g
   Start

6. While the machine is mixing and kneading the ingredients, open the lid and use a spatula to scrape down the sides of the pan as needed, pushing any flour that has accumulated around the edges and under the dough into the center. Let the machine mix the dough until it is smooth and has no lumps, about 5 minutes. Press the stop button to cancel the cycle, turn off the machine, and remove the pan.

7. Transfer the dough to a lightly oiled work surface. Oil your hands lightly and shape the dough into a 9 x 12-inch (23 x 30 cm) rectangle.

8. To make the filling, stir together both sugars and the cinnamon. Brush the dough rectangle with the melted nondairy butter. Spread the filling evenly over the dough, leaving a ½-inch (1 cm) border on all the sides. Press the filling into the dough. Starting on the long side, roll the dough into a tight log. If your fingers stick to the dough, lightly moisten them with oil. Pinch the seam to seal the log. Slice evenly into ten rolls.

9. Place the rolls, cut side up, in the pan. Coat a sheet of plastic wrap with nonstick cooking spray and gently lay it over the dough, oiled side down. Set the pan aside to rise at room temperature for 45 minutes to 1 hour. Gluten-free doughs rarely double in size but they do puff up. Bake until the edges begin to turn golden brown, about 20 minutes. Turn out the rolls onto a cooling rack.

10. To make the glaze, whisk together the confectioners' sugar, nondairy butter, and vanilla. Add the water, a teaspoon or so at a time, until you reach the desired consistency. Drizzle the glaze over the warm rolls and serve.

11. Store any leftover cinnamon rolls in an airtight container at room temperature for up to 1 day or in the refrigerator for up to 3 days. Freezing is not recommended.

HOLIDAY STOLLEN

MAKES 2 LOAVES

This is a gluten-free version of the classic German Christmas bread also known as *Weihnachtsstollen* or *Christstollen*, which has been made in one form or another since the 1400s. Citrus zest is usually added to the dough, which is also heavily dotted with candied fruits, making it is a cross between bread and fruitcake. You can prepare a more traditional version by using Paradise brand Old English Fruit & Peel Mix instead of the candied cherries and golden raisins called for here.

DRY INGREDIENTS

1 tablespoon active dry yeast

300 g (10.6 oz or 2½ cups) Light Flour Blend (page 34) or Whole-Grain Flour Blend (page 34)

100 g (3.5 oz or ½ cup) granulated cane sugar

40 g (1.4 oz or ¼ cup) DariFree

38 g (1.3 oz or ¼ cup) potato starch (*not* potato flour)

1 tablespoon psyllium husk flakes or powder

2 teaspoons baking powder

½ teaspoon salt

112 g (4 oz or 8 tablespoons/1 stick) cold unsalted butter, cut into small pieces

75 g (2.6 oz or ½ cup) chopped golden raisins

104 g (3.7 oz or ½ cup) candied cherries, chopped

36 g (1.3 oz or ⅓ cup) slivered almonds, toasted

1 teaspoon dough enhancer

WET INGREDIENTS

188 g (6.6 oz or ¾ cup) part-skim ricotta cheese

3 large eggs, at room temperature (see page 39), beaten

2 teaspoons pure vanilla extract

Grated zest of 1 lemon

TOPPING

42 g (1.5 oz or 3 tablespoons) unsalted butter, melted and slightly cooled

60 g (2.1 oz or ½ cup) confectioners' sugar

1. Preheat the oven to 325°F (163°C). Line a baking sheet with parchment.

2. Set the bread pan on the counter and insert the beater paddle(s). Unless otherwise directed by your machine's manufacturer, add the liquids first, then the dry ingredients, and finally the yeast.

3. Measure the yeast into a small bowl and set aside. In a large bowl, whisk the flour blend, cane sugar, milk powder, potato starch, psyllium, baking powder, and salt together. Incorporate the cold butter into the dry ingredients with two forks, two knives, or a pastry blender until it resembles coarse crumbs. Add the raisins, candied cherries, and almonds and toss. Set aside.

4. In a 2-cup (0.5 liter) glass measuring cup, whisk the wet ingredients together and pour into the bread pan. Add the dry ingredients, spreading them out with a spatula until all the wet ingredients are covered. Make a shallow well in the center and pour in the yeast.

5. Place the bread pan in the machine, settle it in the center, and lock it in place. Close the lid and select:

   Dough cycle
   Loaf size: 1½ pounds/750 g
   Start

6. While the machine is mixing and kneading the ingredients, open the lid and use a spatula to scrape down the sides of the pan as needed, pushing any flour that has accumulated around the edges and under the dough into the center. Let the machine mix the dough until it is smooth and has no lumps, about 5 minutes. Press the stop button to cancel the cycle, turn off the machine, and remove the pan.

7. Turn out the dough onto a lightly floured work surface and divide it into two equal pieces. Lightly oil or wet your hands and shape each piece of dough into an oval about 8 inches (20 cm) long and ½ inch (1 cm) thick. Then fold each piece of dough almost in half lengthwise, leaving a ½-inch (1 cm) edge so the top half doesn't completely cover the bottom half. Press the edges to seal the dough.

8. Place the breads on the baking sheet. Bake for 35 to 40 minutes, or until an instant-read thermometer inserted into the center of the loaf reads 206°F to 210°F (97°C to 99°C), 35 to 40 minutes. Carefully transfer the loaves to a wire rack to cool.

9. Once the stollen have cooled, brush each loaf with half of the melted butter and sprinkle the tops with the confectioners' sugar.

10. Store the bread in a resealable plastic bag or airtight container on the counter for up to 1 week. For longer storage, cut into even slices, double-wrap tightly in plastic, place in a resealable plastic bag, and freeze for up to 3 months.

CHOCOLATE CHERRY STOLLEN

MAKES 1 (1½-POUND/680 G) LOAF

This dense bread adapts very easily to a gluten-free version. Traditionally, it contains dried fruits or golden raisins, but adding chocolate and dried cherries makes for a delightful change of pace. Sift the chocolate in a coarse strainer after you chop it so the chocolate dust won't turn the loaf a murky color. This recipe is for a loaf made entirely in the bread machine. If you want the classic stollen shape, preheat the oven to 325°F (170°C), line a baking sheet with parchment, and follow the instructions in the Holiday Stollen recipe (page 110), beginning with step 7.

DRY INGREDIENTS

1 tablespoon active dry yeast

300 g (10.6 oz or 2½ cups) Light Flour Blend (page 34) or Whole-Grain Flour Blend (page 34)

59 g (2.1 oz or ½ cup) millet flour

100 g (3.5 oz or ½ cup) granulated cane sugar

1 tablespoon psyllium husk flakes or powder

2 teaspoons baking powder

½ teaspoon kosher or fine sea salt

130 g (4.6 oz or ¾ cup) chopped chocolate (dark, milk, or a combination)

100 g (3.5 oz or ⅔ cup) dried cherries or cranberries

67 g (2.4 oz or ⅔ cup) slivered almonds, toasted

WET INGREDIENTS

56 g (2 oz or 4 tablespoons/½ stick) unsalted butter, coarsely chopped

3 large eggs, at room temperature (see page 39), beaten

2 teaspoons pure vanilla extract

Grated zest of 1 lemon

TOPPING

1 tablespoon unsalted butter, melted

1 tablespoon confectioners' sugar

1. Set the bread pan on the counter and insert the beater paddle(s). Unless otherwise directed by your machine's manufacturer, add the liquids first, then the dry ingredients, and finally the yeast.

2. Measure the yeast into a small bowl and set aside. In a large mixing bowl, whisk the flour blend, millet, cane sugar, psyllium, baking powder, and salt together. Cut the butter into the dry ingredients with two forks, two knives, or a pastry blender until it resembles coarse crumbs. Set aside.

3. In a 2-cup (0.5 liter) glass measuring cup, whisk the wet ingredients together and pour into the bread pan. Use a spatula to spread the dry ingredients over the wet ingredients, covering completely. Make a shallow well in the center and pour in the yeast.

4. Place the bread pan in the machine, settle it in the center, and lock it in place. Close the lid and select:

   Quick bread/cake cycle
   Loaf size: 1½ pounds/750 g
   Light crust
   Start

5. After the first knead cycle, scrape the sides and bottom of the pan with a spatula to make sure all the dry ingredients are incorporated. Add the chocolate, cherries, and almonds and let the machine finish kneading the dough. If your machine has alerts, when you hear the signal that the machine is transitioning from the knead to bake cycle, you can remove the paddle and reshape the loaf if you want. If the dough seems sticky, wet your hands with a little water to help with reshaping the loaf and smoothing the top. Close the lid and let the bread finish baking.

6. At the end of the bake cycle, lift the lid and check the temperature. The bread is done when it registers 206°F to 210°F (97°C to 99°C) on an instant-read thermometer inserted in the center. Remove the pan from the machine and place it on its side on a wire rack. Leave the bread in the pan for a couple of minutes, then turn the pan upside down and slide the loaf onto the wire rack. Carefully remove the paddle if it is embedded in the bottom of the loaf. Lay the bread on its side and cool it for at least 2 hours. When the bread is fully cooled, brush the top with melted butter and sprinkle with confectioners' sugar.

7. Store the bread in a resealable plastic bag or airtight container on the counter for up to 1 week. For longer storage, cut into even slices, double-wrap tightly in plastic, place in a resealable plastic bag, and freeze for up to 3 months.

ITALIAN CIABATTA

MAKES 1 (2-POUND/910 G) LOAF • DAIRY-FREE OPTION

The word *ciabatta* means "slipper" in Italian and refers to the shape of the bread. The traditional version usually has enormous holes inside, making it hard to use for sandwiches, but the bubbles in ours are more evenly distributed, so it's easier to spread the condiments. While you can form this soft dough into the traditional oval shape on a baking sheet, it tends to spread. You will get the best results if you use a slender rectangular baking pan, which contains the dough and offers much needed support on the sides as it rises. We recommend the "biscotti pan" (12 x 5½ x 2 inches/30 x 14 x 5 cm) from USA Pan (see Resources, page 376).

DRY INGREDIENTS

4 teaspoons active dry yeast

480 g (4 cups) Light Flour Blend (page 34) or Whole-Grain Flour Blend (page 34)

½ cup milk powder (44 g/1.6 oz) or DariFree (69 g/2.4 oz)

39 g (1.4 oz or 3 tablespoons) granulated cane sugar

2 teaspoons psyllium husk flakes or powder

2 teaspoons baking powder

2 teaspoons kosher or fine sea salt

⅛ teaspoon ascorbic acid, optional

WET INGREDIENTS

180 to 240 ml (¾ to 1 cup) water, warmed to about 80°F (27°C)

3 large eggs, at room temperature (see page 39), beaten

45 ml (3 tablespoons) vegetable or olive oil

2 teaspoons apple cider vinegar

TOPPING

Olive or vegetable oil

Coarse sea salt, optional

1. Generously brush a slender baking pan (see headnote) with vegetable oil. You can line the pan with parchment, leaving it extended over two sides to create "handles" that make it easy to remove the bread from the pan. If you do, lightly oil the parchment.

2. Set the bread pan on the counter and insert the beater paddle(s). Unless otherwise directed by your machine's manufacturer, add the liquids first, then the dry ingredients, and finally the yeast.

3. Measure the yeast into a small bowl and set aside. In a large mixing bowl, whisk the remaining dry ingredients together.

4. In a 2-cup (0.5 liter) glass measuring cup, whisk the wet ingredients (start with the water) together and pour into the bread pan. Use a spatula to spread the dry ingredients over the wet ingredients, covering completely. Make a shallow well in the center and pour in the yeast.

5. Place the bread pan in the machine and lock it in place. Close the lid and select:

   Dough cycle
   Loaf size: 1½ pounds/750 g
   Start

6. While the machine is mixing and kneading the ingredients, open the lid and use the spatula to scrape down the sides of the pan as needed, pushing any flour that has accumulated around the edges and under the dough into the center. If the dough looks too dry, add up to 60 ml/ ¼ cup more water, 1 tablespoon at a time, until the texture is what you are looking for. Let the machine mix the dough until it is smooth and has no lumps, about 5 minutes.

7. When the dough is ready, press the stop button to cancel the cycle, turn off the machine, and remove the pan. Use a spatula to scoop the dough into the baking pan. Smooth the top. Brush the top gently with a little oil and sprinkle lightly with coarse salt if desired. Set the pan aside to rest and let the dough rise, uncovered, for about 30 minutes. It will not double, but it will puff up.

8. Preheat the oven to 350°F (180°C).

9. Bake the bread, rotating the pan halfway through the baking time, until puffed and golden brown, and the temperature on an instant-read thermometer inserted in the center reaches 206°F to 210°F (97°C to 99°C), 30 to 45 minutes. Remove the bread from the pan and place on a wire rack to cool for at least 1 hour.

10. Store the bread in a resealable plastic bag or airtight container on the counter for up to 1 day. For longer storage, double-wrap tightly in plastic, place in a resealable plastic bag, and freeze for up to 3 months.

VARIATIONS

To Use for Sandwiches
When fully cooled, cut the loaf into three or four sections. Cut each section in half horizontally to create two slices to use for sandwiches.

To Use as Sliced Bread
Wait until the loaf is cool and cut perpendicular to the long side into 1- to 2-inch-wide (3 to 5 cm) slices. Serve alongside your meal or with Italian Herb Dipping Sauce (page 189) as an appetizer.

BUTTERY CHALLAH

MAKES 2 LARGE CHALLAH BRAIDS OR 1 (1½-POUND/680 G) LOAF

Challah is an egg bread similar to French brioche, but a little lighter, and traditionally served during Jewish holidays. These days its popularity has expanded well beyond New York's Lower East Side. It makes beautiful toast and some of the best French toast imaginable. This challah is light, airy, and tender, with just enough sweetness for a beautiful gluten-free alternative during the holidays or any time of year. To make this bread entirely in the machine, use the gluten-free cycle, 1½-pound (750 g) loaf, and medium crust settings and follow the instructions in the other recipes. If you want a more traditional braided look, use a silicone form to mold the soft gluten-free dough.

DRY INGREDIENTS

21 g (0.7 oz or 2 tablespoons) active dry yeast

360 g (12.7 oz or 3 cups) Light Flour Blend (page 34)

48 g (1.7 oz or ¼ cup) granulated cane sugar

1 tablespoon baking powder

1 teaspoon xanthan gum

1 teaspoon kosher or fine sea salt

WET INGREDIENTS

85 g (3 oz or ¼ cup) honey

255 ml (1 cup plus 1 tablespoon) 1% milk or water, warmed to about 80°F (27°C)

56 g (2 oz or 4 tablespoons/½ stick) unsalted butter, melted and slightly cooled

3 large eggs, at room temperature (see page 39), beaten

2 teaspoons champagne vinegar

TOPPING

1 large egg

1 tablespoon water

2 teaspoons sesame seeds or poppy seeds, optional

1. Set the bread pan on the counter and insert the beater paddle(s). Unless otherwise directed by your machine's manufacturer, add the liquids first, then the dry ingredients, and finally the yeast.

2. Measure the yeast into a small bowl and set aside. In a large mixing bowl, whisk the remaining dry ingredients together.

3. In a 4-cup (1 liter) glass measuring cup, whisk the honey and milk together to dissolve the honey. Add the remaining wet ingredients and whisk again. Pour into the bread pan. Use a spatula to spread the dry ingredients over the wet ingredients, covering completely. Make a shallow well in the center and pour in the yeast.

4. Place the bread pan in the machine, settle it in the center, and lock it in place. Close the lid and select:

   Dough cycle
   Loaf size: 1½ pounds/750 g
   Start

5. While the machine is mixing and kneading the ingredients, open the lid and use a spatula to scrape down the sides of the pan as needed, pushing any flour that has accumulated around the edges and under the dough into the center. Let the machine mix the dough until it is smooth and has no lumps, about 5 minutes.

6. While the dough is being kneaded, coat the inside of two large (9 x 5-inch/23 x 13 cm) silicone challah baking pans (see Note, page 118) with nonstick cooking spray, being careful to cover all the surfaces. Set out two sheets of plastic wrap and coat one side with cooking spray (to cover the molds).

7. When the dough is ready, press the stop button to cancel the cycle, turn off the machine, and remove the bread pan. Use a spatula to scoop half of the dough into each baking pan, filling them halfway. Do not overfill. Cover each with a sheet of oiled plastic wrap, oiled side down. Place in a warm area and let them rise until the dough has nearly doubled in size and is just about up to the top edge of the pans, about 1 hour.

8. While the dough is rising, set a rack in the center of the oven and preheat to 325°F (170°C).

9. Make an egg wash by whisking together the egg and water. Set the egg wash and a pastry brush next to the oven.

> **NOTE:** You can purchase silicone challah molds on baking supply websites such as www.thekoshercook.com. This bread can also be baked in any high-sided loaf pan of a similar size.

10. Place the filled bread molds on a baking sheet, rounded side down. Bake for 30 minutes. Remove the bread from the oven, invert the molds onto the baking sheet, and lift off the molds. Brush the top of the bread with the egg wash and sprinkle with the seeds if desired. Tent loosely with aluminum foil and bake for 10 minutes. Remove the foil and bake until the top is deeply golden brown and the temperature on an instant-read thermometer inserted in the center registers 208°F to 212°F (98°C to 100°C), another 5 to 10 minutes. If your oven tends to run hot, watch these very carefully. With the higher sugar content, they can get very dark quickly. You may want to lower the temperature a little to compensate.

11. Carefully transfer the loaves to a wire cooling rack. Cool for at least 2 hours before slicing.

12. Store the bread in a resealable plastic bag or airtight container on the counter for up to 1 day. For longer storage, double-wrap tightly in plastic, place in a resealable plastic bag, and freeze for up to 3 months.

FRENCH BAGUETTES

MAKES 2 (15-INCH/38 CM) BAGUETTES   •   DAIRY-FREE OPTION

In Paris, every block seems to have a *boulangerie*, or bread bakery. Each one is dedicated to bringing customers the best breads they can. Nearly all of them are independently owned, often run by the same family for generations. They are so proud of their breads that they will not sell anything that isn't freshly baked. If they've run out, you're out of luck. It was important to us to make a gluten-free baguette that we could take just as much pride in.

For the best results, use a perforated double baguette pan (see page 120). The perforations allow the steam to escape, resulting in a lovely, light loaf with a crunchy crust. The sides of the channels will help the bread spread less and rise vertically. The narrower the channels, the more structure it will give the loaves. If you have a solid nonstick pan, you can forego the parchment paper, but if your pan tends to stick, use parchment or oil the pan. For a true French experience, split the baked and cooled loaf in half length-wise, smear the insides with plenty of fresh soft butter (see page 69), and add thin slices of ham. This is the most popular sandwich in France, one you can find in every single bread shop. Now you can share this French classic with your family and friends.

DRY INGREDIENTS

21 g (0.7 oz or 2 tablespoons) active dry yeast

300 g (10.6 oz or 2½ cups) Light Flour Blend (page 34)

96 g (3.4 oz or ¾ cup) cornstarch, potato starch (*not* potato flour), or tapioca starch

¼ cup milk powder (22 g/0.8 oz) or DariFree (40 g/1.4 oz)

1 tablespoon granulated cane sugar

2 teaspoons kosher or fine sea salt

2 teaspoons psyllium husk flakes or powder

⅛ teaspoon ascorbic acid, optional

WET INGREDIENTS

3 large egg whites, at room temperature

240 ml (1 cup) water, warmed to about 80°F (27°C)

15 ml (1 tablespoon) vegetable or olive oil

2 teaspoons champagne vinegar or apple cider vinegar

SHAPING

45 ml (3 tablespoons) vegetable or olive oil

1. Set the bread pan on the counter and insert the beater paddle(s). Unless otherwise directed by your machine's manufacturer, add the liquids first, then the dry ingredients, and finally the yeast.

2. Measure the yeast into a small bowl and set aside. In a large mixing bowl, whisk the remaining dry ingredients together.

3. In a 2-cup (0.5 liter) glass measuring cup, whisk the wet ingredients together and pour into the bread pan. Use a spatula to spread the dry ingredients over the wet ingredients, covering completely. Make a shallow well in the center and pour in the yeast.

4. Place the bread pan in the machine, settle it in the center, and lock it in place. Close the lid and select:
   Dough cycle
   Loaf size: 1½ pounds/750 g
   Start

5. While the machine is mixing and kneading the ingredients, open the lid and use a spatula to scrape down the sides of the pan as needed, pushing any flour that has accumulated around the edges, in the corners, and under the dough into the center to be blended. This dough is drier than other breads, making it heavier and harder for the paddle to blend. The dough tends to be pushed out to the edges of the pan, no longer being beaten. Use the spatula to lift the dough onto the paddle repeatedly to get as much mixing done as possible. Let the machine mix the dough until it is smooth and has no lumps, 5 to 6 minutes. Press the stop button to cancel the cycle, turn off the machine, and remove the bread pan.

6. Line both channels of the baguette pan with parchment. For shaping the dough, pour the oil into a large mixing bowl. Use a spatula to scoop the dough into the oiled bowl. Use the spatula to fold the oiled parts of the dough up and over the top, creating a disk of dough that is oiled on all sides.

7. Use the oiled spatula to divide the dough into two equal portions. Use your hands to form each half into an elongated oval, like a football, and lay them in the parchment-lined baguette pan channels. Starting in the center and working out to the ends, gently squeeze the dough with your fingers to lengthen it into a more even shape. Pinch it slightly on both sides as you lengthen it, pulling it away from the edges of the pan. Smooth the tops gently with your oiled hands. With a sharp, oiled knife or a specially designed razor blade called a bread lame, make two or three diagonal slashes on the top of each loaf.

> **NOTE:** The extra starch in the dry ingredients lightens the dough, giving it the softness to be able to easily form into baguettes and rise to give you a tender, delicious bread.

8. Coat a sheet of plastic wrap with nonstick cooking spray and gently lay it over the dough, oiled side down. Set the pan aside to rise at room temperature for 45 minutes to 1 hour. Gluten-free doughs rarely double in size but they do puff up and get taller.

9. While the loaves are rising, preheat the oven to 400°F (200°C).

10. Bake the loaves for 30 minutes, then rotate the pan. Bake until the loaves are deep golden brown, firm on the outside, and reach an internal temperature of about 210°F (97°C) on an instant-read thermometer, about 15 minutes longer. For an even crisper crust, fill a spray bottle with water and spritz the inside of the oven (not hitting the dough) several times right after you've added the baguette pan. Close the oven door quickly to trap the steam.

11. Cool the loaves in the pan for 3 to 5 minutes, then use the parchment as a sling to help you transfer the loaves to a wire rack. Slip them off the parchment and cool for at least 30 minutes before slicing. If you cut one and it seems a little gummy in the center, put it back in the oven for another 15 minutes or so, then cool completely before slicing. You may need to reduce the liquid by a tablespoon the next time you make the recipe.

12. These baguettes are best eaten on the day they are baked. If you have any left over, store in a plastic bag for up to 2 days at room temperature, then wrap tightly in plastic and transfer to the refrigerator for another couple of days. For longer storage, double-wrap in plastic and freeze for up to 3 months.

VARIATION

If you prefer seeded bread, sprinkle a seed blend of your choice on the dough after you've formed it into loaves. Gently press the seeds into the dough. Set the bread aside to rise and continue as directed.

MONKEY BREAD

MAKES 1 (1½-POUND/680 G) LOAF • DAIRY FREE

Monkey bread is a sweet, sticky bread that is reminiscent of a cinnamon roll that has been broken up into small pieces and baked together. It's perfect for brunch or an afternoon treat. Pinch off pieces of dough, roll them into balls, and then coat them with cinnamon-sugar. Switch out the cinnamon-sugar for butter and herbs to transform it into a savory bread (see Variation). A Bundt pan gives the dough structure and forms the dough balls into the shape of a crown. Be sure to grease your pan well so all of that caramely goodness winds up on the bread and not stuck to the pan. Then watch it disappear in the blink of an eye.

DRY INGREDIENTS

2 tablespoons instant yeast

300 g (10.6 oz or 2½ cups) Light Flour Blend (page 34) or Whole-Grain Flour Blend (page 34)

60 g (2.1 oz or ½ cup) millet flour

48 g (1.7 oz or ¼ cup) granulated cane sugar

1 tablespoon baking powder

1 tablespoon psyllium husk flakes or powder

1 teaspoon dough enhancer

½ teaspoon kosher or fine sea salt

WET INGREDIENTS

120 ml (½ cup) unsweetened coconut milk

3 large eggs, at room temperature (see page 39), beaten

56 g (2 oz or 4 tablespoons/½ stick) nondairy butter substitute, melted and slightly cooled

2 teaspoons apple cider vinegar

TOPPING

85 g (3 oz or 6 tablespoons/¾ stick) nondairy butter substitute, melted

225 g (7.9 oz or 1 cup firmly packed) brown sugar

2 tablespoons ground cinnamon

1. Set the bread pan on the counter and insert the beater paddle(s). Unless otherwise directed by your machine's manufacturer, add the liquids first, then the dry ingredients, and finally the yeast.

2. Measure the yeast into a small bowl and set aside. In a large mixing bowl, whisk the remaining dry ingredients together.

3. In a 4-cup (0.5 liter) glass measuring cup, whisk the wet ingredients together and pour into the bread pan. Use a spatula to spread the dry ingredients over the wet ingredients. Make a shallow well in the center and pour in the yeast.

4. Place the bread pan in the machine, settle it in the center, and lock it in place. Close the lid and select:

   Dough cycle
   Loaf size: 1½ pounds/750 g
   Start

5. While the machine is mixing and kneading, open the lid and use a spatula to scrape down the sides of the pan, pushing any flour that has accumulated around the edges and under the dough into the center. Let the machine mix the dough until it is smooth and has no lumps, about 5 minutes. Press the stop button to cancel the cycle, turn off the machine, and remove the pan.

6. Put the melted butter for the topping in a shallow bowl. In a separate shallow bowl, mix the brown sugar and cinnamon together. Oil a 10-cup (2.4 liter) Bundt pan and set it next to the butter and cinnamon-sugar.

7. Turn out the dough onto a lightly oiled work surface. With lightly oiled hands, pat or roll the dough into an 8 x 12-inch (20 x 30 cm) rectangle. Cut into 1½-inch (4 cm) pieces and roll each piece into a ball. Dip the dough balls into butter, then roll them in cinnamon-sugar. Arrange the dough balls evenly in the Bundt pan, building the layers by placing them slightly offset from the row below. Cover with plastic wrap and let rest for 30 to 40 minutes.

8. Preheat the oven to 350°F (180°C).

9. Bake until an instant-read thermometer inserted into the center of the loaf reads at least 190°F (88°C), 30 to 35 minutes. Transfer the pan to a wire rack. Leave the bread in the pan for 3 minutes, then set a plate on top and, holding the two together with pot holders to protect your hands, quickly flip them so that the bread falls out of the pan and onto the plate. Let the bread cool slightly before serving. This bread is best on the day it is baked.

VARIATION

Savory Monkey Bread

The difference is in the topping. Use any combination of herbs and seasonings for an addictve bread your family will beg you to make. Here's our favorite version:

Stir 1 minced garlic clove into the melted butter. Replace the cinnamon-sugar with a mix of 2 tablespoons minced fresh parsley, 2 tablespoons minced fresh basil, and 2 tablespoons minced fresh chives. Add a few red pepper flakes if you'd like some heat.

POLISH BABKA

MAKES 1 (1½-POUND/680 G) LOAF ◆ DAIRY FREE

Babka is an Eastern and Central European sweetened bread that is somewhere between panettone and coffee cake flavor-wise, but is soaked with a rum syrup. Though considered a Jewish holiday tradition, it is also commonly seen at Easter and other holiday feasts. But it is so delicious, why limit it to only a few times a year? When served with a cup of hot espresso or coffee, it is the perfect midmorning pick-me-up.

DRY INGREDIENTS

1 tablespoon instant yeast

300 g (10.6 oz or 2½ cups) Light Flour Blend (page 34) or Whole-Grain Flour Blend (page 34)

48 g (1.7 oz or ¼ cup) granulated cane sugar

1 tablespoon psyllium husk flakes or powder

2 teaspoons baking powder

1 teaspoon dough enhancer

½ teaspoon kosher salt

35 g (1.2 oz or ¼ cup) golden raisins

35 g (1.2 oz or ¼ cup) chopped mixed dried fruit or candied citron

WET INGREDIENTS

120 ml (½ cup) unsweetened coconut milk

3 large eggs, at room temperature (see page 39), beaten

56 g (2 oz or 4 tablespoons/½ stick) nondairy butter substitute, melted and slightly cooled

2 teaspoons apple cider vinegar

RUM SYRUP

100 g (3.5 oz or ½ cup) granulated cane sugar

60 ml (¼ cup) water

1 to 2 tablespoons rum (preferably dark, although light will work fine too)

1. Set the bread pan on the counter and insert the beater paddle(s). Unless otherwise directed by your machine's manufacturer, add the liquids first, then the dry ingredients, and finally the yeast.

2. Measure the yeast into a small bowl and set aside. In a large mixing bowl, whisk together the flour blend, sugar, psyllium husk flakes or powder, baking powder, dough enhancer, and salt. Add the raisins and dried fruit and toss. Set aside.

3. In a 2-cup (0.5 liter) glass measuring cup, whisk the wet ingredients together and pour into the bread pan. Use a spatula to spread the dry ingredients over the wet ingredients, covering completely. Make a shallow well in the center and pour in the yeast.

4. Place the bread pan in the machine, settle it in the center, and lock it in place. Close the lid and select:

   Dough cycle
   Loaf size: 1½ pounds/750 g
   Start

5. While the machine is mixing and kneading, open the lid and use a spatula to scrape down the sides of the pan as needed, pushing any flour that has accumulated around the edges and under the dough into the center. Let the machine mix the dough until it is smooth and has no lumps, about 5 minutes. Press the stop button to cancel the cycle, turn off the machine, and remove the pan.

6. Transfer the dough to a well-oiled 10-cup (2.4 liter) Bundt pan. Cover the pan with an oiled sheet of plastic wrap, oiled side down, and let the dough rest for 30 to 45 minutes.

OPTIONAL GLAZE

Make a quick glaze by whisking together 1 cup (120 g/4.2 oz) confectioners' sugar, 2 tablespoons nondairy milk, and a pinch of salt until smooth. Once the bread is cool, drizzle with the glaze.

---

7. Preheat the oven to 350°F (180°C). Bake until an instant-read thermometer inserted into the center of the loaf reads at least 190°F (88°C), 35 to 40 minutes.

8. While the babka is baking, combine the ingredients for the rum syrup in a small saucepan. Bring to a boil over medium-high heat, stirring, until the sugar dissolves. Remove from the heat.

9. Set the babka, still in its pan, on a cooling rack. Poke it all over gently with a toothpick or fork and slowly pour the syrup over the surface. When the syrup is absorbed (about 30 minutes) turn the babka out onto a rack. Cool for about 1 hour before slicing.

10. Store in a resealable plastic bag or airtight container on the counter for up to 3 days. For longer storage, cut into even slices, double-wrap tightly in plastic, place in a resealable plastic bag, and freeze for up to 3 months.

DUKKAH SPICE BREAD

MAKES 1 (1½-POUND/680 G) LOAF   •   DAIRY FREE

If you are looking for a change of pace, this bread flavored with dukkah seasoning is a great option. Grilled eggplant and sweet peppers, egg salad, or lamb burgers would all be lovely with the flavors in the bread. If you want a new appetizer for your next party, slice this bread thin and cut each slice into thirds. Brush both sides lightly with olive oil, sprinkle with a little kosher salt, and bake until golden brown. Top the toasts with hummus for the perfect blending of flavor, creaminess, and a touch of crunch.

DRY INGREDIENTS

21 g (0.7 oz or 2 tablespoons) active dry yeast

360 g (12.7 oz or 3 cups) Light Flour Blend (page 34)

26 g (0.9 oz or 2 tablespoons) granulated cane sugar

4 teaspoons dukkah seasoning (see opposite)

1 tablespoon baking powder

2 teaspoons xanthan gum

2 teaspoons kosher or fine sea salt

1 teaspoon onion powder

⅛ teaspoon ascorbic acid, optional

WET INGREDIENTS

3 large eggs, at room temperature (see page 39), beaten

255 ml (1 cup plus 1 tablespoon) water, heated to about 80°F (27°C)

60 ml (¼ cup) olive oil

2 teaspoons apple cider vinegar

1. Set the bread pan on the counter and insert the beater paddle(s). Unless otherwise directed by your machine's manufacturer, add the liquids first, then the dry ingredients, and finally the yeast.

2. Measure the yeast into a small bowl and set aside. In a large mixing bowl, whisk the remaining dry ingredients together.

3. In a 4-cup (1 liter) glass measuring cup, whisk the wet ingredients together and pour into the bread pan. Use a spatula to spread the dry ingredients over the wet ingredients, covering completely. Make a shallow well in the center and pour in the yeast.

4. Place the bread pan in the machine, settle it in the center, and lock it in place. Close the lid and select:

   Gluten-free cycle (see page 14 if your machine does not have this setting)
   Loaf size: 1½ pounds/750 g
   Medium crust
   Start

5. About 3 minutes after the machine has started the mix/knead cycle, open the lid and use a spatula to scrape the sides of the pan, pushing any loose flour into the center. Check again once or twice during the knead cycle, scraping the edges, corners, and under the dough. If the dough/batter looks too wet or too dry, add a little flour blend or tiny amounts of warm water. Once the mixing/kneading is done, leave the lid closed during the rise and bake cycles.

6. At the end of the bake cycle, lift the lid and check the temperature. When the bread reaches 206°F to 210°F (97°C to 99°C) on an instant-read thermometer inserted in the center, it is done. Remove the bread pan from the machine and set it on its side on a wire cooling rack. Leave the bread in the pan for a couple of minutes, then turn the pan upside down and slide the loaf onto the wire rack. Carefully remove the paddle if it is embedded in the bottom of the loaf. Let the bread cool upside down for at least 2 hours before slicing.

7. Store the bread in a resealable plastic bag or airtight container on the counter for up to 3 days. For longer storage, cut into even slices, double-wrap tightly in plastic, place in a resealable plastic bag, and freeze for up to 3 months.

WHAT IS DUKKAH?

Dukkah is an Egyptian seasoning blend that is often a combination of very finely chopped nuts, sesame seeds, coriander, and cumin. The exact mixture varies depending on who is making it, so the brand you purchase may have a different combination. Our personal favorite is from Spice Ace in San Francisco (see Resources, page 376). You can also add it to olive oil to use as a dip for bread or to drizzle over grilled meats and steamed vegetables. Versatile and addicting, dukkah transforms an ordinary dish into something special!

Specialty
BREADS

Specialty breads put a fun spin on sandwich breads, each with a different flavor combination to tantalize your taste buds. Cheeses, onions, herbs, chilies, and special seasonings make certain these loaves will stand out. There is nothing commonplace or boring in this collection!

These recipes are just as easy to make as regular sandwich breads—simply change up some of the ingredients and make a few additions. Mix all the dry ingredients together, add them to the liquids in the bread machine, set it, and walk away. No rising, kneading, or forming required. Let the machine do its thing and in a couple of hours you have a beautiful loaf of freshly made bread!

When you bake the Pizza Pie Bread, the aromas of oregano and garlic wafting through your house will make you swear there is pizza in the oven. And the Mexican Salsa Bread, with its cumin, onion, and tomato, will set the scene for a fiesta. Prepping for the Caramelized Onion Bread or Roasted Garlic Bread will make your kitchen smell as if you spent all day making a gourmet meal. The onions and garlic can be made a few days before you make the bread, saving you time on baking day. If you have any extras, you can always create a homemade version of onion dip and serve it with a couple of cocktails.

We have included a variety of savory and sweet cornbreads, so whether you're from the Southern states or New England, there's a recipe for you. If you don't want to add the cheese or peppers we recommend, feel free to leave them out. You are welcome to adapt any recipe to suit your preferences, but remember: if you make major changes, you may need to make adjustments to the amounts of flour, liquid, and/or fats. Keeping the ratios the same is critical in gluten-free baking for the best possible loaves every time.

These breads are delightful sliced and toasted with simple melted butter, as an after-school treat, or used to make a sandwich. Consider turning them into croutons to add a pop of flavor to your salads. And many of them are excellent when turned into stuffing or bread crumbs.

SOUTHWESTERN CHILE-CHEESE BREAD

MAKES 1 (1½-POUND) LOAF

The flavors of the Southwest are bold and dynamic. The blending of three different cultures—Native American, Anglo, and Hispanic—created a fascinating amalgam of culinary traditions. A wide variety of chilli peppers grows well in the heat of the high desert and they find their way into nearly every dish. In this bread you can use any variety of pepper cheese you can find locally to add a burst of spice and flavor. If you want more heat, add more of the hot oil or some finely chopped jalapeño, serrano, or even habanero chillies. Just be careful to wash your hands well after handling fresh peppers—if the oil gets into your eyes, they will burn!

DRY INGREDIENTS

21 g (0.7 oz or 2 tablespoons) active dry yeast

360 g (12.7 oz or 3 cups) Light Flour Blend (page 34)

48 g (1.7 oz or ¼ cup) granulated cane sugar

1 tablespoon baking powder

2 teaspoons xanthan gum

1 teaspoon kosher salt

⅛ teaspoon ascorbic acid, optional

56 g (2 oz or ½ cup) grated chipotle Havarti, pepper jack, or other cheese with chillies

WET INGREDIENTS

285 ml (1 cup plus 3 tablespoons) 1% milk or water, heated to about 80°F (27°C)

3 large eggs, at room temperature (see page 39), beaten

60 ml (¼ cup) olive oil

2 teaspoons apple cider vinegar

1 teaspoon hot green chilli oil, such as Tunisian Baklouti oil (available from Amphora Nueva—see Resources, page 376)

1. Set the bread pan on the counter and insert the beater paddle(s). Unless otherwise directed by your machine's manufacturer, add the liquids first, then the dry ingredients, and finally the yeast.

2. Measure the yeast into a small bowl and set aside. Whisk the remaining dry ingredients— *except* the cheese—together in a large mixing bowl. Add the cheese and toss to disperse evenly.

3. In a 4-cup (1 liter) glass measuring cup, whisk the wet ingredients together and pour into the bread pan. Use a spatula to spread the dry ingredients over the wet ingredients, covering completely. Make a shallow well in the center and pour in the yeast.

4. Place the bread pan in the machine, settle it in the center, and lock it in place. Close the lid and select:

    Gluten-free cycle (see page 14 if your machine does not have this setting)
    Loaf size: 1½ pounds/750 g
    Medium crust
    Start

5. About 3 minutes into the mixing process, open the lid and use a spatula to scrape down the sides of the pan, avoiding the paddle. Push any flour that has accumulated around the edges and under the dough into the center. Check again once or twice during kneading, scraping the edges, corners, and under the dough. If the dough looks too wet or too dry, add a little flour blend or tiny amounts of warm water. Once the mix/knead cycle is done, leave the lid closed during the rise and bake cycles.

6. At the end of the bake cycle, lift the lid and check the temperature. When the bread reaches 206°F to 210°F (97°C to 99°C) on an instant-read thermometer inserted in the center, it is done. Remove the pan from the machine and set it on its side on a wire cooling rack. Leave the bread in the pan for a couple of minutes, then turn the pan upside down and slide the loaf onto the wire rack. Carefully remove the paddle if it is embedded in the bottom of the loaf. Let the bread cool upside down for at least 2 hours before slicing.

7. Store the bread in a resealable plastic bag or airtight container on the counter for up to 3 days. For longer storage, cut into evenly thick slices, double-wrap tightly in plastic, place in a resealable plastic bag, and freeze for up to 3 months.

ASIAGO BREAD

MAKES 1 (1½-POUND/680 G) LOAF

Asiago bread is a staple at bakeries everywhere. And no wonder! With the slightly sharp, pungent flavor of the cheese permeating the bread and an extra sprinkle on the top for good measure, there is cheesy goodness in every bite. And, wow, does your house smell good when it is baking! Add a few slices to the plate when you serve up bowls of chili, baked potato soup, or any hearty stew.

DRY INGREDIENTS

21 g (0.7 oz or 2 tablespoons) active dry yeast

240 g (8.5 oz or 2 cups) Light Flour Blend (page 34)

110 g (3.9 oz or 1 cup) sorghum flour

44 g (1.6 oz or ½ cup) milk powder

26 g (0.9 oz or ¼ cup) flaxseed meal or ground flaxseed

39 g (1.4 oz or 3 tablespoons) granulated cane sugar

1 tablespoon baking powder

2 teaspoons xanthan gum

1½ teaspoons kosher or fine sea salt

⅛ teaspoon ascorbic acid

50 g (1.8 oz or ½ cup) shredded Asiago cheese

WET INGREDIENTS

3 large eggs, at room temperature (see page 39), beaten

270 ml (1 cup plus 2 tablespoons) water, heated to about 80°F (27°C)

45 ml (3 tablespoons) olive oil

2 teaspoons apple cider vinegar

TOPPINGS

25 g (0.8 oz or ¼ cup) shredded Asiago cheese

1 tablespoon minced fresh parsley

1. Set the bread pan on the counter and insert the beater paddle(s). Unless otherwise directed by your machine's manufacturer, add the liquids first, then the dry ingredients, and finally the yeast.

2. Measure the yeast into a small bowl and set aside. Whisk the remaining dry ingredients—*except* the cheese—together in a large mixing bowl. Add the cheese and toss to disperse evenly.

3. In a 4-cup (1 liter) glass measuring cup, whisk the wet ingredients together and pour into the bread pan. Use a spatula to spread the dry ingredients over the wet ingredients, covering completely. Make a shallow well in the center and pour in the yeast.

4. Place the bread pan in the machine, settle it in the center, and lock it in place. Close the lid and select:

   Gluten-free cycle (see page 14 if your machine does not have this setting)
   Loaf size: 1½ pounds/750 g
   Medium crust
   Start

5. About 3 minutes into the mixing process, open the lid and use a spatula to scrape down the sides of the pan, avoiding the paddle. Push any flour that has accumulated around the edges and under the dough into the center. Check again once or twice during kneading, scraping the edges, corners, and under the dough. If the dough looks too wet or too dry, add a little flour blend or tiny amounts of warm water.

6. Once the mix/knead cycle is done, scatter the shredded cheese over the top (try not to get any pieces on the sides of the pan or they may burn), sprinkle on the parsley, and close the lid for the remainder of the rise and bake cycles.

7. At the end of the bake cycle, lift the lid and check the temperature. When the bread reaches 206°F to 210°F (97°C to 99°C) on an instant-read thermometer inserted in the center, it is done. Remove the pan from the machine and set it on its side on a wire cooling rack. Leave the bread in the pan for a couple of minutes, then turn the pan upside down and slide the loaf onto the wire rack. Carefully remove the paddle if it is embedded in the bottom of the loaf. Set the bread back on its side and let it cool for at least 2 hours before slicing.

8. Store the bread in a resealable plastic bag or airtight container on the counter for up to 3 days. For longer storage, cut into evenly thick slices, double-wrap tightly in plastic, place in a resealable plastic bag, and freeze for up to 3 months.

BLUE CHEESE AND WALNUT BREAD

MAKES 1 (1½-POUND/680 G) LOAF

There always seems to be that random piece of cheese, usually blue, left on the cheese tray after a party. Crumble it and use it in this bread to serve alongside tomato-basil soup and a salad of mixed greens, or slice the bread and top with some gooey Brie and fig jam.

DRY INGREDIENTS

21 g (0.7 oz or 2 tablespoons) active dry yeast

240 g (8.5 oz or 2 cups) Light Flour Blend (page 34)

120 g (4.2 oz or 1 cup) teff flour

44 g (1.6 oz or ½ cup) Better Than Milk soy powder

39 g (1.4 oz or 3 tablespoons) granulated cane sugar

1 tablespoon baking powder

2 teaspoons xanthan gum

1 teaspoon kosher or fine sea salt

⅛ teaspoon ascorbic acid, optional

WET INGREDIENTS

3 large eggs, at room temperature (see page 39), beaten

240 ml (1 cup) water, heated to about 80°F (27°C)

45 ml (3 tablespoons) vegetable oil

2 teaspoons apple cider vinegar

90 g (3.2 oz or ¾ cup) crumbled blue cheese

ADD-IN

120 g (4.2 oz or 1 cup) chopped toasted walnuts

1. Set the bread pan on the counter and insert the beater paddle(s). Unless otherwise directed by your machine's manufacturer, add the liquids first, then the dry ingredients, and finally the yeast.

2. Measure the yeast into a small bowl and set aside. In a large mixing bowl, whisk the remaining dry ingredients together.

3. In a 4-cup (1 liter) glass measuring cup, whisk the wet ingredients—*except* the blue cheese—together and pour into the bread pan. Scatter the crumbled blue cheese over the top. Use a spatula to spread the dry ingredients over the wet ingredients, covering completely. Make a shallow well in the center and pour in the yeast.

4. Place the bread pan in the machine, settle it in the center, and lock it in place. Close the lid and select:

   Gluten-free cycle (see page 14 if your machine does not have this setting)
   Loaf size: 1½ pounds/750 g
   Medium crust
   Start

5. About 3 minutes into the mixing process, open the lid and use a spatula to scrape down the sides of the pan, avoiding the paddle. Push any flour that has accumulated around the edges and under the dough into the center. Check again once or twice during kneading, scraping the edges, corners, and under the dough. If the dough looks too wet or too dry, add a little flour blend or tiny amounts of warm water.

6. After the first kneading cycle, add the walnuts. Once the mix/knead cycle is done, leave the lid closed during the rise and bake cycles.

7. At the end of the bake cycle, lift the lid and check the temperature. When the bread reaches 206°F to 210°F (97°C to 99°C) on an instant-read thermometer inserted in the center, it is done. Remove the pan from the machine and set it on its side on a wire cooling rack. Leave the bread in the pan for a couple of minutes, then turn the pan upside down and slide the loaf onto the wire rack. Carefully remove the paddle if it is embedded in the bottom of the loaf. Let the bread cool upside down for at least 2 hours before slicing.

8. Store the bread in a resealable plastic bag or airtight container on the counter for up to 3 days. For longer storage, cut into even slices, double-wrap tightly in plastic, place in a resealable plastic bag, and freeze for up to 3 months.

CHORIZO AND CHEDDAR CORNBREAD

MAKES 1 (1½-POUND/680 G) LOAF

Think of this loaf as a taco turned into bread. It's filled with tasty crumbled chorizo and shredded cheese. For this recipe, you want Mexican (uncooked) chorizo as opposed to Spanish (smoked) chorizo. Mexican chorizo is available in many supermarkets in both spicy and non-spicy versions. This bread is the perfect accompaniment to a bowl of steaming hot tortilla soup or spicy chili, rounding out your meal and making your whole family happy.

ADD-IN

170 g (6 oz) Mexican (uncooked) chorizo, crumbled

DRY INGREDIENTS

21 g (0.7 oz or 2 tablespoons) active dry yeast

240 g (8.5 oz or 2 cups) Light Flour Blend (page 34)

156 g (5.5 oz or 1½ cups) corn flour

26 g (0.9 oz or 2 tablespoons) granulated cane sugar

1 tablespoon baking powder

1 teaspoon kosher salt

1 teaspoon xanthan gum

WET INGREDIENTS

¼ cup vegetable oil (60 ml) or unsalted butter (55 g or 2 oz/½ stick), melted and slightly cooled

3 large eggs, at room temperature (see page 39), beaten

180 ml (¾ cup) water, heated to about 80°F (27°C)

2 teaspoons apple cider vinegar

84 g (3 oz or ¾ cup) shredded cheddar cheese

1. Set a skillet over medium heat and fry the meat, breaking it up into large chunks with a spoon, until cooked through and starting to brown, about 8 minutes. Remove from the heat, drain thoroughly on a a plate lined with a few layers of paper towels, and let cool.

2. Set the bread pan on the counter and insert the beater paddle(s). Unless otherwise directed by your machine's manufacturer, add the liquids first, then the dry ingredients, and finally the yeast.

3. Measure the yeast into a small bowl and set aside. In a large mixing bowl, whisk the remaining dry ingredients together. Stir in the chorizo and set the bowl aside.

4. In a 4-cup (1 liter) glass measuring cup, whisk the wet ingredients—*except* the cheese—together. Stir in the cheese and pour into the bread pan. Use a spatula to spread the dry ingredients over the wet ingredients. Make a shallow well in the center and pour in the yeast.

5. Place the bread pan in the machine, settle it in the center, and lock it in place. Close the lid and select:

   Gluten-free cycle (see page 14 if your machine does not have this setting)
   Loaf size: 1½ pounds/750 g
   Medium crust
   Start

6. About 3 minutes into the mixing process, open the lid and use a spatula to scrape down the sides of the pan, avoiding the paddle. Push any flour that has accumulated around the edges and under the dough into the center. Check again once or twice during kneading, scraping the edges, corners, and under the dough. If the dough looks too wet or too dry, add a little flour blend or tiny amounts of warm water.

7. At the end of the bake cycle, lift the lid and check the temperature. The bread is done when it registers 206°F to 210°F (97°C to 99°C) on an instant-read thermometer inserted in the center of the loaf. Remove the pan from the machine and place it on its side on a wire rack. Leave the bread in the pan for a couple of minutes, then turn the pan upside down and slide the loaf onto the wire rack. Carefully remove the paddle if it is embedded in the bottom of the loaf. Let the bread cool upside down for at least 2 hours before slicing.

8. Store the bread in a resealable plastic bag or airtight container on the counter for up to 3 days. For longer storage, cut into even slices, double-wrap tightly in plastic, place in a resealable plastic bag, and freeze for up to 3 months.

SCALLION AND CILANTRO CORNBREAD

MAKES 1 (1½-POUND/680 G) LOAF ◆ DAIRY-FREE OPTION

The corn flavor really shines through in this savory cornbread. The scallion and cilantro add gentle flecks of flavor to every bite. This slightly pungent bread is perfect with grilled bratwurst. Or serve it toasted, topped with fried eggs or scrambled eggs and chorizo.

DRY INGREDIENTS

240 g (8.5 oz or 2 cups) Light Flour Blend (page 34)

104 g (3.6 oz or 1 cup) masa harina or corn flour

48 g (1.7 oz or ¼ cup) granulated cane sugar

1 tablespoon baking powder

1 teaspoon kosher salt

1 teaspoon xanthan gum or psyllium husk flakes or powder

WET INGREDIENTS

¼ cup vegetable oil (60 ml) or nondairy butter substitute (55 g or 2 oz/½ stick), melted and slightly cooled

3 large eggs, at room temperature (see page 39), beaten

240 ml (1 cup) water, heated to about 80°F (27°C)

ADD-INS

2 scallions, finely chopped

1 tablespoon finely chopped fresh cilantro

1. Set the bread pan on the counter and insert the beater paddle(s). Unless otherwise directed by your machine's manufacturer, add the liquids first and then the dry ingredients.

2. In a large mixing bowl, whisk the dry ingredients together.

3. In a 4-cup (1 liter) glass measuring cup, whisk the wet ingredients together and pour into the bread pan. Use a spatula to spread the dry ingredients over the wet ingredients.

4. Place the bread pan in the machine, settle it in the center, and lock it in place. Close the lid and select:

   Quick bread/cake cycle
   Loaf size: 1½ pounds/750 g
   Medium crust
   Start

5. About 3 minutes into the mixing process, open the lid and use a spatula to scrape down the sides of the pan, avoiding the paddle. Push any flour that has accumulated around the edges and under the dough into the center. Check again once or twice during kneading, scraping the edges, corners, and under the dough. If the dough looks too wet or too dry, add a little flour blend or tiny amounts of warm water. Add the scallions and cilantro. Once the mix/knead cycle is done, leave the lid closed for the remainder of the rise and bake cycles.

> **NOTE:** Since this is a quick bread, you can remove the paddle before the baking cycle.

6. At the end of the bake cycle, lift the lid and check the temperature. When the bread reaches 206°F to 210°F (97°C to 99°C) on an instant-read thermometer inserted in the center, it is done. Remove the pan from the machine and place it on its side on a wire rack. Leave the bread in the pan for a couple of minutes, then turn the pan upside down and slide the loaf onto the wire rack. Carefully remove the paddle if it is embedded in the bottom of the loaf. Let the bread cool upside down for at least 2 hours before slicing.

7. Store the bread in a resealable plastic bag or airtight container on the counter for up to 3 days. For longer storage, cut into even slices, double-wrap tightly in plastic, place in a resealable plastic bag, and freeze for up to 3 months.

JALAPEÑO-CHEESE CORNBREAD

MAKES 1 (1½-POUND/680 G) LOAF • DAIRY-FREE OPTION

While some parts of the country swear by their sweet cornbread, others prefer a savory and spicy version. The pickled jalapeños add a slight tang to this cheesy cornbread. You can find pickled jalapeños in the international aisle of most supermarkets or in the Latin section. This bread is perfect to serve with carnitas (shredded pork) or barbecued beef topped with pickled red onions.

DRY INGREDIENTS

21 g (0.7 oz or 2 tablespoons) active dry yeast

240 g (8.5 oz or 2 cups) Light Flour Blend (page 34)

156 g (5.5 oz or 1½ cups) corn flour

39 g (1.4 oz or 3 tablespoons) granulated cane sugar

2 teaspoons baking powder

1 teaspoon kosher or fine sea salt

1 teaspoon psyllium husk flakes or powder

WET INGREDIENTS

⅓ cup vegetable oil (80 ml) or unsalted butter (75 g or 2.6 oz), melted and slightly cooled

3 large eggs, at room temperature (see page 39), beaten

180 ml (¾ cup) water, heated to about 80°F (27°C)

2 teaspoons apple cider vinegar

84 g (3 oz or ¾ cup) shredded Colby or cheddar jack cheese or dairy-free cheese substitute (such as Daiya brand)

135 g (4.8 oz or 1 cup) pickled jalapeños, finely chopped

1. Set the bread pan on the counter and insert the beater paddle(s). Unless otherwise directed by your machine's manufacturer, add the liquids first, then the dry ingredients, and finally the yeast.

2. Measure the yeast into a small bowl and set aside. In a large mixing bowl, whisk the remaining dry ingredients together.

3. In a 4-cup (1 liter) glass measuring cup, whisk the wet ingredients—*except* the cheese and jalapeños—together. Stir in the cheese and jalapeños and pour into the bread pan. Use a spatula to spread the dry ingredients over the wet ingredients. Make a shallow well in the center and pour in the yeast.

4. Place the bread pan in the machine, settle it in the center, and lock it in place. Close the lid and select:

   Gluten-free cycle (see page 14 if your machine does not have this setting)
   Loaf size: 1½ pounds/750 g
   Light crust
   Start

5. About 3 minutes into the mixing process, open the lid and use a spatula to scrape down the sides of the pan, avoiding the paddle. Push any flour that has accumulated around the edges and under the dough into the center. Check again once or twice during kneading, scraping the edges, corners, and under the dough. If the dough looks too wet or too dry, add a little flour blend or tiny amounts of warm water.

> **NOTE:** Cornmeal and corn flour are both made from ground corn. The difference is corn flour is ground to a much finer texture than cornmeal.

6. At the end of the bake cycle, lift the lid and check the temperature. The bread is done when it registers 206°F to 210°F (97°C to 99°C) on an instant-read thermometer inserted into the center of the loaf. Remove the pan from the machine and place it on its side on a wire rack. Leave the bread in the pan for a couple of minutes, then turn the pan upside down and slide the loaf onto the wire rack. Carefully remove the paddle if it is embedded in the bottom of the loaf. Let the bread cool upside down for at least 2 hours before slicing.

7. Store the bread in a resealable plastic bag or airtight container on the counter for up to 3 days. For longer storage, cut into even slices, double-wrap tightly in plastic, place in a resealable plastic bag, and freeze for up to 3 months.

FRESH ROSEMARY BREAD

MAKES 1 (1½-POUND/680 G) LOAF • DAIRY-FREE OPTION

Many Italian restaurants offer rosemary bread or rolls with their meals, and it is always such a beautiful way to start dinner. Slip a couple of slices of this fragrant gluten-free bread into a plastic bag and take it with you when you're going out for Italian so you can enjoy rosemary bread along with everyone else!

DRY INGREDIENTS

21 g (0.7 oz or 2 tablespoons) active dry yeast

360 g (12.7 oz or 3 cups) Light Flour Blend (page 34)

½ cup milk powder (44 g/1.6 oz) or DariFree (69 g/2.4 oz)

48 g (1.7 oz or ¼ cup) granulated cane sugar

1 heaping tablespoon minced fresh rosemary

1 tablespoon baking powder

2 teaspoons xanthan gum

2 teaspoons kosher salt

⅛ teaspoon ascorbic acid, optional

WET INGREDIENTS

3 large eggs, at room temperature (see page 39), beaten

285 ml (1 cup plus 3 tablespoons) water, heated to about 80°F (27°C)

60 ml (¼ cup) olive oil

2 teaspoons apple cider vinegar

1. Set the bread pan on the counter and insert the beater paddle(s). Unless otherwise directed by your machine's manufacturer, add the liquids first, then the dry ingredients, and finally the yeast.

2. Measure the yeast into a small bowl and set aside. In a large mixing bowl, whisk the remaining dry ingredients together.

3. In a 4-cup (1 liter) glass measuring cup, whisk the wet ingredients together and pour into the bread pan. Use a spatula to spread the dry ingredients over the wet ingredients, covering completely. Make a shallow well in the center and pour in the yeast.

4. Place the bread pan in the machine, settle it in the center, and lock it in place. Close the lid and select:

    Gluten-free cycle (see page 14 if your machine does not have this setting)
    Loaf size: 1½ pounds/750 g
    Medium crust
    Start

5. About 3 minutes into the mixing process, open the lid and use a spatula to scrape down the sides of the pan, avoiding the paddle. Push any flour that has accumulated around the edges and under the dough into the center. Check again once or twice during kneading, scraping the edges, corners, and under the dough. If the dough looks too wet or too dry, add a little flour blend or tiny amounts of warm water. Once the mix/knead cycle is done, leave the lid closed during the rise and bake cycles.

6. At the end of the bake cycle, lift the lid and check the temperature. When the bread reaches 206°F to 210°F (97°C to 99°C) on an instant-read thermometer inserted in the center, it is done. Remove the pan from the machine and set it on its side on a wire cooling rack. Leave the bread in the pan for a couple of minutes, then turn the pan upside down and slide the loaf onto the wire rack. Carefully remove the paddle if it is embedded in the bottom of the loaf. Let the bread cool upside down for at least 2 hours before slicing.

7. Store the bread in a resealable plastic bag or airtight container on the counter for up to 3 days. For longer storage, cut into even slices, double-wrap tightly in plastic, place in a resealable plastic bag, and freeze for up to 3 months.

LEMON-THYME BREAD

One of the best traits of the breads in this book is that they are sturdy enough to hold up to sandwich fillings, giving us back one of our favorite lunchtime meals. Give this bread a try the next time you make chicken salad sandwiches (page 350). The lemon and thyme perfectly complement the flavors in the salad, each enhancing the other. Using lemon zest (just the yellow part of the peel) adds a pop of bright lemon flavor without throwing off the wet-to-dry balance of the bread.

DRY INGREDIENTS

21 g (0.7 oz or 2 tablespoons) active dry yeast

360 g (12.7 oz or 3 cups) Light Flour Blend (page 34)

58 g (2 oz or ½ cup) buttermilk powder

39 g (1.4 oz or 3 tablespoons) granulated cane sugar

1 tablespoon baking powder

1 tablespoon fresh thyme leaves

2 teaspoons xanthan gum

2 teaspoons kosher or fine sea salt

⅛ teaspoon ascorbic acid, optional

WET INGREDIENTS

56 g (2 oz or 4 tablespoons/½ stick) unsalted butter, melted and slightly cooled

3 large eggs, at room temperature (see page 39), beaten

240 ml (1 cup) water, warmed to about 80°F (27°C)

1½ teaspoons very finely grated lemon zest

1 teaspoon apple cider vinegar

1. Set the bread pan on the counter and insert the beater paddle(s). Unless otherwise directed by your machine's manufacturer, add the liquids first, then the dry ingredients, and finally the yeast.

2. Measure the yeast into a small bowl and set aside. In a large mixing bowl, whisk the remaining dry ingredients together.

3. In a 4-cup (1 liter) glass measuring cup, whisk the wet ingredients together and pour into the bread pan. Use a spatula to spread the dry ingredients over the wet ingredients, covering completely. Make a shallow well in the center and pour in the yeast.

4. Place the bread pan in the machine, settle it in the center, and lock it in place. Close the lid and select:

   Gluten-free cycle (see page 14 if your machine does not have this setting)
   Loaf size: 1½ pounds/750 g
   Medium crust
   Start

5. About 3 minutes into the mixing process, open the lid and use a spatula to scrape down the sides of the pan, avoiding the paddle. Push any flour that has accumulated around the edges and under the dough into the center. Check again once or twice during kneading, scraping the edges, corners, and under the dough. If the dough looks too wet or too dry, add a little flour blend or tiny amounts of warm water. Once the mix/knead cycle is done, leave the lid closed during the rise and bake cycles.

ZEST SUCCESS

In recipes calling for citrus zests, add them to the liquids so they will be more evenly dispersed. Use a microplane or other rasp-style grater for the finest zest possible.

---

6. At the end of the bake cycle, lift the lid and check the temperature. When the bread reaches 206°F to 210°F (97°C to 99°C) on an instant-read thermometer inserted in the center, it is done. Remove the pan from the machine and set it on its side on a wire cooling rack. Leave the bread in the pan for a couple of minutes, then turn the pan upside down and slide the loaf onto the wire rack. Carefully remove the paddle if it is embedded in the bottom of the loaf. Let the bread cool upside down for at least 2 hours before slicing.

7. Store the bread in a resealable plastic bag or airtight container on the counter for up to 3 days. For longer storage, cut into even slices, double-wrap tightly in plastic, place in a resealable plastic bag, and freeze for up to 3 months.

SAVORY MOCHA BREAD

MAKES 1 (1½-POUND/680 G) LOAF • DAIRY-FREE OPTION

This savory bread has a gentle chocolate flavor with a hint of coffee. It's a perfect treat when you want to indulge your kids and give them chocolate toast for breakfast—or any time of day. You can boost the chocolate quotient by adding a few chocolate chips. Watch their faces light up when you serve this bread.

DRY INGREDIENTS

21 g (0.7 oz or 2 tablespoons) active dry yeast

360 g (12.7 oz or 3 cups) Light Flour Blend (page 34)

45 g (1.6 oz or ½ cup) unsweetened cocoa powder

¼ cup milk powder (22 g/0.8 oz) or DariFree (40 g/1.4 oz)

115 g (4.1 oz or ½ cup firmly packed) light brown sugar

2 tablespoons tapioca starch

2 teaspoons baking powder

2 teaspoons xanthan gum

2 teaspoons instant espresso powder

1 teaspoon kosher salt

85 g (3 oz or ½ cup) gluten-free, dairy-free semisweet chocolate chips (such as Enjoy Life brand), optional

WET INGREDIENTS

2 large eggs, at room temperature (see page 39), beaten

255 ml (1 cup plus 1 tablespoon) water, heated to about 80°F (27°C)

60 ml (¼ cup) olive oil

85 g (3 oz or ¼ cup) molasses

1 teaspoon apple cider vinegar

1. Set the bread pan on the counter and insert the beater paddle(s). Unless otherwise directed by your machine's manufacturer, add the liquids first, then the dry ingredients, and finally the yeast.

2. Measure the yeast into a small bowl and set aside. In a large mixing bowl, whisk the remaining dry ingredients—*except* the chocolate chips—together. Stir in the chocolate chips, if using.

3. In a 4-cup (1 liter) glass measuring cup, whisk the wet ingredients together and pour into the bread pan. Use a spatula to spread the dry ingredients over the wet ingredients, covering completely. Make a shallow well in the center and pour in the yeast.

4. Place the bread pan in the machine, settle it in the center, and lock it in place. Close the lid and select:

   Gluten-free cycle (see page 14 if your machine does not have this setting)
   Loaf size: 1½ pounds/750 g
   Medium crust
   Start

5. About 3 minutes into the mixing process, open the lid and use a spatula to scrape down the sides of the pan, avoiding the paddle. Push any flour that has accumulated around the edges and under the dough into the center. Check again once or twice during kneading, scraping the edges and corners. The dough should create a dome in the center as it is being kneaded and the edges may look a little wet and shiny. If the dough looks too wet or too dry, add a little flour blend or tiny amounts of warm water during kneading. When the consistency looks good, close the lid and do not open it during the rise and bake cycles.

6. At the end of the bake cycle, lift the lid and check the temperature. When the bread reaches 206°F to 210°F (97°C to 99°C) on an instant-read thermometer inserted in the center, it is done. Remove the bread pan from the machine and set it on its side on a wire cooling rack. Leave the bread in the pan for a couple of minutes, then turn the pan upside down and slide the loaf onto the wire rack. Carefully remove the paddle if it is embedded in the bottom of the loaf. Place the bread back on its side and let it cool for at least 2 hours before slicing.

7. Store the bread in a resealable plastic bag or airtight container on the counter for up to 3 days. For longer storage, cut into even slices, double-wrap tightly in plastic, place in a resealable plastic bag, and freeze for up to 3 months.

CARAMELIZED ONION BREAD

MAKES 1 (1½-POUND/680 G) LOAF • DAIRY FREE

Caramelized onions lend a subtle sweetness to this savory loaf. Serve it with a *salade Niçoise* or make yourself a salad sandwich. In the south of France, they stuff salad into bread and sell it at carts on the beach.

DRY INGREDIENTS

21 g (0.7 oz or 2 tablespoons) active dry yeast

360 g (12.7 oz or 3 cups) Light Flour Blend (page 34)

44 g (1.6 oz or ½ cup) Better Than Milk soy powder

26 g (0.9 oz or 2 tablespoons) granulated cane sugar

1 tablespoon baking powder

2 teaspoons xanthan gum

1 teaspoon kosher salt

⅛ teaspoon ascorbic acid, optional

WET INGREDIENTS

3 large eggs, at room temperature (see page 39), beaten

240 ml (1 cup) water, heated to about 80°F (27°C)

60 ml (¼ cup) vegetable oil

2 teaspoons ume plum vinegar

1 recipe Caramelized Onions (see opposite)

1. Set the bread pan on the counter and insert the beater paddle(s). Unless otherwise directed by your machine's manufacturer, add the liquids first, then the dry ingredients, and finally the yeast.

2. Measure the yeast into a small bowl and set aside. In a large mixing bowl, whisk the remaining dry ingredients together.

3. In a 4-cup (1 liter) glass measuring cup, whisk the wet ingredients—*except* the onions—together. Stir in the onions and pour into the bread pan. Use a spatula to spread the dry ingredients over the wet ingredients, covering completely. Make a shallow well in the center and pour in the yeast.

4. Place the bread pan in the machine and lock it in place. Close the lid and select:

   Gluten-free cycle (see page 14 if your machine does not have this setting)
   Loaf size: 1½ pounds/750 g
   Medium crust
   Start

5. About 3 minutes into the mixing process, open the lid and use a spatula to scrape down the sides of the pan, avoiding the paddle. Push any flour that has accumulated around the edges and under the dough into the center. Check again once or twice during kneading, scraping the edges, corners, and under the dough. If the dough looks too wet or too dry, add a little flour blend or tiny amounts of warm water. Once the mix/knead cycle is done, leave the lid closed during the rise and bake cycles.

6. At the end of the bake cycle, lift the lid and check the temperature. When the bread reaches 206°F to 210°F (97°C to 99°C) on an instant-read thermometer inserted in the center, it is done. Remove the pan from the machine and set it on its side on a wire cooling rack. Wait a couple of minutes, then turn the pan upside down and slide the loaf onto the wire rack. Carefully remove the paddle if it is embedded in the bottom of the loaf. Let the bread cool upside down for at least 2 hours before slicing.

7. Store the bread in a resealable plastic bag or airtight container on the counter for up to 3 days. For longer storage, cut into even slices, double-wrap tightly in plastic, place in a resealable plastic bag, and freeze for up to 3 months.

CARAMELIZED ONIONS

MAKES 1 TO 1½ CUPS (240 TO 360 G)

Heat ¼ cup (60 ml) vegetable oil in a large skillet over medium heat. Add 3 large chopped Vidalia or other sweet onions, 2 tablespoons chopped fresh parsley, and ½ cup (100 g) granulated cane sugar. Cook, stirring occasionally, until the onions are softened and golden brown, 15 to 20 minutes. Stir in ¼ cup (60 ml) balsamic vinegar and 2 tablespoons water. Turn the heat up to high and cook, stirring often, until thickened, 5 to 6 minutes. Season with salt and pepper to taste.

ROASTED GARLIC BREAD

MAKES 1 (1½-POUND/680 G) LOAF   ◆   DAIRY-FREE OPTION

The sweetness and mellowness of roasted garlic makes it a perfect addition to bread. A head of garlic is the entire bulb from which you can extract individual cloves. This recipe calls for two heads of roasted garlic, which sounds like a lot, but roasting mellows the flavor dramatically. The heady aroma will entice even the most reluctant garlic eater to try it. The flecks of golden-brown garlic create bursts of flavor with each bite. Serve topped with your favorite Italian salami, prosciutto, or mortadella.

DRY INGREDIENTS

21 g (0.7 oz or 2 tablespoons) active dry yeast

240 g (8.5 oz or 2 cups) Light Flour Blend (page 34)

½ cup milk powder (44 g/1.6 oz) or DariFree (69 g/2.4 oz)

26 g (0.9 oz or 2 tablespoons) granulated cane sugar

1 tablespoon baking powder

2 teaspoons xanthan gum

1 teaspoon kosher salt

⅛ teaspoon ascorbic acid, optional

WET INGREDIENTS

2 large eggs, at room temperature (see page 39), beaten

285 ml (1 cup plus 3 tablespoons) water, heated to about 80°F (27°C)

60 ml (¼ cup) olive oil

2 teaspoons apple cider vinegar

2 heads Roasted Garlic (see opposite), peeled and chopped

1. Set the bread pan on the counter and insert the beater paddle(s). Unless otherwise directed by your machine's manufacturer, add the liquids first, then the dry ingredients, and finally the yeast.

2. Measure the yeast into a small bowl and set aside. In a large mixing bowl, whisk the remaining dry ingredients together.

3. In a 4-cup (1 liter) glass measuring cup, whisk the wet ingredients—*except* the garlic—together. Stir in the garlic and pour into the bread pan. Use a spatula to spread the dry ingredients over the wet ingredients, covering completely. Make a shallow well in the center and pour in the yeast.

4. Place the bread pan in the machine and lock it in place. Close the lid and select:

   Gluten-free cycle (see page 14 if your machine does not have this setting)
   Loaf size: 1½ pounds/750 g
   Medium crust
   Start

5. About 3 minutes into the mixing process, open the lid and use a spatula to scrape down the sides of the pan, avoiding the paddle. Push any flour that has accumulated around the edges and under the dough into the center. Check again once or twice during kneading, scraping the edges, corners, and under the dough. If the dough looks too wet or too dry, add a little flour blend or tiny amounts of warm water. Once the mix/knead cycle is done, leave the lid closed during the rise and bake cycles.

6. At the end of the bake cycle, lift the lid and check the temperature. When the bread reaches 206°F to 210°F (97°C to 99°C) on an instant-read thermometer inserted in the center, it is done. Remove the pan from the machine and set it on its side on a wire cooling rack. Wait a couple of minutes, then turn the pan upside down and slide the loaf onto the wire rack. Carefully remove the paddle if it is embedded in the bottom of the loaf. Let the bread cool upside down for at least 2 hours before slicing.

7. Store the bread in a resealable plastic bag or airtight container on the counter for up to 3 days. For longer storage, cut into even slices, double-wrap tightly in plastic, place in a resealable plastic bag, and freeze for up to 3 months.

ROASTED GARLIC

Roast as many heads of garlic as you want. A few extra always come in handy. You can store any extra roasted garlic in an airtight container in the refrigerator for up to 1 week and use as an alternative to butter for slathering on bread.

Preheat the oven to 400°F (200°C). Slice the top third off each garlic head to expose the cloves. Drizzle with olive oil and sprinkle with salt. Wrap each head tightly in aluminum foil. Place in the oven and roast until the cloves are soft and golden brown, 45 to 50 minutes. Cool. When you can handle them, remove the garlic heads from the foil and squeeze the pulp into a bowl.

KALAMATA OLIVE AND OREGANO BREAD

MAKES 1 (1½-POUND/680 G) LOAF • DAIRY FREE

This beautiful loaf is packed with the flavors of the Mediterranean. One bite and you will be transported to olive country and the coastline, with the brilliant blue seas stretching to the horizon. This is a perfect bread to serve with bouillabaisse or a Spanish-style *sopa de mariscos*. If you like, switch out the Kalamata olives for pitted Niçoise olives (which are smaller) and leave them whole for a pretty visual when slicing.

DRY INGREDIENTS

21 g (0.7 oz or 2 tablespoons) active dry yeast

240 g (8.5 oz or 2 cups) Light Flour Blend (page 34)

120 g (4.2 oz or 1 cup) millet flour

48 g (1.7 oz or ¼ cup) granulated cane sugar

1 tablespoon baking powder

2 teaspoons psyllium husk flakes or powder

1 teaspoon dried oregano (preferably Greek)

1 teaspoon kosher or fine sea salt

⅛ teaspoon ascorbic acid, optional

WET INGREDIENTS

2 large eggs, at room temperature (see page 39), beaten

285 ml (1 cup plus 3 tablespoons) water, heated to about 80°F (27°C)

60 ml (¼ cup) vegetable oil

2 teaspoons ume plum vinegar

1 cup pitted Kalamata olives, chopped, or pitted Niçoise olives

1. Set the bread pan on the counter and insert the beater paddle(s). Unless otherwise directed by your machine's manufacturer, add the liquids first, then the dry ingredients, and finally the yeast.

2. Measure the yeast into a small bowl and set aside. In a large mixing bowl, whisk the remaining dry ingredients together.

3. In a 4-cup (1 liter) glass measuring cup, whisk the wet ingredients—*except* the olives—together. Stir in the olives and pour into the bread pan. Use a spatula to spread the dry ingredients over the wet ingredients, covering completely. Make a shallow well in the center and pour in the yeast.

4. Place the bread pan in the machine, settle it in the center, and lock it in place. Close the lid and select:

    Gluten-free cycle (see page 14 if your machine does not have this setting)
    Loaf size: 1½ pounds/750 g
    Medium crust
    Start

5. About 3 minutes into the mixing process, open the lid and use a spatula to scrape down the sides of the pan, avoiding the paddle. Push any flour that has accumulated around the edges and under the dough into the center. Check again once or twice during kneading, scraping the edges, corners, and under the dough. If the dough looks too wet or too dry, add a little flour blend or tiny amounts of warm water. Once the mixing/kneading is done, leave the lid closed during the rise and bake cycles.

6. At the end of the bake cycle, lift the lid and check the temperature. When the bread reaches 206°F to 210°F (97°C to 99°C) on an instant-read thermometer inserted in the center, it is done. Remove the pan from the machine and set it on its side on a wire cooling rack. Leave the bread in the pan for a couple of minutes, then turn the pan upside down and slide the loaf onto the wire rack. Carefully remove the paddle if it is embedded in the bottom of the loaf. Let the bread cool upside down for at least 2 hours before slicing.

7. Store the bread in a resealable plastic bag or airtight container on the counter for up to 3 days. For longer storage, cut into even slices, double-wrap tightly in plastic, place in a resealable plastic bag, and freeze for up to 3 months.

MEXICAN SALSA BREAD

MAKES 1 (1½-POUND/680 G) LOAF   ◆   DAIRY FREE

All the flavors of pico de gallo in a slice of bread—is there anything better? This rosy loaf, studded with chopped cilantro and chilli peppers, is always a great conversation starter. While not required, smoked salt adds an extra touch of interest; it will also boost the flavor of your grilled meats and vegetables. The next time you make fajitas, fill slices of this bread with grilled flank steak or chicken and vegetables. Add a spicy mayonnaise or aioli and it will totally change the way you think about fajitas. For a less spicy version, you can cut back on the chillies or leave them out.

DRY INGREDIENTS

21 g (0.7 oz or 2 tablespoons) active dry yeast

360 g (12.7 oz or 3 cups) Light Flour Blend (page 34)

30 g (1.1 oz or ¼ cup) corn flour or masa harina

48 g (1.7 oz or ¼ cup) granulated cane sugar

1 tablespoon baking powder

1 tablespoon chopped fresh cilantro

2½ teaspoons tomato powder (see Resources, page 376)

2 teaspoons xanthan gum

1 teaspoon red pepper flakes, or to taste

1 teaspoon onion powder

1 teaspoon smoked sea salt or kosher salt

⅛ teaspoon ascorbic acid, optional

WET INGREDIENTS

3 large eggs, at room temperature (see page 39), beaten

285 ml (1 cup plus 3 tablespoons) water, warmed to about 80°F (27°C)

60 ml (¼ cup) olive oil

2 teaspoons apple cider vinegar

1. Set the bread pan on the counter and insert the beater paddle(s). Unless otherwise directed by your machine's manufacturer, add the liquids first, then the dry ingredients, and finally the yeast.

2. Measure the yeast into a small bowl and set aside. In a large mixing bowl, whisk the remaining dry ingredients together.

3. In a 4-cup (1 liter) glass measuring cup, whisk the wet ingredients together and pour into the bread pan. Use a spatula to spread the dry ingredients over the wet ingredients, covering completely. Make a shallow well in the center and pour in the yeast.

4. Place the bread pan in the machine, settle it in the center, and lock it in place. Close the lid and select:

   Gluten-free cycle (see page 14 if your machine does not have this setting)
   Loaf size: 1½ pounds/750 g
   Medium crust
   Start

5. About 3 minutes into the mixing process, open the lid and use a spatula to scrape down the sides of the pan, avoiding the paddle. Push any flour that has accumulated around the edges and under the dough into the center. Check again once or twice during kneading, scraping the edges, corners, and under the dough. If the dough looks too wet or too dry, add a little flour blend or tiny amounts of warm water. Once the mix/knead cycle is done, leave the lid closed during the rise and bake cycles.

6. At the end of the bake cycle, lift the lid and check the temperature. When the bread reaches 206°F to 210°F (97°C to 99°C) on an instant-read thermometer inserted in the center, it is done. Remove the pan from the machine and set it on its side on a wire cooling rack. Leave the bread in the pan for a couple of minutes, then turn the pan upside down and slide the loaf onto the wire rack. Carefully remove the paddle if it is embedded in the bottom of the loaf. Let the bread cool upside down for at least 2 hours before slicing.

7. Store the bread in a resealable plastic bag or airtight container on the counter for up to 3 days. For longer storage, cut into even slices, double-wrap tightly in plastic, place in a resealable plastic bag, and freeze for up to 3 months.

PIZZA PIE BREAD

MAKES 1 (1½-POUND/680 G) LOAF

Pizza is one of America's favorite foods, especially for children. This bread has all the same flavors and can be a simple after-school treat or accompaniment to your favorite Italian dinner. The secret ingredient is tomato powder, which adds all the flavor of ripe tomatoes without the liquid and without any chopping. You can use it to boost flavors in soups, stews, chilis, and casseroles, too. The aroma of tomatoes, herbs, and cheese baking in the oven always brings the kids running. The hardest thing will be resisting cutting the loaf before it has completely cooled!

DRY INGREDIENTS

21 g (0.7 oz or 2 tablespoons) active dry yeast

360 g (12.7 oz or 3 cups) Light Flour Blend (page 34)

44 g (1.6 oz or ½ cup) milk powder

39 g (1.4 oz or 3 tablespoons) granulated cane sugar

2 tablespoons very finely grated Parmesan cheese or powdered cheddar cheese (see Note opposite)

1 tablespoon baking powder

1 tablespoon dried oregano

2 teaspoons xanthan gum

2 teaspoons kosher salt

2 teaspoons dried basil

1½ teaspoons onion powder

1½ teaspoons tomato powder (see Resources, page 376)

¼ teaspoon garlic powder

⅛ teaspoon ascorbic acid, optional

WET INGREDIENTS

3 large eggs, at room temperature (see page 39), beaten

270 ml (1 cup plus 2 tablespoons) water, heated to about 80°F (27°C)

60 ml (¼ cup) olive oil

2 teaspoons apple cider vinegar

1. Set the bread pan on the counter and insert the beater paddle(s). Unless otherwise directed by your machine's manufacturer, add the liquids first, then the dry ingredients, and finally the yeast.

2. Measure the yeast into a small bowl and set aside. In a large mixing bowl, whisk the remaining dry ingredients together.

3. In a 4-cup (1 liter) glass measuring cup, whisk the wet ingredients together and pour into the bread pan. Use a spatula to spread the dry ingredients over the wet ingredients, covering completely. Make a shallow well in the center and pour in the yeast.

4. Place the bread pan in the machine, settle it in the center, and lock it in place. Close the lid and select:

   Gluten-free cycle (see page 14 if your machine does not have this setting)
   Loaf size: 1½ pounds/750 g
   Medium crust
   Start

5. About 3 minutes into the mixing process, open the lid and use a spatula to scrape down the sides of the pan, avoiding the paddle. Push any flour that has accumulated around the edges and under the dough into the center. Check again once or twice during kneading, scraping the edges, corners, and under the dough. If the dough looks too wet or too dry, add a little flour blend or tiny amounts of warm water. Close the lid and do not open it during the rise and bake cycles.

NOTE: Cabot sells a gluten-free powdered cheddar that boosts the flavor of baked goods. It is also great sprinkled over popcorn, pizza, and pasta (see Resources, page 376).

6. At the end of the bake cycle, lift the lid and check the temperature. When the bread reaches 206°F to 210°F (97°C to 99°C) on an instant-read thermometer inserted in the center, it is done. Remove the bread pan from the machine and set it on its side on a wire cooling rack. Leave the bread in the pan for a couple of minutes, then turn the pan upside down and slide the loaf onto the wire rack. Carefully remove the paddle if it is embedded in the bottom of the loaf. Let the loaf cool upside down for at least 2 hours before slicing.

7. Store the bread in a resealable plastic bag or airtight container on the counter for up to 3 days. For longer storage, cut into even slices, double-wrap tightly in plastic, place in a resealable plastic bag, and freeze for up to 3 months.

SWEET CORNBREAD

MAKES 1 (1½-POUND/680 G) LOAF ◆ DAIRY FREE

The delicate texture of this bread comes from using corn flour instead of the more customary cornmeal. Slices of this sweet cornbread are perfect for breakfast or an afternoon snack, smeared with butter and fruit jam. Another favorite topping is whipped honey butter (see opposite). It also makes a great dessert base. Slice it about 1 inch (3 cm) thick, toast it or grill it in the summer, then top with fresh berries or grilled peaches and ice cream or sorbet. Drizzle with a little caramel sauce and you'll never eat cornbread plain again.

DRY INGREDIENTS

172 g (6.1 oz or 1½ cups) corn flour

120 g (4.2 oz or 1 cup) Light Flour Blend (page 34)

60 g (2.1 oz or ½ cup) millet flour

200 g (7.1 oz or 1 cup) granulated cane sugar

1 tablespoon baking powder

1 teaspoon kosher or fine sea salt

1 teaspoon xanthan gum or psyllium husk flakes or powder

WET INGREDIENTS

⅓ cup vegetable oil (80 ml) or nondairy butter substitute (75 g or 2.6 oz/ ⅔ stick), melted and slightly cooled

240 ml (1 cup) unsweetened soy or coconut milk

3 large eggs, beaten

1. Set the bread pan on the counter and insert the beater paddle(s). Unless otherwise directed by your machine's manufacturer, add the liquids first and then the dry ingredients.

2. In a large mixing bowl, whisk the dry ingredients together.

3. In a 2-cup (0.5 liter) glass measuring cup, whisk the wet ingredients together and pour into the bread pan. Use a spatula to spread the dry ingredients over the wet ingredients, covering completely.

4. Place the bread pan in the machine, settle it in the center, and lock it in place. Close the lid and select:

Quick bread/cake cycle
Loaf size: 1½ pounds/750 g
Light crust
Start

5. After the first kneading cycle, scrape the sides and bottom of the pan, lifting the dough with a spatula to check underneath and make sure all the dry ingredients are incorporated. If your machine has alerts, when you hear the signal for the machine transitioning from the knead to the bake cycle, you can remove the paddle and reshape the loaf if you want. If the dough seems sticky, wet your hands with a little water to help with reshaping the loaf and smoothing the top. Close the lid and let the bread finish baking undisturbed.

6. At the end of the bake cycle, lift the lid and check the temperature. The bread is done when it registers 206°F to 210°F (97°C to 99°C) on an instant-read thermometer inserted in the center of the loaf. Remove the pan from the machine and place it on its side on a wire rack. Leave the bread in the pan for a couple of minutes, then turn the pan upside down and slide the loaf onto the wire rack. Carefully remove the paddle if it is embedded in the bottom of the loaf. Set the loaf back on its side. Let the bread cool for at least 2 hours before slicing.

7. Store the bread in a resealable plastic bag or airtight container on the counter for up to 3 days. For longer storage, cut into even slices, double-wrap tightly in plastic, place in a resealable plastic bag, and freeze for up to 3 months.

WHIPPED HONEY BUTTER

You can transform your homemade butter (page 69) into whipped honey butter in a matter of moments. But you can also make this with butter from the grocery store.

Put ½ cup (112 g or 4 oz/1 stick) softened butter in the bowl of a stand mixer fitted with the paddle attachment. Beat on low speed until smooth. Add 2 tablespoons (40 g or 1.4 oz) honey and beat on low to combine. Turn the speed up to medium and beat until light and fluffy, about 30 seconds.

Transfer to a serving bowl. This will keep in the refrigerator, covered, for a week or two.

IRISH SODA BREAD

MAKES 1 (1½-POUND/680 G) LOAF • DAIRY FREE

Traditional Irish soda bread has only four ingredients: flour, baking soda, salt, and buttermilk. It takes more than four ingredients to create a gluten-free loaf that tastes as good as the original. There is yeast and baking powder in this recipe, as baking soda alone doesn't provide enough lift. We have also added extra potato starch to lighten the bread. Irish Americans usually add embellishments, which might be currants, raisins, golden raisins, dried cranberries, or caraway seeds. Serve the bread alongside a bowl of beef stew and a pint of ale, and all you'll be missing is a band playing an Irish jig to get your toes tapping.

DRY INGREDIENTS

21 g (0.7 oz or 2 tablespoons) active dry yeast

180 g (6.3 oz or 1½ cups) Light Flour Blend (page 34) or Whole-Grain Flour Blend (page 34)

120 g (4.2 oz or 1 cup) sorghum flour

60 g (2.1 oz ½ cup) potato starch (*not* potato flour)

26 g (0.9 oz or 2 tablespoons) granulated cane sugar

1 tablespoon baking powder

2 teaspoons psyllium husk flakes or powder

2 teaspoons baking soda

1 teaspoon kosher or fine sea salt

⅛ teaspoon ascorbic acid, optional

WET INGREDIENTS

59 ml (4 tablespoons) nondairy butter substitute, melted and slightly cooled

350 ml (1½ cups) unsweetened soy or coconut milk

1 tablespoon apple cider vinegar

1 tablespoon freshly squeezed lemon juice

ADD-IN

1 cup dried currants

1. Set the bread pan on the counter and insert the beater paddle(s). Unless otherwise directed by your machine's manufacturer, add the liquids first, then the dry ingredients, and finally the yeast.

2. Measure the yeast into a small bowl and set aside. In a large mixing bowl, whisk the remaining dry ingredients together.

3. In a 2-cup (0.5 liter) glass measuring cup, whisk the wet ingredients together and pour into the bread pan. Use a spatula to spread the dry ingredients over the wet ingredients, covering completely.

4. Place the bread pan in the machine, settle it in the center, and lock it in place. Close the lid and select:

   Gluten-free cycle (see page 14 if your machine does not have this setting)
   Loaf size: 1½ pounds/750 g
   Light crust
   Start

5. After the first kneading cycle, scrape the sides and bottom of the pan with a spatula to make sure all the dry ingredients are incorporated. Add the currants. If your machine has alerts, when you hear the signal for the machine transitioning from the knead to the rise cycle, you can remove the paddle and reshape the loaf if you want. If the dough seems sticky, wet your hands with a little water to help with reshaping the loaf and smoothing the top. Close the lid and do not open during the rise and bake cycles.

6. At the end of the bake cycle, lift the lid and check the temperature. When the bread reaches 206°F to 210°F (97°C to 99°C) on an instant-read thermometer inserted in the center, it is done. Remove the pan from the machine and set it on its side on a wire rack. Leave the bread in the pan for 3 minutes, then turn the loaf out of the pan. Carefully remove the paddle if it is embedded in the bottom of the loaf. Set the loaf on its side and cool for at least 1 hour before slicing.

7. Store the bread in a resealable plastic bag or airtight container on the counter for up to 3 days. For longer storage, cut into even slices, double-wrap tightly in plastic, place in a resealable plastic bag, and freeze for up to 3 months.

BROWN IRISH SODA BREAD

MAKES 1 (1½-POUND/680 G) LOAF

This beautiful soda bread—packed with oats, oat flour, sorghum flour, and a bit of molasses to add a touch of sweetness—is a perfect breakfast treat. It is a must-make every year for St. Patrick's Day. With the combination of yeast, baking powder, and baking soda, the bread will be taller with a looser crumb, for luscious flavor without the heaviness often found in traditional loaves. Splurge on some Kerrygold salted butter and spread a thick layer over each slice for a treat you'll thank the Irish for!

DRY INGREDIENTS

21 g (0.7 oz or 2 tablespoons) active dry yeast

120 g (4.2 oz or 1 cup) Light Flour Blend (page 34)

137 g (4.8 oz or 1¼ cups) sorghum flour

125 g (4.4 oz or 1 cup) gluten-free oat flour

30 g (1.1 oz or ⅓ cup) gluten-free oats

45 g (1.6 oz or 3 tablespoons firmly packed) brown sugar

1 tablespoon baking soda

1 tablespoon baking powder

2 teaspoons xanthan gum

1 teaspoon kosher salt

⅛ teaspoon ascorbic acid, optional

WET INGREDIENTS

20 g (0.7 oz or 1 tablespoon) molasses (*not* blackstrap)

320 ml (1⅓ cups) buttermilk, warmed to about 80°F (27°C)

3 large eggs, at room temperature (see page 39), beaten

60 ml (¼ cup) olive oil

1 teaspoon apple cider vinegar

ADD-INS (OPTIONAL)

27 g (1 oz or 3 tablespoons) golden raisins

1 tablespoon caraway seeds

1. Set the bread pan on the counter and insert the beater paddle(s). Unless otherwise directed by your machine's manufacturer, add the liquids first, then the dry ingredients, and finally the yeast.

2. Measure the yeast into a small bowl and set aside. In a large mixing bowl, whisk the remaining dry ingredients together. Set aside.

3. In a 4-cup (1 liter) glass measuring cup, whisk the molasses and buttermilk together to dissolve the molasses. Add the remaining wet ingredients and whisk again. Pour into the bread pan. Use a spatula to spread the dry ingredients over the wet ingredients, covering completely. Make a shallow well in the center of the dry ingredients and pour in the yeast.

4. Place the bread pan in the machine, settle it in the center, and lock it in place. Close the lid and select:

   Gluten-free cycle (see page 14 if your machine does not have this setting)
   Loaf size: 1½ pounds/750 g
   Medium crust
   Start

5. After the first kneading cycle, scrape the sides and bottom of the pan with a spatula to make sure all the dry ingredients are incorporated. Add the raisins and caraway seeds (if using them), letting the machine mix them into the dough. If your machine has alerts, when you hear the signal for the machine transitioning from the knead to the rise cycle, you can remove the paddle and reshape the loaf if you want. If the dough seems sticky, wet your hands with a little water to help with reshaping the loaf and smoothing the top. Close the lid and do not open during the rise and bake cycles.

6. At the end of the bake cycle, lift the lid and check the temperature. When the bread reaches 206°F to 210°F (97°C to 99°C) on an instant-read thermometer inserted in the center, it is done. Remove the pan from the machine and set it on its side on a wire cooling rack. Leave the bread in the pan for a couple of minutes, then turn the pan upside down and slide the loaf onto the wire rack. Carefully remove the paddle if it is embedded in the bottom of the loaf. Let the bread cool upside down for at least 2 hours before slicing.

7. Store the bread in a resealable plastic bag or airtight container on the counter for up to 3 days. For longer storage, cut into even slices, double-wrap tightly in plastic, place in a resealable plastic bag, and freeze for up to 3 months.

SWEET HAWAIIAN BREAD

MAKES 1 (1½-POUND/680 G) LOAF

Trade winds blowing, the grace of hula dancers, breathtaking sunsets, friendly and generous people, pineapple plantations stretching for miles—these are the images of Hawaii. Delicate sweetness and a hint of pineapple make this soft and tender bread reminiscent of the flavors of Hawaii. You can enjoy it plain or toasted with a little butter or topped with a dab of pineapple jam. You could even add some finely chopped macadamia nuts. It is good all year long and adds a touch of paradise to any meal.

DRY INGREDIENTS

21 g (0.7 oz or 2 tablespoons) active dry yeast

360 g (12.7 oz or 3 cups) Light Flour Blend (page 34)

48 g (1.7 oz or ¼ cup) granulated cane sugar

22 g (0.8 oz or ¼ cup) milk powder

1 tablespoon baking powder

2 teaspoons xanthan gum

1 teaspoon kosher salt

¼ teaspoon ground ginger

⅛ teaspoon ascorbic acid, optional

WET INGREDIENTS

60 g (2 oz or 3 tablespoons) honey

270 ml (1 cup plus 2 tablespoons) 1% milk or water, heated to 80°F (27°C)

56 g (2 oz or 4 tablespoons/½ stick) unsalted butter, melted and slightly cooled

2 large eggs, at room temperature (see page 39), beaten

2 teaspoons apple cider vinegar

⅛ teaspoon pineapple flavoring (see opposite)

1. Set the bread pan on the counter and insert the beater paddle(s). Unless otherwise directed by your machine's manufacturer, add the liquids first, then the dry ingredients, and finally the yeast.

2. Measure the yeast into a small bowl and set aside. In a large mixing bowl, whisk the remaining dry ingredients together.

3. in a 4-cup (1 liter) glass measuring cup, Whisk the honey and milk together to dissolve the honey. Add the remaining wet ingredients and whisk again. Pour into the bread pan. Use a spatula to spread the dry ingredients over the wet ingredients, covering completely. Make a shallow well in the center of the dry ingredients and pour in the yeast.

4. Place the bread pan in the machine, settle it in the center, and lock it in place. Close the lid and select:

   Gluten-free cycle (see page 14 if your machine does not have this setting)
   Loaf size: 1½ pounds/750 g
   Medium crust
   Start

5. About 3 minutes into the mixing process, open the lid and use a spatula to scrape down the sides of the pan, avoiding the paddle. Push any flour that has accumulated around the edges or under the dough into the center. Check again once or twice during kneading, scraping the edges, corners, and under the dough. If the dough looks too wet or too dry, add a little flour blend or tiny amounts of warm water. Once the mixing/kneading is done, leave the lid closed during the rise and bake cycles.

> **NOTE:** LorAnn Oils and Flavors makes high-quality gluten-free flavorings, including pineapple. Their products are very concentrated, so always measure carefully—you might consider replacing the lids with eye-dropper lids for the most accurate measuring.

6. At the end of the bake cycle, lift the lid and check the temperature. When the bread reaches 206°F to 210°F (97°C to 99°C) on an instant-read thermometer inserted in the center, it is done. Remove the pan from the machine and set it on its side on a wire cooling rack. Leave the bread in the pan for a couple of minutes, then turn the pan upside down and slide the loaf onto the wire rack. Carefully remove the paddle if it is embedded in the bottom of the loaf. Flip the loaf back onto its side and let cool for at least 2 hours before slicing.

7. Store the bread in a resealable plastic bag or airtight container on the counter for up to 3 days. For longer storage, cut into even slices, double-wrap tightly in plastic, place in a resealable plastic bag, and freeze for up to 3 months.

PORTUGUESE SWEET BREAD

MAKES 1 (1½-POUND/680 G) LOAF • DAIRY FREE

Many of us know of King's Hawaiian sweet rolls. Despite the name, they are more like a cross between Portuguese bread and Hawaiian, with sweetening added. Soft and tender, they are a staple on buffets everywhere. You will be surprised how much this loaf tastes like those wheat rolls, but without the gluten. Use this bread to make salty sliced ham and spicy mustard sandwiches and relish that wonderful flavor combination!

DRY INGREDIENTS

21 g (0.7 oz or 2 tablespoons) active dry yeast

360 g (12.7 oz or 3 cups) Light Flour Blend (page 34)

48 g (1.7 oz or ¼ cup) granulated cane sugar

1 tablespoon baking powder

2 teaspoons xanthan gum

1 teaspoon kosher salt

WET INGREDIENTS

60 g (2 oz or 3 tablespoons) honey

255 ml (1 cup plus 1 tablespoon) water, warmed to about 80°F (27°C)

56 g (2 oz or 4 tablespoons/½ stick) nondairy butter substitute, melted and slightly cooled

2 large eggs, at room temperature (see page 39), beaten

2 teaspoons apple cider vinegar

1. Set the bread pan on the counter and insert the beater paddle(s). Unless otherwise directed by your machine's manufacturer, add the liquids first, then the dry ingredients, and finally the yeast.

2. Measure the yeast into a small bowl and set aside. In a large mixing bowl, whisk the remaining dry ingredients together.

3. In a 4-cup (1 liter) glass measuring cup, whisk the honey and milk together to dissolve the honey. Add the remaining wet ingredients and whisk again. Pour into the bread pan. Use a spatula to spread the dry ingredients over the wet ingredients, covering completely. Make a shallow well in the center of the dry ingredients and pour in the yeast.

4. Place the bread pan in the machine, settle it in the center, and lock it in place. Close the lid and select:

   Gluten-free cycle (see page 14 if your machine does not have this setting)
   Loaf size: 1½ pounds/750 g
   Medium crust
   Start

5. About 3 minutes into the mixing process, open the lid and use a spatula to scrape down the sides of the pan, avoiding the paddle. Push any flour that has accumulated around the edges and under the dough into the center. Check again once or twice during kneading, scraping the edges, corners, and under the dough. If the dough looks too wet or too dry, add a little flour blend or tiny amounts of warm water. Close the lid and do not open it during the rise and bake cycles. The bread should rise to about ½ inch (1 cm) below the level of your bread pan and then will settle and the top will flatten. This is normal.

6. At the end of the bake cycle, lift the lid and check the temperature. When the bread reaches 206°F to 210°F (97°C to 99°C) on an instant-read thermometer inserted in the center, it is done. Remove the bread pan from the machine and set it on its side on a wire cooling rack. Leave the bread in the pan for a couple of minutes, then turn the pan upside down and slide the loaf onto the wire rack. Carefully remove the paddle if it is embedded in the bottom of the loaf. Place the bread back on its side and let cool for at least 2 hours before slicing.

7. Store the bread in a resealable plastic bag or airtight container on the counter for up to 3 days. For longer storage, cut into even slices, double-wrap tightly in plastic, place in a resealable plastic bag, and freeze for up to 3 months.

SAVORY ROASTED PECAN AND CRANBERRY BREAD

MAKES 1 (1½-POUND/680 G) LOAF • DAIRY FREE

The combination of nuts and cranberries sings of winter holidays. Slightly tart dried cranberries and spiced pecans add just the right balance of sweet and savory. Toast up some slices and top with melting butter for a bite of pure heaven. Spread the toasted slices with cranberry sauce left over from holiday dinners for the perfect afternoon treat or quick breakfast. Make sandwiches with leftover turkey and extra cranberry sauce for the quintessential post-Thanksgiving meal.

DRY INGREDIENTS

21 g (0.7 oz or 2 tablespoons) active dry yeast

360 g (12.7 oz or 3 cups) Light Flour Blend (page 34)

48 g (1.7 oz or ¼ cup) granulated cane sugar

3 teaspoons baking powder

2 teaspoons xanthan gum

1 teaspoon kosher salt

60 g (2.1 oz or ½ cup) dried sweetened cranberries

37 g (1.3 oz or ⅓ cup) chopped Savory Roasted Pecans (see opposite)

WET INGREDIENTS

2 large eggs, at room temperature (see page 39), beaten

240 ml (1 cup) water, warmed to about 80°F (27°C)

45 ml (3 tablespoons) olive oil

2 teaspoons apple cider vinegar

1. Set the bread pan on the counter and insert the beater paddle(s). Unless otherwise directed by your machine's manufacturer, add the liquids first, then the dry ingredients, and finally the yeast.

2. Measure the yeast into a small bowl and set aside. In a large mixing bowl, whisk the dry ingredients—*except* the cranberries and nuts—together. Add the cranberries and nuts and toss. Set aside.

3. In a 4-cup (1 liter) glass measuring cup, whisk the wet ingredients together and pour into the bread pan. Use a spatula to spread the dry ingredients over the wet ingredients, covering completely. Make a shallow well in the center and pour in the yeast.

4. Place the bread pan in the machine and lock it in place. Close the lid and select:

   Gluten-free cycle (see page 14 if your machine does not have this setting)
   Loaf size: 1½ pounds/750 g
   Medium crust
   Start

5. About 3 minutes into the mixing cycle, open the lid and use a spatula to scrape down the sides of the pan, avoiding the paddle. Push any flour that has accumulated around the edges and under the dough into the center. Repeat once or twice more during kneading. The dough should create a dome in the center, and the edges may look a little wet and shiny. If the dough looks too wet or too dry, add small amounts of flour blend or warm water during kneading. Once the mix/knead cycle is done, leave the lid closed.

6. At the end of the bake cycle, lift the lid and check the temperature. When the bread reaches 206°F to 210°F (97°C to 99°C) on an instant-read thermometer inserted in the center, it is done. Remove the bread pan from the machine and set it on its side on a wire cooling rack. Leave the bread in the pan for a couple of minutes, then turn the pan upside down and slide the loaf onto the wire rack. Carefully remove the paddle if it is embedded in the bottom of the loaf. Place the bread back on its side and let cool for at least 2 hours before slicing.

7. Store the bread in a resealable plastic bag or airtight container on the counter for up to 3 days. For longer storage, cut into even slices, double-wrap tightly in plastic, place in a resealable plastic bag, and freeze for up to 3 months.

SAVORY ROASTED PECANS

MAKES 1 CUP (110 G OR 3.8 OZ)

110 g (3.8 oz or 1 cup) chopped pecans
1½ teaspoons dried thyme
½ teaspoon onion powder
½ teaspoon kosher salt
2 tablespoons (30 ml) olive oil

Preheat the oven to 350°F (180°C). Line a rimmed baking sheet with parchment. Put the pecans on the baking sheet and sprinkle with the thyme, onion powder, and salt. Drizzle with the olive oil and toss to make sure the nuts are evenly coated. Spread the nuts out in a single layer.

Bake for 10 minutes. Remove from the oven, toss again, and continue baking until fragrant and lightly golden, about 10 minutes longer. Set aside to cool. Store in a resealable plastic bag at room temperature for several days, in the refrigerator for up to a week, or in the freezer for longer storage.

Put any extra nuts into a bowl. You'll find yourself reaching for them as the bread bakes—they are irresistible, and you'll be surprised how quickly they disappear.

WALNUT-CRANBERRY OAT BREAD

MAKES 1 (1½-POUND/680 G) LOAF ◆ DAIRY FREE

The tartness of fresh cranberries, the crunch of toasted walnuts, and the hominess of oats are combined in this bread for one of our favorite ways to celebrate the harvest season. Fresh cranberries are one of only a few produce items that are not available year-round, but if you need a fix during the rest of the year, use dried sweetened cranberries to make this bread. Enjoy it with jam and a cup of tea in the afternoon. Toasted and brushed with a little butter or mascarpone cheese, it is a perfect treat for breakfast, especially when you are snuggled in a comfy chair by the warm fire.

DRY INGREDIENTS

21 g (0.7 oz or 2 tablespoons) active dry yeast

240 g (8.5 oz or 2 cups) Light Flour Blend (page 34)

125 g (4.4 oz or 1 cup) gluten-free oat flour

48 g (1.7 oz or ¼ cup) granulated cane sugar

1 tablespoon baking powder

1 teaspoon xanthan gum

1 teaspoon kosher or fine sea salt

⅛ teaspoon ascorbic acid, optional

100 g (3.5 oz or 1 cup) fresh cranberries

60 g (2.1 oz or ½ cup) toasted chopped walnuts

WET INGREDIENTS

3 large eggs, at room temperature (see page 39), beaten

255 ml (1 cup plus 1 tablespoon) water or seltzer water, warmed to about 80°F (27°C)

60 ml (¼ cup) olive oil

2 teaspoons apple cider vinegar

TOPPING

1 tablespoon water

Gluten-free oats

1. Set the bread pan on the counter and insert the beater paddle(s). Unless otherwise directed by your machine's manufacturer, add the liquids first, then the dry ingredients, and finally the yeast.

2. Measure the yeast into a small bowl and set aside. In a large mixing bowl, whisk the dry ingredients—*except* the cranberries and nuts—together. Add the cranberries and nuts and toss. Set aside.

3. In a 4-cup (1 liter) glass measuring cup, whisk the wet ingredients together and pour into the bread pan. Use a spatula to spread the dry ingredients over the wet ingredients, covering completely. Make a shallow well in the center and pour in the yeast.

4. Place the bread pan in the machine, settle it in the center, and lock it in place. Close the lid and select:
   Gluten-free cycle (see page 14 if your machine does not have this setting)
   Loaf size: 1½ pounds/750 g
   Medium crust
   Start

5. About 3 minutes into the mixing process, open the lid and use a spatula to scrape down the sides of the pan, avoiding the paddle. Push any flour that has accumulated around the edges and under the dough into the center. Check again once or twice during kneading, scraping the edges, corners, and under the dough. If the dough looks too wet or too dry, add a little flour blend or tiny amounts of warm water.

6. Once the mix/knead cycle is done, brush the top of the dough very gently with some water and sprinkle with oats. Close the lid and do not open it during the rise and bake cycles.

BREADS WITH TOPPINGS

It's always best to cool breads with toppings on their sides.

---

7. At the end of the bake cycle, lift the lid and check the temperature. When the bread reaches 207°F to 210°F (97°C to 99°C) on an instant-read thermometer inserted in the center, it is done. Remove the pan from the machine and set it on its side on a wire cooling rack. Leave the bread in the pan for a couple of minutes, then turn the pan upside down and slide the loaf onto the wire rack. Carefully remove the paddle if it is embedded in the bottom of the loaf. Set the loaf back on its side and let cool for at least 2 hours before slicing.

8. Store the bread in a resealable plastic bag or airtight container on the counter for up to 3 days. For longer storage, cut into even slices, double-wrap tightly in plastic, place in a resealable plastic bag, and freeze for up to 3 months.

Sourdough

BREADS

THE ART OF SOURDOUGH

Sourdough starter is the original bread leavener, used for millennia before commercial yeast was developed. Wild yeasts and lactobacilli naturally occur in the environment. These yeasts are attracted to a mixture of flour and water, creating what is called a starter, a culture of microorganisms that will naturally leaven bread.

Ancient Egyptians were the first to record the use of sourdough, around 1500 CE. Sourdough was used for centuries in the United States of America, by cooks on chuck wagons following cattle drives from Texas to Kansas along the Chisholm Trail, by pioneers on wagon trains crossing the nation, by trappers who spent months on their own in the wilderness, and by the California Gold Rush prospectors, who called themselves Sourdoughs.

Sourdough baking is an art, not a science. It is part water, part flour, part care, and part luck. Most recipes tell you to add an equal amount of flour and water (usually by weight), stir it in, and set aside to let the yeast feed. This is a simple formula for how to feed it, so it should turn out perfect every time, right? Wrong. The challenge lies in the starter itself.

Most recipes in other cookbooks call for a specific weighed amount of starter. However, the starter's weight varies from day to day and sometimes even hour to hour depending on when it was last fed, the amount of activity, the moisture content, and even the weather. A test we did on 1 cup (240 ml) of starter resulted in weights of 282 g one day, 270 g the next day, and over 300 g another day. It sounds like a huge difference—and it is in weight, but not in volume. This is why we use volume in our recipes. This difference does mean that your results will vary from one batch to the next. So, you need to learn what gluten-free dough should look like in the machine and make adjustments as needed to get the results you want.

GET HELP FROM H_2O

Using distilled water instead of tap water is especially helpful when working with your sourdough starter and in making sourdough breads. The starter is even more sensitive to chemicals in distilled water than regular gluten-free bread doughs. Distilled water will help your starter grow, make it bubbly, and keep it happy.

If you haven't already, make the Simple Sandwich Bread on page 38 to learn how gluten-free doughs differ from traditional wheat dough and to discover how your machine works in your kitchen. We have tried to be as descriptive as possible about what to look for, but machines vary widely, and every environment is unique. In addition, the humidity in your kitchen will change from day to day. It won't take long to know by the look of the dough as it mixes when it needs an extra tablespoon of water or flour. If you think it looks good while mixing but the top sinks as it bakes, then it has too much liquid. Try reducing the amount by 1 to 2 tablespoons the next time you make it and see how it turns out. After a couple of tries, you should have it pretty well dialed in.

Once you are comfortable with what works for your kitchen, give one of the sourdough recipes a try. Because the starter is a blend of water and flour, we've adjusted the amounts of both dry and wet ingredients. And because the starter is fickle, you are likely going to have to make more small adjustments. But by now, if you've made other breads from this book, you'll have the experience to know what to look for and make judgment calls. Even professional bakers can spend years perfecting their sourdough breads, so don't be discouraged. The more you make, the better it will get!

Since sourdough starter is a leavening agent, you may be wondering why the recipes also call for yeast. Bread machines have set rising times, so yeast (and sometimes other leaveners) helps achieve the lift we need within the time available. In this case, the sourdough is mostly for flavor.

MAKING A SOURDOUGH STARTER

You can attempt to make a wild yeast starter from scratch, which means you are depending on the yeasts that naturally occur in the air and the flour to create a colony and happily grow and ferment. But most of us don't have the patience to wait the amount of time this usually takes, so we turn to sourdough starter kits.

Most kits on the market are made from a wheat flour base, so you have to look for a gluten-free version. These recipes were developed using a starter made with our Whole-Grain Flour Blend (page 34) and the gluten-free brown rice sourdough starter kit from Cultures for Health (see Resources, page 376). This kit comes with instructions that walk you through every step of the process, as well as videos online to help show the consistency you should be looking for. If your house is cool when you make the starter, utilize a heating pad with a couple of towels between it and the bowl of starter to give it the warmth it needs for the active cultures to grow.

Each starter kit behaves differently and has unique requirements for feeding. Generally it will take 3 to 7 days for you to get a fully active starter. Don't worry if it takes longer—sometimes it does. If it seems to be stalled, try using King Arthur Flour's gluten-free Ancient Grains Flour Blend (see Resources, page 376) for a couple of feedings to kick-start the yeasts.

Your starter must be "fed" regularly with fresh gluten-free flour and water to keep it alive and maintain its strength. When the mixture bubbles within a few hours of feeding, you know it is active and ready to be used as a leavener in breads, pancakes, rolls, and other baked goods.

TIPS FOR SUCCESS

- Many municipal water companies use chlorine to clean water, and it may interfere with yeast growth and the flavor of your bread. If your tap water tastes good, use it, but if there is any scent of chemicals in your tap water, we recommend using distilled water.

- Use wooden, plastic, or silicone utensils when working with your starter to avoid possible chemical interactions with some metals.

- Whisking when you feed the starter helps aerate the mixture. Once all the flour and water have been incorporated and the mixture is smooth, use a silicone whisk to whisk vigorously for 30 to 60 seconds to oxygenate the mixture.

- Keeping the starter in a warm but not hot area will help it grow in the expected timeframe. The best conditions are 70°F to 90°F (21°C to 32°C). If the temperature falls below 65°F (18°C), the starter will take longer to develop and won't have as strong a sour flavor.

- Using a glass container, such as a 1-quart (1 liter) mason jar, to store your starter helps you keep an eye on activity and easily see when it needs to be fed. Cover the opening with a coffee filter secured with a rubber band to allow the gases to escape and keep things from dropping in.

- If your starter isn't very active after a week, try using King Arthur Flour's Ancient Grains Flour Blend for one or two feedings. It is a gluten-free combination of amaranth, millet, sorghum, and quinoa flours. It adds protein, fiber, vitamins, and minerals, as well as a complex taste. The blending of these flours makes a great booster for sourdough starters.

STEPS TO A HEALTHY STARTER

While your kit will have detailed directions that you should follow, here are some general guidelines of the steps to building your sourdough starter.

- Combine the starter with equal amounts of room-temperature distilled water and gluten-free flour, whisking with a silicone whisk until there are no lumps and the mixture is smooth. (Metal whisks can react with the starter and cause havoc.)

- Cover the container with a clean kitchen towel or coffee filter secured with a rubber band to keep anything from dropping into the container.

- Place the starter in a warm area—ideally, 70°F to 80°F (21°C to 27°C)—and let rest for 18 to 20 hours.

- Feed the starter with equal parts water and gluten-free flour, whisk vigorously, then cover and let rest for 4 to 8 hours.

- Discard all but ¾ to 1 cup (180 to 240 ml) of the starter. Add equal parts water and gluten-free flour, cover, and let rest for 4 to 8 hours.

- Repeat the feeding and resting steps for 3 to 7 days until the mixture becomes light and bubbly.

- Once the starter is bubbling reliably within a few hours of feeding, feed it twice more before using for baking.

- The hardest part of growing a starter is giving it enough time to fully develop. Don't rush it, and you will have a starter that will keep your family happily in luscious breads and pancakes for years to come.

- The liquid that forms on top is alcohol, a natural by-product of the fermentation process. Called hooch, it is a sign that the starter needs to be fed. If it is light colored and there isn't much of it, you can stir it in before feeding the starter. It will add more sourness. If it is dark colored or there is a lot, pour it off before feeding.

- A mild vinegar odor is an indication that the pH of the starter is too acidic and it needs an extra feeding to rebalance.

- If the starter goes bad (it does happen occasionally) and develops an off aroma—different from a pleasant sour smell—throw it out and start over. Having an extra packet of sourdough starter mix handy will make starting over a little less frustrating.

KEEPING YOUR SOURDOUGH STARTER HAPPY

There is a lot of discussion and guidance about throwing away all but a certain amount of your starter each time you feed it. That is helpful when you are maintaining it between baking sessions. Removing a portion helps maintain the pH balance and reduces the total number of yeasts so there is plenty of food for them, keeping your starter happy and healthy.

But if you are going to be using a lot of it for a big baking project, you need more starter. This means adding more water and flour without discarding any of the starter. If you are planning on making multiple loaves of sourdough bread, build your starter for a few days, feeding it regularly and keeping it at room temperature. This will give you enough starter for your baking projects plus enough left over to keep the starter going. Never use all your starter or you will have to start over again from scratch. When you are going to take a break from baking for a while, go back to discarding (or using) most of the starter, feeding, resting, and then storing it in the refrigerator.

Even when you are storing it in the refrigerator between baking sessions, you still need to feed it at least once a week. Put it on your calendar, but if you are a little late, don't worry too much. Sourdough is very hardy; with a couple of feedings, it should be bubbling happily again. If you are feeding your starter by weight, the weight will likely be different each time. Make a note of your starting weight so you can adjust the other ingredients as needed.

USING SOURDOUGH STARTER

The day before you plan to bake, take the starter out of the refrigerator and bring it to room temperature. Feed it two or three times to reactivate it and get it bubbling. It is ready to use when it is active within a couple of hours of feeding. Remove the amount you will need for your recipe and return the rest to the refrigerator. Be sure to feed this portion as well to keep it bubbly and happy before baking.

If you are going to be baking over several days, you can keep the whole starter at room temperature, but you will have to feed it twice a day, about 12 hours apart. If you keep your house cool, you may want to set your starter in a warmer area, such as near an appliance (your refrigerator, for example) or a radiator that gives off ambient heat. If that isn't possible, set up a heating pad on its lowest setting, cover it with a couple of folded kitchen towels, and set the container of starter on top. If your heating pad has an automatic shut-off, you will have to keep an eye on it and restart it whenever needed.

If you have a convection bread maker—which warms up your ingredients before starting the mixing cycle—you can use starter that isn't quite room temperature and let the machine finish warming it. This will save you a little advance time and planning.

WAYS TO USE EXCESS SOURDOUGH STARTER

When you are ready to feed your starter and have to remove a portion of it, there are a number of ways to use it instead of discarding it. You can use it to make any of the sourdough recipes in this book or any recipe you like. To add it to a non-sourdough recipe, weigh ½ to 1 cup (120 to 240 ml) of the starter and reduce the flour and water measures in the recipe by half that weight. As the machine is mixing and kneading the dough, be prepared to make adjustments with additional flour or water until you have the right consistency. Make notes of what you used (measurements and ingredients) and what your results were to get consistency in the future.

ALMOST SAN FRANCISCO SOURDOUGH SANDWICH BREAD

MAKES 1 (1½-POUND/680 G) LOAF

With a higher percentage of starter, this sourdough bread packs a nice little punch. When you are getting ready to make this loaf, don't pour off the liquid on top of the starter (the hooch); stir it in and then measure out 2 cups (480 ml) of starter. The hooch will intensify the sourness and add more tang to your bread. It's not quite the bread some of us remember, but it's pretty darn close.

DRY INGREDIENTS

21 g (0.7 oz or 2 tablespoons) active dry yeast

120 g (4.2 oz or 1 cup) Light Flour Blend (page 34)

58 g (2 oz or ½ cup) buttermilk powder

39 g (1.4 oz or 3 tablespoons) granulated cane sugar

16 g (0.6 oz or 2 tablespoons) potato starch (*not* potato flour)

2 teaspoons kosher or fine sea salt

1 teaspoon baking powder

1 teaspoon xanthan gum

WET INGREDIENTS

480 ml (2 cups) sourdough starter, at room temperature

28 g (1 oz or 2 tablespoons/¼ stick) unsalted butter, melted and slightly cooled

3 large eggs, at room temperature (see page 39), beaten

30 ml (2 tablespoons) water, warmed to 80°F (27°C)

Sourdough starter must be at room temperature before using. If your starter has been refrigerated, pull out 2 cups (480 ml) and set it on the counter for about 2 hours to warm up to room temperature. You do not have to have recently fed the starter, but if you are taking out a cup or two, it's always a good idea to go ahead and feed the remaining starter (see directions on page 176).

1. Set the bread pan on the counter and insert the beater paddle(s). Unless otherwise directed by your machine's manufacturer, add the liquids first, then the dry ingredients, and finally the yeast.

2. Measure the yeast into a small bowl and set aside. In a large mixing bowl, whisk the remaining dry ingredients together.

3. In a 4-cup (1 liter) glass measuring cup, whisk the wet ingredients together and pour into the bread pan. Use a spatula to spread the dry ingredients over the wet ingredients, covering completely. Make a shallow well in the center and pour in the yeast.

4. Place the bread pan in the machine, settle it in the center, and lock it in place. Close the lid and select:

    Gluten-free cycle (see page 14 if your machine does not have this setting)
    Loaf size: 1½ pounds/750 g
    Medium crust
    Start

5. About 3 minutes after the machine has started mixing/kneading, open the lid and use a spatula to scrape the sides of the pan, avoiding the paddle. Push any flour that has accumulated around the edges onto the dough. Check again once or twice during kneading, scraping any loose flour into the dough. This dough is much wetter than many of the others you may be used to working with—that is because the sourdough starter is halfway between a wet and a dry ingredient. As it mixes it will fill the bottom of the bread pan in an even layer with a mound in the center around the beater blade. If it looks as if it needs a little more warm water or flour blend, add them 1 tablespoon at a time until you get the consistency you want. Once the machine has finished the mix/knead cycles, leave the lid closed during the baking cycle.

6. At the end of the bake cycle, lift the lid and check the temperature. When the bread reaches 206°F to 210°F (97°C to 99°C) on an instant-read thermometer inserted in the center, it is done. Remove the bread pan from the machine and set it on its side on a wire cooling rack. Leave the bread in the pan for a couple of minutes, then turn the pan upside down and slide the loaf onto the wire rack. Remove the paddle if it is embedded in the bottom of the loaf. Cool the loaf upside down for at least 2 hours before slicing.

7. Store the bread in a resealable plastic bag or airtight container on the counter for up to 3 days. For longer storage, cut into even slices, double-wrap tightly, place in a resealable plastic bag, and freeze for up to 3 months.

SOURDOUGH SANDWICH BREAD

MAKES 1 (1½-POUND/680 G) LOAF

This bread has just a hint of sourdough, perfect for those who are not enamored with traditional San Francisco sourdough bread.

DRY INGREDIENTS

21 g (0.7 oz or 2 tablespoons) active dry yeast

240 g (8.5 oz or 2 cups) Light Flour Blend (page 34)

½ cup milk powder (44 g/1.6 oz) or buttermilk powder (58 g/2 oz) (see opposite)

39 g (1.4 oz or 3 tablespoons) granulated cane sugar

1 tablespoon baking powder

2 teaspoons kosher or fine sea salt

1 teaspoon xanthan gum

WET INGREDIENTS

240 ml (1 cup) sourdough starter, at room temperature

56 g (2 oz or 4 tablespoons/½ stick) unsalted butter, melted and slightly cooled

3 large eggs, at room temperature (see page 39), beaten

60 ml (¼ cup) water, warmed to 80°F (27°C)

Sourdough starter must be at room temperature before using. If your starter has been refrigerated, pull out 1 cup (240 ml) and set it on the counter for about 2 hours to warm up to room temperature. You do not have to have recently fed the starter, but if you are taking out a cup, it's always a good idea to go ahead and feed the remaining starter (see directions on page 176).

> **NOTE:** If your sourdough starter is young and fairly mild, or if you like more assertive sourness in your bread, use the buttermilk powder. If your starter has a very strong sour aroma, you will get good results with either regular milk powder or buttermilk powder.

1. Set the bread pan on the counter and insert the beater paddle(s). Unless otherwise directed by your machine's manufacturer, add the liquids first, then the dry ingredients, and finally the yeast.

2. Measure the yeast into a small bowl and set aside. In a large mixing bowl, whisk the remaining dry ingredients together.

3. In a 4-cup (1 liter) glass measuring cup, whisk the wet ingredients together and pour into the bread pan. Use a spatula to spread the dry ingredients over the wet ingredients. Make a shallow well in the center and pour in the yeast.

4. Place the bread pan in the machine, settle it in the center, and lock it in place. Close the lid and select:

   Gluten-free cycle (see page 14 if your machine does not have this setting)
   Loaf size: 1½ pounds/750 g
   Medium crust
   Start

5. About 3 minutes after the machine has started mixing/kneading, open the lid and use a spatula to scrape the sides of the pan. Push any flour that has accumulated around the edges onto the dough. Check again once or twice during kneading, scraping any loose flour into the dough, avoiding the beater. The dough will look like a very sticky pancake batter with a slightly dull surface. If the dough looks too wet or too dry, add a little of the flour blend or tiny amounts of warm water. Once the mixing/kneading is done, leave the lid closed during the rise and bake cycles.

6. At the end of the bake cycle, lift the lid and check the temperature. When the bread reaches 206°F to 210°F (97°C to 99°C) on an instant-read thermometer inserted in the center, it is done. Remove the bread pan from the machine and set it on its side on a wire cooling rack. Leave the bread in the pan for a couple of minutes, then turn the pan upside down and slide the loaf onto the wire rack. Remove the paddle if it is embedded in the bottom of the loaf. Cool the loaf upside down for at least 2 hours before slicing.

7. Store the bread in a resealable plastic bag or airtight container on the counter for up to 3 days. For longer storage, cut into even slices, double-wrap tightly, place in a resealable plastic bag, and freeze for up to 3 months.

SOURDOUGH WALNUT BREAD

<u>MAKES 1 (1½-POUND/680 G) LOAF</u>

Bakers in the San Francisco Bay area use sourdough bread as a jumping-off point, adding many different ingredients for variety and interest, and so do we. The nuts add a pleasant, unexpected crunch and richness. Feel free to try adding other ingredients in place of the walnuts—fresh herbs, dried fruits, or other nuts and seeds are all fun choices to experiment with. Who knows, maybe you'll come up with the next new bread craze!

DRY INGREDIENTS

21 g (0.7 oz or 2 tablespoons) active dry yeast

240 g (8.5 oz or 2 cups) Light Flour Blend (page 34)

58 g (2 oz or ½ cup) buttermilk powder

39 g (1.4 oz or 3 tablespoons) granulated cane sugar

1 tablespoon baking powder

2 teaspoons kosher or fine sea salt

1 teaspoon xanthan gum

120 g (4.2 oz or 1 cup) finely chopped walnuts

WET INGREDIENTS

240 ml (1 cup) sourdough starter, at room temperature

56 g (2 oz or 4 tablespoons/½ stick) unsalted butter, melted and slightly cooled

3 large eggs, at room temperature (see page 39), beaten

60 ml (¼ cup) water, warmed to 80°F (27°C)

1 teaspoon apple cider vinegar

Sourdough starter must be at room temperature before using. If your starter has been refrigerated, pull out 1 cup (240 ml) and set it on the counter for about 2 hours to warm up to room temperature. You do not have to have recently fed the starter, but if you are taking out a cup, it's always a good idea to go ahead and feed the remaining starter (see directions on page 176).

1. Set the bread pan on the counter and insert the beater paddle(s). Unless otherwise directed by your machine's manufacturer, add the liquids first, then the dry ingredients, and finally the yeast.

2. Measure the yeast into a small bowl and set aside. In a large mixing bowl, whisk the remaining dry ingredients—*except* the walnuts—together. Stir in the walnuts. Set aside.

3. In a 4-cup (1 liter) glass measuring cup, whisk the wet ingredients together and pour into the bread pan. Use a spatula to spread the dry ingredients over the wet ingredients, covering completely. Make a shallow well in the center and pour in the yeast.

4. Place the bread pan in the machine, settle it in the center, and lock it in place. Close the lid and select:

   Gluten-free cycle (see page 14 if your machine does not have this setting)
   Loaf size: 1½ pounds/750 g
   Medium crust
   Start

5. About 3 minutes after the machine has started mixing/kneading, open the lid and use a spatula scrape the sides of the pan. Push any flour that has accumulated around the edges onto the dough. Check again once or twice during kneading, scraping any loose flour into the dough but avoiding the beater. The dough should look like a very sticky pancake batter with a slightly dull surface. If the dough looks too wet or too dry, add a little flour blend or tiny amounts of warm water. Once the mix/knead cycle is done, leave the lid closed during the rise and bake cycles.

6. At the end of the bake cycle, lift the lid and check the temperature. When the bread reaches 206°F to 210°F (97°C to 99°C) on an instant-read thermometer inserted in the center, it is done. Remove the bread pan from the machine and set it on its side on a wire cooling rack. Leave the bread in the pan for a couple of minutes, then turn the pan upside down and slide the loaf onto the wire rack. Remove the paddle if it is embedded in the bottom of the loaf. Cool the loaf upside down for at least 2 hours before slicing.

7. Store the bread in a resealable plastic bag or airtight container on the counter for up to 3 days. For longer storage, cut into even slices, double-wrap tightly, place in a resealable plastic bag, and freeze for up to 3 months.

SOURDOUGH ENGLISH MUFFIN BREAD

MAKES 1 (1½-POUND/680 G) LOAF ◆ DAIRY-FREE OPTION

This loaf has all the flavor and all the nooks and crannies we love, although when we use a knife to slice it, the bread isn't quite as craggy as a fork-split English muffin. It is chewy, a touch tangy, and a lovely way to start your day. It is especially good when lightly toasted and spread with jam—try our Tomato Jam (page 329) for an unusual and delicious treat.

DRY INGREDIENTS

2 teaspoons active dry yeast

180 g (6.3 oz or 1½ cups) Light Flour Blend (page 34) or Whole-Grain Flour Blend (page 34)

234 g (8.3 oz or 1½ cups) potato starch (*not* potato flour)

1 tablespoon kosher or fine sea salt

2 teaspoons psyllium husk flakes or powder

WET INGREDIENTS

1 teaspoon honey

180 to 240 ml (¾ to 1 cup) water, warmed to about 80°F (27°C)

240 ml (1 cup) sourdough starter, at room temperature

2 large eggs, at room temperature (see page 39), beaten

60 ml (¼ cup) olive or vegetable oil

1 teaspoon apple cider vinegar

TOPPING

1 to 2 teaspoons unsalted butter or nondairy butter substitute, melted

Fine-ground cornmeal

Sourdough starter must be at room temperature before using. If your starter has been refrigerated, pull out 1 cup (240 ml) and set it on the counter for about 2 hours to warm up to room temperature. You do not have to have recently fed the starter, but if you are taking out a cup, it's always a good idea to go ahead and feed the remaining starter (see directions on page 176).

1. Set the bread pan on the counter and insert the beater paddle(s). Unless otherwise directed by your machine's manufacturer, add the liquids first, then the dry ingredients, and finally the yeast.

2. Measure the yeast into a small bowl and set aside. In a large mixing bowl, whisk the remaining dry ingredients together.

3. In a 4-cup (1 liter) glass measuring cup, whisk the honey and 180 ml (¾ cup) water together to dissolve the honey. Add the remaining wet ingredients and whisk again. Pour into the bread pan. Use a spatula to spread the dry ingredients over the wet ingredients, covering completely. Make a shallow well in the center and pour in the yeast.

4. Place the bread pan in the machine, settle it in the center, and lock it in place. Close the lid and select:

   Gluten-free cycle (see page 14 if your machine does not have this setting)
   Loaf size: 1½ pounds/750 g
   Medium crust
   Start

5. About 3 minutes into the mixing process, open the lid and use a spatula to scrape down the sides of the pan, avoiding the paddle. Push any flour that has accumulated around the edges into the center. Check again once or twice during kneading, scraping the edges, corners, and under the dough. If the dough looks too wet (shiny surface) or too dry (not moving easily around the paddle), add a little flour blend or as much of the remaining 60 ml (¼ cup) warm water as needed. Once the mix/knead cycle is done, gently brush the top of the dough with melted butter and lightly sprinkle it with a little cornmeal. Close the lid and do not open it during the rise and bake cycles.

6. At the end of the bake cycle, lift the lid and check the temperature. When the bread reaches 206°F to 210°F (97°C to 99°C) on an instant-read thermometer inserted in the center, it is done. You may need to add baking time to get it to the right temperature (see page 41). Remove the pan from the machine and set it on its side on a wire cooling rack. If the bread sticks to the sides of the pan, use a long plastic spatula or spreader to release it. You may need to rap it on the counter to get it out of the pan and slide it onto the wire rack. Carefully remove the paddle if it is embedded in the bottom of the loaf. Let the bread cool upside down for at least 2 hours before slicing.

7. Store the bread in a resealable plastic bag or airtight container on the counter for 1 day, then refrigerate for another day or two. For longer storage, either leave the loaf whole or cut it into evenly thick slices, double-wrap tightly in plastic, place in a resealable plastic bag, and freeze for up to 3 months.

SOURDOUGH ENGLISH MUFFINS

MAKES 12 MUFFINS ◆ DAIRY-FREE OPTION

Line two baking sheets with parchment paper. Set 12 English muffin rings or 4-inch (10 cm) cake pans on the baking sheets. Coat them thoroughly with nonstick cooking spray or brush with oil and set aside.

Follow the bread recipe through step 3, adding 2 teaspoons baking soda to the dry ingredients. Place the bread pan in the machine, settle it in the center, and lock it in place. Close the lid and select:

Dough cycle
Loaf size: 1½ pounds/750 g
Start

While the machine is mixing and kneading the ingredients, open the lid and use a spatula to scrape down the sides of the pan, pushing any flour that has accumulated around the edges and under the dough into the center. Let the machine mix the dough until it is smooth and has no lumps, and all the dry ingredients have been incorporated, about 5 minutes.

When the dough is ready, press the stop button to cancel the cycle, turn off the machine, and remove the bread pan. Scoop the dough into each muffin ring, dividing as evenly as possible. Fill each muffin ring about halfway to two-thirds full. Using damp fingers, pat each one until flattened; they will not necessarily reach the edges of the rings. Let the muffins rest, uncovered, for 30 to 45 minutes. They will not double in size, but they will puff up and will continue to rise once in the oven.

While the dough is resting, preheat the oven to 350°F (180°C).

Bake until the bottoms are set and the muffins have pulled away from the sides of the rings, about 15 minutes. Remove from the oven and gently remove the rings. Brush the tops with melted butter to help them brown and sprinkle with a little cornmeal if you like. Return to the oven and continue baking until the muffins are golden brown on top and an instant-read thermometer inserted in the center (through the side) registers 210°F (99°C), 12 to 15 minutes. Remove any that reached the desired temperature and set them on a wire rack. If others need more baking, put them back in the oven, checking often until they are done.

Cool completely before cutting and/or freezing. To store any leftovers, wrap tightly in plastic wrap and store in an airtight container on the counter for a day or two or in the refrigerator for up to 4 days. Freeze for longer storage.

To get the best "nooks and crannies," use a fork to perforate a circle around the outside, about halfway up the side. Repeat poking with the fork until you can start to open the muffins, using the fork to split all the way to the center. Put the two halves in a toaster and toast lightly once. Lower the temperature slightly and toast for a second time until golden and crispy.

SOURDOUGH CIABATTA

MAKES 1 (2-POUND/910 G) LOAF

Ciabatta is a wonderful Italian bread traditionally shaped in a long oval that resembles a slipper. When you use a sourdough starter to make it, you add another dimension, depth, and richness to the flavor. This is a wonderful way to use the starter that you remove before feeding. There is no reason to throw it down the drain when you can be enjoying breads like this! Because this gluten-free dough is so soft, you will get the best results if you use a slender baking pan with sides. This contains the dough, and the sides support it as it rises. We found one called a "biscotti pan" (12 x 5½ x 2 inches/30 x 14 x 5 cm) from USA Pan that works like a champ (see Resources, page 376). This pan is extremely efficient at heat distribution, so keep an eye on the bread; if it is baking and browning too quickly, turn down the oven temperature by 25 degrees.

DRY INGREDIENTS

4 teaspoons active dry yeast

360 g (12.7 oz or 3 cups) Light Flour Blend (page 34) or Whole-Grain Flour Blend (page 34)

44 g (1.6 oz or ½ cup) milk powder

39 g (1.4 oz or 3 tablespoons) granulated cane sugar

2 teaspoons psyllium husk flakes or powder

2 teaspoons kosher or fine sea salt

WET INGREDIENTS

240 ml (1 cup) sourdough starter, at room temperature

3 large eggs, at room temperature (see page 39), beaten

90 ml (¼ cup plus 2 tablespoons) water, warmed to about 80°F (27°C)

45 ml (3 tablespoons) vegetable or olive oil

TOPPING

Vegetable oil

Coarse sea salt, optional

Sourdough starter must be at room temperature before using. If your starter has been refrigerated, pull out 1 cup (240 ml) and set it on the counter for about 2 hours to warm up to room temperature. You do not have to have recently fed the starter, but if you are taking out a cup, it's always a good idea to go ahead and feed the remaining starter (see directions on page 176).

1. Brush a long slender baking pan (see headnote) generously with vegetable oil. For extra insurance you can line the pan with parchment, leaving it extended over two sides to create "handles" that makes it very easy to remove the bread from the pan. Lightly oil the parchment.

2. Set the bread pan on the counter and insert the beater paddle(s). Unless otherwise directed by your machine's manufacturer, add the liquids first, then the dry ingredients, and finally the yeast.

3. Measure the yeast into a small bowl and set aside. In a large mixing bowl, whisk the remaining dry ingredients together.

4. In a 4-cup (1-liter) glass measuring cup, whisk the wet ingredients together and pour into the bread pan. Use a spatula to spread the dry ingredients over the wet ingredients, covering completely. Make a shallow well in the center and pour in the yeast.

5. Place the bread pan in the machine, settle it in the center, and lock it in place. Close the lid and select:

   Dough cycle
   Loaf size: 1½ pounds/750 g
   Start

6. While the machine is mixing and kneading the ingredients, open the lid and use a spatula to scrape down the sides of the pan, pushing any flour that has accumulated around the edges and under the dough into the center. If the dough looks really dry (sometimes this happens with a less hydrated starter), add 1 to 2 tablespoons water. Let the machine mix the dough until it is smooth and has no lumps, about 5 minutes.

7. When the dough is ready, press the stop button to cancel the cycle, turn off the machine, and remove the pan. Use a spatula to scoop the dough into the oiled baking pan. Smooth the dough with damp fingers and brush the top with a teaspoon of vegetable oil.

8. Let the dough rise, uncovered, to the top of the pan or just above it, 30 to 45 minutes.

9. While the dough is rising, preheat the oven to 350°F (180°C).

10. Sprinkle the top lightly with coarse salt if desired. Bake the bread until golden brown and the center registers 206°F to 210°F (97°C to 99°C) on an instant-read thermometer, 30 to 45 minutes. Remove from the oven and immediately flip the bread out of the pan. Cool right side up on a wire rack for 30 to 60 minutes before slicing. To store, wait until the bread is thoroughly cooled, then wrap tightly in plastic and store overnight on the counter or for up to 3 days in the refrigerator. Freeze for longer storage.

To Use for Sandwiches
When fully cooled, cut the loaf into three or four sections. Cut each section in half horizontally to create two slices to use for sandwiches.

To Use as Sliced Bread
Simply wait until the loaf is cool and cut into 1- to 2-inch-wide (3 to 5 cm) slices. Serve alongside your meal or with Italian Herb Dipping Sauce (see opposite) as an appetizer.

ITALIAN HERB DIPPING SAUCE

MAKES ABOUT 1 CUP (240 ML)

When you sit down at the table in an Italian restaurant in the United States, chances are you will be served a basket of breads and the waiter will pour olive oil and balsamic vinegar into a container for dipping. This is definitely an American invention and very popular. To take that dipping sauce up a level, we have added herbs and seasonings. Feel free to change the combination to suit your personal tastes.

Whisk 1 cup (240 ml) extra-virgin olive oil and 2 tablespoons balsamic vinegar with 1 teaspoon dried oregano, 1 teaspoon dried basil, ½ teaspoon garlic paste, ¼ teaspoon kosher salt, ⅛ teaspoon freshly ground black pepper, and a pinch of red pepper flakes. Set aside at room temperature for 1 hour so the flavors infuse.

Store leftovers, covered, in the refrigerator for up to 1 week. Bring to room temperature before serving.

SOURDOUGH FOCACCIA

MAKES 1 (1½-POUND/680 G) LOAF

Focaccia is an Italian bread that is similar in some ways to a bready pizza crust but baked in a shallow, flat pan. The surface is dimpled by your fingertips and—at its simplest—brushed with fresh olive oil and sprinkled with coarse salt. Other versions are studded with garlic or herbs, but the pure flavor of this loaf needs no enhancement. This focaccia has a definite tanginess coupled with wonderful chewiness that comes from the psyllium. It will rise to about 4 inches (10 cm) tall and turn golden brown, and all it needs is a slathering of homemade butter (page 69).

DRY INGREDIENTS

2 teaspoons active dry yeast

150 g (5.3 oz or 1¼ cups) Light Flour Blend (page 34) or Whole-Grain Flour Blend (page 34)

22 g (0.8 oz or ¼ cup) milk powder

1 tablespoon granulated cane sugar

2 teaspoons psyllium husk flakes or powder

1 teaspoon kosher or fine sea salt

⅛ teaspoon ascorbic acid, optional

WET INGREDIENTS

180 ml (¾ cup) sourdough starter, at room temperature

2 large eggs, at room temperature (see page 39), beaten

60 ml (¼ cup) water, warmed to about 80°F (27°C)

30 ml (2 tablespoons) vegetable or olive oil

2 teaspoons apple cider vinegar

TOPPING

Olive oil

Coarse sea salt

Sourdough starter must be at room temperature before using. If your starter has been refrigerated, pull out ¾ cup (180 ml) and set it on the counter for about 2 hours to warm up to room temperature. You do not have to have recently fed the starter, but if you are taking out a cup or two, it's always a good idea to go ahead and feed the remaining starter (see directions on page 176).

1. Line a baking sheet with parchment and brush the parchment generously with oil.

2. Set the bread pan on the counter and insert the beater paddle(s). Unless otherwise directed by your machine's manufacturer, add the liquids first, then the dry ingredients, and finally the yeast.

3. Measure the yeast into a small bowl and set aside. In a large mixing bowl, whisk the remaining dry ingredients together.

4. In a 2-cup (0.5 liter) glass measuring cup, whisk the wet ingredients together and pour into the bread pan. Use a spatula to spread the dry ingredients over the wet ingredients, covering completely. Make a shallow well in the center and pour in the yeast.

5. Place the bread pan in the machine, settle it in the center, and lock it in place. Close the lid and select:

Dough cycle
Loaf size: 1½ pounds/750 g
Start

6. While the machine is mixing and kneading the ingredients, open the lid and use the spatula to scrape down the sides of the pan, pushing any flour that has accumulated around the edges into the center. Let the machine mix the dough until it is smooth and has no lumps, about 5 minutes.

7. When the dough is ready, press the stop button to cancel the cycle, turn off the machine, and remove the pan. Scoop the dough out of the pan and onto the oiled baking sheet. Brush the top with a little more oil and use your hands to press the dough out into a rectangle about 12 x 8 inches (30 x 20 cm). Use your fingertips or knuckles to press dimples all over the surface of the dough. Brush a piece of plastic wrap with oil and place it, oiled side down, over the dough.

8. Set the pan aside to rest and let the dough rise for 1 hour. It will not double, but it will get puffy.

9. While the dough is rising, preheat the oven to 350°F (180°C).

10. Remove the plastic wrap and sprinkle the dough liberally with coarse salt. Bake until the focaccia is puffed and golden brown, 20 to 25 minutes.

11. Set the bread on a wire rack to cool for at least 30 minutes. Cut into squares or slender rectangles to serve.

12. To store, wrap either the uncut loaf or pieces tightly in plastic wrap and leave on the counter overnight, or in the refrigerator for up to 3 days. Freeze for longer storage.

SOURDOUGH FLATBREAD WITH FRESH TOMATOES AND ZA'ATAR

MAKES 4 MEDIUM FLATBREADS OR 8 INDIVIDUAL FLATBREADS   ◆   DAIRY-FREE OPTION

Sourdough starter gives our Basic Flatbread recipe (page 226) a nice zing. It's also a terrific way to utilize the starter you have to remove when you give your starter its weekly feeding. While you can top this bread with whatever you like, pick up a jar of za'atar if you've never tried it. It is a Middle Eastern spice mixture that can vary but is usually a blend of thyme, oregano, marjoram, toasted sesame seeds, ground sumac, and salt. This may become your favorite seasoning to sprinkle over vegetables and eggs or add to baked goods. These flatbreads are perfect for summertime lunches or an appetizer for dinner when the garden is overflowing with ripe tomatoes.

DRY INGREDIENTS

½ teaspoon active dry yeast

120 g (4.2 oz or 1 cup) Light Flour Blend (page 34) or Whole-Grain Flour Blend (page 34)

1 teaspoon granulated cane sugar

¾ teaspoon kosher or fine sea salt

½ teaspoon xanthan gum

WET INGREDIENTS

120 ml (½ cup) sourdough starter, at room temperature

60 to 120 ml (¼ to ½ cup) water, warmed to about 80°F (27°C)

1 large egg, at room temperature (see page 39), beaten

1 tablespoon olive or vegetable oil

TOPPING

120 ml (½ cup) olive oil

2 tablespoons za'atar

25 g (0.8 oz or ¼ cup) finely grated Parmesan cheese, optional

300 g (10.6 oz or 2 cups) cherry tomatoes, cut in half

70 g (2.5 oz or ½ cup) pine nuts

Kosher or fine sea salt

Sourdough starter must be at room temperature before using. If your starter has been refrigerated, pull out ½ cup (120 ml) and set it on the counter for about 2 hours to warm up to room temperature. You do not have to have recently fed the starter, but if you are taking out a cup or two, it's always a good idea to go ahead and feed the remaining starter (see directions on page 176).

1. Set the bread pan on the counter and insert the beater paddle(s). Unless otherwise directed by your machine's manufacturer, add the liquids first, then the dry ingredients, and finally the yeast.

2. Measure the yeast into a small bowl and set aside. In a large mixing bowl, whisk the remaining dry ingredients together.

3. In a 2-cup (0.5 liter) glass measuring cup, whisk the wet ingredients (start with 60 ml/¼ cup water) together. Pour into the bread pan. Use a spatula to spread the dry ingredients over the wet ingredients, covering completely. Make a shallow well in the center and pour in the yeast.

4. Place the bread pan in the machine, settle it in the center, and secure. Close the lid and select:

   Dough cycle
   Loaf size: 1 pound/500 g (if available)
   or 1½ pounds/750 g
   Start

5. While the machine is mixing and kneading, open the lid and use a spatula to scrape down the sides of the pan, pushing any flour that has accumulated around the edges and under the dough into the center. If needed, add enough of the remaining 60 ml (¼ cup) water, 1 tablespoon at a time, to make dough that resembles a thick batter. Let the machine mix the dough until it is smooth and has no lumps, about 5 minutes.

6. Meanwhile, oil a large bowl.

7. When the dough is ready, cancel the cycle, turn off the machine, and remove the bread pan. Use a spatula to transfer the dough to the oiled bowl. Brush a little more oil over the top and sides. Cover the bowl with a clean kitchen towel and set aside to rest and rise for 1 to 1½ hours. It won't double in size, but it will puff up.

8. While the dough is rising, preheat the oven to 500°F (250°C). Line two baking sheets with parchment and oil the parchment lightly.

9. For the topping, mix the olive oil, za'atar, and Parmesan cheese, if using, in a small bowl.

10. When the dough is done rising, stir it gently with a spoon to deflate it. Portion the dough, using ¼ cup dough for each medium flatbread or 2 tablespoons for each individual flatbread. Place the dough on the baking sheets, leaving plenty of room between them. Oil your hands and press each medium flatbread into a flat oval and each individual flatbread into a flat circle about ¼ inch (6 mm) thick. Forming the dough into ovals makes it easier to fit two on each baking sheet.

11. Bake until the flatbreads are golden brown and cooked through in the center, 8 to 10 minutes. Remove from the oven and cool on wire racks for 15 to 20 minutes.

12. While the flatbreads are cooling, divide the tomatoes and pine nuts evenly between the flatbreads, spreading them out on each one. Sprinkle with a little of the za'atar mixture and sprinkle lightly with a little salt if desired. Cut each bread into quarters and serve while warm.

SOURDOUGH "RYE" BREAD

MAKES 1 (1½-POUND/680 G) LOAF • DAIRY-FREE OPTION

The soft rye breads you find in New York City's Jewish delis have a little tang, but the sourdough here adds a touch of delightful sourness. Think of this bread when you're in the mood for a Reuben. But who's to say that it isn't the ideal bread for a roast beef sandwich with coleslaw and Russian dressing, too?

DRY INGREDIENTS

21 g (0.7 oz or 2 tablespoons) active dry yeast

120 g (4.2 oz or 1 cup) Light Flour Blend (page 34)

155 g (5.5 oz or 1 cup plus 2 tablespoons) buckwheat flour

¼ cup milk powder (22 g/0.8 oz) or DariFree (40 g/1.4 oz)

30 g (1.1 oz or 2 tablespoons firmly packed) brown sugar

2 tablespoons caraway seeds, optional

14 g (0.5 oz or 2 tablespoons) flaxseed meal or ground flaxseed (double this amount if not using caraway seeds)

3 teaspoons baking powder

2 teaspoons xanthan gum

2 teaspoons dried minced onions or shallots

1 teaspoon caraway powder

1 teaspoon kosher salt

½ teaspoon dried dill weed

WET INGREDIENTS

60 g (2 oz or 3 tablespoons) honey

135 ml (½ cup plus 1 tablespoon) water, heated to about 80°F (27°C)

240 ml (1 cup) sourdough starter, at room temperature

3 large eggs, at room temperature (see page 39), beaten

45 ml (3 tablespoons) olive oil

2 teaspoons apple cider vinegar

1 teaspoon finely grated orange zest, optional

Sourdough starter must be at room temperature before using. If your starter has been refrigerated, pull out 1 cup (240 ml) and set it on the counter for about 2 hours to warm up to room temperature. You do not have to have recently fed the starter, but if you are taking out a cup or two, it's always a good idea to go ahead and feed the remaining starter (see directions on page 176).

1. Set the bread pan on the counter and insert the beater paddle(s). Unless otherwise directed by your machine's manufacturer, add the liquids first, then the dry ingredients, and finally the yeast.

2. Measure the yeast into a small bowl and set aside. In a large mixing bowl, whisk the remaining dry ingredients together.

3. In a 4-cup (1 liter) glass measuring cup, whisk the honey and water together to dissolve the honey. Add the remaining wet ingredients and whisk again. Pour into the bread pan. Use a spatula to spread the dry ingredients over the wet ingredients, covering completely. Make a shallow well in the center and pour in the yeast.

4. Place the bread pan in the machine, settle it in the center, and lock it in place. Close the lid and select:

   Gluten-free cycle (see page 14 if your machine does not have this setting)
   Loaf size: 1½ pounds/750 g
   Medium crust
   Start

5. About 3 minutes into the mixing process, open the lid and use a spatula to scrape down the sides of the pan, avoiding the paddle. Push any flour that has accumulated around the edges into the center. Check again once or twice during kneading, scraping the edges, corners, and under the dough. If the dough looks too wet or too dry, add a little flour blend or tiny amounts of warm water. Once the mix/knead cycle is done, leave the lid closed during the rise and bake cycles.

6. At the end of the bake cycle, lift the lid and check the temperature. When the bread reaches 206°F to 210°F (97°C to 99°C) on an instant-read thermometer inserted in the center, it is done. Remove the pan from the machine and set it on its side on a wire cooling rack. Leave the bread in the pan for a couple of minutes, then turn the pan upside down and slide the loaf onto the wire rack. Carefully remove the paddle if it is embedded in the bottom of the loaf. Let the bread cool upside down for at least 2 hours before slicing.

7. Store the bread in a resealable plastic bag or airtight container on the counter for up to 3 days. For longer storage, cut into even slices, double-wrap tightly in plastic, place in a resealable plastic bag, and freeze for up to 3 months.

SOUR PUMPERNICKEL BREAD

MAKES 1 (1½-POUND/680 G) LOAF   ◆   DAIRY FREE

The addition of sourdough starter takes dark pumpernickel to a whole new level of deliciousness. If you have made a number of breads from this book already, you may be surprised that there is no vinegar in this recipe. Between the sourdough starter and cocoa powder, there is plenty of acid to make the yeast happy. Don't leave out the caraway powder—it gives this bread the flavor we associate with rye and pumpernickel without using rye flour.

DRY INGREDIENTS

21 g (0.7 oz or 2 tablespoons) active dry yeast

165 g (5.8 oz or 1¼ cups) Light Flour Blend (page 34)

95 g (3.4 oz or ¾ cup) buckwheat flour

30 g (1.1 oz or 2 tablespoons firmly packed) brown sugar

21 g (0.7 oz or 3 tablespoons) flaxseed meal or ground flaxseed

2 teaspoons unsweetened cocoa powder

2 teaspoons baking powder

2 teaspoons xanthan gum

1 teaspoon kosher or fine sea salt

1 teaspoon onion powder

½ teaspoon caraway powder

WET INGREDIENTS

120 ml (½ cup) water, heated to about 80°F (27°C)

60 g (2.1 oz or 3 tablespoons) molasses (*not* blackstrap)

240 ml (1 cup) sourdough starter, at room temperature

3 large eggs, at room temperature (see page 39), beaten

60 ml (¼ cup) olive oil

Sourdough starter must be at room temperature before using. If your starter has been refrigerated, pull out 1 cup (240 ml) and set it on the counter for about 2 hours to warm up to room temperature. You do not have to have recently fed the starter, but if you are taking out a cup or two, it's always a good idea to go ahead and feed the remaining starter (see directions on page 176).

1. Set the bread pan on the counter and insert the beater paddle(s). Unless otherwise directed by your machine's manufacturer, add the liquids first, then the dry ingredients, and finally the yeast.

2. Measure the yeast into a small bowl and set aside. In a large mixing bowl, whisk the remaining dry ingredients together.

3. In a 4-cup (1 liter) glass measuring cup, whisk the water and molasses together to dissolve the molasses. Add the remaining wet ingredients and whisk again. Pour into the bread pan. Use a spatula to spread the dry ingredients over the wet ingredients, covering completely. Make a shallow well in the center and pour in the yeast.

4. Place the bread pan in the machine, settle it in the center, and lock it in place. Close the lid and select:

   Gluten-free cycle (see page 14 if your machine does not have this setting)
   Loaf size: 1½ pounds/750 g
   Medium crust
   Start

5. About 3 minutes into the mixing process, open the lid and use a spatula to scrape down the sides of the pan, avoiding the paddle. Push any flour that has accumulated around the edges into the center. Check again once or twice during kneading, scraping the edges, corners, and under the dough. If the dough looks too wet or too dry, add a little flour blend or tiny amounts of warm water. Once the mix/knead cycle is done, leave the lid closed during the rise and bake cycles.

6. At the end of the bake cycle, lift the lid and check the temperature. When the bread reaches 206°F to 210°F (97°C to 99°C) on an instant-read thermometer inserted in the center, it is done. Remove the pan from the machine and set it on its side on a wire cooling rack. Leave the bread in the pan for a couple of minutes, then turn the pan upside down and slide the loaf onto the wire rack. Carefully remove the paddle if it is embedded in the bottom of the loaf. Let the bread cool upside down for at least 2 hours before slicing.

7. Store the bread in a resealable plastic bag or airtight container on the counter for up to 3 days. For longer storage, cut into even slices, double-wrap tightly in plastic, place in a resealable plastic bag, and freeze for up to 3 months.

Pizza, Focaccia, AND Flatbread

Flatbreads in all their incarnations have been a food staple for millennia. From grains beaten between rocks and cooked over fire to pita bread, focaccia, and pizza, our baking has stayed pretty close to the original. Flatbreads are more about texture and are less dependent on leavening than regular breads. They often serve as the foundation for other foods or are used for dipping into sauces.

Out of all the breads in this book, these doughs behave the most like wheat doughs. Softer and stickier, thanks to the help of psyllium, these doughs are much easier to form and the breads have a chewier texture. Don't be tempted to add liquid to make these doughs look like those in the rest in this book. This chapter's doughs are drier and will form a ball, cleaning the sides of the pan and needing help to stay on the beater blade and get fully kneaded.

Pizza is a world favorite and an American standard, and it's also one of the foods people miss the most when they discover they can no longer eat gluten. But now you can have it again! Most of our pizza doughs have extra

TIP: Kitchen scissors work as well as a pizza wheel or knife to cut pizza—and they're safer for children to use.

starch added to the dry ingredients to lighten them. In addition to helping the crusts rise more quickly and bake through completely, it reduces the gumminess often found in gluten-free breads. You can make the dough in advance—just place it in an oiled bowl and brush all the surfaces with more oil. Then cover the bowl with plastic wrap and refrigerate overnight. This slow rise will develop deeper flavor and give you more flexibility on busy days. Since these recipes are big enough for two crusts, you can make one pizza for dinner and refrigerate the second half of the dough for an easy meal the next day. Because the dough contains raw eggs, you don't want to let this dough sit any longer than that in the refrigerator.

Another Italian invention, focaccia is somewhere between a flatbread and a regular bread. The slightly dense crumb bakes up to be about 2 inches (5 cm) thick, and is often topped with tantalizing goodies. Focaccia is sturdy enough to transport, making it a great contribution to potlucks and other social events. It is a wonderful feeling to be able to bring food to an event knowing that it is safe for those with celiac disease and gluten intolerance to enjoy.

We are delighted to bring you the ability to not only enjoy pizza and other breads again, but also to make them the way you love them, using the best ingredients and serving foods that put a smile on everyone's face.

POKE SOME HOLES

If you make pizza and pastry doughs regularly, a docker can save you time and effort. This tool made specifically for working with dough looks like a small paint roller with spikes that poke holes in the dough to prevent big bubbles from forming. It helps keep the center of the pizza flatter, giving you a crispier crust. You can do the same thing with a fork, but using the docker is quicker—and your kids will think it's a lot of fun.

CLASSIC PIZZA

MAKES 1 (10 X 12-INCH/25 X 30 CM) OR 2 (9-INCH/23 CM) ROUND PIZZA CRUSTS

Pizza is an American standard, great for a quick dinner, lunch at the office, late evening snack, or even breakfast—especially when cooked with an egg on top. It is a go-to option for many families on busy weeknights. Top it with your favorites and you will have a custom pizza that will earn you a round of applause from a table of happy campers. Adding oregano to the dough bumps up the flavor and makes your kitchen smell like a pizzeria.

DRY INGREDIENTS

21 g (0.7 oz or 2 tablespoons) active dry yeast

300 g (10.6 oz or 2½ cups) Light Flour Blend (page 34) or Whole-Grain Flour Blend (page 34)

64 g (2.3 oz or ½ cup) cornstarch, potato starch (*not* potato flour), or arrowroot

1 tablespoon dried oregano

2½ teaspoons psyllium husk flakes or powder

2 teaspoons kosher or fine sea salt

1½ teaspoons granulated cane sugar

⅛ teaspoon ascorbic acid, optional

Finely ground cornmeal, for the bottom of the dough (substitute coarsely ground oats or finely ground nuts if you cannot have corn)

WET INGREDIENTS

240 ml (1 cup) water, warmed to about 80°F (27°C)

3 large egg whites, at room temperature

2 teaspoons apple cider vinegar

TOPPINGS (OPTIONAL)

Pizza Sauce (page 203) or pesto

Shredded mozzarella and/or grated Parmesan cheese

Chopped and blanched vegetables such as bell peppers, onions, broccoli, and zucchini

Fresh ingredients such as arugula, mushrooms, sliced olives, sliced tomatoes, pineapple, and basil leaves

Sliced cured meats such as pepperoni, salami, prosciutto, ham, or sautéed sausage chunks

Red pepper flakes

1. Set the bread pan on the counter and insert the beater paddle(s). Unless otherwise directed by your machine's manufacturer, add the liquids first, then the dry ingredients, and finally the yeast.

2. Measure the yeast into a small bowl and set aside. Whisk the remaining dry ingredients—*except* the cornmeal—together in a large bowl. Set aside.

3. In a 2-cup (0.5 liter) glass measuring cup, whisk the wet ingredients together and pour into the bread pan. Use a spatula to spread the dry ingredients over the wet ingredients. Make a shallow well in the center of the flour blend and pour in the yeast.

4. Place the bread pan in the machine, settle it in the center, and lock it in place. Close the lid and select:
Dough cycle
Loaf size: 1½ pounds/750 g
Start

MAKE AHEAD

You can make the dough a day ahead. Mix it in the machine and transfer to an oiled bowl. Brush the top with a little more oil, making sure that all surfaces are coated. Cover the bowl with plastic wrap and refrigerate. When you are ready to make your pizzas, bring the dough to room temperature. Form, let rise, and bake as directed. You may need to increase the rise time by about 20 minutes.

5. Let the machine mix and knead until all the dry ingredients have been incorporated. Use a spatula to move any flour caught in the corners or under the dough to the center so the paddle can mix it in. Because this is such a heavy dough, it will move to the edges and stay there without being properly beaten. You have to keep pushing the dough onto the beater paddle. Once the dough is smooth and has no lumps, hit stop to cancel the cycle and turn off the machine. Remove the pan from the machine.

6. Shape the dough.

To make 1 rectangular pizza

a. Line a baking sheet with parchment and lightly oil it.

b. Scoop out the dough with a rubber spatula and place it on the baking sheet. Use your lightly oiled or damp hands to press into a 10 x 12-inch (25 x 30 cm) rectangle.

c. With one hand supporting the outside of the dough and the other on the inside about 1 inch (2.5 cm) from the edge, push the dough outward around the edges to create a lip. This will help contain the toppings and give you a chewy crust. Your outside hand will help keep it from expanding too much. Don't make the center too thin or it will be more like a cracker crust.

To make 2 round pizzas

a. Line two baking sheets with parchment and lightly oil them.

b. Use an oiled bench scraper or knife to divide the dough into two equal pieces. Transfer one piece to each of the baking sheets.

c. Press the dough into a 9-inch (23 cm) circle, working from the center out. Sprinkle the top with cornmeal.

d. Set a nonstick or oiled pizza pan upside down over the dough, and with one hand under the parchment and the other on top of the pan, flip them both together, inverting the dough onto the pan. Carefully remove the parchment from the dough.

e. With one hand supporting the outside of the dough and the other on the inside about 1 inch (2.5 cm) from the edge, push the dough outward around the edge to create a lip to help contain the toppings—your outside hand will help keep it from expanding too much.

f. Repeat with the other piece of dough.

7. Use the tines of a fork or a docker (see Resources, page 376) to poke holes all over the center of the crust (not the thicker edge) to help prevent bubbles. Set aside, uncovered, to rise for about 20 minutes.

8. While the dough is resting, place a rack in the upper third of the oven and preheat to 350°F (180°C).

9. Poke the center of the dough again in multiple places. Bake until brown on top, about 30 minutes. The crust should sound hollow when tapped on the edge.

10. Once ready, remove the crust from the oven. Brush a light coating of pizza sauce over the center of the dough, spreading it to the raised edge. Sprinkle with grated cheese and finish with any toppings you desire. The pizza will not be in the oven long, so make sure all your toppings are already cooked.

11. Bake until the crust is deep golden brown and sounds hollow when you tap it, about another 25 minutes. If the cheese is not fully melted, put the pizza under the broiler for a few minutes. Watch carefully so it does not burn.

12. Transfer the pizza to a wire rack to cool for 10 minutes (this allows the steam to escape, keeping the crust crispy). Slide onto a cutting board, cut into wedges, and serve.

PIZZA SAUCE

MAKES ENOUGH SAUCE FOR
2 TO 4 PIZZAS, DEPENDING ON SIZE

Pour 28 ounces (794 g) canned San Marzano tomatoes into a bowl and crush with your hands or a spoon. (Alternatively, you can use chopped ripe plum tomatoes.) Heat 1 tablespoon (15 ml) olive oil in a large saucepan over medium-high heat. Add 1 chopped onion and sauté until translucent, about 3 minutes. Add 1 minced garlic clove and sauté until fragrant, about 30 seconds. Add the tomatoes and their juices, 1 teaspoon dried basil, 1 teaspoon dried oregano, 1 teaspoon kosher salt, and freshly ground black pepper to taste. Cook, stirring often, until the sauce is reduced and thickened, about 15 minutes.

Transfer to a food processor or use an immersion blender to puree the sauce. (Skip this step if you prefer a chunkier sauce.) Taste and adjust the seasonings. Store in an airtight container in the refrigerator for up to 1 week or freeze for up to 3 months.

This recipe can be doubled or tripled, but do not increase the salt incrementally. Start with 1½ teaspoons and then add to taste.

This pizza sauce works equally well tossed with hot pasta—make a double batch and have a second dinner ready to go.

TIPS FOR MAKING THE BEST GLUTEN-FREE PIZZA

- Prebaking the crust gives it some structure and helps ensure the center is fully cooked at the same time the toppings are ready.

- Using a thoroughly cooked tomato sauce, with most of the excess liquid cooked off, will result in a crisper crust.

- For the most flavorful, crispy crust, don't add too many toppings.

- Use dry cheeses like shredded mozzarella, provolone, Parmesan, Grana Padano, or pecorino instead of wetter ones such as fresh mozzarella or ricotta.

- Most vegetables need to be cooked to remove excess liquid before using as a pizza topping.

- You can also add raw vegetables to the pizza, such as sliced tomatoes, after it's baked and then sprinkle on a little Parmesan for flavor.

CHEESY HERBED PIZZA

MAKES 2 (10- TO 12-INCH/25 TO 30 CM) PIZZAS

Sometimes we just "need" a little cheese, especially when it complements the other ingredients in a dish. Mixing cheddar cheese powder, Parmesan, and herbs into this pizza dough adds a wonderful richness and boosts the flavor quotient, making the crust just as tantalizing as the toppings!

DRY INGREDIENTS

1 tablespoon active dry yeast

360 g (12.7 oz or 3 cups) Light Flour Blend (page 34) or Whole-Grain Flour Blend (page 34)

64 g (2.3 oz or ½ cup) cornstarch, potato starch (*not* potato flour), or arrowroot

22 g (0.8 oz or ¼ cup) milk powder

21 g (0.7 oz or ¼ cup) cheddar cheese powder (see Resources, page 376)

25 g (0.8 oz or ¼ cup) lightly packed finely grated Parmesan cheese

1 tablespoon psyllium husk flakes or powder

2 teaspoons granulated cane sugar

2 teaspoons baking powder

1½ teaspoons kosher or fine sea salt

½ teaspoon dried oregano

½ teaspoon onion powder

½ teaspoon garlic powder

⅛ teaspoon ascorbic acid, optional

WET INGREDIENTS

360 ml (1½ cups) water, warmed to about 80°F (27°C)

1 teaspoon apple cider vinegar

TOPPING

Any of your favorites, such as Pizza Sauce (page 203), pesto, shredded cheese, chopped vegetables, fresh herbs, and thinly sliced meats

Chopped fresh basil, optional

> NOTE: Cheddar cheese powder tends to clump in the jar. Be sure to whisk it first for the most accurate measuring.

1. Set the bread pan on the counter and insert the beater paddle(s). Unless otherwise directed by your machine's manufacturer, add the liquids first, then the dry ingredients, and finally the yeast.

2. Line two baking sheets lined with parchment paper and lightly oil them. Set oven racks in the upper and lower thirds of the oven and preheat to 400°F (200°C).

3. Measure the yeast into a small bowl and set aside. In a large mixing bowl, whisk the remaining dry ingredients together.

4. In a 2-cup (0.5 liter) glass measuring cup, whisk the wet ingredients together and pour into the bread pan. Use a spatula to spread the dry ingredients over the wet ingredients. Make a shallow well in the center and pour in the yeast.

5. Place the bread pan in the machine, settle it in the center, and lock it in place. Close the lid and select:

Dough cycle
Loaf size: 1½ pounds/750 g
Start

6. While the machine is mixing and kneading the ingredients, occasionally open the lid and use a spatula to scrape down the sides of the pan, pushing any flour that has accumulated around the edges and under the dough into the center. Let the machine mix the dough until it is smooth and has no lumps, about 5 minutes. Press the stop button to cancel the cycle, turn off the machine, and remove the bread pan.

7. Use a spatula to scoop the dough out of the bread pan and onto one of the baking sheets. Press it into a flattened disk and divide into two equal pieces. Move half to the second baking sheet.

8. Lightly oil your hands and press each piece of dough into a 10- to 12-inch (25 to 30 cm) rectangle (the thinner you make it, the crispier the crust). Use your fingers to press a shallow "moat" about ½ inch (1 cm) from the edge, which will help hold the toppings on the baked pizza and make the edge just a little thicker than the middle. Use the tines of a fork or a docker (see Resources, page 376) to poke holes all over the center of the crust (not the thicker edge). Set the crusts aside to rest, uncovered, until they have risen slightly, 30 to 45 minutes. They will not rise dramatically but will puff up.

9. Bake until the center of each crust is fully cooked, 15 to 20 minutes, rotating the pans and swapping racks halfway through and docking the center again to pop any bubbles that have formed and flatten the dough. Remove the pans from the oven and reduce the heat to 350°F (180°C). Add whatever toppings you like, using only a little of each one so they won't weigh down the dough or make it soggy.

10. Return the pizzas to the oven and bake until the crust is golden brown on the top and bottom, the toppings are hot and bubbly, and any added cheese is melted, 15 to 20 minutes.

11. Use the parchment to transfer the pizzas to wire cooling racks, then slip the parchment out to allow the steam to escape. Sprinkle a little chopped fresh basil over the top if desired. Let the pizzas rest for at least 5 minutes before cutting and serving.

PRETZEL PIZZA

MAKES 3 (8-INCH/20 CM) INDIVIDUAL PIZZAS OR 1 (12- TO 14-INCH/30 TO 36 CM) PIZZA

This crust is a beautiful cross between a regular pizza crust and a soft pretzel. It has the chewiness and rich brown color of pretzels, plus a sprinkling of coarse salt on the edges. Beware, one bite and you may never be satisfied with any other style of pizza crust!

DRY INGREDIENTS

1 tablespoon active dry yeast

360 g (12.7 oz or 3 cups) Light Flour Blend (page 34) or Whole-Grain Flour Blend (page 34)

64 g (2.3 oz or ½ cup) cornstarch, potato starch (*not* potato flour), or arrowroot

2 teaspoons psyllium husk flakes or powder

2 teaspoons kosher or fine sea salt

½ teaspoon baking powder

⅛ teaspoon ascorbic acid, optional

WET INGREDIENTS

320 to 360 ml (1⅓ to 1½ cups) water, warmed to about 80°F (27°C)

2 teaspoons apple cider vinegar

1 teaspoon honey

BAKING SODA WASH

60 ml (¼ cup) water

¼ teaspoon baking soda

TOPPING

Melted butter or olive oil, for brushing

Pretzel salt

Any of your favorite additions, such as Pizza Sauce (page 203), pesto, shredded cheese, chopped vegetables, fresh herbs, and thinly sliced meats

1. Set the bread pan on the counter and insert the beater paddle(s). Unless otherwise directed by your machine's manufacturer, add the liquids first, then the dry ingredients, and finally the yeast.

2. Line a baking sheet with parchment and brush lightly with vegetable oil.

3. Measure the yeast into a small bowl and set aside. In a large mixing bowl, whisk the remaining dry ingredients together.

4. In a 2-cup (0.5 liter) glass measuring cup, whisk the wet ingredients (start with 320 ml/ 1⅓ cups water) together and pour into the bread pan. Use a spatula to spread the dry ingredients on top. Make a shallow well in the center and pour in the yeast.

5. Place the bread pan in the machine, settle it in the center, and lock it in place. Close the lid and select:

   Dough cycle
   Loaf size: 1½ pounds/750 g
   Start

6. While the machine is mixing and kneading the ingredients, open the lid and use a spatula to scrape down the sides of the pan, pushing any flour that has accumulated around the edges and under the dough into the center. If there is a lot of extra flour and the dough is not gathering into a ball, add the remaining water, 1 tablespoon at a time, until it comes together. Let the machine mix the dough until it is smooth and has no lumps, about 3 minutes, pushing the dough onto the beater blade as it tends to move to the edges of the pan. This dough will be very soft and slightly sticky. Press the stop button to cancel the cycle, turn off the machine, and remove the bread pan.

7. Use a spatula to scoop the dough out of the pan and onto the baking sheet. Brush the top with more oil and press into a flattened disk.

8. Preheat the oven to 400°F (200°C).

9. For individual pizzas, divide the dough into thirds. Set one of the balls of dough on one end of a baking sheet. Oil your hands and use your palms to press the dough into an 8-inch (20 cm) circle. Use your fingers to press a shallow "moat" about ½ inch (1 cm) from the edge, which will help hold the toppings on the baked pizza and make the edge just a little thicker than the middle. Smooth the center as much as possible. Add a little more oil if your hands are sticking. Repeat with the remaining dough. For a large pizza, shape the dough in the same way, pressing it into a 12- to 14-inch (30 to 36 cm) circle. Use the tines of a fork or a docker (see Resources, page 376) to poke holes all over the center of the crust (not the thicker edge). Set aside to rise, uncovered, for 30 to 45 minutes.

10. Whisk the baking soda and water together in a small bowl until completely dissolved. Lightly brush the top and edges of each crust.

11. Bake individual crusts for 10 minutes or one large crust for 12 minutes. Remove from the oven, dock the center again if needed, brush the rims with melted butter, and sprinkle liberally with pretzel salt. Add your desired toppings to the center. Bake until the crust is browned on the top and bottom, the toppings are hot and bubbly, and any added cheese has melted, 10 to 15 minutes. Transfer to a wire rack, slipping the parchment out from under the crust, and cool for about 10 minutes before slicing and serving.

THIN-CRUST PIZZA

MAKES 4 (10-INCH/25 CM) PIZZAS OR 2 (14-INCH/36 CM) PIZZAS

Some people like a thick, chewy, bready pizza crust. Others prefer a thin, almost cracker-like crust. We aim to please, so here is one that is crispier. The larger you make the crusts, the thinner and crispier they will be. Partially baking the crust helps give it structure and starts the cooking process so it gets fully cooked.

DRY INGREDIENTS

1 tablespoon active dry yeast

270 g (9.5 oz or 2¼ cups) Light Flour Blend (page 34) or Whole-Grain Flour Blend (page 34)

96 g (3.4 oz or ¾ cup) cornstarch, potato starch (*not* potato flour), or arrowroot

1 tablespoon psyllium husk flakes or powder

2 teaspoons kosher or fine sea salt

½ teaspoon baking powder

⅛ teaspoon ascorbic acid, optional

WET INGREDIENTS

375 ml (1½ cups plus 1 tablespoon) water, warmed to about 80°F (27°C)

2 teaspoons apple cider vinegar

1 teaspoon honey

TOPPING

Any of your favorites, such as Pizza Sauce (page 203), pesto, shredded cheese, chopped vegetables, fresh herbs, and thinly sliced meats

1. Set the bread pan on the counter and insert the beater paddle(s). Unless otherwise directed by your machine's manufacturer, add the liquids first, then the dry ingredients, and finally the yeast.

2. Line one or two baking sheets with parchment and brush lightly with vegetable oil.

3. Measure the yeast into a small bowl and set aside. In a large mixing bowl, whisk the remaining dry ingredients together.

4. In a 2-cup (0.5 liter) glass measuring cup, whisk the wet ingredients together and pour into the bread pan. Use a spatula to spread the dry ingredients over the wet ingredients. Make a shallow well in the center and pour in the yeast.

5. Place the bread pan in the machine and lock it in place. Close the lid and select:
   Dough cycle
   Loaf size: 1½ pounds/750 g
   Start

6. While the machine is mixing and kneading the ingredients, open the lid and use a spatula to scrape down the sides of the pan, pushing any flour that has accumulated around the edges and under the dough into the center. This dough looks and behaves more like regular wheat doughs so stay by the machine and keep pushing the dough back onto the beater blade. Let the machine mix the dough until it is smooth and has no lumps, about 3 minutes. This dough will be very soft and slightly sticky. Press the stop button to cancel the cycle, turn off the machine, and remove the bread pan.

7. Use a spatula to scoop the dough out of the bread pan and onto an oiled baking sheet. Lightly brush the top of the dough with a little oil and press out into a flattened disk.

8. Preheat the oven to 400°F (200°C).

9. For smaller pizzas, divide the dough in quarters. Set two balls of dough on one of the baking sheets. Oil your hands and press the dough gently into two 10-inch (25 cm) circles. Use your fingers to press a shallow "moat" about ½ inch (1 cm) from the edge, which will help hold the toppings on the baked pizza and make the edge just a little thicker than the middle. Smooth the center as much as possible using light strokes and gentle pressure. Repeat with the remaining dough. For a large pizza, shape the dough in the same way, pressing it into a 14-inch (36 cm) circle or rectangle.

10. Poke holes in the center of the crust with the tines of a fork or a docker (see Resources, page 376) to keep it from forming bubbles. Set aside to rise, uncovered, for 30 minutes.

11. Bake small crusts for 12 minutes, a single large crust for about 20 minutes. Remove from the oven and spread a light coating of sauce (if using) in the center section. Scatter your desired toppings over the sauce. Return to the oven and continue baking until the crust is crispy and golden brown and sounds hollow when you tap on it, 25 to 30 minutes. The browner the crust, the crispier it will be. If you used a lot of sauce or wet toppings, make sure you cook it thoroughly.

12. Slide onto a wire cooling rack, slip the parchment out from underneath to help steam escape, and let rest for about 5 minutes. Transfer to a work surface, cut into wedges, and serve.

CRISPY CRUSTS

You can bake these thin-crust pizzas right on your baking sheet and get very good results. But if you want them really crisp, look into getting a pizza stone (or splurging on a baking steel—see Resources, page 376). Because gluten-free doughs are so sticky, form them on the parchment and slip the parchment and crust straight onto the preheated stone or steel. Both surfaces require a long preheating to get to maximum temperature and give you great results, but the baking steel will never break and has much greater thermal conductivity. If you are using a pizza stone or baking steel, your bake times will likely be shorter.

BREAKFAST PIZZA

SERVES 2 TO 4

Pizza is for dinner, right? Not anymore. Once you make this fun breakfast version, you'll want it for any meal—especially Sunday brunch! It is light but bursting with rich flavors. Who wouldn't love melted cheese, prosciutto, and eggs? And the best part: you can make the crust the night before and finish the pizzas quickly in the morning, so breakfast will be on the table in no time.

1 recipe Classic Pizza crust (page 200, see Make Ahead instructions)

230 g (8.1 oz or 2 cups) shredded mozzarella

150 g (5.3 oz or 1 cup) finely chopped prosciutto

4 large eggs

Kosher or fine sea salt

Freshly ground black pepper

Freshly grated Parmesan cheese

Finely chopped fresh parsley or basil

1. Preheat the oven to 400°F (200°C). Line two baking sheets with parchment paper and lightly oil them.

2. Divide the dough into two equal pieces and press each one into a 9-inch (23 cm) circle on the baking sheets.

3. Bake the crusts for the first cooking as directed, adding an extra 15 minutes bake time, rotating them halfway through. Remove from the oven and spread a layer of mozzarella over the top of each crust, leaving a ½-inch (1 cm) border at the edges. Sprinkle the prosciutto around the outside of the crust, leaving the center open. Crack two eggs next to each other in the center of each pizza. Season the eggs with salt and pepper and a light sprinkling of Parmesan.

4. Bake until the cheese is melted, the egg whites are firm, and the yolks are done to your liking, 5 to 8 minutes. Place on a wire rack to cool for 3 minutes. Sprinkle the pizzas with a little more Parmesan and some parsley or basil. Transfer to a cutting board and cut the pizzas in half (between the eggs, not breaking the yolks). You can serve two people (a whole pizza per person) or four people (a half pizza). Serve hot.

CHEWY FOCACCIA

MAKES 1 (8 X 12-INCH/20 X 30 CM) FOCACCIA • DAIRY-FREE OPTION

Focaccia, a member of the flatbread family, is a staple at many meals served in Italy. It can be seasoned and topped with any combination of cheeses, herbs, and vegetables, which makes it a great way to use up small amounts of ingredients that wouldn't be enough for a regular recipe. This is one of the easiest breads to make because it doesn't need any special forming—just shape it loosely with your hands into a long oval on a baking sheet. Even beginners will find this dough easy to work with and will be proud of their baking efforts. This bread is so delicious that it doesn't need anything added, but try it with the Fresh Basil Oil (see opposite). A drizzle over the slices just before serving adds a beautiful bright green accent, and the intense aromas and flavors of the fresh basil make each bite a revelation.

DRY INGREDIENTS

2 teaspoons active dry yeast

240 g (8.5 oz or 2 cups) Light Flour Blend (page 34) or Whole-Grain Flour Blend (page 34)

¼ cup milk powder (22 g/0.8 oz) or DariFree (40 g/1.4 oz)

1 tablespoon granulated cane sugar

2 teaspoons psyllium husk flakes or powder

1 teaspoon baking powder

1 teaspoon kosher or fine sea salt

⅛ teaspoon ascorbic acid, optional

WET INGREDIENTS

2 large eggs, at room temperature (see page 39), beaten

120 ml (½ cup) water, warmed to about 80°F (27°C)

30 ml (2 tablespoons) vegetable or olive oil

2 teaspoons apple cider vinegar

TOPPING

Olive oil, for brushing

Coarse sea salt

1. Set the bread pan on the counter and insert the beater paddle(s). Unless otherwise directed by your machine's manufacturer, add the liquids first, then the dry ingredients, and finally the yeast.

2. Line a baking sheet with parchment and brush it lightly with oil.

3. Measure the yeast into a small bowl and set aside. In a large mixing bowl, whisk the remaining dry ingredients together.

4. In a 2-cup (0.5 liter) glass measuring cup, whisk the wet ingredients together and pour into the bread pan. Use a spatula to spread the dry ingredients over the wet ingredients. Make a shallow well in the center and pour in the yeast.

5. Place the bread pan in the machine and lock it in place. Close the lid and select:

Dough cycle
Loaf size: 1½ pounds/750 g
Start

6. While the machine is mixing and kneading the ingredients, open the lid and use a spatula to scrape down the sides of the pan, pushing any flour that has accumulated around the edges and under the dough into the center. Repeat scraping down the pan several times during mixing. Let the machine mix the dough until it is smooth and has no lumps, about 5 minutes. Press the stop button to cancel the cycle, turn off the machine, and remove the pan.

7. Scoop the dough out of the bread pan and onto the baking sheet. Brush the top lightly with olive oil and use your hands to press the dough out into an 8 x 12-inch (20 x 30 cm) rectangle. Use your fingertips to press dimples all over the surface of the dough. Sprinkle it liberally with coarse salt. Set the pan aside and let the dough rise, uncovered, until puffy, about 30 minutes. If you want a higher loaf, cover the pan with an oiled piece of plastic wrap and let it rise for up to an hour.

8. While the dough is rising, preheat the oven to 350°F (180°C).

9. Bake until puffed and golden brown, 20 to 25 minutes, rotating the pan halfway through.

10. Remove the baking sheet from the oven and use the parchment to help slide the focaccia onto a wire cooling rack. Remove the parchment to let the steam escape and keep the crust crispy. Set aside to cool for at least 30 minutes. Cut into squares or slender rectangles to serve.

11. Tightly wrap any leftovers in plastic wrap and store in the refrigerator for a day or two.

FRESH BASIL OIL

MAKES ABOUT 1½ CUPS (360 ML)

Drizzle this oil over sliced bread and focaccia or put it out as a dipping oil. Add it to fresh tomato salads, soups, marinades—or even over vanilla ice cream for an unusual dessert. Even though it has a lot more parsley than basil, parsley is fairly neutral flavored, so basil is the dominant flavor.

Place 1½ cups firmly packed (100 g) Italian parsley leaves and ½ cup firmly packed (40 g) basil leaves into a blender and pour in 1 cup (240 ml) neutral-flavored oil (such as canola, safflower, or light olive oil). Pulse until coarse. Slowly pour in another ½ cup (60 ml) oil and puree until smooth.

Pour the oil through a fine-mesh strainer into a bowl. Press on the solids with the back of a ladle or spoon to extract as much of the oil as possible. You can use the remaining solids in other recipes such as salsas, sauces, or compound butters, or toss it with roasted potatoes.

Transfer the strained oil to a jar with a tight-fitting lid. Store in the refrigerator for up to 2 weeks.

PIZZA FOCACCIA

MAKES 1 (8 X 12-INCH/20 X 30 CM) FOCACCIA

Inspiration for this bread comes from the San Francisco bakery Liguria, which is legendary for tomato focaccia. Our version—with tomato and cheese powders flavoring the bread and a simple tomato sauce and basil—is just like a loaf of pizza! This may remind you of frozen French bread pizzas, but it's so much better. It's the perfect treat for a picnic in the park. All you need to add is a bottle of wine and some friends to share it with.

DRY INGREDIENTS

2 teaspoons active dry yeast

240 g (8.5 oz or 2 cups) Light Flour Blend (page 34) or Whole-Grain Flour Blend (page 34)

¼ cup milk powder (22 g/0.8 oz) or DariFree (40 g/1.4 oz)

4 teaspoons cheddar cheese powder (see Resources, page 376)

1 tablespoon granulated cane sugar

2 teaspoons psyllium husk flakes or powder

2 teaspoons baking powder

2 teaspoons dried oregano

2 teaspoons onion powder

1½ teaspoons tomato powder (see Resources, page 376)

1 teaspoon kosher or fine sea salt

⅛ teaspoon ascorbic acid, optional

WET INGREDIENTS

80 ml (⅓ cup) water, warmed to about 80°F (27°C)

2 large eggs, at room temperature (see page 39), beaten

30 ml (2 tablespoons) vegetable or olive oil

2 teaspoons apple cider vinegar

TOPPING

Olive oil, for brushing

60 ml (¼ cup) Pizza Sauce (page 203)

2 tablespoons minced fresh basil

1. Set the bread pan on the counter and insert the beater paddle(s). Unless otherwise directed by your machine's manufacturer, add the liquids first, then the dry ingredients, and finally the yeast.

2. Line a baking sheet with parchment and brush it with oil.

3. Measure the yeast into a small bowl and set aside. In a large mixing bowl, whisk the remaining dry ingredients together.

4. In a 2-cup (0.5 liter) glass measuring cup, whisk the wet ingredients together and pour into the bread pan. Use a spatula to spread the dry ingredients over the wet ingredients. Make a shallow well in the center and pour in the yeast.

5. Place the bread pan in the machine, settle it in the center, and lock it in place. Close the lid and select:
Dough cycle
Loaf size: 1½ pounds/750 g
Start

6. While the machine is mixing and kneading the ingredients, open the lid and use a spatula to scrape down the sides of the pan as needed, pushing any flour that has accumulated around the edges and under the dough into the center. Let the machine mix the dough until it is smooth and has no lumps, about 5 minutes. Press the stop button to cancel the cycle, turn off the machine, and remove the pan.

7. Scoop the dough out of the bread pan and onto the baking sheet. Brush the top lightly with olive oil and use your hands to press the dough out into an 8 x 12-inch (20 x 30 cm) rectangle. Use your fingers or knuckles to press dimples all over the surface of the dough. Spread the sauce gently over the top of the dough and sprinkle basil across the top. Set the pan aside and let the dough rise, uncovered, for about 30 minutes. It will not double, but it will get puffy.

8. While the dough is rising, preheat the oven to 350°F (180°C).

9. Bake until puffed and golden brown, 20 to 25 minutes. Remove from the oven and use the parchment to transfer the bread to a wire cooling rack. Slip the parchment out from under the bread to let the steam escape. Cool for about 20 minutes before cutting into squares or slender rectangles to serve.

10. Tightly wrap any leftovers in plastic wrap and store in the refrigerator for a day or two.

ITALIAN HERB FOCACCIA

MAKES 1 (8 X 12-INCH/20 X 30 CM) FOCACCIA   •   DAIRY-FREE OPTION

This flavorful bread—seasoned with basil, oregano, and fresh garlic—is perfect for sopping up pasta sauce or drizzled with a little Fresh Basil Oil (page 213) as a snack, appetizer, or first course. Feel free to switch up the toppings at any time for a change of pace.

DRY INGREDIENTS

2 teaspoons active dry yeast

240 g (8.5 oz or 2 cups) Light Flour Blend (page 34) or Whole-Grain Flour Blend (page 34)

¼ cup milk powder (22 g/0.8 oz) or DariFree (40 g/1.4 oz)

1 tablespoon granulated cane sugar

1 tablespoon dried oregano

2 to 3 teaspoons dried basil

2 teaspoons psyllium husk flakes or powder

1 teaspoon baking powder

1 teaspoon kosher or fine sea salt

⅛ teaspoon ascorbic acid, optional

WET INGREDIENTS

2 large eggs, at room temperature (see page 39), beaten

120 ml (½ cup) water, warmed to about 80°F (27°C)

30 ml (2 tablespoons) vegetable or olive oil

2 teaspoons apple cider vinegar

½ teaspoon minced garlic

TOPPING

Olive oil, for brushing

Coarse sea salt, optional

2 teaspoons chopped fresh rosemary

2 to 3 teaspoons grated Parmesan cheese, optional

1. Set the bread pan on the counter and insert the beater paddle(s). Unless otherwise directed by your machine's manufacturer, add the liquids first, then the dry ingredients, and finally the yeast.

2. Line a baking sheet with parchment and brush it with oil.

3. Measure the yeast into a small bowl and set aside. In a large mixing bowl, whisk the remaining dry ingredients together.

4. In a 2-cup (0.5 liter) glass measuring cup, whisk the wet ingredients together and pour into the bread pan. Use a spatula to spread the dry ingredients over the wet ingredients. Make a shallow well in the center and pour in the yeast.

5. Place the bread pan in the machine, settle it in the center, and lock it in place. Close the lid and select:
   Dough cycle
   Loaf size: 1½ pounds/750 g
   Start

6. While the machine is mixing and kneading, open the lid and use a spatula to scrape down the sides of the pan as needed, pushing any flour that has accumulated around the edges and under the dough into the center. Let the machine mix the dough until it is smooth and has no lumps, about 5 minutes. Press the stop button to cancel the cycle, turn off the machine, and remove the pan.

7. Scoop the dough out of the bread pan and onto the baking sheet. Brush the top with olive oil and use your hands to press the dough out into an 8 x 12-inch (20 x 30 cm) rectangle. Use your fingers or knuckles to press dimples all over the surface of the dough. Sprinkle it with the coarse salt and rosemary. Set the pan aside and let the dough rise, uncovered, for about 30 minutes. It will not double, but it will get a little puffy.

8. While the dough is rising, preheat the oven to 350°F (180°C).

9. Bake until puffed and golden brown, 20 to 25 minutes. Remove from the oven and use the parchment to help transfer the loaf to a wire rack. Slip the parchment out from under the bread to allow the steam to escape, sprinkle with Parmesan, if desired, and set aside to cool for at least 20 minutes before cutting into squares or slender rectangles to serve.

10. Tightly wrap any leftovers in plastic wrap and store in the refrigerator for a day or two.

ROSEMARY FOCACCIA

MAKES 1 (8 X 12-INCH/20 X 30 CM) FOCACCIA • DAIRY-FREE OPTION

Did you ever notice how many homes have rosemary bushes as hedges? This may be due to the healing benefits of rosemary or the belief that it enhances memory. Whatever the reason, any bread made with fresh rosemary is always popular. The distinctive aroma of rosemary, earthy and with a hint of pine, is one of dining's greatest pleasures. Use this hardy herb sparingly because it can become overwhelming. Resist the urge to completely cover the surface with it—in this case, less is definitely more.

DRY INGREDIENTS

2 teaspoons active dry yeast

240 g (8.5 oz or 2 cups) Light Flour Blend (page 34) or Whole-Grain Flour Blend (page 34)

¼ cup milk powder (22 g/0.8 oz) or DariFree (40 g/1.4 oz)

2 tablespoons finely minced fresh rosemary

1 tablespoon granulated cane sugar

2 teaspoons psyllium husk flakes or powder

1 teaspoon baking powder

1 teaspoon kosher or fine sea salt

⅛ teaspoon ascorbic acid, optional

WET INGREDIENTS

2 large eggs, at room temperature (see page 39), beaten

120 ml (½ cup) water, warmed to about 80°F (27°C)

30 ml (2 tablespoons) vegetable or olive oil

2 teaspoons apple cider vinegar

TOPPING

Olive oil, for brushing

Fresh rosemary sprigs (see opposite)

Coarse sea salt

1. Set the bread pan on the counter and insert the beater paddle(s). Unless otherwise directed by your machine's manufacturer, add the liquids first, then the dry ingredients, and finally the yeast.

2. Line a baking sheet with parchment and brush it with oil.

3. Measure the yeast into a small bowl and set aside. In a large mixing bowl, whisk the remaining dry ingredients together.

4. In a 2-cup (0.5 liter) glass measuring cup, whisk the wet ingredients together and pour into the bread pan. Use a spatula to spread the dry ingredients over the wet ingredients. Make a shallow well in the center and pour in the yeast.

5. Place the bread pan in the machine, settle it in the center, and lock it in place. Close the lid and select:

   Dough cycle
   Loaf size: 1½ pounds/750 g
   Start

6. While the machine is mixing and kneading the ingredients, open the lid and use a spatula to scrape down the sides of the pan as needed, pushing any flour that has accumulated around the edges and under the dough into the center. Let the machine mix the dough until it is smooth and has no lumps, about 5 minutes. Press the stop button to cancel the cycle, turn off the machine, and remove the pan.

7. Scoop the dough out of the bread pan and onto the baking sheet. Brush the top with a little more oil and use your hands to press the dough out into an 8 x 12-inch (20 x 30 cm) rectangle. Use your fingertips or knuckles to press dimples all over the surface of the dough. Stud it randomly with fresh rosemary sprigs and sprinkle the top with coarse salt. Set the pan aside to rest and let the dough rise, uncovered, for about 30 minutes. It will not double, but it will get puffy.

8. While the dough is rising, preheat the oven to 350°F (180°C).

USING ROSEMARY

This recipe calls for rosemary sprigs. Look closely at a branch of rosemary and you will notice that each one is made up of little clusters of leaves or needles. Each one of these little clusters is called a sprig. The sprigs are attached to a single thin stem. Snap the stems off the main branches and rinse well. Pat dry before using.

Garnishing your serving platters with an ingredient used in the foods being served, like sprigs of fresh herbs, enhances the appearance and helps guests anticipate the flavors they will experience with each bite.

For a professional presentation, you can insert a sprig of rosemary in many of the dimples. If you don't have fresh rosemary, you can use 2 teaspoons dried rosemary. But if you can, use fresh. There is nothing like it!

9. Bake the bread until puffed and golden brown, 20 to 25 minutes. Remove from the oven and use the parchment to transfer the bread to a wire cooling rack. Slip the parchment out from beneath to let the steam to escape. Set aside to cool for at least 20 minutes before cutting into squares or slender rectangles to serve. Garnish the basket or tray with fresh rosemary sprigs if desired.

10. Tightly wrap any leftovers in plastic wrap and store in the refrigerator for a day or two.

OLIVE FOCACCIA

MAKES 1 (8 X 12-INCH/20 X 30 CM) FOCACCIA ◆ DAIRY-FREE OPTION

Olives and bread are two staples of the Mediterranean diet. Rich, heady olives, with their earthiness and slight saltiness from the brine, complement the flavor and chewy texture of this focaccia. While black olives are traditional, you can use any pitted olives in this recipe. And feel free to add fresh herbs, too. The joy of interpreting recipes is making a dish that is unique to you.

DRY INGREDIENTS

2 teaspoons active dry yeast

240 g (8.5 oz or 2 cups) Light Flour Blend (page 34) or Whole-Grain Flour Blend (page 34)

¼ cup milk powder (22 g/0.8 oz) or DariFree (40 g/1.4 oz)

1 tablespoon granulated cane sugar

2 teaspoons psyllium husk flakes or powder

1 teaspoon baking powder

1 teaspoon kosher or fine sea salt

⅛ teaspoon ascorbic acid, optional

WET INGREDIENTS

2 large eggs, at room temperature (see page 39), beaten

120 ml (½ cup) water, warmed to about 80°F (27°C)

30 ml (2 tablespoons) vegetable or olive oil

2 teaspoons apple cider vinegar

TOPPING

Olive oil, for brushing

50 g (1.8 oz or ½ cup) pitted black olives, drained well and coarsely chopped

Coarse sea salt, optional

1. Set the bread pan on the counter and insert the beater paddle(s). Unless otherwise directed by your machine's manufacturer, add the liquids first, then the dry ingredients, and finally the yeast.

2. Line a baking sheet with parchment and brush it with oil.

3. Measure the yeast into a small bowl and set aside. In a large mixing bowl, whisk the remaining dry ingredients together.

4. In a 2-cup (0.5 liter) glass measuring cup, whisk the wet ingredients together and pour into the bread pan. Use a spatula to spread the dry ingredients over the wet ingredients. Make a shallow well in the center and pour in the yeast.

5. Place the bread pan in the machine, settle it in the center, and lock it in place. Close the lid and select:

   Dough cycle
   Loaf size: 1½ pounds/750 g
   Start

6. While the machine is mixing and kneading, open the lid and use a spatula to scrape down the sides of the pan as needed, pushing any flour that has accumulated around the edges and under the dough into the center. Let the machine mix the dough until it is smooth and has no lumps, about 5 minutes. Press the stop button to cancel the cycle, turn off the machine, and remove the pan.

7. Scoop the dough out of the bread pan and onto the baking sheet. Brush the top with olive oil and use your hands to press the dough out into an 8 x 12-inch (20 x 30 cm) rectangle. Use your fingertips or knuckles to press dimples all over the surface of the dough. Arrange the olives evenly over the top, pressing them gently into the dough. Sprinkle lightly with coarse salt, if desired. Set the pan aside to let the dough rise, uncovered, for about 30 minutes. It will not double, but it will get puffy.

8. While the dough is rising, preheat the oven to 350°F (180°C).

9. Bake the bread until puffed and golden brown, 20 to 25 minutes. Remove from the oven and use the parchment to transfer the bread to a wire cooling rack. Slip the parchment out from beneath to let the steam to escape. Set aside to cool for at least 20 minutes before cutting into squares or slender rectangles to serve.

10. Tightly wrap any leftovers in plastic wrap and store in the refrigerator for a day or two.

TRIPLE GARLIC FOCACCIA

MAKES 1 (8 X 12-INCH/20 X 30 CM) FOCACCIA • DAIRY-FREE OPTION

Here's a treat for those who cannot get enough garlic. This focaccia is flavored with garlic, studded with fresh garlic, and then slathered with garlic butter before serving. This will keep the vampires at bay. Make sure everyone at the party has a piece!

DRY INGREDIENTS

2 teaspoons active dry yeast

240 g (8.5 oz or 2 cups) Light Flour Blend (page 34) or Whole-Grain Flour Blend (page 34)

¼ cup milk powder (22 g/0.8 oz) or DariFree (40 g/1.4 oz)

1 tablespoon granulated cane sugar

2 teaspoons psyllium husk flakes or powder

1 teaspoon baking powder

1 teaspoon kosher or fine sea salt

1 teaspoon garlic powder

⅛ teaspoon ascorbic acid, optional

WET INGREDIENTS

2 large eggs, at room temperature (see page 39), beaten

120 ml (½ cup) water, warmed to about 80°F (27°C)

30 ml (2 tablespoons) vegetable or olive oil

2 teaspoons apple cider vinegar

TOPPING

Olive oil, for brushing

Garlic cloves (as many as you like), peeled and quartered lengthwise

1 teaspoon minced garlic or Roasted Garlic (see page 151)

28–42 g (1–1.5 oz or 2–3 tablespoons) unsalted butter or nondairy butter substitute, melted, or olive oil

Coarse sea salt

1. Set the bread pan on the counter and insert the beater paddle(s). Unless otherwise directed by your machine's manufacturer, add the liquids first, then the dry ingredients, and finally the yeast.

2. Line a baking sheet with parchment and brush it with oil.

3. Measure the yeast into a small bowl and set aside. In a large mixing bowl, whisk the remaining dry ingredients together.

4. In a 2-cup (0.5 liter) glass measuring cup, whisk the wet ingredients together and pour into the bread pan. Use a spatula to spread the dry ingredients over the wet ingredients. Make a shallow well in the center and pour in the yeast.

5. Place the bread pan in the machine, settle it in the center, and lock it in place. Close the lid and select:

   Dough cycle
   Loaf size: 1½ pounds/750 g
   Start

6. While the machine is mixing and kneading, open the lid and use a spatula to scrape down the sides of the pan as needed, pushing any flour that has accumulated around the edges and under the dough into the center. Let the machine mix the dough until it is smooth and has no lumps, about 5 minutes, scraping the sides as needed. Press the stop button to cancel the cycle, turn off the machine, and remove the pan.

7. Scoop the dough out of the bread pan and onto the baking sheet. Brush the top with olive oil and use your hands to press the dough out into an 8 x 12-inch (20 x 30 cm) rectangle. Use your fingertips or knuckles to press dimples all over the surface of the dough. Tuck pieces of garlic into the dimples, adding as many as you and your family like. Set the pan aside and let the dough rise, uncovered, for about 30 minutes. It will not double, but it will get puffy.

8. While the dough is rising, preheat the oven to 350°F (180°C). Stir the minced garlic and melted butter together in a small bowl.

9. Bake until puffed and golden brown, 20 to 25 minutes. Brush the top with the garlic butter, sprinkle with a little coarse salt, and use the parchment to transfer the bread to a wire cooling rack. Slip the parchment out from under the bread to let the steam escape. Set aside to cool for at least 20 minutes before slicing. Cut into squares or rectangles to serve.

10. Tightly wrap any leftovers in plastic wrap and store in the refrigerator for a day or two.

SUMMER FOCACCIA WITH GRILLED NECTARINES, FRESH MOZZARELLA, AND ARUGULA

MAKES 1 (8 X 12-INCH/20 X 30 CM) FOCACCIA

When the weather heats up, we all look for ways to create delicious, light meals. Inspired by a photo posted by Los Angeles–based chef Suzanne Goin on Instagram, we put together a beautiful combination of bright summer flavors, using focaccia as a "plate" on which to serve them. One bite and you will never think of focaccia the same way again! Serve this as a starter or as a side dish with grilled chicken. If you have the grill fired up, brush the nectarine with a little oil and grill it cut side down to add a touch of smokiness and beautiful markings. If you can't find arugula (also called rocket) at your local farmers' market or gourmet grocery store, you can use watercress or baby spinach in its place.

1 recipe Chewy Focaccia dough (page 212), prepared through step 6 but before rising

2 to 3 teaspoons fresh thyme leaves

Coarse sea salt

1 large shallot, sliced

Olive oil

1 ripe nectarine, halved and pitted

1 (2-inch/5 cm) ball fresh mozzarella or burrata

1 handful baby arugula or spinach, washed and patted dry

Kosher or fine sea salt

Freshly ground black pepper

Mosto cotto (see opposite) or aged balsamic vinegar, for drizzling

1. Sprinkle the top of the focaccia with the thyme leaves and coarse salt before setting aside to rise.

2. While the dough is rising, preheat the oven to 350°F (180°C).

3. Separate the shallot slices into rings and toss with a little olive oil. When the focaccia has risen, scatter the shallots over the top.

4. Bake until puffed and golden brown, 20 to 25 minutes, rotating the pan halfway through.

5. While the focaccia is baking, heat a stove-top grill pan over high heat (or use your outdoor grill if you are already grilling the rest of your meal). Brush the cut sides of the nectarine lightly with oil. Turn the heat down to medium. Place on the grill pan, cut side down, and do not move until you have nice grill marks and the fruit releases easily when you lift it with tongs or a spatula, 2 to 3 minutes. If it sticks, leave it for another minute or two. It will release on its own when the sugars in the fruit have caramelized. Cut into wedges about ⅛ inch (3 mm) thick.

6. Set the focaccia on a wire rack and slide the parchment out from underneath to allow the steam to escape. Cut the mozzarella into small pieces, pat dry, and scatter over the top, but don't cover the entire surface or it will add too much liquid. Cool for at least 20 minutes.

WHAT IS MOSTO COTTO?

Mosto cotto is thick Italian grape juice, made from the first steps of the wine-making process. Originally from the Abruzzo region, it is made by pressing grapes with a sugar content too high for wine. The juice is filtered and cooked slowly for hours to reduce and concentrate the flavors. It can be added to nonalcoholic drinks, drizzled over salad greens, or used in breads like this focaccia.

7. When you are ready to serve, toss the baby arugula with 1 teaspoon of olive oil, until evenly coated. Scatter evenly over the top of the bread and season lightly with salt and a few grinds of black pepper. Add about half of the grilled nectarine slices (save the rest for breakfast cereal) and drizzle very lightly with mosto cotto. Cut into squares with a serrated knife and serve warm or at room temperature.

8. Tightly wrap any leftovers in plastic wrap and store in the refrigerator for a day or two.

BASIC FLATBREAD

MAKES 6 INDIVIDUAL FLATBREADS

Flatbreads are one of the most utilized bread products in the world. In one form or another, they're found in nearly every cuisine. Softer than a traditional pizza crust, foldable, and tender, they are incredibly versatile and can be eaten plain, dipped in a flavored oil or sauce, or used as the base for a myriad of topping combinations. Take this recipe, put your own spin on it, and create a memorable and unique meal!

DRY INGREDIENTS

2 teaspoons active dry yeast

240 g (8.5 oz or 2 cups) Light Flour Blend (page 34) or Whole-Grain Flour Blend (page 34)

2 teaspoons granulated cane sugar

1 teaspoon kosher or fine sea salt, plus more for sprinkling, optional

½ teaspoon xanthan gum

½ teaspoon baking powder

¼ teaspoon baking soda

⅛ teaspoon ascorbic acid, optional

WET INGREDIENTS

160 ml (⅔ cup) water, warmed to about 80°F (27°C)

56 g (2 oz or 4 tablespoons/½ stick) unsalted butter, melted and slightly cooled

2 teaspoons apple cider vinegar

1. Set the bread pan on the counter and insert the beater paddle(s). Unless otherwise directed by your machine's manufacturer, add the liquids first, then the dry ingredients, and finally the yeast.

2. Line a baking sheet with parchment and brush lightly with oil.

3. Measure the yeast into a small bowl and set aside. In a large mixing bowl, whisk the remaining dry ingredients together.

4. In a 2-cup (0.5 liter) glass measuring cup, whisk the wet ingredients together and pour into the bread pan. Use a spatula to spread the dry ingredients over the wet ingredients, covering completely. Because there are fewer ingredients than normal, make a shallow well to the side of the beater blade and pour in the yeast. **Note: This is a change from our usual method.**

5. Place the bread pan in the machine and lock it in place. Close the lid and select:
Dough cycle
Loaf size: 1 pound/500 g (if available)
or 1½ pounds/750 g
Start

6. While the machine is mixing and kneading, open the lid and use a spatula to scrape down the sides of the pan as needed. This dough tends to break apart, so you will have to constantly push it back onto the beater blade to be sure all the ingredients are fully incorporated. Let the machine mix and knead for about 3 minutes. Press the stop button to cancel the cycle, turn off the machine, and remove the bread pan.

7. Use a spatula to transfer the dough to the prepared baking sheet. Form the dough into a ball and divide into six equal pieces.

8. Press each piece of dough into a flat circle about 4 inches (10 cm) in diameter, staggering them on the baking sheet so they are not touching. Dock the center of each circle. Sprinkle lightly with salt, if desired.

9. Preheat the oven to 400°F (200°C).

10. Place the baking sheet in the oven and bake until the flatbreads are browned around the edges and puff up slightly, 15 to 20 minutes, rotating the pan halfway through. Remove from the oven and use the parchment to help transfer the bread to a wire cooling rack. Slip the parchment out from under the breads to let the steam escape. Cool for about 15 minutes before serving.

11. If you make these ahead, you can wrap them tightly, place in resealable plastic bags, press all the air out, and freeze for up to 1 month.

LAHMAJOUNE (ARMENIAN TOMATO, PEPPER, AND MEAT SAUCE ON FLATBREAD)

SERVES 6

Lahmajoune is a thick, savory mix of tomatoes, beef, and bell pepper baked on top of flatbread—almost like Armenian pizza. This is a delightful afternoon snack or dinner-time treat and a nice change of pace. Thanks to Nancy Buchanan, author of the blog "A Communal Table," for this wonderful recipe, one of her childhood favorites.

SAUCE

1 cup (175 g) chopped red bell pepper (or a mix of red and orange)

¾ cup (120 g) chopped onion

3 garlic cloves, chopped

¼ cup (15 g) Italian parsley, chopped

1 cup (180 g) drained canned diced tomatoes

¼ cup (65 g) tomato paste

1 teaspoon kosher salt

1 teaspoon freshly ground black pepper

1 teaspoon dried mint

½ teaspoon grated lemon zest

8 ounces (225 g) ground beef (or substitute uncooked Italian sausage or Mexican chorizo)

BASE

1 recipe Basic Flatbread (page 226)

1. For the sauce, in a food processor, mince the bell pepper, onion, garlic, and parsley.

2. Add the parsley, diced tomatoes, tomato paste, salt, black pepper, mint, and lemon zest. Pulse three or four times to combine.

3. Put the ground beef in a large bowl, add the sauce, and blend. Set aside.

4. Preheat the oven to 450°F (230°C). Line a baking sheet with parchment.

5. Divide the flatbread dough into six equal pieces and press into 4-inch (10 cm) disks on the prepared baking sheet. Dock the dough or poke all over with a fork. Slip into the oven and bake for 15 minutes, rotating the pan halfway through.

6. Remove from the oven and top each flatbread with about 3 tablespoons of meat sauce, spreading it into a thin layer. Return to the oven and bake for 3 minutes. Rotate the baking sheet.

7. Bake until the meat is cooked through and browned at the edges, 5 to 8 minutes. Serve hot.

MAKE AHEAD TIP

While they are best on the day they are baked, the flatbreads can be prepared a day ahead; wrap them individually in plastic and refrigerate.

Fruit

BREADS

The bread recipes in this chapter are geared toward seasonal ingredients. Summer ushers in fresh berries and herbs. Blueberry Quick Bread with Brown Sugar Crumble Topping will thrill everyone at your brunch or picnic. Our Fruitcake, a dense, spicy, aromatic bread, is so good your friends and family will be clamoring for it all year long. As the seasons change and citrus comes into the picture, try the Orange-Glazed Quick Bread. It will delight guests at tea or for an afternoon snack.

Once you understand the base recipe, the combination of sweet and savory from fruits and nuts will entice you to create whimsical variations. It's important not to overload a dough with fresh fruits, as their moisture will change its consistency. Dried fruits and nuts tend to be more forgiving. You can also dress up your breads. Sprinkle a cinnamon-brown sugar crumble on top of the dough before the rise or bake cycle has begun, or make a coffee, raspberry, or lemon glaze for the finished loaf.

These quick bread recipes can be tailored to other dietary needs, though most of them are dairy free. We like using unsweetened coconut milk, but rice, soy, hemp, or almond milk are all fine substitutes for milk in our recipes.

Xanthan gum and psyllium husk flakes or powder are also interchangeable in these recipes, just in different proportions: use 1 teaspoon xanthan for the psyllium. (When substituting one for the other in other recipes in this book, the general ratio is 1:2 xanthan to psyllium.) We use psyllium husk flakes or powder in these recipes. If you want to experiment with whole psyllium husks, you will likely get different results.

If you want beautiful loaves without the paddle in the bottom, use the quick bread recipes. They are less temperamental than yeast-raised breads. Once the knead cycle is done, pull out the paddle, but be quick so you do not tamper too much with the temperature for the rise and bake cycles. Smooth out the loaf, top with something special if desired, close the lid, and get ready to enjoy the smell of luscious bread baking.

APPLE BACON QUINOA BREAD

Quinoa cereal flakes are great in quick breads and yeast breads for those with oat allergies. Quinoa gives this apple bread a nutty taste and a denser crumb. The grated apple adds sweetness and texture to the finished loaf.

DRY INGREDIENTS

21 g (0.7 oz or 2 tablespoons) active dry yeast

240 g (8.5 oz or 2 cups) Light Flour Blend (page 34)

104 g (3.7 oz or 1 cup) quinoa flakes

44 g (1.6 oz or ½ cup) Better than Milk soy powder

133 g (4.7 oz or ⅔ cup) granulated cane sugar

1 tablespoon baking powder

1 tablespoon psyllium husk flakes or powder

2 teaspoons kosher salt

⅛ teaspoon ascorbic acid, optional

6 slices bacon, cooked, crumbled

WET INGREDIENTS

3 large eggs, at room temperature (see page 39), beaten

180 ml (¾ cup) water, heated to about 80°F (27°C)

60 ml (¼ cup) vegetable oil

2 teaspoons apple cider vinegar

220 g (7.8 oz or 2 cups) finely grated peeled apple (preferably Granny Smith)

1. Set the bread pan on the counter and insert the beater paddle(s). Unless otherwise directed by your machine's manufacturer, add the liquids first, then the dry ingredients, and finally the yeast.

2. Measure the yeast into a small bowl and set aside. In a large mixing bowl, whisk the remaining dry ingredients together.

3. In a 4-cup (1 liter) glass measuring cup, whisk the wet ingredients—*except* the apples—together. Stir in the apples and pour into the bread pan. Use a spatula to spread the dry ingredients over the wet ingredients, covering completely. Make a shallow well in the center and pour in the yeast.

4. Place the bread pan in the machine, settle it in the center, and lock it in place. Close the lid and select:

   Gluten-free cycle (see page 14 if your machine does not have this setting)
   Loaf size: 1½ pounds/750 g
   Medium crust
   Start

5. About 3 minutes into the mixing process, open the lid and use a spatula to scrape down the sides of the pan, avoiding the paddle. Push any flour that has accumulated around the edges into the center. Check again once or twice during kneading, scraping the edges, corners, and under the dough. If the dough looks too wet or too dry, add a little flour blend or tiny amounts of warm water. Once the mix/knead cycle is done, leave the lid closed during the rise and bake cycles.

6. At the end of the bake cycle, lift the lid and check the temperature. When the bread reaches 206°F to 210°F (97°C to 99°C) on an instant-read thermometer inserted in the center, it is done. Remove the pan from the machine and set it on its side on a wire cooling rack. Leave the bread in the pan for a couple of minutes, then turn the pan upside down and slide the loaf onto the wire rack. Carefully remove the paddle if it is embedded in the bottom of the loaf. Let the bread cool upside down for at least 2 hours before slicing.

7. Store the bread in a resealable plastic bag or airtight container on the counter for up to 3 days. For longer storage, cut into even slices, double-wrap tightly in plastic, place in a resealable plastic bag, and freeze for up to 3 months.

APRICOT-WALNUT QUICK BREAD

MAKES 1 (1½-POUND/680 G) LOAF ◆ DAIRY FREE

This bread is slightly sweet and perfect for breakfast, as a snack, or at teatime. You can steep the dried apricots in boiling water for 10 to 15 minutes, then drain and reserve ½ cup (120 ml) of the water to use in the recipe instead of apricot nectar or plain water. The softening of the apricots makes their flavor more pronounced.

DRY INGREDIENTS

270 g (9.5 oz or 2¼ cups) Light Flour Blend (page 34)

200 g (7.1 oz or 1 cup) granulated cane sugar

90 g (3.2 oz or ¾ cup) millet flour

1 tablespoon baking powder

2 teaspoons psyllium husk flakes or powder

1 teaspoon ground ginger

½ teaspoon kosher or fine sea salt

WET INGREDIENTS

¼ cup vegetable oil (60 ml) or nondairy butter substitute (55 g/2 oz or ½ stick), melted and slightly cooled

120 ml (½ cup) apricot nectar or water (see headnote)

3 large eggs, at room temperature (see page 39), beaten

130 g (4.6 oz or 1 cup) chopped dried apricots

60 g (2 oz or ½ cup) chopped walnuts, toasted

1. Set the bread pan on the counter and insert the beater paddle(s). Unless otherwise directed by your machine's manufacturer, add the liquids first, then the dry ingredients.

2. In a large mixing bowl, whisk the dry ingredients together.

3. Whisk the oil, apricot nectar, and eggs together in a large bowl. Stir in the chopped apricots and walnuts. Scrape into the bread pan. Use a spatula to spread the dry ingredients over the wet ingredients.

4. Place the bread pan in the machine, settle it in the center, and lock it in place. Close the lid and select:

   Express bake cycle
   Loaf size: 1½ pounds/750 g
   Light crust
   Start

5. After the first knead cycle, scrape the sides and bottom of the pan with the spatula to make sure all the dry ingredients are incorporated. Once the mixing/kneading is done, leave the lid closed during the rise and bake cycles.

6. At the end of the bake cycle, lift the lid and check the temperature. The bread is done when it registers 206°F to 210°F (97°C to 99°C) on an instant-read thermometer inserted in the center of the loaf. Remove the pan from the machine and place it on its side on a wire rack. Leave the bread in the pan for 3 minutes, then turn the pan upside down and slide the loaf onto the wire rack on its side. Carefully remove the paddle if it is embedded in the bottom of the loaf. Let the bread cool upside down for at least 2 hours before slicing.

7. Store the bread in a resealable plastic bag or airtight container on the counter for up to 1 day. For longer storage, cut into even slices, double-wrap tightly in plastic, place in a resealable plastic bag, and freeze for up to 3 months.

BANANA QUICK BREAD

MAKES 1 (1½-POUND/680 G) LOAF ◆ DAIRY FREE

Cocoa powder and instant espresso powder really "wake up" this banana bread. They are an interesting and unusual addition, but give it a try and we bet you'll get requests for this bread all year long. Buy your bananas a few days before you plan to make the bread. The blacker their peels turn, the easier they are to mash and the sweeter the resulting bread.

DRY INGREDIENTS

240 g (8.5 oz or 2 cups) Light Flour Blend (page 34)

200 g (7.1 oz or 1 cup) granulated cane sugar

60 g (2.1 oz or ½ cup) millet flour

23 g (0.8 oz or ¼ cup) unsweetened cocoa powder

1 tablespoon baking powder

1 tablespoon psyllium husk flakes or powder

2 teaspoons instant espresso powder

½ teaspoon kosher or fine sea salt

WET INGREDIENTS

3 large ripe bananas

⅓ cup vegetable oil (80 ml) or nondairy butter substitute (75 g or 2.6 oz/ ⅔ stick), melted and slightly cooled

3 large eggs, at room temperature (see page 39), beaten

1. Set the bread pan on the counter and insert the beater paddle(s). Unless otherwise directed by your machine's manufacturer, add the liquids first, then the dry ingredients.

2. In a large mixing bowl, whisk the dry ingredients together.

3. In a large bowl, mash the bananas into a paste using a fork or potato masher. Add the oil and eggs and whisk until smooth. Scrape into the bread pan. Use a spatula to spread the dry ingredients over the wet ingredients.

4. Place the bread pan in the machine, settle it in the center, and lock it in place. Close the lid and select:

   Express bake cycle
   Loaf size: 1½ pounds/750 g
   Light crust
   Start

5. After the first knead cycle, scrape the sides and bottom of the pan with the spatula to make sure all the dry ingredients are incorporated. Once the mixing/kneading is done, leave the lid closed during the rise and bake cycles.

6. At the end of the bake cycle, lift the lid and check the temperature. The bread is done when it registers 206°F to 210°F (97°C to 99°C) on an instant-read thermometer inserted in the center of the loaf. Remove the pan from the machine and place it on its side on a wire rack. Leave the bread in the pan for 3 minutes, then turn the pan upside down and slide the loaf onto the wire rack on its side. Carefully remove the paddle if it is embedded in the bottom of the loaf. Let the bread cool upside down for at least 2 hours before slicing.

7. Store the bread in a resealable plastic bag or airtight container on the counter for up to 3 days. For longer storage, cut into even slices, double-wrap tightly in plastic, place in a resealable plastic bag, and freeze for up to 3 months.

BANANA-CHOCOLATE CHIP QUICK BREAD

MAKES 1 (1½-POUND/680 G) LOAF ◆ DAIRY FREE

This recipe was inspired by the chocolate-covered frozen bananas you find at summer fairs. Drizzle the sliced bread with hot fudge, warmed Nutella, or chocolate sauce and serve for dessert with a scoop of vanilla ice cream. You will have the flavors you love all year long with no wait for the county fair!

DRY INGREDIENTS

240 g (8.5 oz or 2 cups) Light Flour Blend (page 34)

200 g (7.1 oz or 1 cup) granulated cane sugar

65 g (2.3 oz or ½ cup) teff flour

60 g (2.1 oz or ½ cup) buckwheat flour

1 tablespoon baking powder

1 tablespoon psyllium husk flakes or powder

1 teaspoon kosher or fine sea salt

WET INGREDIENTS

3 large ripe bananas

⅓ cup vegetable oil (80 ml) or nondairy butter substitute (75 g or 2.6 oz/ ⅔ stick), melted and slightly cooled

3 large eggs, at room temperature (see page 39), beaten

ADD-IN

255 g (9 oz or 1½ cups) gluten-free, dairy-free semisweet chocolate chips (such as Enjoy Life brand)

1. Set the bread pan on the counter and insert the beater paddle(s). Unless otherwise directed by your machine's manufacturer, add the liquids first, then the dry ingredients.

2. In a large mixing bowl, whisk the dry ingredients together.

3. In a large bowl, mash the bananas into a paste using a fork or potato masher. Add the oil and eggs and whisk until smooth. Scrape into the bread pan. Use a spatula to spread the dry ingredients over the wet ingredients.

4. Place the bread pan in the machine, settle it in the center, and lock it in place. Close the lid and select:

   Quick bread/cake cycle
   Loaf size: 1½ pounds/750 g
   Light crust
   Start

5. After the first knead cycle, scrape the sides and bottom of the pan with the spatula to make sure all the dry ingredients are incorporated. Add the chocolate chips. Once the mixing/kneading is done, leave the lid closed during the rise and bake cycles.

6. At the end of the bake cycle, lift the lid and check the temperature. The bread is done when it registers 206°F to 210°F (97°C to 99°C) on an instant-read thermometer inserted in the center of the loaf. Remove the pan from the machine and place it on its side on a wire rack. Leave the bread in the pan for 3 minutes, then turn the pan upside down and slide the loaf onto the wire rack on its side. Carefully remove the paddle if it is embedded in the bottom of the loaf. Let the bread cool upside down for at least 2 hours before slicing.

7. Store the bread in a resealable plastic bag or airtight container on the counter for up to 3 days. For longer storage, cut into even slices, double-wrap tightly in plastic, place in a resealable plastic bag, and freeze for up to 3 months.

BLUEBERRY QUICK BREAD WITH BROWN SUGAR CRUMBLE TOPPING

MAKES 1 (1½-POUND/680 G) LOAF • DAIRY FREE

This bread looks like a decadent coffee cake. Fresh, tangy blueberries are the perfect foil for the sweetness of the brown sugar. If you do not have fresh blueberries you can substitute ¾ cup dried blueberries that you have steeped in warm water and drained. You can also skip the crumble topping.

DRY INGREDIENTS

180 g (6.3 oz or 1½ cups) Light Flour Blend (page 34) or Whole-Grain Flour Blend (page 34)

120 g (4.2 oz or 1 cup) millet flour

200 g (7.1 oz or 1 cup) granulated cane sugar

1 tablespoon baking powder

2 teaspoons psyllium husk flakes or powder

1 teaspoon kosher or fine sea salt

WET INGREDIENTS

120 ml (½ cup) unsweetened coconut milk, warmed to about 80°F (27°C)

80 ml (⅓ cup) vegetable oil

3 large eggs, at room temperature (see page 39), beaten

1 teaspoon pure vanilla extract

ADD-IN

180 g (6.3 oz or 1¼ cups) fresh blueberries, rinsed and patted dry

TOPPING

75 g (2.6 oz or ⅓ cup) brown sugar

2 tablespoons Light Flour Blend (page 34) or Whole-Grain Flour Blend (page 34)

⅛ teaspoon ground cinnamon, nutmeg, mace, or cardamom

1. Set the bread pan on the counter and insert the beater paddle(s). Unless otherwise directed by your machine's manufacturer, add the liquids first, then the dry ingredients.

2. In a large mixing bowl, whisk the dry ingredients together.

3. In a 4-cup (1 liter) glass measuring cup, whisk the wet ingredients together and pour into the bread pan. Use a spatula to spread the dry ingredients over the wet ingredients.

4. Place the bread pan in the machine, settle it in the center, and lock it in place. Close the lid and select:

   Quick bread/cake cycle
   Loaf size: 1½ pounds/750 g
   Light crust
   Start

5. After the first knead cycle, scrape the sides and bottom of the pan with the spatula to make sure all the dry ingredients are incorporated. Stir in the blueberries. Close the lid and continue to knead.

6. Meanwhile, mix the topping ingredients together in a small bowl with a fork.

7. When you hear the signal as the machine transitions from the knead to the bake cycle, remove the kneading paddle and reshape the loaf. If the dough seems sticky, wet your hands with a little water to help with reshaping the loaf. Scatter the topping evenly over the dough. Close the lid and let the bread finish baking.

8. At the end of the bake cycle, lift the lid and check the temperature. The bread is done when it registers 206°F to 210°F (97°C to 99°C) on an instant-read thermometer inserted in the center of the loaf. Remove the pan from the machine and place it on its side on a wire rack. Leave the bread in its pan for 3 minutes. Then slide the loaf out of the pan. Set it on its side on the rack and cool for at least 1 hour before slicing.

9. Store the bread in a resealable plastic bag or airtight container on the counter for up to 3 days. For longer storage, cut into even slices, double-wrap tightly in plastic, place in a resealable plastic bag, and freeze for up to 3 months.

CARAMEL APPLE QUICK BREAD

MAKES 1 (1½-POUND/680 G) LOAF ◆ DAIRY-FREE OPTION

This caramel apple bread is more like a pound cake than bread. It's dense and rich with bits of caramel throughout that make each bite a sweet adventure. The teff flour adds a slight molasses flavor that enhances the apples and caramel. Serve it for brunch— or for dessert, drizzled with chocolate or caramel sauce.

DRY INGREDIENTS

300 g (10.6 oz or 2½ cups) Light Flour Blend (page 34)

200 g (7.1 oz or 1 cup) granulated cane sugar

65 g (2.3 oz or ½ cup) teff flour

44 g (1.6 oz or ½ cup) Better Than Milk soy powder

1 tablespoon baking powder

1 tablespoon psyllium husk flakes or powder

1 teaspoon kosher or fine sea salt

WET INGREDIENTS

3 large eggs, at room temperature (see page 39), beaten

120 ml (½ cup) applesauce

80 ml (⅓ cup) vegetable oil

220 g (7.8 oz or 2 cups) grated peeled apples (preferably Granny Smith)

312 g (11 oz or 1½ cups) gluten-free caramel bits or quartered standard caramel squares

NOTE: For dairy free, use coconut caramels; check the label to be sure there are no hidden dairy ingredients.

1. Set the bread pan on the counter and insert the beater paddle(s). Unless otherwise directed by your machine's manufacturer, add the liquids first, then the dry ingredients.

2. In a large mixing bowl, whisk the dry ingredients together.

3. In another large mixing bowl, whisk the eggs, applesauce, and oil together. Stir in the apples and caramel bits and scrape into the bread pan. Use a spatula to spread the dry ingredients over the wet ingredients, covering completely.

4. Place the bread pan in the machine, settle it in the center, and lock it in place. Close the lid and select:

   Quick bread/cake cycle
   Loaf size: 1½ pounds/750 g
   Medium crust
   Start

5. About 3 minutes into the mixing process, open the lid and use a spatula to scrape down the sides of the pan, avoiding the paddle. Push any flour that has accumulated around the edges into the center. Check again once or twice during kneading, scraping the edges, corners, and under the dough. If the dough looks too wet or too dry, add a little flour blend or tiny amounts of warm water.

6. At the end of the bake cycle, lift the lid and check the temperature. When the bread reaches 206°F to 210°F (97°C to 99°C) on an instant-read thermometer inserted in the center, it is done. Remove the pan from the machine and set it on its side on a wire cooling rack. Leave the bread in the pan for a couple of minutes, then turn the pan upside down and slide the loaf onto the wire rack. Carefully remove the paddle if it is embedded in the bottom of the loaf. Let the bread cool upside down for at least 2 hours before slicing.

7. Store the bread in a resealable plastic bag or airtight container on the counter for up to 3 days. For longer storage, cut into even slices, double-wrap tightly in plastic, place in a resealable plastic bag, and freeze for up to 3 months.

"DIRTY" CHAI DATE AND WALNUT QUICK BREAD WITH CHAI GLAZE

MAKES 1 (1½-POUND/680 G) LOAF • DAIRY FREE

Chai powder, typically comprised of black tea mixed with cinnamon, fennel, ginger, black pepper, cloves, coriander, and star anise, gives you a balanced spicy flavor; a bit of espresso powder makes it "dirty." In this bread, it complements the nuttiness of the walnuts and the sweetness of the dates for a perfect breakfast, brunch addition, or snack. Toast the walnuts beforehand to enhance the nuttiness of this bread. Be sure to save a few to sprinkle on top of the glaze.

DRY INGREDIENTS

240 g (8.5 oz or 2 cups) Light Flour Blend (page 34) or Whole-Grain Flour Blend (page 34)

118 g (4.2 oz or 1 cup) millet flour

200 g (7.1 oz or 1 cup) granulated cane sugar

46 g (1.6 oz or ¼ cup) dairy-free chai powder

40 g (1.4 oz or ¼ cup) DariFree

1 tablespoon baking powder

1 tablespoon psyllium husk flakes or powder

2 teaspoons instant espresso powder

1 teaspoon kosher or fine sea salt

WET INGREDIENTS

3 large eggs, at room temperature (see page 39), beaten

120 ml (½ cup) unsweetened soy or coconut milk

80 ml (⅓ cup) vegetable oil

1 teaspoon pure vanilla extract

ADD-INS

178 g (6.3 oz or 1 cup) chopped dates

120 g (4.2 oz or 1 cup) coarsely chopped walnuts

CHAI GLAZE

90 g (3.2 oz or ¾ cup) confectioners' sugar

30 ml (2 tablespoons) hot chai tea

1. Set the bread pan on the counter and insert the beater paddle(s). Unless otherwise directed by your machine's manufacturer, add the liquids first, then the dry ingredients.

2. In a large mixing bowl, whisk the dry ingredients together.

3. In a 4-cup (1 liter) glass measuring cup, whisk the wet ingredients together and pour into the bread pan. Use a spatula to spread the dry ingredients over the wet ingredients.

4. Place the bread pan in the machine, settle it in the center, and lock it in place. Close the lid and select:

   Quick bread/cake cycle
   Loaf size: 1½ pounds/750 g
   Medium crust
   Start

5. After the first kneading cycle, scrape the sides and bottom of the pan with the spatula to make sure all the dry ingredients are incorporated. Add the dates and nuts.

6. If your machine has alerts, when you hear the signal for the machine transitioning from the knead to the bake cycle, remove the kneading paddle and reshape the loaf. If the dough seems sticky, wet your hands with a little water to help with reshaping the loaf; smooth the top with a lightly oiled spatula. Close the lid and let the bread finish baking.

7. At the end of the bake cycle, lift the lid and check the temperature. The bread is done when it registers 206°F to 210°F (97°C to 99°C) on an instant-read thermometer inserted in the center of the loaf. Remove the pan from the machine and place it on its side on a wire rack. Leave the bread in the pan for a couple of minutes, then turn the pan upside down and slide the loaf onto the wire rack. Set the loaf on its side and cool for at least 2 hours before slicing.

8. Whisk the glaze ingredients together to form a drizzle-like consistency, adding a little more chai or hot water if necessary. After the bread has cooled, drizzle with the glaze; let set. Slice and serve.

9. Store the bread in a resealable plastic bag or airtight container on the counter for up to 3 days. For longer storage, cut into even slices, double-wrap tightly in plastic, place in a resealable plastic bag, and freeze for up to 3 months.

DOUBLE CRANBERRY-APPLESAUCE QUINOA QUICK BREAD

MAKES 1 (1½-POUND/680 G) LOAF • DAIRY FREE

Dried cranberries add some sweetness and chewiness to this bread, while the fresh cranberries give it a tart, bright flavor. Serve it alongside carved chicken or turkey, or cut it into small squares, toast, and use as the base for holiday canapés.

DRY INGREDIENTS

240 g (8.5 oz or 2 cups) Light Flour Blend (page 34)

104 g (3.7 oz or 1 cup) quinoa flakes

200 g (7.1 oz or 1 cup) granulated cane sugar

44 g (1.6 oz or ½ cup) Better Than Milk soy powder

1 tablespoon baking powder

1 tablespoon psyllium husk flakes or powder

1 teaspoon kosher salt

WET INGREDIENTS

3 large eggs, at room temperature (see page 39), beaten

120 ml (½ cup) unsweetened applesauce, plain or cinnamon

80 ml (⅓ cup) vegetable oil

110 g (4 oz or 1 cup) fresh or frozen cranberries (no need to thaw if frozen)

60 g (2 oz or ½ cup) dried cranberries

1. Set the bread pan on the counter and insert the beater paddle(s). Unless otherwise directed by your machine's manufacturer, add the liquids first, then the dry ingredients.

2. In a large mixing bowl, whisk the dry ingredients together.

3. In a 4-cup (1 liter) glass measuring cup, whisk the wet ingredients—*except* the cranberries—together. Stir in the cranberries and scrape into the bread pan. Use a spatula to spread the dry ingredients over the wet ingredients, covering completely.

4. Place the bread pan in the machine, settle it in the center, and lock it in place. Close the lid and select:

   Quick bread/cake cycle
   Loaf size: 1½ pounds/750 g
   Medium crust
   Start

5. About 3 minutes into the mixing process, open the lid and use a spatula to scrape down the sides of the pan, avoiding the paddle. Push any flour that has accumulated around the edges into the center. Check again once or twice during kneading, scraping the edges, corners, and under the dough. If the dough looks too wet or too dry, add a little flour blend or tiny amounts of warm water. Once the mix/knead cycle is done, leave the lid closed during the bake cycle.

6. At the end of the bake cycle, lift the lid and check the temperature. When the bread reaches 206°F to 210°F (97°C to 99°C) on an instant-read thermometer inserted in the center, it is done. Remove the pan from the machine and set it on its side on a wire cooling rack. Leave the bread in the pan for a couple of minutes, then turn the pan upside down and slide the loaf onto the wire rack. Carefully remove the paddle if it is embedded in the bottom of the loaf. Let the bread cool upside down for at least 2 hours before slicing.

7. Store the bread in a resealable plastic bag or airtight container on the counter for up to 3 days. For longer storage, cut into even slices, double-wrap tightly in plastic, place in a resealable plastic bag, and freeze for up to 3 months.

CRANBERRY-ORANGE BREAD

MAKES 1 (1½-POUND) LOAF • DAIRY FREE

Love fresh cranberry sauce with Thanksgiving dinner? Now you can have all that flavor in a bread! This is more savory than the Double Cranberry-Applesauce Quinoa Quick Bread on page 246. It's more versatile, too—use it for sliced turkey or roast beef sandwiches.

DRY INGREDIENTS

21 g (0.7 oz or 2 tablespoons) active dry yeast

360 g (12.7 oz or 3 cups) Light Flour Blend (page 34)

150 g (5.3 oz or ¾ cup) granulated cane sugar

1 tablespoon psyllium husk flakes or powder

2 teaspoons baking powder

1 teaspoon kosher or fine sea salt

⅛ teaspoon ascorbic acid, optional

WET INGREDIENTS

3 large eggs, at room temperature (see page 39), beaten

120 ml (½ cup) water, heated to about 80°F (27°C)

120 ml (½ cup) orange juice, at room temperature (see Note)

60 ml (¼ cup) vegetable or canola oil

2 teaspoons apple cider vinegar

220 g (8 oz or 2 cups) fresh or frozen cranberries (thawed first if frozen)

> NOTE: If you are using freshly squeezed orange juice, grate the zest first and add it to the wet ingredients for an extra layer of flavor.

1. Set the bread pan on the counter and insert the beater paddle(s). Unless otherwise directed by your machine's manufacturer, add the liquids first, then the dry ingredients, and finally the yeast.

2. Measure the yeast into a small bowl and set aside. In a large mixing bowl, whisk the remaining dry ingredients together.

3. In a 4-cup (1 liter) glass measuring cup, whisk the wet ingredients—*except* the cranberries—together. Stir in the cranberries and pour into the bread pan. Use a spatula to spread the dry ingredients over the wet ingredients, covering completely. Make a shallow well in the center and pour in the yeast.

4. Place the bread pan in the machine, settle it in the center, and lock it in place. Close the lid and select:

   Gluten-free cycle (see page 14 if your machine does not have this setting)
   Loaf size: 1½ pounds/750 g
   Medium crust
   Start

5. About 3 minutes into the mixing process, open the lid and use a spatula to scrape down the sides of the pan, avoiding the paddle. Push any flour that has accumulated around the edges into the center. Check again once or twice during kneading, scraping the edges, corners, and under the dough. If the dough looks too wet or too dry, add a little flour blend or tiny amounts of warm water. Once the mix/knead cycle is done, leave the lid closed during the rise and bake cycles.

6. At the end of the bake cycle, lift the lid and check the temperature. When the bread reaches 206°F to 210°F (97°C to 99°C) on an instant-read thermometer inserted in the center, it is done. Remove the pan from the machine and set it on its side on a wire cooling rack. Leave the bread in the pan for a couple of minutes, then turn the pan upside down and slide the loaf onto the wire rack. Carefully remove the paddle if it is embedded in the bottom of the loaf. Let the bread cool upside down for at least 2 hours before slicing.

7. Store the bread in a resealable plastic bag or airtight container on the counter for up to 3 days. For longer storage, cut into even slices, double-wrap tightly in plastic, place in a resealable plastic bag, and freeze for up to 3 months.

CURRANT-WALNUT QUICK BREAD

MAKES 1 (1½-POUND/680 G) LOAF ◆ DAIRY FREE

Currants are like tiny raisins, but tarter. You may find a product called Zante currants in your grocery store—these are actually miniature grapes and much sweeter than true currants. Either version will work in this recipe, but if you can't find them, you can use dark raisins. Toast the walnuts if you want to play up the nuttiness of this bread. The buckwheat flour adds an earthy quality without heaviness.

DRY INGREDIENTS

300 g (10.6 oz or 2½ cups) Light Flour Blend (page 34) or Whole-Grain Flour Blend (page 34)

60 g (2.1 oz or ½ cup) buckwheat flour

200 g (7.1 oz or 1 cup) granulated cane sugar

1 tablespoon psyllium husk flakes or powder

2 teaspoons baking powder

½ teaspoon kosher or fine sea salt

WET INGREDIENTS

125 g (4.4 oz or ½ cup) applesauce, at room temperature

80 ml (⅓ cup) vegetable oil

3 large eggs, at room temperature (see page 39), beaten

1 teaspoon pure vanilla extract

ADD-INS

120 g (4.2 oz or 1 cup) coarsely chopped walnuts

110 g (4 oz or ¾ cup) dried currants or dark raisins (see headnote)

1. Set the bread pan on the counter and insert the beater paddle(s). Unless otherwise directed by your machine's manufacturer, add the liquids first, then the dry ingredients.

2. In a large mixing bowl, whisk the dry ingredients together.

3. In a 4-cup (1 liter) glass measuring cup, whisk the wet ingredients together and pour into the bread pan. Use a spatula to spread the dry ingredients over the wet ingredients.

4. Place the bread pan in the machine, settle it in the center, and lock it in place. Close the lid and select:

   Quick bread/cake cycle
   Loaf size: 1½ pounds/750 g
   Light crust
   Start

5. After the first kneading cycle, scrape the sides and bottom of the pan with the spatula to make sure all the dry ingredients are incorporated. Add the walnuts and currants.

6. If your machine has alerts, when you hear the signal for the machine transitioning from the knead to the bake cycle, remove the kneading paddle and reshape the loaf. If the dough seems sticky, wet your hands with a little water to help with reshaping the loaf and smoothing the top. Close the lid and let the bread finish baking.

7. At the end of the bake cycle, lift the lid and check the temperature. The bread is done when it registers 206°F to 210°F (97°C to 99°C) on an instant-read thermometer inserted in the center of the loaf. Remove the pan from the machine and place it on its side on a wire rack. Leave the bread in the pan for a couple of minutes, then turn the pan upside down and slide the loaf onto the wire rack. Turn the loaf onto its side and cool for at least 2 hours before slicing.

8. Store the bread in a resealable plastic bag or airtight container on the counter for up to 3 days. For longer storage, cut into even slices, double-wrap tightly in plastic, place in a resealable plastic bag, and freeze for up to 3 months.

FRUITCAKE

MAKES 1 (1½-POUND/680 G) LOAF ◆ DAIRY FREE

This bread/cake was inspired by groom's cakes, which traditionally were fruitcakes. It is possible that the typical wedding cake was also a fruitcake up until the eighteenth century, when processed flour and baking soda were introduced. Traditionally, the groom's cake is not served; slices are boxed up and sent to family and guests who were unable to attend the ceremony. We made this recipe with orange extract to give it more citrusy flavor without adding extra dried fruit. Feel free to slice and ship to all your friends during the holiday season.

FRUIT MIXTURE

455 g (1 pound or 2½ cups) dried fruit of your choice, diced

210 g (7.4 oz or 1 cup) candied cherries, coarsely chopped or left whole

80 ml (⅓ cup) brandy, rum, or whiskey

1 tablespoon pure vanilla extract

DRY INGREDIENTS

21 g (0.7 oz or 2 tablespoons) active dry yeast

240 g (8.5 oz or 2 cups) Light Flour Blend (page 34) or Whole-Grain Flour Blend (page 34)

133 g (4.7 oz or ⅔ cup) granulated cane sugar

1 tablespoon baking powder

1 tablespoon psyllium husk flakes or powder

1 teaspoon ground nutmeg

¾ teaspoon ground cinnamon

¾ teaspoon kosher or fine sea salt

WET INGREDIENTS

112 g (4 oz or 8 tablespoons/1 stick) nondairy butter substitute, melted and slightly cooled

85 g (3 oz or ¼ cup) molasses (*not* blackstrap)

3 large eggs, at room temperature (see page 39), beaten

2 teaspoons orange extract

ADD-IN

56 g (2 oz or ½ cup) chopped pecans or other any other nut

ADDING ADD-INS

With regular breads made with wheat flour, additional ingredients are often added later in the kneading process because the gluten can support additions right at the end of kneading. With gluten-free yeast doughs, adding nuts or chocolate chips too late in the mixing process will weigh the dough down. Depending on what we are mixing in, sometimes we will recommend you add them to the dry or wet ingredients and other times they are added during mixing. If your machine has an automatic add-in feature, ignore it for your gluten-free baking.

1. Combine the fruit mixture ingredients in a heatproof bowl and microwave for 5 minutes. Set aside to macerate while you put together the rest of the ingredients.

2. Set the bread pan on the counter and insert the beater paddle(s). Unless otherwise directed by your machine's manufacturer, add the liquids first, then the dry ingredients, and finally the yeast.

3. Measure the yeast into a small bowl and set aside. In a large mixing bowl, whisk the remaining dry ingredients together.

4. In a 4-cup (1 liter) glass measuring cup, whisk the wet ingredients together and pour into the bread pan. Use a spatula to spread the dry ingredients over the wet ingredients. Make a shallow well in the center and sprinkle in the yeast.

5. Place the bread pan in the machine, settle it in the center, and lock it in place. Close the lid and select:

   Gluten-free cycle (see page 14 if your machine does not have this setting)
   Loaf size: 1½ pounds/750 g
   Medium crust
   Start

6. After the first knead cycle, scrape the sides and bottom of the pan with a spatula to make sure all the dry ingredients are incorporated. Add the macerated fruits with their soaking liquid, and the nuts. Once the mix/knead cycle is done, leave the lid closed and do not open it during the rise and bake cycles.

7. At the end of the bake cycle, lift the lid and check the temperature. The bread is done when it registers 206°F to 210°F (97°C to 99°C) on an instant-read thermometer inserted in the center of the loaf. Remove the pan from the machine and place it on its side on a wire rack. Leave the bread in the pan for a couple of minutes, then turn the pan upside down and slide the loaf onto the wire rack. Carefully remove the paddle if it is embedded in the bottom of the loaf. Lay the bread on its side and cool for at least 2 hours before slicing.

8. Store the bread in a resealable plastic bag or airtight container on the counter for up to 2 weeks. For longer storage, cut into even slices, double-wrap tightly in plastic, place in a resealable plastic bag, and freeze for up to 3 months.

LEMON QUICK BREAD

MAKES 1 (1½-POUND/680 G) LOAF • DAIRY FREE

Pucker up for this bread. Fresh lemon juice and lemon zest create a delightful loaf that makes a great snack or breakfast on the go. Add a lemon glaze to the top and you can serve it as a light, refreshing dessert. Almond flour adds nuttiness, a slightly chewy texture, and some additional protein. If your household has nut allergies, use an equal amount by weight of the Light Flour Blend in place of the almond flour.

DRY INGREDIENTS

300 g (10.6 oz or 2½ cups) Light Flour Blend (page 34)

56 g (2 oz or ½ cup) almond flour/meal

½ cup Better Than Milk soy powder (44 g/1.6 oz) or coconut milk powder (40 g/1.4 oz)

250 g (8.8 oz or 1¼ cups) granulated cane sugar

1 tablespoon baking powder

1 tablespoon psyllium husk flakes or powder

1 teaspoon kosher or fine sea salt

WET INGREDIENTS

3 large eggs, at room temperature (see page 39), beaten

Grated zest of 1 lemon

120 ml (½ cup) freshly squeezed lemon juice

80 ml (⅓ cup) vegetable or canola oil

1. Set the bread pan on the counter and insert the beater paddle(s). Unless otherwise directed by your machine's manufacturer, add the liquids first, then the dry ingredients.

2. In a large mixing bowl, whisk the dry ingredients together.

3. In a 4-cup (1 liter) glass measuring cup, whisk the wet ingredients together and pour into the bread pan. Use a spatula to spread the dry ingredients over the wet ingredients, covering completely.

4. Place the bread pan in the machine, settle it in the center, and lock it in place. Close the lid and select:

   Quick bread/cake cycle
   Loaf size: 1½ pounds/750 g
   Medium crust
   Start

5. About 3 minutes into the mixing process, open the lid and use a spatula to scrape down the sides of the pan, avoiding the paddle. Push any flour that has accumulated around the edges or under the dough into the center. Check again once or twice during kneading, scraping the edges, corners, and under the dough. If the dough looks too wet or too dry, add a little flour blend or tiny amounts of warm water.

6. At the end of the bake cycle, lift the lid and check the temperature. When the bread reaches 206°F to 210°F (97°C to 99°C) on an instant-read thermometer inserted in the center, it is done. Remove the pan from the machine and set it on its side on a wire cooling rack. Leave the bread in the pan for a couple of minutes, then turn the pan upside down and slide the loaf onto the wire rack. Carefully remove the paddle if it is embedded in the bottom of the loaf. Let the bread cool upside down for at least 2 hours before slicing.

7. Store the bread in a resealable plastic bag or airtight container on the counter for up to 3 days. For longer storage, cut into even slices, double-wrap tightly in plastic, place in a resealable plastic bag, and freeze for up to 3 months.

LEMON-BLUEBERRY BREAD

MAKES 1 (1½-POUND/680 G) LOAF • DAIRY FREE

Fresh blueberries are so naturally sweet that the lemon flavor tempers them perfectly in this bread, but you can also use frozen wild blueberries. Wild blueberries are smaller than the cultivated ones, which means more berry goodness throughout your loaf of bread. Thaw frozen wild blueberries in a bowl at room temperature for approximately 30 minutes, or defrost in the microwave for about 1 minute. This makes a great breakfast or tea bread with whipped cream cheese.

DRY INGREDIENTS

21 g (0.7 oz or 2 tablespoons) active dry yeast

360 g (12.7 oz or 3 cups) Light Flour Blend (page 34)

44 g (1.6 oz or ½ cup) Better Than Milk soy powder

150 g (5.3 oz or ¾ cup) granulated cane sugar

1 tablespoon psyllium husk flakes or powder

2 teaspoons baking powder

1 teaspoon kosher or fine sea salt

⅛ teaspoon ascorbic acid, optional

WET INGREDIENTS

3 large eggs, at room temperature (see page 39), beaten

180 ml (¾ cup) water, heated to about 80°F (27°C)

60 ml (¼ cup) vegetable or canola oil

2 teaspoons ume plum vinegar

2 teaspoons lemon extract

2 cups fresh or frozen blueberries (thawed first if frozen)

1. Set the bread pan on the counter and insert the beater paddle(s). Unless otherwise directed by your machine's manufacturer, add the liquids first, then the dry ingredients, and finally the yeast.

2. Measure the yeast into a small bowl and set aside. In a large mixing bowl, whisk the remaining dry ingredients together.

3. In a 4-cup (1 liter) glass measuring cup, whisk the wet ingredients—*except* the blueberries—together. Stir in the blueberries and pour into the bread pan. Use a spatula to spread the dry ingredients over the wet ingredients, covering completely. Make a shallow well in the center and pour in the yeast.

4. Place the bread pan in the machine, settle it in the center, and lock it in place. Close the lid and select:

   Gluten-free cycle (see page 14 if your machine does not have this setting)
   Loaf size: 1½ pounds/750 g
   Medium crust
   Start

5. About 3 minutes into the mixing process, open the lid and use a spatula to scrape down the sides of the pan, avoiding the paddle. Push any flour that has accumulated around the edges into the center. Check again once or twice during kneading, scraping the edges, corners, and under the dough. If the dough looks too wet or too dry, add a little flour blend or tiny amounts of warm water. Once the mixing/kneading is done, leave the lid closed during the rise and bake cycles.

6. At the end of the bake cycle, lift the lid and check the temperature. When the bread reaches 206°F to 210°F (97°C to 99°C) on an instant-read thermometer inserted in the center, it is done. Remove the pan from the machine and set it on its side on a wire cooling rack. Leave the bread in the pan for a couple of minutes, then turn the pan upside down and slide the loaf onto the wire rack. Carefully remove the paddle if it is embedded in the bottom of the loaf. Let the bread cool upside down for at least 2 hours before slicing.

7. Store the bread in a resealable plastic bag or airtight container on the counter for up to 3 days. For longer storage, cut into even slices, double-wrap tightly in plastic, place in a resealable plastic bag, and freeze for up to 3 months.

LIME-POPPY SEED QUICK BREAD

MAKES 1 (1½-POUND/680 G) LOAF • DAIRY FREE

Poppy seeds add a crunchy texture and a slightly nutty taste to this bright lime quick bread. Sprinkle the top with confectioners' sugar or spread on some Raspberry Frosting (page 283) for a delightful springtime celebration. This bread would be perfect served at a tea party, a bridal or baby shower, or alongside a cup of coffee any time of year.

DRY INGREDIENTS

300 g (10.6 oz or 2½ cups) Light Flour Blend (page 34)

60 g (2.1 oz or ½ cup) millet flour

44 g (1.6 oz or ½ cup) Better Than Milk soy powder

200 g (7.1 oz or 1 cup) granulated cane sugar

2 tablespoons poppy seeds

1 tablespoon baking powder

1 tablespoon psyllium husk flakes or powder

1 teaspoon kosher or fine sea salt

WET INGREDIENTS

3 large eggs, at room temperature (see page 39), beaten

120 ml (½ cup) water, heated to about 80°F (27°C)

Grated zest of 1 lime

90 ml (¼ cup plus 2 tablespoons) freshly squeezed lime juice

60 ml (¼ cup) vegetable or canola oil

1. Set the bread pan on the counter and insert the beater paddle(s). Unless otherwise directed by your machine's manufacturer, add the liquids first, then the dry ingredients.

2. In a large mixing bowl, whisk the dry ingredients together.

3. In a 4-cup (1 liter) glass measuring cup, whisk the wet ingredients together and pour into the bread pan. Use a spatula to spread the dry ingredients over the wet ingredients, covering completely.

4. Place the bread pan in the machine, settle it in the center, and lock it in place. Close the lid and select:

   Quick bread/cake cycle
   Loaf size: 1½ pounds/750 g
   Medium crust
   Start

5. About 3 minutes into the mixing process, open the lid and use a spatula to scrape down the sides of the pan, avoiding the paddle. Push any flour that has accumulated around the edges into the center. Check again once or twice during kneading, scraping the edges, corners, and under the dough. If the dough looks too wet or too dry, add a little flour blend or tiny amounts of warm water. Once the mix/knead cycle is done, leave the lid closed during the bake cycle.

6. At the end of the bake cycle, lift the lid and check the temperature. When the bread reaches 206°F to 210°F (97°C to 99°C) on an instant-read thermometer inserted in the center, it is done. Remove the pan from the machine and set it on its side on a wire cooling rack. Leave the bread in the pan for a couple of minutes, then turn the pan upside down and slide the loaf onto the wire rack. Carefully remove the paddle if it is embedded in the bottom of the loaf. Let the bread cool upside down for at least 2 hours before slicing.

7. Store the bread in a resealable plastic bag or airtight container on the counter for up to 3 days. For longer storage, cut into even slices, double-wrap tightly in plastic, place in a resealable plastic bag, and freeze for up to 3 months.

NUT 'N' FRUIT BREAD

MAKES 1 (1½-POUND/680 G) LOAF ◆ DAIRY FREE

Are you tired of eating gluten-free crackers with cheese and dream of a nutty bread to have with a glass of wine? Thin slices of this bread are the perfect addition to cheese boards, but they're equally delicious with tea at breakfast. This extremely dense loaf is loaded with so many dried fruits and nuts that it is hard to imagine how it holds together—thank goodness for sticky fruit! With only one wet ingredient, it will look very dry as it mixes, but don't add any more liquid. If your machine has a beeper that alerts you when the bake cycle is starting, we suggest you remove the paddle at that point and smooth out the top.

DRY INGREDIENTS

240 g (8.5 oz or 2 cups) Light Flour Blend (page 34) or Whole-Grain Flour Blend (page 34)

2 teaspoons active dry yeast (see Note, opposite)

1 tablespoon psyllium husk flakes or powder

½ teaspoon kosher or fine sea salt

145 g (5 oz or 1 cup) golden raisins

145 g (5 oz or 1 cup) dark raisins or currants

145 g (5 oz or 1 cup) chopped dates

145 g (1 oz or 1 cup) quartered dried apricots

55 g (2 oz or ½ cup) chopped pecans

55 g (2 oz or ½ cup) chopped walnuts

55 g (2 oz or ½ cup) sliced almonds

WET INGREDIENT

400 ml (1¾ cups) unsweetened coconut milk, warmed to about 80°F (27°C)

> **NOTE:** The yeast is added merely for flavor, not for lift, so it is okay to mix it with the other dry ingredients instead of adding it on top as usual. Given the density of this bread, do not expect it to rise at all.

1. Set the bread pan on the counter and insert the beater paddle(s). Unless otherwise directed by your machine's manufacturer, add the liquids first, then the dry ingredients.

2. Whisk the flour blend, yeast, psyllium, and salt together in a large mixing bowl. Add the dried fruit and nuts. Stir and toss to coat the fruit and nuts well with the dry ingredients.

3. Pour the coconut milk into the bread pan. Add the dry ingredients to the pan, spreading them out with a spatula until all the milk is covered.

4. Place the bread pan in the machine, settle it in the center, and lock it in place. Close the lid and select:

   Quick bread/cake cycle
   Loaf size: 1½ pounds/750 g
   Medium crust
   Start

5. After the first knead cycle, scrape the sides and bottom of the pan with a spatula to make sure all the dry ingredients are incorporated. It will look dry, but that's fine; this bread is very dense. After the second knead cycle, remove the paddle and smooth the top of the dough. Close the lid and do not open during the bake cycle.

6. At the end of the bake cycle, lift the lid and check the temperature. The bread is done when it registers 206°F to 210°F (97°C to 99°C) on an instant-read thermometer inserted in the center of the loaf. Remove the pan from the machine and place it on its side on a wire rack. Leave the bread in the pan for 3 minutes, then turn the pan upside down and slide the loaf onto the wire rack on its side. Let the bread cool on its side for at least 2 hours before slicing.

7. Store the bread in a resealable plastic bag or airtight container on the counter for up to 3 days. For longer storage, cut into even slices, double-wrap tightly in plastic, place in a resealable plastic bag, and freeze for up to 3 months.

ORANGE-GLAZED QUICK BREAD

MAKES 1 (1½-POUND/680 G) LOAF • DAIRY FREE

Winter is a great time to make this bread, since citrus is plentiful and cheap. It will bring a taste of sunshine to your kitchen. Glazing a bread makes it more festive for brunch or a special breakfast celebration. Sprinkle the top with some finely chopped candied peel to add even more color and texture.

DRY INGREDIENTS

300 g (10.6 oz or 2½ cups) Light Flour Blend (page 34) or Whole-Grain Flour Blend (page 34)

200 g (7.1 oz or 1 cup) granulated cane sugar

60 g (2.1 oz or ½ cup) millet flour

20 g (0.7 oz or ¼ cup) coconut milk powder

1 tablespoon baking powder

1 tablespoon psyllium husk flakes or powder

1 teaspoon kosher or fine sea salt

WET INGREDIENTS

80 ml (⅓ cup) vegetable oil

3 large eggs, at room temperature (see page 39), beaten

120 ml (½ cup) freshly squeezed orange juice or water, warmed to about 80°F (27°C)

1 teaspoon orange extract

44 g (1.6 oz or ¼ cup) finely chopped candied orange peel (see Note)

GLAZE

90 g (3.2 oz or ¾ cup) confectioners' sugar

30 ml (2 tablespoons) freshly squeezed orange juice

15 to 30 ml (1 to 2 tablespoons) hot water, as needed

NOTE: Candied orange peel can be found in the supermarket—no need to make it yourself. Just chop it up.

1. Set the bread pan on the counter and insert the beater paddle(s). Unless otherwise directed by your machine's manufacturer, add the liquids first, then the dry ingredients.

2. In a large mixing bowl, whisk the dry ingredients together.

3. In a 4-cup (1 liter) glass measuring cup, whisk the wet ingredients—*except* the candied orange peel—together. Stir in the orange peel and pour into the bread pan. Use a spatula to spread the dry ingredients over the wet ingredients.

4. Place the bread pan in the machine, settle it in the center, and lock it in place. Close the lid and select:

   Quick bread/cake cycle
   Loaf size: 1½ pounds/750 g
   Medium crust
   Start

5. After the first knead cycle, scrape the sides and bottom of the pan with the spatula to make sure all the dry ingredients are incorporated.

6. If your machine has alerts, when you hear the signal for the machine transitioning from the knead to the bake cycle, remove the kneading paddle and reshape the loaf. If the dough seems sticky, wet your hands with a little water to help with reshaping the loaf and smoothing the top. Close the lid and let the bread finish baking undisturbed.

7. At the end of the bake cycle, lift the lid and check the temperature. The bread is done when it registers 206°F to 210°F (97°C to 99°C) on an instant-read thermometer inserted in the center of the loaf. Remove the pan from the machine and place it on its side on a wire rack. Leave the bread in the pan for a couple of minutes, then turn the pan upside down and slide the loaf onto the wire rack. Lay the bread on its side and cool for at least 2 hours before glazing and slicing.

8. To make the glaze, whisk the confectioners' sugar and orange juice together in a small bowl. Add the water, a little at a time, until you achieve the desired consistency. Drizzle the bread with the glaze and let it set for about 15 minutes before slicing.

9. Store the bread in a resealable plastic bag or airtight container on the counter for up to 3 days. For longer storage, cut into even slices, double-wrap tightly in plastic, place in a resealable plastic bag, and freeze for up to 3 months.

PEAR-GINGER QUICK BREAD

MAKES 1 (1½-POUND/680 G) LOAF • DAIRY FREE

Use Bosc pears in this recipe for their crisp-dense texture and pleasantly sweet flavor, which is balanced with hints of fall spices and both fresh and crystallized ginger. Pears are at their peak from September to March, so this bread is a lovely treat on a blustery winter day. Grating the pears ensures a fine texture and moistness, making it a wonderful bread to serve sliced with butter for breakfast.

DRY INGREDIENTS

360 g (12.7 oz or 3 cups) Light Flour Blend (page 34)

44 g (1.6 oz or ½ cup) Better Than Milk soy powder

200 g (7.1 oz or 1 cup) granulated cane sugar

1 tablespoon psyllium husk flakes or powder

2 teaspoons baking powder

1 teaspoon kosher or fine sea salt

WET INGREDIENTS

3 large eggs, at room temperature (see page 39), beaten

180 ml (¾ cup) water, warmed to about 80°F (27°C)

60 ml (¼ cup) vegetable or canola oil

2 teaspoons pure vanilla extract

2 teaspoons grated peeled fresh ginger

ADD-INS

220 g (7.8 oz or 2 cups) grated peeled Bosc pear

118 g (4.2 oz or ½ cup) finely chopped crystallized or candied ginger

1. Set the bread pan on the counter and insert the beater paddle(s). Unless otherwise directed by your machine's manufacturer, add the liquids first, then the dry ingredients.

2. In a large mixing bowl, whisk the dry ingredients together.

3. In a 4-cup (1 liter) glass measuring cup, whisk the wet ingredients together and pour into the bread pan. Use a spatula to spread the dry ingredients over the wet ingredients, covering completely.

4. Place the bread pan in the machine, settle it in the center, and lock it in place. Close the lid and select:

   Quick bread/cake cycle
   Loaf size: 1½ pounds/750 g
   Medium crust
   Start

5. About 3 minutes into the mixing process, open the lid and use a spatula to scrape down the sides of the pan, avoiding the paddle. Push any flour that has accumulated around the edges or under the dough into the center. Check again once or twice during kneading, scraping the edges, corners, and under the dough. If the dough looks too wet or too dry, add a little flour blend or tiny amounts of warm water.

6. After the first knead cycle, add the pear and crystallized ginger. Once the mix/knead cycle is done, leave the lid closed during the bake cycle.

7. At the end of the bake cycle, lift the lid and check the temperature. When the bread reaches 206°F to 210°F (97°C to 99°C) on an instant-read thermometer inserted in the center, it is done. Remove the pan from the machine and set it on its side on a wire cooling rack. Leave the bread in the pan for a couple of minutes, then turn the pan upside down and slide the loaf onto the wire rack. Carefully remove the paddle if it is embedded in the bottom of the loaf. Let the bread cool on its side for least 2 hours before slicing.

8. Store the bread in a resealable plastic bag or airtight container on the counter for up to 3 days. For longer storage, cut into even slices, double-wrap tightly in plastic, place in a resealable plastic bag, and freeze for up to 3 months.

PINEAPPLE-COCONUT QUICK BREAD

MAKES 1 (1½-POUND/680 G) LOAF ◆ DAIRY FREE

This bread is like a giant pineapple-scented macaroon. Loaded with sweetened shredded coconut, coconut flour, and coconut milk, this pineapple-studded loaf is reminiscent of the breads you find in Brazil, called *rosca de coco*. It's sweet but not too sweet, soft but with a sweet, crunchy crust. Don't be surprised if you find yourself singing "The Girl from Ipanema" while it bakes.

DRY INGREDIENTS

300 g (10.6 oz or 2½ cups) Light Flour Blend (page 34)

59 g (2.1 oz or ½ cup) coconut flour

200 g (7.1 oz or 1 cup) granulated cane sugar

1 tablespoon psyllium husk flakes or powder

2 teaspoons baking powder

1 teaspoon kosher or fine sea salt

WET INGREDIENTS

3 large eggs, at room temperature (see page 39), beaten

240 ml (1 cup) unsweetened coconut milk, warmed to about 80°F (27°C)

80 ml (⅓ cup) vegetable or canola oil

2 teaspoons pure vanilla extract

ADD-INS

170 g (6 oz or 2 cups) sweetened shredded coconut

168 g (6.3 oz or 1 cup) chopped dried pineapple

1. Set the bread pan on the counter and insert the beater paddle(s). Unless otherwise directed by your machine's manufacturer, add the liquids first, then the dry ingredients.

2. In a large mixing bowl, whisk the dry ingredients together.

3. In a 4-cup (1 liter) glass measuring cup, whisk the wet ingredients together and pour into the bread pan. Use a spatula to spread the dry ingredients over the wet ingredients, covering completely.

4. Place the bread pan in the machine, settle it in the center, and lock it in place. Close the lid and select:

   Quick bread/cake cycle
   Loaf size: 1½ pounds/750 g
   Medium crust
   Start

5. About 3 minutes into the mixing process, open the lid and use a spatula to scrape down the sides of the pan, avoiding the paddle. Push any flour that has accumulated around the edges into the center. Check again once or twice during kneading, scraping the edges, corners, and under the dough. If the dough looks too wet or too dry, add a little flour blend or tiny amounts of warm water.

6. After the first kneading cycle, add the coconut and pineapple. Once the mix/knead cycle is done, leave the lid closed during the bake cycle.

7. At the end of the bake cycle, lift the lid and check the temperature. When the bread reaches 206°F to 210°F (97°C to 99°C) on an instant-read thermometer inserted in the center, it is done. Remove the pan from the machine and set it on its side on a wire cooling rack. Leave the bread in the pan for a couple of minutes, then turn the pan upside down and slide the loaf onto the wire rack. Carefully remove the paddle if it is embedded in the bottom of the loaf. Let the bread cool on its side for at least 2 hours before slicing.

8. Store the bread in a resealable plastic bag or airtight container on the counter for up to 3 days. For longer storage, cut into even slices, double-wrap tightly in plastic, place in a resealable plastic bag, and freeze for up to 3 months.

RASPBERRY QUICK BREAD
WITH STREUSEL TOPPING

MAKES 1 (1½-POUND/680 G) LOAF ◆ DAIRY-FREE OPTION

With their rich color and sweet juicy taste, raspberries remain one of the world's most consumed berries. Stored in the refrigerator, raspberries are at their peak for about two days. Bake them in this bread and enjoy raspberries for breakfast for at least a week.

DRY INGREDIENTS

240 g (8.5 oz or 2 cups) Light Flour Blend (page 34) or Whole-Grain Flour Blend (page 34)

118 g (4.2 oz or 1 cup) millet flour

200 g (7.1 oz or 1 cup) granulated cane sugar

1 tablespoon baking powder

1 tablespoon psyllium husk flakes or powder

1 teaspoon kosher or fine sea salt

WET INGREDIENTS

120 ml (½ cup) unsweetened coconut milk, warmed to about 80°F (27°C)

¼ cup vegetable oil (60 ml) or unsalted butter or nondairy butter substitute (55 g/2 oz or ½ stick), melted and slightly cooled

2 large eggs, at room temperature (see page 39), beaten

2 teaspoons pure vanilla extract

ADD-IN

170 g (6 oz or 1⅓ cups) fresh raspberries

STREUSEL TOPPING

170 g (6 oz or ¾ cup firmly packed) light brown sugar

30 g (1.1 oz or ¼ cup) Light Flour Blend (page 34) or Whole-Grain Flour Blend (page 34)

⅛ teaspoon kosher or fine sea salt

28 g (1 oz or 2 tablespoons/¼ stick) unsalted butter or nondairy butter substitute, chilled and cubed

1. Set the bread pan on the counter and insert the beater paddle(s). Unless otherwise directed by your machine's manufacturer, add the liquids first, then the dry ingredients.

2. In a large mixing bowl, whisk the dry ingredients together.

3. In a 4-cup (1 liter) glass measuring cup, whisk the wet ingredients together and pour into the bread pan. Use a spatula to spread the dry ingredients over the wet ingredients.

4. Place the bread pan in the machine, settle it in the center, and lock it in place. Close the lid and select:

   Quick bread/cake cycle
   Loaf size: 1½ pounds/750 g
   Light crust
   Start

5. After the first kneading cycle, scrape the sides and bottom of the pan with a spatula to make sure all the dry ingredients are incorporated. Add the raspberries. Close the lid and let the machine finish mixing and kneading.

6. Meanwhile, in a small bowl, mix the streusel ingredients together with a fork. It should look like wet sand.

7. If your machine has alerts, when you hear the signal for the machine transitioning from the knead to the bake cycle, remove the kneading paddle and reshape the loaf. If the dough seems sticky, wet your hands with a little water to help with reshaping the loaf and smoothing the top. Scatter the streusel evenly over the top. Close the lid and let the bread finish baking undisturbed.

8. At the end of the bake cycle, lift the lid and check the temperature. The bread is done when it registers 206°F to 210°F (97°C to 99°C) on an instant-read thermometer inserted in the center of the loaf. Remove the pan from the machine and place it on its side on a wire rack. Leave the bread in the pan for a couple of minutes, then turn the pan upside down and slide the loaf onto the wire rack. Turn the loaf on its side and cool for at least 2 hours before slicing.

9. Store the bread in a resealable plastic bag or airtight container on the counter for up to 1 week. For longer storage, cut into even slices, double-wrap tightly in plastic, place in a resealable bag, and freeze for up to 3 months.

TRAIL MIX BREAD

MAKES 1 (1½-POUND/680 G) LOAF ◆ DAIRY FREE

This bread is denser than the Honey Granola Bread (page 298), and with a different combination of ingredients. Packed with healthy fruits and nuts, it is great to take along on a hike, keeping you feeling full longer and giving you added energy. Pick a trail mix that contains lots of the good stuff, like nuts, seeds, dried fruits, and whole-grain cereals, without high-fructose corn syrup, starches, or gums. And make sure the brand you choose is certified gluten free.

DRY INGREDIENTS

21 g (0.7 oz or 2 tablespoons) active dry yeast

360 g (12.7 oz or 3 cups) Light Flour Blend (page 34)

44 g (1.6 oz or ½ cup) Better Than Milk soy powder

100 g (3.5 oz or ½ cup) granulated cane sugar

1 tablespoon psyllium husk flakes or powder

2 teaspoons baking powder

1 teaspoon kosher or fine sea salt

⅛ teaspoon ascorbic acid, optional

WET INGREDIENTS

3 large eggs, at room temperature (see page 39), beaten

240 ml (1 cup) water, heated to about 80°F (27°C)

60 ml (¼ cup) vegetable or canola oil

2 teaspoons ume plum vinegar

2 teaspoons pure vanilla extract

ADD-IN

300 g (10.6 oz or 2 cups) gluten-free, dairy-free trail mix

1. Set the bread pan on the counter and insert the beater paddle(s). Unless otherwise directed by your machine's manufacturer, add the liquids first, then the dry ingredients, and finally the yeast.

2. Measure the yeast into a small bowl and set aside. In a large mixing bowl, whisk the remaining dry ingredients together.

3. In a 4-cup (1 liter) glass measuring cup, whisk the wet ingredients together and pour into the bread pan. Use a spatula to spread the dry ingredients over the wet ingredients, covering completely. Make a shallow well in the center and pour in the yeast.

4. Place the bread pan in the machine, settle it in the center, and lock it in place. Close the lid and select:

   Gluten-free cycle (see page 14 if your machine does not have this setting)
   Loaf size: 1½ pounds/750 g
   Medium crust
   Start

5. About 3 minutes into the mixing process, open the lid and use a spatula to scrape down the sides of the pan, avoiding the paddle. Push any flour that has accumulated around the edges or under the dough into the center. Check again once or twice during kneading, scraping the edges, corners, and under the dough. If the dough looks too wet or too dry, add a little flour blend or tiny amounts of warm water.

6. After the first kneading cycle, add the trail mix. Once the mix/knead cycle is done, leave the lid closed during the rise and bake cycles.

7. At the end of the bake cycle, lift the lid and check the temperature. When the bread reaches 206°F to 210°F (97°C to 99°C) on an instant-read thermometer inserted in the center, it is done. Remove the pan from the machine and set it on its side on a wire cooling rack. Leave the bread in the pan for a couple of minutes, then turn the pan upside down and slide the loaf onto the wire rack. Carefully remove the paddle if it is embedded in the bottom of the loaf. Let the bread cool upside down for at least 2 hours before slicing.

8. Store the bread in a resealable plastic bag or airtight container on the counter for up to 3 days. For longer storage, cut into even slices, double-wrap tightly in plastic, place in a resealable plastic bag, and freeze for up to 3 months.

ZUCCHINI-APPLESAUCE QUICK BREAD

MAKES 1 (1½-POUND/680 G) LOAF • DAIRY FREE

Freshly grated zucchini creates a classic quick bread spiced with cinnamon. It often contains raisins, but we're using nondairy chocolate chips instead! Adding applesauce gives it more flavor and moisture while reducing some of the fat, since it replaces a portion of the oil. This bread is a great opportunity to finish off a nearly-empty jar of applesauce and to make use of a bounty of zucchini from your garden. It is also a delicious, if slightly sneaky, way to get picky eaters to eat their vegetables. After a bite or two, they may be more willing to accept "green foods" on their plates.

DRY INGREDIENTS

180 g (6.3 oz or 1½ cups) Light Flour Blend (page 34) or Whole-Grain Flour Blend (page 34)

118 g (4.2 oz or 1 cup) millet flour

250 g (8.8 oz or 1¼ cups) granulated cane sugar

2 teaspoons baking powder

2 teaspoons psyllium husk flakes or powder

1 teaspoon kosher or fine sea salt

¾ teaspoon ground cinnamon

WET INGREDIENTS

3 large eggs, at room temperature (see page 39), beaten

125 g (4.4 oz or ½ cup) applesauce

80 ml (⅓ cup) vegetable oil

2 teaspoons pure vanilla extract

120 g (4.2 oz or 1 cup) grated peeled zucchini

ADD-IN

85 g (3 oz or ½ cup) gluten-free, dairy-free semisweet chocolate chips (such as Enjoy Life brand)

1. Set the bread pan on the counter and insert the beater paddle(s). Unless otherwise directed by your machine's manufacturer, add the liquids first, then the dry ingredients.

2. In a large mixing bowl, whisk the dry ingredients together.

3. In a 4-cup (1 liter) glass measuring cup, whisk the wet ingredients—*except* the zucchini—together. Stir in the grated zucchini and pour into the bread pan. Use a spatula to spread the dry ingredients over the wet ingredients.

4. Place the bread pan in the machine, settle it in the center, and lock it in place. Close the lid and select:

   Quick bread/cake cycle
   Loaf size: 1½ pounds/750 g
   Medium crust
   Start

5. After the first knead cycle, scrape the sides and bottom of the pan with a spatula to make sure all the dry ingredients are incorporated. Add the chocolate chips. Once the mix/knead cycle is done, leave the lid closed during the bake cycle.

6. At the end of the bake cycle, lift the lid and check the temperature. The bread is done when it registers 206°F to 210°F (97°C to 99°C) on an instant-read thermometer inserted in the center of the loaf. Remove the pan from the machine and place it on its side on a wire rack. Leave the bread in the pan for a couple of minutes, then turn the pan upside down and slide the loaf onto the wire rack. Carefully remove the paddle if it is embedded in the bottom of the loaf. Lay the bread on its side and cool for at least 2 hours before slicing.

7. Store the bread in a resealable plastic bag or airtight container on the counter for up to 3 days. For longer storage, cut into even slices, double-wrap tightly in plastic, place in a resealable plastic bag, and freeze for up to 3 months.

Sweet

BREADS

The majority of the breads in this chapter are quick breads. Since you aren't using yeast, there's no need to bring the ingredients—other than the eggs—to room temperature. Set the machine to the quick bread/cake cycle and smell the wonderful aromas in a matter of minutes.

In summer and fall, we scout the farmers' markets for late-harvest fruits and vegetables like tomatoes, zucchini, and butternut squash. They are perfect for making dense, flavorful quick breads to serve for breakfast or an after-school snack. What better way to start the day than with a slice of White Chocolate–Pistachio Quick Bread or Honey Granola Bread paired with sliced melon or berries and yogurt?

Pumpkin Quick Bread, Gingerbread, and Italian Panettone Holiday Bread usher in the holiday season for many who tend not to bake year-round. The scent of cinnamon, cloves, allspice, and nutmeg will make your house smell festive in no time. Many of the recipes in this chapter are so aromatic that they not only evoke the holidays but conjure exotic places as well. The Coconut Curry Quick Bread and the Almond Quick Bread with Cardamom each have a heady perfume like you would find in a wonderful spice market.

Coffee and tea shops provide inspiration for breads that mirror the flavors of the products they sell. The Chai Latte Bread and Matcha Green Tea Quick Bread are new "classics" for our weekend brunches and as hostess gifts. Unconventional pairings and flavors really spark conversations.

Most of the recipes in this chapter are wonderful topped with ice cream, hot fudge, or caramel sauce. If you're feeling really indulgent, make a bread sundae with whipped cream, nuts, and cherries. You can also layer these breads to make trifles, bread puddings, or even French toast.

These sweet breads are not only delicious, but they are also less delicate than the sandwich breads. The structure is denser, so they don't suffer from being handled as much. While we don't recommend removing the paddle from sandwich breads, you have the option to do that with these quick breads. You might lose a little of the lift and rise if you stop the machine, remove the paddle, and smooth the top of the dough before baking, but some people prefer that to having a hole in the finished bread.

You're in for a treat—in more ways than one—with the breads in this chapter.

SIMPLIFY YOUR BAKING

The bread machine not only simplifies making your own breads from scratch, but it also helps save on counter space, because the mixing and baking takes place in the machine. If space is at a premium in your kitchen, think outside the box. Utilize other areas of your home, such as plugging the machine in and setting it on your dining room table while you use your kitchen to prepare the rest of the meal. On nice days, you might even consider placing it outside in a covered area where the aromas will attract your neighbors.

ALMOND QUICK BREAD WITH CARDAMOM

MAKES 1 (1½-POUND/680 G) POUND LOAF • DAIRY FREE

Cardamom is a member of the ginger family, used as a spice and also medicinally in many parts of the world. It is often used in Scandinavian cakes and pastries as well as Indian sweets. It's the perfect spice to pair with the almonds in this bread. It is wonderful sliced and toasted, but try grilling it for a touch of smokiness. For a simple and delicious dessert, top it with vanilla ice cream or frozen yogurt.

DRY INGREDIENTS

300 g (10.6 oz or 2½ cups) Light Flour Blend (page 34)

56 g (2 oz or ½ cup) almond flour

20 g (0.7 oz or ¼ cup) coconut milk powder

200 g (7.1 oz or 1 cup) granulated cane sugar

1 tablespoon baking powder

1 tablespoon psyllium husk flakes or powder

2 teaspoons ground cardamom

1 teaspoon kosher or fine sea salt

110 g (3.8 oz or 1 cup) slivered almonds, toasted

WET INGREDIENTS

3 large eggs, at room temperature (see page 39), beaten

180 ml (¾ cup) water

60 ml (¼ cup) vegetable or canola oil

1. Set the bread pan on the counter and insert the beater paddle(s). Unless otherwise directed by your machine's manufacturer, add the liquids first, then the dry ingredients.

2. In a large mixing bowl, whisk the dry ingredients—*except* the slivered almonds—together. Stir in the almonds and set aside.

ALMOND FLOUR

If you have never worked with almond flour before, you are in for a treat. Made from peeled and very finely ground fresh almonds, it is sometimes called almond meal. You get a delectable nuttiness, and the extra oils add a lushness to your baked goods. It is coarser than other flours and can be used in much the same way, but for gluten-free breads, it is wisest to use it in combination with a flour blend. If someone in your household is allergic to almonds, you can substitute hazelnut meal—both are readily available from Bob's Red Mill (see Resources, page 376). Always store nut meals in an airtight container in the freezer to keep them as fresh as possible.

3. In a 4-cup (1 liter) glass measuring cup, whisk the wet ingredients together and pour into the bread pan. Use a spatula to spread the dry ingredients over the wet ingredients, covering completely.

4. Place the bread pan in the machine, settle it in the center, and lock it in place. Close the lid and select:

   Quick bread/cake cycle
   Loaf size: 1½ pounds/750 g
   Medium crust
   Start

5. About 3 minutes into the mixing process, open the lid and use a spatula to scrape down the sides of the pan, avoiding the paddle. Push any flour that has accumulated around the edges and under the paddle into the center. Check again once or twice during kneading, scraping the edges, corners, and under the dough. If the dough looks too wet or too dry, add a little flour blend or tiny amounts of warm water.

6. If your machine has alerts, when you hear the signal for the machine transitioning from the knead to the bake cycle, remove the paddle and reshape the loaf. If the dough seems sticky, wet your hands with a little water to help with reshaping the loaf and smoothing the top. Close the lid and let the bread finish baking undisturbed.

7. At the end of the bake cycle, lift the lid and check the temperature. When the bread reaches 206°F to 210°F (97°C to 99°C) on an instant-read thermometer inserted in the center, it is done. Remove the pan from the machine and set it on its side on a wire cooling rack. Leave the bread in the pan for a couple of minutes, then turn the pan upside down and slide the loaf onto the wire rack. Let the bread cool upside down for at least 2 hours before slicing.

8. Store the bread in a resealable plastic bag or airtight container on the counter for up to 3 days. For longer storage, cut into even slices, double-wrap tightly in plastic, place in a resealable plastic bag, and freeze for up to 3 months.

BUTTERNUT SQUASH QUICK BREAD

MAKES 1 (1½-POUND/680 G) LOAF ◆ DAIRY FREE

With its natural sweetness, butternut squash makes a wonderful addition to quick breads. All-natural butternut squash flour is 100 percent butternut squash with no gluten fillers. It adds an extra serving of vegetables to this bread, as well as a delightful chewiness. The freshly grated squash lends texture and freshness in addition to moisture. If you do not have squash flour, you can substitute ½ cup of any nut flour you have on hand.

DRY INGREDIENTS

300 g (10.6 oz or 2½ cups) Light Flour Blend (page 34) or Whole-Grain Flour blend (page 34)

56 g (2 oz or ½ cup) butternut squash flour (see Resources, page 376)

100 g (3.5 oz or 1 cup) granulated cane sugar

1 tablespoon baking powder

1 tablespoon psyllium husk flakes or powder

1 teaspoon kosher or fine sea salt

¾ teaspoon ground nutmeg

WET INGREDIENTS

3 large eggs, at room temperature (see page 39), beaten

120 ml (½ cup) unsweetened coconut milk

60 ml (¼ cup) vegetable oil

2 teaspoons pure vanilla extract

140 g (4.9 oz or 1 cup) grated peeled butternut squash

1. Set the bread pan on the counter and insert the beater paddle(s). Unless otherwise directed by your machine's manufacturer, add the liquids first, then the dry ingredients.

2. In a large mixing bowl, whisk the dry ingredients together.

3. In a 4-cup (1 liter) glass measuring cup, whisk the wet ingredients—*except* the grated squash—together. Stir in the squash and pour into the bread pan. Use a spatula to spread the dry ingredients over the wet ingredients, covering completely.

4. Place the bread pan in the machine, settle it in the center, and lock it in place. Close the lid and select:

   Quick bread/cake cycle
   Loaf size: 1½ pounds/750 g
   Light crust
   Start

5. After the first knead cycle, scrape the sides and bottom of the pan with the spatula to make sure all the dry ingredients are incorporated.

6. If your machine has alerts, when you hear the signal for the machine transitioning from the knead to the bake cycle, remove the paddle and reshape the loaf. If the dough seems sticky, wet your hands with a little water to help with reshaping the loaf and smoothing the top. Close the lid and let the bread finish baking.

7. At the end of the bake cycle, lift the lid and check the temperature. When the bread reaches 206°F to 210°F (97°C to 99°C) on an instant-read thermometer inserted in the center, it is done. Remove the pan from the machine and set it on its side on a wire rack. Leave the bread in the pan for 3 minutes, then slide the loaf out of the pan. Cool the bread on its side for at least 1 hour before slicing.

8. Store the bread in a resealable plastic bag or airtight container on the counter for up to 3 days. For longer storage, cut into even slices, double-wrap tightly in plastic, place in a resealable plastic bag, and freeze for up to 3 months.

CARROT-RAISIN BREAD

MAKES 1 (1½-POUND/680 G) LOAF • DAIRY FREE

This carrot-raisin bread is closer to sandwich bread than a quick bread. A new variation of raisin bread, this yeast version gives an otherwise dense bread a more cake-like consistency and savory flavor. A great way to use up those extra carrots in your fridge, it will no doubt become a new favorite for toast in the morning—especially when covered with a thick layer of cream cheese.

DRY INGREDIENTS

21 g (0.7 oz or 2 tablespoons) active dry yeast

360 g (12.7 oz or 3 cups) Light Flour Blend (page 34)

44 g (1.6 oz or ½ cup) Better than Milk soy powder

100 g (3.5 oz or ½ cup) granulated cane sugar

2 tablespoons baking powder

1 tablespoon psyllium husk flakes or powder

1 teaspoon kosher or fine sea salt

⅛ teaspoon ascorbic acid, optional

WET INGREDIENTS

3 large eggs, at room temperature (see page 39), beaten

180 ml (¾ cup) carrot juice, heated to about 80°F (27°C)

60 ml (¼ cup) vegetable or canola oil

2 teaspoons ume plum vinegar

180 g (6.3 oz or 1½ cups) shredded peeled carrots

145 g (5 oz or 1 cup) golden raisins

1. Set the bread pan on the counter and insert the beater paddle(s). Unless otherwise directed by your machine's manufacturer, add the liquids first, then the dry ingredients, and finally the yeast.

2. Measure the yeast into a small bowl and set aside. In a large mixing bowl, whisk the remaining dry ingredients together.

3. In a 4-cup (1 liter) glass measuring cup, whisk the wet ingredients—*except* the carrots and raisins—together. Stir in the carrots and raisins and pour into the bread pan. Use a spatula to spread the dry ingredients over the wet ingredients, covering completely. Make a shallow well in the center and pour in the yeast.

4. Place the bread pan in the machine, settle it in the center, and lock it in place. Close the lid and select:

   Gluten-free cycle (see page 14 if your machine does not have this setting)
   Loaf size: 1½ pounds/750 g
   Medium crust
   Start

5. About 3 minutes into the mixing process, open the lid and use a spatula to scrape down the sides of the pan, avoiding the paddle. Push any flour that has accumulated around the edges into the center. Check again once or twice during kneading, scraping the edges, corners, and under the dough. If the dough looks too wet or too dry, add a little flour blend or tiny amounts of warm water. Once the mixing/kneading is done, leave the lid closed during the rise and bake cycles.

6. At the end of the bake cycle, lift the lid and check the temperature. When the bread reaches 206°F to 210°F (97°C to 99°C) on an instant-read thermometer inserted in the center, it is done. Remove the pan from the machine and set it on its side on a wire cooling rack. Leave the bread in the pan for a couple of minutes, then turn the pan upside down and slide the loaf onto the wire rack. Carefully remove the paddle if it is embedded in the bottom of the loaf. Let the bread cool upside down for at least 2 hours before slicing.

7. Store the bread in a resealable plastic bag or airtight container on the counter for up to 3 days. For longer storage, cut into even slices, double-wrap tightly in plastic, place in a resealable plastic bag, and freeze for up to 3 months.

SWEET CHOCOLATE QUICK BREAD

MAKES 1 (1½-POUND/680 G) LOAF • DAIRY FREE

This is a sweet, dense, rich quick bread, something like a very decadent brownie only more versatile. For the simplest presentation, sprinkle it with some sifted confectioners' sugar, or make it more decadent by spreading a thick layer of Raspberry Frosting (see opposite) over the top. You can slice the bread and turn it into a dessert panino with hazelnut spread or almond butter or chocolate bread pudding, or go whole hog and make s'mores French toast with melted marshmallow crème over the top.

DRY INGREDIENTS

360 g (12.7 oz or 3 cups) Light Flour Blend (page 34) or Whole-Grain Flour Blend (page 34)

200 g (7.1 oz or 1 cup) granulated cane sugar

55 g (1.9 oz or ½ cup) sweet ground chocolate, such as Ghirardelli brand

40 g (1.4 oz or ¼ cup) DariFree

2 teaspoons baking powder

1 tablespoon psyllium husk flakes or powder

1 teaspoon kosher salt

85 g (3 oz or ½ cup) gluten-free, dairy-free chocolate chunks (such as Enjoy Life brand), optional

WET INGREDIENTS

⅓ cup vegetable oil (80 ml) or nondairy butter substitute (75 g or 2.6 oz/ ⅔ stick), melted and slightly cooled

80 ml (⅓ cup) chocolate coconut milk

3 large eggs, at room temperature (see page 39), beaten

2 teaspoons pure vanilla extract

1. Set the bread pan on the counter and insert the beater paddle(s). Unless otherwise directed by your machine's manufacturer, add the liquids first, then the dry ingredients.

2. Whisk the dry ingredients—*except* the chocolate chunks—together in a large mixing bowl. Stir in the chunks, if using.

3. In a 4-cup (1 liter) glass measuring cup, whisk the wet ingredients together and pour into the bread pan. Use a spatula to spread the dry ingredients over the wet ingredients.

4. Place the bread pan in the machine, settle it in the center, and lock it in place. Close the lid and select:

   Quick bread/cake cycle
   Loaf size: 1½ pounds/750 g
   Light crust
   Start

5. After the first knead cycle, scrape the sides and bottom of the pan with the spatula to make sure all the dry ingredients are incorporated.

6. At the end of the bake cycle, lift the lid and check the temperature. The bread is done when it registers 206°F to 210°F (97°C to 99°C) on an instant-read thermometer inserted in the center of the loaf. Remove the pan from the machine and place it on its side on a wire rack. Leave the bread in the pan for a couple of minutes, then turn the pan upside down and slide the loaf onto the wire rack. Carefully remove the paddle if it is embedded in the bottom of the loaf. Turn the bread on its side and cool for at least 2 hours before slicing.

7. Store the bread in a resealable plastic bag or airtight container on the counter for up to 3 days. For longer storage, cut into even slices, double-wrap tightly in plastic, place in a resealable plastic bag, and freeze for up to 3 months

---

RASPBERRY FROSTING

MAKES ENOUGH TO COVER 1 LOAF OF SWEET BREAD OR A SMALL CAKE

Puree ¾ cup (95 g) raspberries with 1 tablespoon granulated cane sugar in a food processor. Press through a fine-mesh strainer to remove the seeds.

Beat 12 tablespoons (1½ sticks/ 170 g) softened unsalted butter (or nondairy butter substitute) with an electric mixer until fluffy. Add 2 cups (240 g) sifted confectioners' sugar, 1 cup at a time, beating well after each addition. Add the berry puree and mix until smooth.

CHOCOLATE–PEANUT BUTTER QUICK BREAD

MAKES 1 (1½-POUND/680 G) LOAF ◆ DAIRY-FREE OPTION

This bread—inspired by peanut butter cup candies—is slightly sweet, nutty in flavor, and light brown in color. Toast some up and spread with peanut butter and jelly for an updated sandwich classic. Layer a couple of slices with some bananas and a scoop of ice cream and you're mighty close to the flavors of a hot fudge sundae.

DRY INGREDIENTS

300 g (10.6 oz or 2½ cups) Light Flour Blend (page 34) or Whole-Grain Flour Blend (page 34)

200 g (7.1 oz or 1 cup) granulated cane sugar

55 g (1.9 oz or ½ cup) sweet ground chocolate, such as Ghirardelli brand

24 g (0.8 oz or ¼ cup) powdered peanut butter (see Note, opposite)

40 g (1.4 oz or ¼ cup) DariFree

1 tablespoon baking powder

1 teaspoon xanthan gum

¾ teaspoon salt

WET INGREDIENTS

⅓ cup vegetable oil (80 ml) or nondairy butter substitute (75 g or 2.6 oz/ ⅔ stick), melted and slightly cooled

3 large eggs, at room temperature (see page 39), beaten

180 ml (¾ cup) chocolate coconut or hemp milk

2 teaspoons apple cider vinegar

ADD-IN

255 g (9 oz or 1½ cups) peanut butter chips

NOTE: PB2 brand powdered peanut butter comes in regular and chocolate flavors and is available in the same aisle as the regular nut butters at the grocery store. It can be used in a wide variety of recipes to add a subtle peanut butter flavor without adding any extra liquid. You can also use it to enhance the flavor in any recipe containing peanut butter.

1. Set the bread pan on the counter and insert the beater paddle(s). Unless otherwise directed by your machine's manufacturer, add the liquids first, then the dry ingredients.

2. In a large mixing bowl, whisk the dry ingredients together.

3. In a 4-cup (1 liter) glass measuring cup, whisk the wet ingredients together and pour into the bread pan. Use a spatula to spread the dry ingredients over the wet ingredients, covering completely.

4. Place the bread pan in the machine, settle it in the center, and lock it in place. Close the lid and select:

   Quick bread/cake cycle
   Loaf size: 1½ pounds/750 g
   Medium crust
   Start

5. After the first knead cycle, scrape the sides and bottom of the pan with the spatula to make sure all the dry ingredients are incorporated. Add the peanut butter chips, if using. Close the lid and let the machine finish kneading, rising, and baking.

6. At the end of the bake cycle, lift the lid and check the temperature. The bread is done when it registers 206°F to 210°F (97°C to 99°C) on an instant-read thermometer inserted in the center of the loaf. Remove the pan from the machine and place it on its side on a wire rack. Leave the bread in the pan for a couple of minutes, then turn the pan upside down and slide the loaf onto the wire rack. Carefully remove the paddle if it is embedded in the bottom of the loaf. Lay the loaf on its side and cool for at least 1 hour before slicing.

7. Store the bread in a resealable plastic bag or airtight container on the counter for up to 3 days. For longer storage, cut into even slices, double-wrap tightly in plastic, place in a resealable plastic bag, and freeze for up to 3 months.

CINNAMON LOAF

MAKES 1 (1½-POUND/680 G) LOAF   •   DAIRY FREE

If you love cinnamon, this is the bread for you! It does not look like a traditional store-bought cinnamon bread with swirls of cinnamon; it's closer in appearance to whole-wheat bread. The bold aroma will have you imagining cinnamon toast before the bread is finished baking. It's great toasted and brushed with butter, egg-battered for French toast, and, somewhat surprisingly, used for sandwiches—particularly chicken salad.

DRY INGREDIENTS

2 tablespoons instant yeast

360 g (12.7 oz or 3 cups plus 3 tablespoons) Light Flour Blend (page 34) or Whole-Grain Flour Blend (page 34)

72 g (2.5 oz or ⅓ cup) granulated cane sugar

1 tablespoon psyllium husk flakes or powder

1 teaspoon kosher or fine sea salt

3 teaspoons ground cinnamon

1 teaspoon dough enhancer

1 teaspoon ground allspice

WET INGREDIENTS

3 large eggs, at room temperature (see page 39), beaten

300 ml (1¼ cups) water, warmed to about 80°F (27°C)

56 g (2 oz or 4 tablespoons/½ stick) nondairy butter substitute, melted and slightly cooled

2 teaspoons apple cider vinegar

ADD-IN

145 g (5 oz or 1 cup) raisins, optional

ENHANCE YOUR DOUGH

Dough enhancer is another secret weapon in gluten-free baking. It helps the loaves taste and feel just like gluten-containing breads. It also improves rise and texture, while extending shelf life. There are many brands on the market, such as those from King Arthur Flour and Authentic Foods (see Resources, page 376)—just make sure you get one that is guaranteed gluten free.

1. Set the bread pan on the counter and insert the beater paddle(s). Unless otherwise directed by your machine's manufacturer, add the liquids first, then the dry ingredients, and finally the yeast.

2. Measure the yeast into a small bowl and set aside. In a large mixing bowl, whisk the remaining dry ingredients together.

3. In a 4-cup (1 liter) glass measuring cup, whisk the wet ingredients together and pour into the bread pan. Use a spatula to spread the dry ingredients over the wet ingredients. Make a shallow well in the center and pour in the yeast.

4. Place the bread pan in the machine, settle it in the center, and lock it in place. Close the lid and select:

   Gluten-free cycle (see page 14 if your machine does not have this setting)
   Loaf size: 1½ pounds/750 g
   Medium crust
   Start

5. After the first knead cycle, scrape the sides and bottom of the pan with the spatula to make sure all the dry ingredients are incorporated. Add the raisins if you're using them. Close the lid and let the bread finish kneading and baking.

6. At the end of the bake cycle, lift the lid and check the temperature. The bread is done when it registers 206°F to 210°F (97°C to 99°C) on an instant-read thermometer inserted in the center of the loaf. Remove the pan from the machine and place it on its side on a wire rack. Leave the bread in the pan for a couple of minutes, then turn the pan upside down and slide the loaf onto the wire rack. Carefully remove the paddle if it is embedded in the bottom of the loaf. Turn the bread on its side and cool for at least 2 hours before slicing.

7. Store the bread in a resealable plastic bag or airtight container on the counter for up to 3 days. For longer storage, cut into even slices, double-wrap tightly in plastic, place in a resealable plastic bag, and freeze for up to 3 months.

COCONUT CURRY QUICK BREAD

MAKES 1 (1½-POUND/680 G) LOAF   •   DAIRY FREE

This bread uses the spice blend known as vadouvan to give it unexpected flavor. Vadouvan is a French-inspired curry blend that originated in Southern India that has become popular in the United States over the last few years, gathering an almost cult following. It has curry flavors, but the addition of toasted onion, shallot, and garlic gives it a deeper, more balanced flavor. It is delicious in both sweet and savory dishes. Coconut is often found in many Indian foods, making it a natural partner to curry. It is often used in celebrations as a symbol of prosperity and to honor Lakshmi, the goddess of wealth in the Hindu culture. The cherries add a sweet note and chewiness to this bread.

DRY INGREDIENTS

360 g (12.7 oz or 3 cups) Light Flour Blend (page 34)

150 g (5.3 oz or ¾ cup) granulated cane sugar

1 tablespoon baking powder

1 tablespoon psyllium husk flakes or powder

2 teaspoons vadouvan or other curry powder

1 teaspoon kosher salt

⅛ teaspoon ascorbic acid, optional

WET INGREDIENTS

3 large eggs, at room temperature (see page 39), beaten

240 ml (1 cup) unsweetened coconut milk, heated to about 80°F (27°C)

60 ml (¼ cup) vegetable or canola oil

2 teaspoons apple cider vinegar

ADD-INS

125 g (4.4 oz or 1½ cups) unsweetened shredded coconut

90 g (3.2 oz or ¾ cup) chopped dried sweet cherries, optional

1. Set the bread pan on the counter and insert the beater paddle(s). Unless otherwise directed by your machine's manufacturer, add the liquids first, then the dry ingredients.

2. In a large mixing bowl, whisk the dry ingredients together.

3. In a 4-cup (1 liter) glass measuring cup, whisk the wet ingredients together and pour into the bread pan. Use a spatula to spread the dry ingredients over the wet ingredients, covering completely.

4. Place the bread pan in the machine, settle it in the center, and lock it in place. Close the lid and select:

   Quick bread/cake cycle
   Loaf size: 1½ pounds/750 g
   Medium crust
   Start

5. About 3 minutes into the mixing process, open the lid and use a spatula to scrape down the sides of the pan, avoiding the paddle. Push any flour that has accumulated around the edges into the center. Check again once or twice during kneading, scraping the edges, corners, and under the dough. If the dough looks too wet or too dry, add a little flour blend or tiny amounts of warm water. Add the coconut and cherries, if using, after the first knead cycle. Once the mix/knead cycle is done, leave the lid closed during the bake cycle.

> **NOTE:** Whenever purchasing and using a spice blend, always check with the manufacturer to be certain there is no chance of cross-contamination or use of gluten fillers.

6. At the end of the bake cycle, lift the lid and check the temperature. When the bread reaches 206°F to 210°F (97°C to 99°C) on an instant-read thermometer inserted in the center, it is done. Remove the pan from the machine and set it on its side on a wire cooling rack. Leave the bread in the pan for a couple of minutes, then turn the pan upside down and slide the loaf onto the wire rack. Carefully remove the paddle if it is embedded in the bottom of the loaf. Let the bread cool upside down for least 2 hours before slicing.

7. Store the bread in a resealable plastic bag or airtight container on the counter for up to 3 days. For longer storage, cut into even slices, double-wrap tightly in plastic, place in a resealable plastic bag, and freeze for up to 3 months.

QUICK COFFEE CAKE LOAF

MAKES 1 (1½-POUND/680 G) CAKE ◆ DAIRY FREE

We used applesauce in place of oil in this recipe for flavor and interest. It is a good option if you are trying to reduce your fat intake. Because it is yeast free, this loaf will wind up a little shorter than the other breads, but it still has a moist, delicate crumb. Millet helps give gluten-free bread that "wheat" color and a delicate texture. And there's *lots* of streusel topping, sure to be popular with your kids and those with a sweet tooth!

DRY INGREDIENTS

240 g (8.5 oz or 2 cups) Light Flour Blend (page 34) or Whole-Grain Flour Blend (page 34)

118 g (4.2 oz or 1 cup) millet flour

200 g (7.1 oz or 1 cup) granulated cane sugar

1 tablespoon baking powder

2 teaspoons psyllium husk flakes or powder

1 teaspoon kosher or fine sea salt

WET INGREDIENTS

125 g (4.4 oz or ½ cup) unsweetened applesauce

¼ cup vegetable oil (60 ml) or nondairy butter substitute (55 g/2 oz or ½ stick), melted and slightly cooled

3 large eggs, at room temperature (see page 39), beaten

2 teaspoons pure vanilla extract

STREUSEL TOPPING

170 g (6 oz or ¾ cup firmly packed) light brown sugar

60 g (2.1 oz or ½ cup) Light Flour Blend (page 34) or Whole-Grain Flour Blend (page 34)

¼ teaspoon kosher or fine sea salt

42 g (1.5 oz or 3 tablespoons) nondairy butter substitute, chilled and cubed

1. Set the bread pan on the counter and insert the beater paddle(s). Unless otherwise directed by your machine's manufacturer, add the liquids first, then the dry ingredients.

2. In a large mixing bowl, whisk the dry ingredients together.

3. In a 4-cup (1 liter) glass measuring cup, whisk the wet ingredients together and pour into the bread pan. Use a spatula to spread the dry ingredients over the wet ingredients.

4. Place the bread pan in the machine, settle it in the center, and lock it in place. Close the lid and select:

   Quick bread/cake cycle
   Loaf size: 1½ pounds/750 g
   Light crust
   Start

5. While the dough is mixing, combine the streusel ingredients with a fork until it looks like wet sand.

6. After the first knead cycle, scrape the sides and bottom of the pan with the spatula to make sure all the dry ingredients are incorporated.

7. If your machine has alerts, when you hear the signal for the machine transitioning from the knead to the rise cycle, remove the kneading paddle and reshape the loaf. If the dough seems sticky, wet your hands with a little water to help with reshaping the loaf and smoothing the top. Sprinkle the top evenly with the streusel topping. Close the lid and let the bread finish baking undisturbed.

8. At the end of the bake cycle, lift the lid and check the temperature. The coffee cake is done when it registers 206°F to 210°F (97°C to 99°C) on an instant-read thermometer inserted in the center of the loaf. Remove the pan from the machine and place it on its side on a wire rack. Leave the bread in the pan for 3 minutes, then turn the pan upside down and slide the loaf onto the wire rack. Turn the loaf on its side and cool for at least 2 hours before slicing.

9. Store in a resealable plastic bag or airtight container on the counter for up to 3 days. For longer storage, cut into even slices, double-wrap tightly in plastic, place in a resealable plastic bag, and freeze for up to 3 months.

CHAI LATTE BREAD

MAKES 1 (1½-POUND/680 G) LOAF • DAIRY FREE

Chai by itself just means "tea," and the spiced-up version that we see in most coffee shops in the United States is masala chai, black tea with a mix of spices. Chai latte powder makes the perfect "tea" bread that is not as spicy as chai tea; it has a more balanced, earthy flavor. For a stronger chai flavor, use prepared chai tea in place of the soy milk and substitute soy powder for the chai powder.

DRY INGREDIENTS

240 g (8.5 oz or 2 cups) Light Flour Blend (page 34) or Whole-Grain Flour Blend (page 34)

118 g (4.2 oz or 1 cup) millet flour

250 g (8.8 oz or 1¼ cups) granulated cane sugar

46 g (1.6 oz or ¼ cup) dairy-free chai powder

1 tablespoon baking powder

2 teaspoons psyllium husk flakes or powder

2 teaspoons instant espresso powder

1 teaspoon kosher salt

WET INGREDIENTS

120 ml (½ cup) unsweetened soy or coconut milk

80 ml (⅓ cup) vegetable oil

3 large eggs, at room temperature (see page 39), beaten

1 teaspoon pure vanilla extract

1. Set the bread pan on the counter and insert the beater paddle(s). Unless otherwise directed by your machine's manufacturer, add the liquids first, then the dry ingredients.

2. In a large mixing bowl, whisk the dry ingredients together.

3. In a 4-cup (1 liter) glass measuring cup, whisk the wet ingredients together and pour into the bread pan. Use a spatula to spread the dry ingredients over the wet ingredients.

4. Place the bread pan in the machine, settle it in the center, and lock it in place. Close the lid and select:

   Quick bread/cake cycle
   Loaf size: 1½ pounds/750 g
   Medium crust
   Start

5. After the first knead cycle, scrape the sides and bottom of the pan with the spatula to make sure all the dry ingredients are incorporated. Once the mix/knead cycle is done, leave the lid closed during the bake cycle.

6. At the end of the bake cycle, lift the lid and check the temperature. The bread is done when it registers 206°F to 210°F (97°C to 99°C) on an instant-read thermometer inserted in the center of the loaf. Remove the pan from the machine and place it on its side on a wire rack. Leave the bread in the pan for a couple of minutes, then turn the pan upside down and slide the loaf onto the wire rack. Carefully remove the paddle if it is embedded in the bottom of the loaf. Turn the bread on its side and cool for at least 2 hours before slicing.

7. Store the bread in a resealable plastic bag or airtight container on the counter for up to 3 days. For longer storage, cut into even slices, double-wrap tightly in plastic, place in a resealable plastic bag, and freeze for up to 3 months.

GINGERBREAD

MAKES 1 (1½-POUND/680 G) LOAF ◆ DAIRY FREE

This bread fills your house with the aromas of the holidays. Don't be surprised if a hungry crowd gathers around when you are taking it out of the machine. Traditional gingerbread is not made with yeast, depending instead on chemical leaveners such as baking soda and baking powder for lift. But gluten-free flours are often heavier and need a little more help, so using yeast is the perfect solution. It also gives this rich, aromatic bread a finer textured crumb. For an intriguing change of pace, slice the bread and use it to make panini with sliced turkey and Pomegranate-Cranberry Relish (page 357).

DRY INGREDIENTS

21 g (0.7 oz or 2 tablespoons) active dry yeast

360 g (12.7 oz or 3 cups) Light Flour Blend (page 34)

200 g (7.1 oz or 1 cup) granulated cane sugar

1 tablespoon baking powder

1 tablespoon psyllium husk flakes or powder

16.5 g (0.6 oz or 3 tablespoons) ground ginger

¾ teaspoon ground cloves

½ teaspoon ground cinnamon

½ teaspoon kosher salt

WET INGREDIENTS

340 g (12 oz or 1 cup) unsulfured molasses (*not* blackstrap)

180 ml (¾ cup) water, heated to about 80°F (27°C)

¼ cup vegetable oil (60 ml) or nondairy butter substitute (55 g/2 oz or ½ stick), melted and slightly cooled

3 large eggs, at room temperature (see page 39), beaten

1. Set the bread pan on the counter and insert the beater paddle(s). Unless otherwise directed by your machine's manufacturer, add the liquids first, then the dry ingredients, and finally the yeast.

2. Measure the yeast into a small bowl and set aside. In a large mixing bowl, whisk the remaining dry ingredients together.

3. In a 4-cup (1 liter) glass measuring cup, whisk the molasses into the water to dissolve the molasses. Add the remaining wet ingredients and whisk again. Pour into the bread pan. Use a spatula to spread the dry ingredients over the wet ingredients. Make a shallow well in the center and sprinkle in the yeast.

4. Place the bread pan in the machine, settle it in the center, and lock it in place. Close the lid and select:

   Quick bread/cake cycle
   Loaf size: 1½ pounds/750 g
   Medium crust
   Start

5. After the first knead cycle, scrape the sides and bottom of the pan with spatula to make sure all the dry ingredients are incorporated. Once the mixing/kneading is done, leave the lid closed during the rise and bake cycles.

6. At the end of the bake cycle, lift the lid and check the temperature. When the bread reaches 206°F to 210°F (97°C to 99°C) on an instant-read thermometer inserted in the center, it is done. Remove the pan from the machine and place it on its side on a wire rack. Leave the bread in the pan for 3 minutes, then turn the pan upside down and slide the loaf onto the wire rack on its side. Carefully remove the paddle if it is embedded in the bottom of the loaf. Let the bread cool upside down for at least 2 hours before slicing.

7. Store the bread in a resealable plastic bag or airtight container on the counter for up to 3 days. For longer storage, cut into even slices, double-wrap tightly in plastic, place in a resealable plastic bag, and freeze for up to 3 months.

HOLIDAY EGGNOG BREAD

MAKES 1 (1½-POUND/680 G) LOAF   ◆   DAIRY-FREE OPTION

Flavors of a classic holiday beverage are a delightful surprise in this lightly sweetened bread. Toasted slices with butter are a great afternoon snack, or use it to make French toast for the perfect holiday breakfast or bread pudding for a dessert everyone will love. If you keep LorAnn's eggnog flavoring (see Resources, page 376) on hand, you can enjoy this treat all year long using half-and-half instead of eggnog.

DRY INGREDIENTS

21 g (0.7 oz or 2 tablespoons) active dry yeast

360 g (12.7 oz or 3 cups) Light Flour Blend (page 34)

48 g (1.7 oz or ¼ cup) granulated cane sugar

1 tablespoon psyllium husk flakes or powder

2 teaspoons baking powder

1 teaspoon kosher salt

¾ teaspoon ground nutmeg

WET INGREDIENTS

60 g (2 oz or 3 tablespoons) mild honey

240 ml (1 cup) eggnog, soy eggnog, or half-and-half, warmed to about 80°F (27°C)

42 g (1.5 oz or 3 tablespoons) unsalted butter or nondairy butter substitute, melted and slightly cooled

3 large eggs, at room temperature (see page 39), beaten

2 teaspoons water

2 teaspoons apple cider vinegar

⅛ to ¼ teaspoon LorAnn eggnog flavoring, *only* if you are using half-and-half

1. Set the bread pan on the counter and insert the beater paddle(s). Unless otherwise directed by your machine's manufacturer, add the liquids first, then the dry ingredients, and finally the yeast.

2. Measure the yeast into a small bowl and set aside. In a large mixing bowl, whisk the remaining dry ingredients together.

3. In a 4-cup (1 liter) glass measuring cup, whisk the honey into the eggnog to dissolve the honey. Add the remaining wet ingredients and whisk again. Pour into the bread pan. Use a spatula to spread the dry ingredients over the wet ingredients, covering completely. Make a shallow well in the center and pour in the yeast.

4. Place the bread pan in the machine, settle it in the center, and lock it in place. Close the lid and select:

   Gluten-free cycle (see page 14 if your machine does not have this setting)
   Loaf size: 1½ pounds/750 g
   Medium crust
   Start

5. About 3 minutes into the mixing process, open the lid and use a spatula to scrape down the sides of the pan and under the paddle. Push any flour that has accumulated around the edges into the center. Check again once or twice during kneading, scraping the edges, corners, and under the dough. If the dough looks too wet or too dry, add a little flour blend or tiny amounts of warm water. Once the mix/knead cycle is done, leave the lid closed during the rise and bake cycles.

6. At the end of the bake cycle, lift the lid and check the temperature. When the bread reaches 206°F to 210°F (97°C to 99°C) on an instant-read thermometer inserted in the center, it is done. Remove the pan from the machine and set it on its side on a wire cooling rack. Leave the bread in the pan for a couple of minutes, then turn the pan upside down and slide the loaf onto the wire rack. Carefully remove the paddle if it is embedded in the bottom of the loaf. Let the bread cool upside down for at least 2 hours before slicing.

7. Store the bread in a resealable plastic bag or airtight container on the counter for up to 3 days. For longer storage, cut into even slices, double-wrap tightly in plastic, place in a plastic bag, and freeze for up to 3 months.

A NOTE ON FLAVORINGS

When you are using concentrated flavorings, you want to be able to control how fast the liquid comes out of the bottle—too much and you'll ruin the entire recipe. It's a good idea to replace the original caps on flavoring bottles with threaded dropper tops that screw onto the top. Store in the refrigerator.

HONEY GRANOLA BREAD

MAKES 1 (1½-POUND/680 G) LOAF • DAIRY FREE

Granola is basically dressed-up toasted oats with dried fruit, nuts, and sometimes chocolate bits. When added to a gluten-free dough, it creates a loaf that tastes like your morning cereal but is much more portable since you don't need a bowl. It is similar to your favorite granola bar but with a soft, bread-like texture that's perfect for breakfast. The granola doesn't have to be sweetened since you are adding honey. Just make sure it's gluten free and has some texture. You can toast the granola before adding it to the bread to provide a really pronounced oat flavor.

DRY INGREDIENTS

21 g (0.7 oz or 2 tablespoons) active dry yeast

240 g (8.5 oz or 2 cups) Light Flour Blend (page 34)

120 g (4.2 oz or 1 cup) oat flour

150 g (5.3 oz or ¾ cup) granulated cane sugar

44 g (1.6 oz or ½ cup) Better Than Milk soy powder

1 tablespoon baking powder

1 tablespoon psyllium husk flakes or powder

1 teaspoon kosher salt

⅛ teaspoon ascorbic acid, optional

WET INGREDIENTS

85 g (3 oz or ¼ cup) honey

180 ml (¾ cup) water, heated to about 80°F (27°C)

3 large eggs, at room temperature (see page 39), beaten

60 ml (¼ cup) vegetable or canola oil

2 teaspoons apple cider vinegar

2 teaspoons pure vanilla extract

200 g (7.1 oz or 2 cups) gluten-free granola

1. Set the bread pan on the counter and insert the beater paddle(s). Unless otherwise directed by your machine's manufacturer, add the liquids first, then the dry ingredients, and finally the yeast.

2. Measure the yeast into a small bowl and set aside. In a large mixing bowl, whisk the remaining dry ingredients together.

3. In a 4-cup (1 liter) glass measuring cup, whisk the honey and water together to dissolve the honey. Add the remaining wet ingredients— *except* the granola—and whisk again. Stir in the granola and pour into the bread pan. Use a spatula to spread the dry ingredients over the wet ingredients, covering completely. Make a shallow well in the center and pour in the yeast.

4. Place the bread pan in the machine, settle it in the center, and lock it in place. Close the lid and select:

   Gluten-free cycle (see page 14 if your machine does not have this setting)
   Loaf size: 1½ pounds/750 g
   Medium crust
   Start

5. About 3 minutes into the mixing process, open the lid and use a spatula to scrape down the sides of the pan, avoiding the paddle. Push any flour that has accumulated around the edges into the center. Check again once or twice during kneading, scraping the edges, corners, and under the dough. If the dough looks too wet or too dry, add a little flour blend or tiny amounts of warm water. Once the mix/knead cycle is done, leave the lid closed during the rise and bake cycles.

6. At the end of the bake cycle, lift the lid and check the temperature. When the bread reaches 206°F to 210°F (97°C to 99°C) on an instant-read thermometer inserted in the center, it is done. Remove the pan from the machine and set it on its side on a wire cooling rack. Leave the bread in the pan for a couple of minutes, then turn the pan upside down and slide the loaf onto the wire rack. Carefully remove the paddle if it is embedded in the bottom of the loaf. Let the bread cool upside down for at least 2 hours before slicing.

7. Store the bread in a resealable plastic bag or airtight container on the counter for up to 3 days. For longer storage, cut into even slices, double-wrap tightly in plastic, place in a resealable plastic bag, and freeze for up to 3 months.

I WANT S'MORE BREAD

MAKES 1 (1½-POUND/680 G) LOAF • DAIRY FREE

Teff flour has a faint molasses flavor and millet has a slight nutty taste. The combination of these flours mirrors the taste of the graham cracker that is the base of the childhood favorite s'mores. Adding mini marshmallows and chocolate to the batter creates a s'more you can eat all year long. No campfire necessary.

DRY INGREDIENTS

21 g (0.7 oz or 2 tablespoons) active dry yeast

240 g (8.5 oz or 2 cups) Light Flour Blend (page 34)

65 g (2.3 oz or ½ cup) teff flour

60 g (2.1 oz or ½ cup) millet flour

44 g (1.6 oz or ½ cup) Better than Milk soy powder

63 g (2.2 oz or ⅓ cup) granulated cane sugar

1 tablespoon baking powder

24 g (0.8 oz or 4 teaspoons) psyllium husk flakes or powder

1 teaspoon kosher or fine sea salt

⅛ teaspoon ascorbic acid, optional

WET INGREDIENTS

3 large eggs, at room temperature (see page 39), beaten

285 ml (1 cup plus 3 tablespoons) water, heated to about 80°F (27°C)

60 ml (¼ cup) vegetable oil

2 teaspoons ume plum vinegar

ADD-INS

90 g (3.2 oz or 2 cups) mini marshmallows

255 g (9 oz or 1½ cups) gluten-free, dairy-free semisweet chocolate chips (such as Enjoy Life brand—see opposite)

> **NOTE:** Enjoy Life chocolate chips are gluten free, dairy free, nut free, and soy free, making them an excellent choice if you are baking for a group with multiple food allergies.

1. Set the bread pan on the counter and insert the beater paddle(s). Unless otherwise directed by your machine's manufacturer, add the liquids first, then the dry ingredients, and finally the yeast.

2. Measure the yeast into a small bowl and set aside. In a large mixing bowl, whisk the remaining dry ingredients together.

3. In a 4-cup (1 liter) glass measuring cup, whisk the wet ingredients together and pour into the bread pan. Use a spatula to spread the dry ingredients over the wet ingredients, covering completely. Make a shallow well in the center and pour in the yeast.

4. Place the bread pan in the machine, settle it in the center, and lock it in place. Close the lid and select:

   Gluten-free cycle (see page 14 if your machine does not have this setting)
   Loaf size: 1½ pounds/750 g
   Medium crust
   Start

5. About 3 minutes into the mixing process, open the lid and use a spatula to scrape down the sides of the pan, avoiding the paddle. Push any flour that has accumulated around the edges into the center. Check again once or twice during kneading, scraping the edges, corners, and under the dough. If the dough looks too wet or too dry, add a little flour blend or tiny amounts of warm water.

6. After first knead cycle, add the marshmallows and chocolate. Once the mix/knead cycle is done, leave the lid closed during the rise and bake cycles.

7. At the end of the bake cycle, lift the lid and check the temperature. When the bread reaches 206°F to 210°F (97°C to 99°C) on an instant-read thermometer inserted in the center, it is done. Remove the pan from the machine and set it on its side on a wire cooling rack. Leave the bread in the pan for a couple of minutes, then turn the pan upside down and slide the loaf onto the wire rack. Carefully remove the paddle if it is embedded in the bottom of the loaf. Let the bread cool upside down for least 2 hours before slicing.

8. Store the bread in a resealable plastic bag or airtight container on the counter for up to 3 days. For longer storage, cut into even slices, double-wrap tightly in plastic, place in a resealable plastic bag, and freeze for up to 3 months.

ITALIAN PANETTONE HOLIDAY BREAD

MAKES 1 (1½-POUND/680 G) LOAF

Italy's favorite holiday baked good is panettone, a tall, sweetened bread studded with candied citrus peels. Panettone, which means "big bread" in Italian, is traditionally baked in round paper shells. Towering above the edge of the paper, the only way for the bread to keep its height is to hang it upside down while it cools. To create a bread machine version, we used Fiori di Sicilia, available from King Arthur Flour (see Resources, page 376), to replicate the unique flavor of Italian baked goods. Fiori di Sicilia ("flowers of Sicily") is best described as a blend of orange and vanilla with floral notes. It is addicting, and you will be tempted to use it in all your sweet baking. Our version of panettone isn't as tall as the traditional treat because we don't have gluten to support it, but it has a beautiful crumb and texture, and the fruit and flavoring are perfect together. One bite and you'll swear you are in Firenze, sipping espresso on the banks of the Arno River.

DRY INGREDIENTS

21 g (0.7 oz or 2 tablespoons) active dry yeast

378 g (13.3 oz or 3 cups plus 2 tablespoons) Light Flour Blend (page 34)

48 g (1.7 oz or ¼ cup) granulated cane sugar

1 tablespoon baking powder

2 teaspoons xanthan gum

1 teaspoon kosher or fine sea salt

½ teaspoon dough enhancer

88 g (3.1 oz or ½ cup) mixed candied fruit peels with citron or other candied fruits

35 g (1.2 oz or ¼ cup) golden raisins (see opposite)

WET INGREDIENTS

40 g (1.4 oz or 2 tablespoons) honey

240 ml (1 cup) water, heated to about 80°F (27°C)

56 g (2 oz or 4 tablespoons/½ stick) unsalted butter, melted and slightly cooled

3 large eggs, at room temperature (see page 39), beaten

2 teaspoons apple cider vinegar

¾ teaspoon Fiori di Sicilia (see headnote) or ¾ teaspoon pure vanilla extract plus several drops orange oil

> **NOTE:** Golden raisins are moister and more tender than regular raisins. If you only have dark raisins, soak them in a bowl of warm water for 3 minutes to partially rehydrate them. Drain well before using.

1. Set the bread pan on the counter and insert the beater paddle(s). Unless otherwise directed by your machine's manufacturer, add the liquids first, then the dry ingredients, and finally the yeast.

2. Measure the yeast into a small bowl and set aside. In a large mixing bowl, whisk the remaining dry ingredients—*except* the candied peel and raisins—together. Add the peel and raisins and toss until evenly distributed.

3. In a 4-cup (1 liter) glass measuring cup, whisk the honey and water together to dissolve the honey. Add the remaining wet ingredients and whisk again. Pour into the bread pan. Use a spatula to spread the dry ingredients over the wet ingredients, covering completely. Make a shallow well in the center and pour in the yeast.

4. Place the bread pan in the machine, settle it in the center, and lock it in place. Close the lid and select:

   Gluten-free cycle (see page 14 if your machine does not have this setting)
   Loaf size: 1½ pounds/750 g
   Medium crust
   Start

5. About 3 minutes into the mixing process, open the lid and use a spatula to scrape down the sides of the pan, avoiding the paddle. Push any flour that has accumulated around the edges into the center. Check again once or twice during kneading, scraping the edges, corners, and under the dough. If the dough looks too wet or too dry, add a little flour blend or tiny amounts of warm water. If the fruits you use are very moist, you will probably need to add 1 tablespoon or more of the flour blend. Once the mix/knead cycle is done, leave the lid closed during the rise and bake cycles.

6. At the end of the bake cycle, lift the lid and check the temperature. When the bread reaches 206°F to 210°F (97°C to 99°C) on an instant-read thermometer inserted in the center, it is done. Remove the pan from the machine and set it on its side on a wire cooling rack. Leave the bread in the pan for a couple of minutes, then turn the pan upside down and slide the loaf onto the wire rack. Carefully remove the paddle if it is embedded in the bottom of the loaf. Let the bread cool upside down for at least 2 hours before slicing.

7. Store the bread in a resealable plastic bag or airtight container on the counter for up to 3 days. For longer storage, cut into even slices, double-wrap tightly in plastic, place in a resealable plastic bag, and freeze for up to 3 months.

MATCHA GREEN TEA QUICK BREAD

MAKES 1 (1½-POUND/680 G) LOAF • DAIRY FREE

One of the most popular beverages in Japan is matcha tea, which is a beautiful shade of green that reminds us of verdant fields and forests. It comes in four grades, the highest of which has been used in traditional tea ceremonies for centuries. The remaining three grades are often used in recipes and for brewing, lending a delicate green color and a unique combination of herbs, slight bitterness, and sweetness. It is readily available at the grocery store in the tea and coffee aisle, or you can buy it online. Try eating your tea!

DRY INGREDIENTS

240 g (8.5 oz or 2 cups) Light Flour Blend (page 34) or Whole-Grain Flour Blend (page 34)

200 g (7.1 oz or 1 cup) granulated cane sugar

60 g (2.1 oz or ½ cup) tigernut flour (see opposite)

60 g (2.1 oz or ½ cup) millet flour

22 g (0.8 oz or ¼ cup) green matcha tea powder

1 tablespoon baking powder

2 teaspoons psyllium husk flakes or powder

1 teaspoon kosher salt

WET INGREDIENTS

120 ml (½ cup) unsweetened soy or coconut milk

80 ml (⅓ cup) vegetable oil

3 large eggs, at room temperature (see page 39), beaten

1 teaspoon pure vanilla extract

1. Set the bread pan on the counter and insert the beater paddle(s). Unless otherwise directed by your machine's manufacturer, add the liquids first, then the dry ingredients.

2. In a large mixing bowl, whisk the dry ingredients together.

3. In a 4-cup glass measuring cup, whisk the wet ingredients together and pour into the bread pan. Use a spatula to spread the dry ingredients over the wet ingredients.

4. Place the bread pan in the machine, settle it in the center, and lock it in place. Close the lid and select:

   Quick bread/cake cycle
   Loaf size: 1½ pounds/750 g
   Medium crust
   Start

5. After the first knead cycle, scrape the sides and bottom of the pan with the spatula to make sure all the dry ingredients are incorporated.

6. If your machine has alerts, when you hear the signal for the machine transitioning from the knead to the bake cycle, remove the paddle and reshape the loaf. If the dough seems sticky, wet your hands with a little water to help with reshaping the loaf and smoothing the top. Close the lid and let the bread finish baking.

7. At the end of the bake cycle, lift the lid and check the temperature. When the bread reaches 206°F to 210°F (97°C to 99°C) on an instant-read thermometer inserted in the center, it is done. Remove the pan from the machine and set it on its side on a wire cooling rack. Leave the bread in the pan for a couple of minutes, then turn the pan upside down and slide the loaf onto the wire rack. Turn the loaf on its side. Cool for at least 1 hour before slicing.

8. Store the bread in a resealable plastic bag or airtight container on the counter for up to 3 days. For longer storage, cut into even slices, double-wrap tightly in plastic, place in a resealable plastic bag, and freeze for up to 3 months.

MORNING GLORY QUICK BREAD

MAKES 1 (1½-POUND/680 G) LOAF ◆ _DAIRY FREE_

Chef Pam McKinstry is credited with making the first Morning Glory muffin decades ago at her Morning Glory Café on Nantucket. Since that time many variations have been created. Our version is like a sliced soft granola bar loaded with fruits, nuts, and vegetables. The pineapple and coconut suggest a tropical taste while adding sweetness. It's the perfect way to start your day.

ADD-IN

75 g (2.6 oz or ½ cup) raisins

DRY INGREDIENTS

270 g (9.5 oz or 2¼ cups) Light Flour Blend (page 34) or Whole-Grain Flour Blend (page 34)

170 g (6 oz or ¾ cup firmly packed) dark brown sugar

2 teaspoons baking powder

2 teaspoons xanthan gum

1 teaspoon ground cinnamon

¾ teaspoon kosher or fine sea salt

½ teaspoon ground ginger

8 ounces (227 g) canned crushed pineapple, drained

82.5 g (2.9 oz or ¾ cup) grated peeled carrots

43 g (1.5 oz or ½ cup) grated sweetened coconut

60 g (2.1 oz or ½ cup) chopped walnuts

WET INGREDIENTS

60 ml (¼ cup) vegetable oil

60 ml (¼ cup) water, heated to about 80°F (27°C)

2 large eggs, at room temperature (see page 39), beaten

1 teaspoon pure vanilla extract

1. Put the raisins in a small bowl, cover with water, microwave for 30 seconds, set aside for 5 minutes to rehydrate, and then drain.

2. Set the bread pan on the counter and insert the beater paddle(s). Unless otherwise directed by your machine's manufacturer, add the liquids first, then the dry ingredients.

3. Whisk together the flour blend, brown sugar, baking powder, xanthan, cinnamon, salt, and ginger in a large mixing bowl. Add the pineapple, carrots, coconut, nuts, and drained raisins. Stir and toss to coat everything well with the dry ingredients.

4. In a 4-cup (1 liter) glass measuring cup, whisk the wet ingredients together and pour into the bread pan. Use a spatula to spread the dry ingredients over the wet ingredients.

5. Place the bread pan in the machine, settle it in the center, and lock it in place. Close the lid and select:

   Quick bread/cake cycle
   Loaf size: 1½ pounds/750 g
   Light crust
   Start

6. After the first kneading cycle, scrape the sides and bottom of the pan with the spatula to make sure all the dry ingredients are incorporated. Once the mix/knead cycle is done, leave the lid closed during the rise and bake cycles.

7. At the end of the bake cycle, lift the lid and check the temperature. The bread is done when it registers 206°F to 210°F (97°C to 99°C) on an instant-read thermometer inserted in the center of the loaf. Remove the pan from the machine and place it on its side on a wire rack. Leave the bread in the pan for 3 minutes, then turn the pan upside down and slide the loaf onto the wire rack on its side. Carefully remove the paddle if it is embedded in the bottom of the loaf. Let the bread cool upside down for at least 2 hours before slicing.

8. Store the bread in a resealable plastic bag or airtight container on the counter for up to 3 days. For longer storage, cut into even slices, double-wrap tightly in plastic, place in a resealable plastic bag, and freeze for up to 3 months.

PAIN D'EPICES

MAKES 1 (1½-POUND/680 G) LOAF • DAIRY FREE

Pain d'epices literally translated means "bread of spices." Like most recipes from different regions of France, the ratios of spices vary. Honey is the traditional sweetener for this bread, and it would often be sold in the French honey shops instead of at the bakery. In this gluten-free version, buckwheat flour stands in for the traditional rye flour. Enjoy this delightful combination that is a cross between a bread and a cake. Sprinkle with confectioners' sugar to serve as dessert.

DRY INGREDIENTS

2 tablespoons instant yeast

360 g (12.7 oz or 3 cups) Light Flour Blend (page 34) or Whole-Grain Flour Blend (page 34)

68 g (2.4 oz or ½ cup) buckwheat flour

1 tablespoon baking powder

1 tablespoon psyllium husk flakes or powder

1 teaspoon kosher or fine sea salt

1 teaspoon ground cinnamon

1 teaspoon ground ginger

1 teaspoon ground nutmeg

½ teaspoon anise seeds

¼ teaspoon ground cloves

¼ teaspoon freshly ground black pepper

WET INGREDIENTS

340 g (12 oz or 1 cup) honey

180 ml (¾ cup) water, heated to about 80°F (27°C)

1 large egg, at room temperature (see page 39), beaten

56 g (2 oz or 4 tablespoons/½ stick) nondairy butter substitute, melted and slightly cooled

2 teaspoons apple cider vinegar

1 tablespoon grated orange zest

1. Set the bread pan on the counter and insert the beater paddle(s). Unless otherwise directed by your machine's manufacturer, add the liquids first, then the dry ingredients, and finally the yeast.

2. Measure the yeast into a small bowl and set aside. In a large mixing bowl, whisk the remaining dry ingredients together.

3. In a 4-cup (1 liter) glass measuring cup, whisk the honey and water together to dissolve the honey. Add the remaining wet ingredients and whisk again. Pour into the bread pan. Use a spatula to spread the dry ingredients over the wet ingredients. Make a shallow well in the center and pour in the yeast.

4. Place the bread pan in the machine, settle it in the center, and lock it in place. Close the lid and select:

   Gluten-free cycle (see page 14 if your machine does not have this setting)
   Loaf size: 1½ pounds/750 g
   Medium crust
   Start

5. After the first kneading cycle, scrape the sides and bottom of the pan with the spatula to make sure all the dry ingredients are incorporated. Once the mix/knead cycle is done, leave the lid closed during the rise and bake cycles.

6. At the end of the bake cycle, lift the lid and check the temperature. The bread is done when it registers 206°F to 210°F (97°C to 99°C) on an instant-read thermometer inserted in the center of the loaf. Remove the pan from the machine and place it on its side on a wire rack. Leave the bread in the pan for a couple of minutes, then turn the pan upside down and slide the loaf onto the wire rack. Carefully remove the paddle if it is embedded in the bottom of the loaf. Lay the bread on its side and cool for at least 2 hours before slicing.

7. Store the bread in a resealable plastic bag or airtight container on the counter for up to 3 days. For longer storage, cut into even slices, double-wrap tightly in plastic, place in a resealable plastic bag, and freeze for up to 3 months.

PUMPKIN QUICK BREAD

MAKES 1 (1½-POUND/680 G) LOAF ◆ DAIRY FREE

Pumpkin bread was traditionally baked in late fall when fresh pumpkins were available. Our version is made from canned pumpkin, which lends a stronger pumpkin flavor that is perfectly balanced by warm spices—so you can bake it year-round. You can add 1 cup (112 g) of toasted walnuts if you like your bread nutty.

DRY INGREDIENTS

300 g (10.6 oz or 2½ cups) Light Flour Blend (page 34)

300 g (10.6 oz or 1½ cups) granulated cane sugar

60 g (2.1 oz or ½ cup) millet flour

1 tablespoon baking powder

2 teaspoons psyllium husk flakes or powder

2 teaspoons ground nutmeg

2 teaspoons ground cinnamon

1 teaspoon kosher salt

1 teaspoon ground allspice

½ teaspoon ground cloves

WET INGREDIENTS

15 ounces (425 g) canned pure pumpkin puree (*not* pumpkin pie filling)

120 ml (½ cup) vegetable or canola oil

3 large eggs, at room temperature (see page 39), beaten

60 ml (¼ cup) water, heated to about 80°F (27°C)

1. Set the bread pan on the counter and insert the beater paddle(s). Unless otherwise directed by your machine's manufacturer, add the liquids first, then the dry ingredients.

2. In a large mixing bowl, whisk the dry ingredients together.

3. Whisk the wet ingredients together in another large bowl and scrape into the bread pan. Use a spatula to spread the dry ingredients over the wet ingredients.

4. Place the bread pan in the machine, settle it in the center, and lock it in place. Close the lid and select:
   Quick bread/cake cycle
   Loaf size: 1½ pounds/750 g
   Medium crust
   Start

5. After the first knead cycle, scrape the sides and bottom of the pan with the spatula to make sure all the dry ingredients are incorporated. Once the mix/knead cycle is done, leave the lid closed during the bake cycle.

6. At the end of the bake cycle, lift the lid and check the temperature. The bread is done when it registers 206°F to 210°F (97°C to 99°C) on an instant-read thermometer inserted in the center of the loaf. Remove the pan from the machine and place it on its side on a wire rack. Leave the bread in the pan for 3 minutes, then turn the pan upside down and slide the loaf onto the wire rack on its side. Carefully remove the paddle if it is embedded in the bottom of the loaf. Let the bread cool upside down for at least 2 hours before slicing.

7. Store the bread in a resealable plastic bag or airtight container on the counter for up to 3 days. For longer storage, cut into even slices, double-wrap tightly in plastic, place in a resealable plastic bag, and freeze for up to 3 months.

SALTED CARAMEL QUICK BREAD

All you have to say is "salted caramel," and your friends will be placing orders for this bread. Salty and sweet seems to be here to stay, especially with all the fancy colored salts from around the world. Himalayan pink salt would work on this bread, as does fleur de sel, but kosher salt works just fine. Try toasting this bread and topping with sliced bananas and whipped cream. Make an almond butter and banana sandwich. Add marshmallow crème, and you'll have a sandwich Elvis would love. Have mercy!

DRY INGREDIENTS

240 g (8.5 oz or 2 cups) Light Flour Blend (page 34) or Whole-Grain Flour Blend (page 34)

118 g (4.2 oz or 1 cup) millet flour

200 g (7.1 oz or 1 cup) granulated cane sugar

2 teaspoons baking powder

1 teaspoon kosher or fine sea salt

1 teaspoon xanthan gum

WET INGREDIENTS

60 ml (¼ cup) vegetable oil

3 large eggs, at room temperature (see page 39), beaten

120 ml (½ cup) unsweetened soy or coconut milk

1 teaspoon pure vanilla extract

ADD-IN

155 g (5.5 ounces or 1 cup) gluten-free caramel bits or quartered standard caramel squares

FOR SERVING

60 g (2.1 oz or ¼ cup) gluten-free caramel sauce

Coarse sea salt (such as fleur de sel)

1. Set the bread pan on the counter and insert the beater paddle(s). Unless otherwise directed by your machine's manufacturer, add the liquids first, then the dry ingredients.

2. In a large mixing bowl, whisk the dry ingredients together.

3. In a 4-cup (1 liter) glass measuring cup, whisk the wet ingredients together and pour into the bread pan. Use a spatula to spread the dry ingredients over the wet ingredients.

4. Place the bread pan in the machine, settle it in the center, and lock it in place. Close the lid and select:
   Quick bread/cake cycle
   Loaf size: 1½ pounds/750 g
   Light crust
   Start

5. After the first knead cycle, scrape the sides and bottom of the pan with the spatula to make sure all of the dry ingredients are incorporated. Add the caramel bits.

6. If your machine has alerts, pay attention for the signal indicating the transition from the knead to the bake cycle. When you hear it, remove the paddle, reshape the loaf, and smooth the top. If the dough seems sticky, wet your hands with a little water to help. Close the lid and let the bread finish baking undisturbed.

7. At the end of the bake cycle, lift the lid and check the temperature. The bread is done when it registers 206°F to 210°F (97°C to 99°C) on an instant-read thermometer inserted in the center of the loaf. Remove the pan from the machine and place it on its side on a wire rack. Leave the bread in the pan for a couple of minutes, then turn the pan upside down and slide the loaf onto the wire rack. Let the bread cool upside down for at least 2 hours before slicing.

8. Drizzle the loaf with caramel sauce and sprinkle with fleur de sel before slicing and serving.

9. If you plan to serve the loaf later, store it in a resealable plastic bag or airtight container on the counter for up to 3 days. For longer storage, cut into even slices, double-wrap tightly in plastic, place in a resealable plastic bag, and freeze for up to 3 months.

SNICKERDOODLE BREAD

MAKES 1 (1½-POUND/680 G) LOAF   •   DAIRY FREE

The term *snickerdoodles* usually refers to sugar cookies dusted with cinnamon and sugar that were very popular in New England and Pennsylvania in the late 1800s. The name is thought to be derived from the German word *schneckennudel*, or cinnamon-dusted sweet roll. This bread uses common gluten-free pantry staples. Not overly sweet, it makes great breakfast toast. And peanut butter and jelly sandwiches.

DRY INGREDIENTS

21 g (0.7 oz or 2 tablespoons) active dry yeast

360 g (12.7 oz or 3 cups) Light Flour Blend (page 34)

44 g (1.6 oz or ½ cup) Better Than Milk soy powder

150 g (5.3 oz or ¾ cup) granulated cane sugar

3 teaspoons ground cinnamon

2 teaspoons baking powder

2 teaspoons xanthan gum

1 teaspoon kosher salt

⅛ teaspoon ascorbic acid, optional

WET INGREDIENTS

3 large eggs, at room temperature (see page 39), beaten

180 ml (¾ cup) water, heated to about 80°F (27°C)

60 ml (¼ cup) vegetable or canola oil

2 teaspoons apple cider vinegar

2 teaspoons pure vanilla extract

TOPPINGS

1 tablespoon granulated cane sugar

½ teaspoon ground cinnamon

1. Set the bread pan on the counter and insert the beater paddle(s). Unless otherwise directed by your machine's manufacturer, add the liquids first, then the dry ingredients, and finally the yeast.

2. Measure the yeast into a small bowl and set aside. In a large mixing bowl, whisk the remaining dry ingredients together.

3. In a 4-cup (1 liter) glass measuring cup, whisk the wet ingredients together and pour into the bread pan. Use a spatula to spread the dry ingredients over the wet ingredients, covering completely. Make a shallow well in the center and pour in the yeast.

4. Place the bread pan in the machine, settle it in the center, and lock it in place. Close the lid and select:

   Gluten-free cycle (see page 14 if your machine does not have this setting)
   Loaf size: 1½ pounds/750 g
   Medium crust
   Start

5. About 3 minutes into the mixing process, open the lid and use a spatula to scrape down the sides of the pan, avoiding the paddle. Push any flour that has accumulated around the edges into the center. Check again once or twice during kneading, scraping the edges, corners, and under the dough. If the dough looks too wet or too dry, add a little flour blend or tiny amounts of warm water.

6. Mix the sugar and cinnamon together to make the topping. After the second knead cycle, just before the rise and bake cycles begin, sprinkle the top of the loaf with the cinnamon sugar. Close the lid and do not open it while it rises and bakes.

7. At the end of the bake cycle, lift the lid and check the temperature. When the bread reaches 206°F to 210°F (97°C to 99°C) in its center, it is done. Remove the pan from the machine and set it on its side on a wire cooling rack. Leave the bread in the pan for a couple of minutes, then turn the pan upside down and slide the loaf onto the wire rack. Carefully remove the paddle if it is embedded in the bottom of the loaf. Let the bread cool upside down for at least 2 hours before slicing.

8. Store the bread in a resealable plastic bag or airtight container on the counter for up to 3 days. For longer storage, cut into even slices, double-wrap tightly in plastic, place in a resealable plastic bag, and freeze for up to 3 months.

TOMATO JAM BREAD

MAKES 1 (1½-POUND/680 G) LOAF ◆ DAIRY FREE

Our tomato jam made in the bread machine (page 329) is so delicious that we had to add it to a bread. A beautiful light red color with flecks of tomato, this loaf is not too sweet and has a slight kick, making it the perfect addition to any meal. Think of serving it toasted for brunch with cream cheese and lox.

DRY INGREDIENTS

21 g (0.7 oz or 2 tablespoons) active dry yeast

360 g (12.7 oz or 3 cups) Light Flour Blend (page 34)

39 g (1.4 oz or 3 tablespoons) granulated cane sugar

1 tablespoon baking powder

2 teaspoons xanthan gum

1 teaspoon kosher salt

WET INGREDIENTS

2 large eggs, at room temperature (see page 39), beaten

240 ml (1 cup) water, heated to about 80°F (27°C)

320 g (11.3 oz or 1 cup) Tomato Jam (page 329)

45 ml (3 tablespoons) olive oil

2 teaspoons ume plum vinegar

1. Set the bread pan on the counter and insert the beater paddle(s). Unless otherwise directed by your machine's manufacturer, add the liquids first, then the dry ingredients, and finally the yeast.

2. Measure the yeast into a small bowl and set aside. In a large mixing bowl, whisk the remaining dry ingredients together.

3. In a 4-cup (1 liter) glass measuring cup, whisk the wet ingredients together and pour into the bread pan. Use a spatula to spread the dry ingredients over the wet ingredients, covering completely. Make a shallow well in the center and pour in the yeast.

4. Place the bread pan in the machine, settle it in the center, and lock it in place. Close the lid and select:

   Gluten-free cycle (see page 14 if your machine does not have this setting)
   Loaf size: 1½ pounds/750 g
   Medium crust
   Start

5. About 3 minutes into the mixing process, open the lid and use a spatula to scrape down the sides of the pan, avoiding the paddle. Push any flour that has accumulated around the edges and under the dough into the center. Check again once or twice during kneading, scraping the edges and corners. The dough should create a dome in the center as it is being kneaded and the edges may look a little wet and shiny. If the dough looks too wet or too dry, add a little flour blend or tiny amounts of warm water during kneading. Once the mix/knead cycle is done, leave the lid closed during the rise and bake cycles.

6. At the end of the bake cycle, lift the lid and check the temperature. When the bread reaches 206°F to 210°F (97°C to 99°C) on an instant-read thermometer inserted in the center, it is done. Remove the bread pan from the machine and set it on its side on a wire cooling rack. Leave the bread in the pan for a couple of minutes, then turn the pan upside down and slide the loaf onto the wire rack. Carefully remove the paddle if it is embedded in the bottom of the loaf. Place the bread back on its side and cool for at least 1 hour before slicing.

7. Store the bread in a resealable plastic bag or airtight container on the counter for up to 3 days. For longer storage, cut into even slices, double-wrap tightly in plastic, place in a resealable plastic bag, and freeze for up to 3 months.

TROPICAL QUICK BREAD

MAKES 1 (1½-POUND/680 G) LOAF   •   DAIRY FREE

When the winds are howling, rain and snow are falling, and you are dreaming of warm summer days, this is the bread to make. The flavors of coconut and pineapple evoke memories of days lounging poolside or digging your feet into the sand of your favorite beach. Make it with sweetened coconut if you'd like a slightly sweeter version. This treat can be enjoyed for breakfast or brunch, or as an after-school snack.

DRY INGREDIENTS

240 g (8.5 oz or 2 cups) Light Flour Blend (page 34) or Whole-Grain Flour Blend (page 34)

118 g (4.2 oz or 1 cup) millet flour

150 g (5.3 oz or ¾ cup) granulated cane sugar

1 tablespoon psyllium husk flakes or powder

2 teaspoons baking powder

¾ teaspoon kosher or fine sea salt

½ cup (63 g or 2.2 oz) grated unsweetened coconut (see headnote)

WET INGREDIENTS

120 ml (½ cup) unsweetened coconut milk

60 ml (¼ cup) vegetable oil

3 large eggs, at room temperature (see page 39), beaten

1 teaspoon pure vanilla extract

8 ounces (227 g) canned crushed pineapple, drained

ADD-IN

⅓ cup (50 g) coarsely chopped macadamia nuts

1. Set the bread pan on the counter and insert the beater paddle(s). Unless otherwise directed by your machine's manufacturer, add the liquids first, then the dry ingredients.

2. In a large mixing bowl, whisk the dry ingredients—*except* the coconut—together. Stir in the coconut and toss until well coated with the dry ingredients.

3. In a 4-cup (1 liter) glass measuring cup, whisk the wet ingredients—*except* the pineapple—together. Stir in the pineapple and pour into the bread pan. Use a spatula to spread the dry ingredients over the wet ingredients.

4. Place the bread pan in the machine, settle it in the center, and lock it in place. Close the lid and select:

   Quick bread/cake cycle
   Loaf size: 1½ pounds/750 g
   Medium crust
   Start

5. After the first knead cycle, scrape the sides and bottom of the pan with the spatula to make sure all the dry ingredients are incorporated. Add the macadamia nuts.

6. If your machine has alerts, when you hear the signal for the machine transitioning from the knead to the bake cycle, remove the kneading paddle and reshape the loaf. If the dough seems sticky, wet your hands with a little water to help with reshaping the loaf and smoothing the top. Close the lid and let the bread finish baking undisturbed.

7. At the end of the bake cycle, lift the lid and check the temperature. The bread is done when it registers 206°F to 210°F (97°C to 99°C) on an instant-read thermometer inserted in the center of the loaf. Remove the pan from the machine and place it on its side on a wire rack. Leave the bread in the pan for a couple of minutes, then turn the pan upside down and slide the loaf onto the wire rack. Turn the loaf on its side and cool for at least 2 hours before slicing.

8. Store the bread in a resealable plastic bag or airtight container on the counter for up to 3 days. For longer storage, cut into even slices, double-wrap tightly in plastic, place in a resealable plastic bag, and freeze for up to 3 months.

WHITE CHOCOLATE–PISTACHIO QUICK BREAD

MAKES 1 (1½-POUND/680 G) LOAF

White chocolate gives a hint of sweetness to this cardamom-scented pistachio bread. A member of the ginger family, cardamom is often used as an aromatic spice in sweet dishes and is common in Swedish pastries. Here it lends a perfumed aroma and spiciness to the bread. This bread is perfect for afternoon tea, either simply spread with a little butter or toasted for a pleasing crunch.

DRY INGREDIENTS

360 g (12.7 oz or 3 cups) Light Flour Blend (page 34)

200 g (7.1 oz or 1 cup) granulated cane sugar

1 tablespoon baking powder

2 teaspoons psyllium husk flakes or powder

1 teaspoon kosher or fine sea salt

1 teaspoon ground cardamom

WET INGREDIENTS

180 ml (¾ cup) unsweetened coconut milk

60 ml (¼ cup) water

2 tablespoons vegetable oil or unsalted butter, melted and slightly cooled

3 large eggs, at room temperature (see page 39), beaten

2 teaspoons pure vanilla extract

ADD-INS

227 g (8 oz or 1⅓ cups) white chocolate chips

60 g (2.1 oz or ½ cup) chopped pistachios

1. Set the bread pan on the counter and insert the beater paddle(s). Unless otherwise directed by your machine's manufacturer, add the liquids first, then the dry ingredients.

3. In a large mixing bowl, whisk the dry ingredients together.

4. In a 4-cup (1 liter) glass measuring cup, whisk the wet ingredients together and pour into the bread pan. Use a spatula to spread the dry ingredients over the wet ingredients.

5. Place the bread pan in the machine, settle it in the center, and lock it in place. Close the lid and select:

   Quick bread/cake cycle
   Loaf size: 1½ pounds/750 g
   Medium crust
   Start

6. After the first knead cycle, scrape the sides and bottom of the pan with the spatula to make sure all the dry ingredients are incorporated. Add the white chocolate chips and pistachios. Close the lid and let the bread finish baking.

7. At the end of the bake cycle, lift the lid and check the temperature. The bread is done when it registers 206°F to 210°F (97°C to 99°C) on an instant-read thermometer inserted in the center of the loaf. Remove the pan from the machine and set it on its side on a wire cooling rack. Leave the bread in the pan for a couple of minutes, then turn the pan upside down and slide the loaf onto the wire rack. Carefully remove the paddle if it is embedded in the bottom of the loaf. Turn the loaf on its side and cool for at least 2 hours before slicing.

8. Store the bread in a resealable plastic bag or airtight container on the counter for up to 3 days. For longer storage, cut into even slices, double-wrap tightly in plastic, place in a resealable plastic bag, and freeze for up to 3 months.

ZUCCHINI BREAD

MAKES 1 (1½-POUND/680 G) LOAF   ◆   DAIRY FREE

There are only so many savory dishes we can prepare when all of the zucchini in our garden seems to ripen at the same time. That's when we pull out this recipe and make zucchini bread for the entire neighborhood. A little sweet, a little healthy, and a bunch of delicious, this bread is perfect to make and freeze, giving you the fresh flavor of summer all winter long!

DRY INGREDIENTS

240 g (8.5 oz or 2 cups) Light Flour Blend (page 34)

118 g (4.2 oz or 1 cup) millet flour

225 g (7.9 oz or 1 cup firmly packed) brown sugar

1 tablespoon baking powder

2 teaspoons psyllium husk flakes or powder

1½ teaspoons ground cinnamon

½ teaspoon kosher salt

WET INGREDIENTS

⅓ cup vegetable oil (80 ml) or nondairy butter substitute (75 g or 2.6 oz/ ⅔ stick), melted and slightly cooled

1 teaspoon pure vanilla extract

3 large eggs, at room temperature (see page 39), beaten

120 g (4.2 oz or 1 cup) grated zucchini

ADD-IN

75 g (2.6 oz or ½ cup) raisins or currants, optional

1. Set the bread pan on the counter and insert the beater paddle(s). Unless otherwise directed by your machine's manufacturer, add the liquids first, then the dry ingredients.

2. In a large mixing bowl, whisk the dry ingredients together.

3. Whisk the wet ingredients—*except* the zucchini—together in a large bowl. Stir in the zucchini. Scrape the wet ingredients into the bread pan. Use a spatula to spread the dry ingredients over the wet ingredients.

4. Place the bread pan in the machine, settle it in the center, and lock it in place. Close the lid and select:

   Express bake or quick bread/cake cycle
   Loaf size: 1½ pounds/750 g
   Medium crust
   Start

5. After the first kneading cycle, scrape the sides and bottom of the pan with a spatula to make sure all the dry ingredients are incorporated. Add the raisins if you are using them. Once the mix/knead cycle is done, leave the lid closed during the rise and bake cycles.

6. At the end of the bake cycle, lift the lid and check the temperature. The bread is done when it registers 206°F to 210°F (97°C to 99°C) on an instant-read thermometer inserted in the center of the loaf. Remove the pan from the machine and place it on its side on a wire rack. Leave the bread in the pan for 3 minutes, then turn the pan upside down and slide the loaf onto the rack. Carefully remove the paddle if it is embedded in the bottom of the loaf. Turn the bread on its side and cool for at least 2 hours before slicing.

7. Store the bread in a resealable plastic bag or airtight container on the counter for up to 3 days. For longer storage, cut into even slices, double-wrap tightly in plastic, place in a resealable plastic bag, and freeze for up to 3 months.

ZUCCHINI OAT BREAD

MAKES 1 (1½-POUND/680 G) LOAF

Most zucchini bread recipes are for sweet quick breads that hide the zucchini. This yeasted bread showcases the flavor of zucchini and enhances it with oat flour. It's a new twist on a sandwich bread; use it for grilled ham and cheese, tuna salad, or even a BLT. Use leftovers to make a breakfast strata (page 366).

DRY INGREDIENTS

21 g (0.7 oz or 2 tablespoons) active dry yeast

240 g (8.5 oz or 2 cups) Light Flour Blend (page 34)

120 g (4.2 oz or 1 cup) oat flour

48 g (1.7 oz or ¼ cup) granulated cane sugar

18 g (0.6 oz or 4 teaspoons) baking powder

1 tablespoon psyllium husk flakes or powder

1¼ teaspoons kosher or fine sea salt

⅛ teaspoon ascorbic acid, optional

150 g (5.3 oz or 1¼ cups) grated zucchini

WET INGREDIENTS

3 large eggs, at room temperature (see page 39), beaten

255 ml (1 cup plus 1 tablespoon) water or seltzer, heated to about 80°F (27°C)

60 ml (¼ cup) olive oil or vegetable oil

2 teaspoons apple cider vinegar

TOPPINGS

Milk, for brushing

1 tablespoon gluten-free oats

1. Set the bread pan on the counter and insert the beater paddle(s). Unless otherwise directed by your machine's manufacturer, add the liquids first, then the dry ingredients, and finally the yeast.

2. Measure the yeast into a small bowl and set aside. In a large mixing bowl, whisk the remaining dry ingredients—*except* the zucchini—together. Add the zucchini and toss.

3. In a 4-cup (1 liter) glass measuring cup, whisk the wet ingredients together and pour into the bread pan. Use a spatula to spread the dry ingredients over the wet ingredients, covering completely. Make a shallow well in the center and pour in the yeast.

4. Place the bread pan in the machine, settle it in the center, and lock it in place. Close the lid and select:

   Gluten-free cycle (see page 14 if your machine does not have this setting)
   Loaf size: 1½ pounds/750 g
   Medium crust
   Start

5. About 3 minutes into the mixing process, open the lid and use a spatula to scrape down the sides of the pan, avoiding the paddle. Push any flour that has accumulated around the edges into the center. Check again once or twice during kneading, scraping the edges, corners, and under the dough. If the dough looks too wet or too dry, add a little flour blend or tiny amounts of warm water.

6. Once the mix/knead cycle is done, gently brush the top of the dough with milk and sprinkle on the oats. Leave the lid closed during the rise and bake cycles.

7. At the end of the bake cycle, lift the lid and check the temperature. When the bread reaches 207°F to 210°F (97°C to 99°C) on an instant-read thermometer inserted in its center, it is done. Remove the pan from the machine and set it on its side on a wire cooling rack. Leave the bread in the pan for a couple of minutes, then turn the pan upside down and slide the loaf onto the wire rack. Carefully remove the paddle if it is embedded in the bottom of the loaf. Turn the bread on its side and let it cool for at least 2 hours before slicing.

8. Store the bread in a resealable plastic bag or airtight container on the counter for up to 3 days. For longer storage, cut into even slices, double-wrap tightly in plastic, place in a resealable plastic bag, and freeze for up to 3 months.

Condiments

FROM THE BREAD MACHINE

Most bread machines have a jam setting, so it warranted mention and exploration for recipes in this book. The jam setting produces delicious spreads in a short time—and not all of them need pectin to set up. The jams and chutneys can be stored without the hassle of sterilizing jars; just use an airtight, freezer-safe, tightly lidded container.

Many of the recipes that follow make great sandwich spreads. The Five-Pepper Jam and Mango Chutney have some crunch, so you can even use them as salsa served with chips. Orange Marmalade originally required special sour oranges from Seville, but we've created a version that incorporates seedless oranges with candied peel for a preserve you can easily make in your bread machine. It's perfect on toast while you have a cup of tea in front of the fire. The Pear-Blueberry-Ginger Chutney and Mixed Berry Jam both work beautifully as ice cream toppings. They are also a delightful addition to a cheese tray or melted into grilled cheese sandwiches.

We've also created gluten-free versions of our two favorite Asian sauces, both of which add a tremendous amount of flavor to grilled foods and give us the tastes we crave. If you love a spicy teriyaki chicken dinner, Pineapple "Bourbon" BBQ Sauce is the one for you! If you prefer a more savory barbecue sauce, you will love our Asian BBQ Sauce. It uses gluten-free soy sauce and a Korean red pepper paste called gochujang, which adds umami as well as heat. One taste and your friends will be begging you for the recipe.

We hope you enjoy taking advantage of one of the lesser-used functions on your bread machine. Before you know it, you'll find yourself hitting that button regularly and may never go back to store-bought jams and sauces again!

FIVE-PEPPER JAM

MAKES 3 CUPS (960 G OR 34 OZ) • DAIRY FREE

The blend of sweet and spicy in this jam makes it the perfect accompaniment for smoky meats hot off the grill. It has a lovely balance of heat and sweet, complementing the caramelization that happens when the natural sugars in meats and vegetables hit a screaming-hot grill. Be sure to cut the peppers very small to give the finished jam the right texture; they won't cook down all the way.

2 red bell peppers, seeded and finely chopped

1 orange bell pepper, seeded and finely chopped

1 yellow bell pepper, seeded and finely chopped

2 serrano peppers, seeded and finely chopped

¼ cup (1.7 oz or 48 g) granulated cane sugar

2 teaspoons distilled white vinegar

2 teaspoons powdered pectin

1 teaspoon red pepper flakes

1. Set the bread pan on the counter and insert the beater paddle(s). Add all of the ingredients to the pan and stir gently to combine.

2. Place the bread pan in your machine and lock it in place. Close the lid and select:
   Jam cycle
   Start

3. Some machines are better than others at stirring the jam while it cooks. Keep an eye on it and stir it if you think it needs it. When the cycle is complete, remove the pan from the machine. Cool for 15 minutes in the pan before transferring to a bowl or clean jars. Cover and refrigerate.

4. Store, covered, in the refrigerator for up to 2 weeks. This jam is not designed to be preserved.

TOMATO JAM

MAKES 2 CUPS (640 G OR 22.5 OZ) • DAIRY FREE

This slightly sweet and tangy jam gives you a taste of summer when tomatoes are no longer in season. It is a great alternative to classic cranberry sauce for your Thanksgiving feast. It is also a delicious accompaniment to roasted chicken or added to a grilled cheese sandwich.

28 ounces (794 g) canned diced tomatoes, drained

½ cup (120 ml) water

2 tablespoons (30 ml) freshly squeezed lemon juice

1 teaspoon minced garlic

¾ cup (5.3 oz or 150 g) granulated cane sugar

2 teaspoons red pepper flakes

1 teaspoon kosher salt

1. Set the bread pan on the counter and insert the beater paddle(s). Add all of the ingredients to the pan and stir gently to combine.

2. Place the bread pan in your machine and lock it in place. Close the lid and select:
   Jam cycle
   Start

3. Some machines are better than others at stirring the jam while it cooks. Keep an eye on it and stir it if you think it needs it. When the cycle is complete, remove the pan from the machine. Ladle ½ to 1 cup (160 to 320 g) jam into clean jars. Cool the jam completely, then cover the jars and refrigerate.

4. Store, covered, in the refrigerator for up to 1 week. This jam is not designed to be preserved.

CHIPOTLE KETCHUP

MAKES ABOUT 3 CUPS (720 ML) • DAIRY FREE

Ketchup is easy to make in the bread machine with the jam setting. Customize the heat level and flavors to your liking—you will never be satisfied with store-bought ketchup again. Since there is no corn syrup in this recipe, it is also healthier.

28 ounces (794 g) crushed tomatoes or tomato puree

6 ounces (170 g) tomato paste or 3 tablespoons tomato powder (see Resources, page 376)

1 or 2 chipotles in adobo sauce, drained and chopped (see Note)

½ cup (120 ml) apple cider vinegar

1 tablespoon (5 g) minced garlic

½ cup firmly packed (115 g or 4.1 oz) brown sugar

2 teaspoons kosher or fine sea salt

1 teaspoon dry mustard

¼ teaspoon cayenne pepper

¼ teaspoon freshly ground black pepper

⅛ teaspoon ground allspice

1. Set the bread pan on the counter and insert the beater paddle(s). Add all of the ingredients and stir gently to combine.

2. Place the bread pan in your machine and lock it in place. Close the lid and select:
   Jam cycle
   Start

3. Some machines are better than others at stirring the jam while it cooks. Keep an eye on it and stir it if you think it needs it. When the cycle is complete, remove the pan from the machine. Cool completely in the pan, then transfer to a blender and puree. Thin out with a little water if it's too thick. Transfer to jars, cover, and refrigerate.

4. This ketchup can be stored, covered, in the refrigerator for up to 2 weeks. This ketchup is not designed to be preserved.

NOTE: Chipotles are smoked and dried jalapeño peppers that are often rehydrated and packed in a savory, vinegar-based sauce called adobo. The sauce adds a pop of smoky heat to any sauce or dish. You can find canned chipotles in adobo sauce in the Mexican food section of the grocery store or online.

PINEAPPLE "BOURBON" BBQ SAUCE

MAKES ABOUT 2 CUPS (480 ML) ◆ DAIRY FREE

Two of the most popular sandwiches served in California are the teriyaki chicken sandwich and the Hawaiian burger—a grilled chicken breast or beef patty topped with a slice of pineapple and teriyaki glaze. That flavor combination inspired this sauce, but we added an extra punch of spice with sambal oelek, a chili paste made of fresh red chillies (often cayenne) flavored with salt, sugar, and vinegar. It's the perfect counterpoint to the sweet pineapple and the earthy bite of the liquor. If you want a milder version, closer in flavor to teriyaki, you can omit the sambal oelek. Though we call this a bourbon BBQ sauce, many producers of dark liquor add caramel coloring, which can contain gluten. In order to be safe for people with celiac disease, we have used a combination of vodka and brown sugar as a substitute. Watch out, this could become your new favorite!

8 ounces (227 g) canned crushed pineapple

¾ cup (180 ml) potato vodka

¼ cup (60 ml) apple cider vinegar

2 tablespoons Worcestershire sauce (Lea & Perrins brand is gluten free)

2 tablespoons (22 g or 0.8 oz) Dijon mustard

2 tablespoons sambal oelek or red chili paste (see headnote)

2 tablespoons (10 g or 0.4 oz) minced garlic

½ cup firmly packed (115 g or 4.1 oz) brown sugar

2 teaspoons tapioca flour/starch, arrowroot, or cornstarch

1. Set the bread pan on the counter and insert the beater paddle(s). Add all of the ingredients and stir gently to combine and partially dissolve the brown sugar.

2. Place the bread pan in your machine and lock it in place. Close the lid and select:
   Jam cycle
   Start

3. No stirring is required for this sauce; the machine will do it for you. When the cycle is complete, remove the pan from the machine. Cool completely in the pan, then transfer to a blender and puree to your desired consistency. Thin out with a little water if it's too thick. Transfer to jars, cover, and refrigerate.

4. This sauce can be stored, covered, in the refrigerator for up to 2 weeks. This sauce is not designed to be preserved.

ASIAN BBQ SAUCE

MAKES ABOUT 2½ CUPS (600 ML) • DAIRY FREE

Gluten-free barbecue sauce is incredibly simple to make using the jam setting on your bread machine. You can now find gluten-free soy sauce and tamari at most grocery stores—look for the designation on the label. Or give the Korean soy sauce ganjang a try; it is naturally wheat free (but still be sure to check the label). The Korean fermented red pepper paste gochujang has a texture similar to miso paste and a very concentrated, pungent, spicy flavor, helping make this sauce thick and luxurious with a nice bite of heat. On its own, it is strong, but when combined with the other ingredients, it becomes a secret weapon! Brush this on chicken wings, ribs, or any other grilled meats. It also helps make oven-baked foods taste as if you've cooked them on the grill. The brown sugar in the sauce has a tendency to burn, so watch your foods carefully once you've basted them with the sauce.

1¼ cups (300 ml) gluten-free soy sauce, tamari, or ganjang (see opposite)

¾ cup (180 ml) rice wine vinegar (Marukan brand is gluten free)

¾ cup (180 ml) mirin (rice cooking wine; Eden Foods brand is gluten free)

¼ cup (106 g or 3.7 oz) gochujang (Korean fermented red pepper paste)

2 tablespoons (10 g or 0.4 oz) minced garlic

1 tablespoon grated peeled ginger

1 tablespoon (15 ml) toasted sesame oil

1 cup firmly packed (225 g or 7.9 oz) brown sugar

2 teaspoons tapioca starch, arrowroot, or cornstarch

1. Set the bread pan on the counter and insert the beater paddle(s). Add all of the ingredients and stir gently to combine and partially dissolve the brown sugar.

2. Place the bread pan in the machine and lock it in place. Close the lid and select:

   Jam cycle
   Start

3. No stirring is required for this sauce; the machine will do it for you. When the cycle is complete, remove the pan from the machine. Cool completely in the pan, then transfer to a blender and puree to your desired consistency. Thin out with a little water if it's too thick. Transfer to jars, cover, and refrigerate.

4. This sauce can be stored, covered, in the refrigerator for up to 2 weeks. This sauce is not designed to be preserved.

GLUTEN IN SOY SAUCE

Many Asian sauces and cooking ingredients contain gluten. Soy sauce, which usually has wheat in it, is often the culprit because it is a common ingredient in other products.

San-J, Kikkoman, and Eden Foods all have gluten-free varieties of soy sauce and tamari. For ganjang, the Wholly Ganjang brand is gluten free.

As with all commercial food products, always read labels carefully, looking for hidden sources of gluten.

MANGO CHUTNEY

MAKES ABOUT 3 CUPS (750 G OR 26.4 OZ)   ◆   DAIRY FREE

Mango chutney usually calls for unripened or dried fruit, but this version is made with fresh, ripe mangoes. This sweet, tropical chutney gets its heat from the red pepper flakes. It's wonderful stirred into mayonnaise or yogurt for a quick dip or spread, or served alongside any curry dish. And try it with grilled fresh fish—swoon-worthy!

3 large mangoes, pitted, peeled, and diced

1½ cups (240 g or 8.5 oz) finely chopped red onion

1 cup (145 g or 5.1 oz) golden raisins

2 teaspoons grated peeled ginger

2 teaspoons minced garlic

¾ cup (150 g or 5.3 oz) granulated cane sugar

2 teaspoons red pepper flakes

1 teaspoon kosher salt

1 teaspoon ground allspice

1 teaspoon ground cinnamon

½ teaspoon ground cloves

½ cup (120 ml) water

¼ cup (60 ml) apple cider vinegar

1. Set the bread pan on the counter and insert the beater paddle(s). Add all of the ingredients and stir gently to combine.

2. Place the bread pan in your machine and lock it in place. Close the lid and select:

   Jam cycle
   Start

3. Some machines are better than others at stirring the jam while it cooks. Keep an eye on it and stir it if you think it needs it. When the cycle is complete, remove the pan from the machine. Ladle the cooked chutney into clean jars. Cool the chutney completely, then cover the jars and refrigerate.

4. The chutney can be stored, covered, in the refrigerator for up to 1 week. This chutney is not designed to be preserved.

PEAR-BLUEBERRY-GINGER CHUTNEY

MAKES ABOUT 3 CUPS (750 G OR 26.4 OZ) • DAIRY FREE

This mild chutney owes the majority of its spice to ginger rather than red pepper flakes. Golden raisins add sweetness, and pears add a nice crunch. Using golden raisins is important in this recipe. They are moister and more tender than regular dark raisins. If you have some Sweet Cornbread (page 158), grill it and top with vanilla ice cream and this chutney for a lovely summer dessert. This is also great spread on top of cream cheese or a wheel of Brie as part of a summer cheese tray.

4 large pears (any variety), peeled, cored, and diced

1¼ cups (180 g) fresh or frozen blueberries (thawed if frozen)

1 cup (145 g or 5.1 oz) golden raisins

2 tablespoons grated peeled ginger

1 teaspoon minced garlic

¾ cup (150 g or 5.3 oz) granulated cane sugar

1 teaspoon kosher salt

1 teaspoon red pepper flakes

2 tablespoons (30 ml) apple cider vinegar

2 tablespoons (30 ml) water

1. Set the bread pan on the counter and insert the beater paddle(s). Add all of the ingredients and stir gently to combine.

2. Place the bread pan in your machine and lock it in place. Close the lid and select:

   Jam cycle
   Start

3. Some machines are better than others at stirring the jam while it cooks. Keep an eye on it and stir it if you think it needs it. When the cycle is complete, remove the pan from the machine. Cool the chutney in the pan for 15 minutes, then transfer to a bowl or jars. Cover and refrigerate.

4. The chutney can be stored, covered, in the refrigerator for up to 2 weeks. This chutney is not designed to be preserved.

MIXED BERRY JAM

MAKES ABOUT 3 CUPS (960 G OR 34 OZ) ◆ DAIRY FREE

This is the perfect use for a bread machine in the summer. It won't heat up your kitchen, and you can have homemade jam made from luscious farmers' market berries. When berries are at their peak and the prices are low, buy some extra just for this addicting treat. Try spreading it on toast, or you can top cheese and crackers or ice cream with this decadent homemade jam.

1 pound (455 g) strawberries, quartered

12 ounces (340 g) blackberries

12 ounces (340 g) blueberries

¾ cup (150 g or 5.3 oz) granulated cane sugar

2 tablespoons (30 ml) freshly squeezed lemon juice

½ teaspoon kosher salt

1. Set the bread pan on the counter and insert the beater paddle(s). Add all of the ingredients and stir gently to combine.

2. Place the bread pan in your machine and lock it in place. Close the lid and select:
   Jam cycle
   Start

3. Some machines are better than others at stirring the jam while it cooks. Keep an eye on it and stir it if you think it needs it. When the cycle is complete, remove the pan from the machine. Ladle the cooked jam into jars. Cool the jam completely, then cover the jars and refrigerate.

4. The jam can be stored, covered, in the refrigerator for up to 2 weeks. This is a refrigerator jam and is not designed to be preserved.

ORANGE MARMALADE

MAKES ABOUT 3 CUPS (960 G OR 34 OZ) ◆ DAIRY FREE

Orange marmalade is different from other popular jams because it includes the peels, giving it a touch of bitterness that nicely balances the sweetness. Our version has three distinct textures—fresh orange peels, candied orange peels, and fresh orange flesh—to pack flavor into every bite. Made with just four ingredients, this marmalade will land on your table in no time. Serve it with our Almond Quick Bread with Cardamom (page 276) for a delightful indulgence. This marmalade will make any breakfast or brunch extra special, with the flavor of sunshine in every bite.

3 large seedless oranges, such as navel, rinsed and patted dry

1 cup (176 g or 6.2 oz) chopped candied orange peel or orange citron

2 cups (400 g or 14.1 oz) granulated cane sugar

½ cup (120 ml) water

1. Use a microplane rasp grater to grate the zest from the oranges. Cut off and discard the remaining skin and pith (white covering). Slice the oranges crosswise and then coarsely chop into small chunks.

2. Set the bread pan on the counter and insert the beater paddle(s). Add the orange zest, fresh orange chunks, candied orange, sugar, and water to the pan, stirring gently to combine.

3. Place the bread pan in your machine and lock it in place. Close the lid and select:
   Jam cycle
   Start

4. Some machines are better than others at stirring the jam while it cooks. Keep an eye on this and stir it occasionally if you think it needs it. When the cycle is complete, remove the pan from the machine. Cool in the pan for 15 minutes, then ladle the marmalade into jars. Cool completely, then cover and refrigerate.

5. This marmalade can be stored, covered, in the refrigerator for up to 2 weeks. This is a refrigerator jam and is not designed to be preserved.

THINGS TO MAKE WITH

Gluten-Free

BREADS

There are so many foods our families love that have bread as a component. From celebrating the holidays with a time-honored family stuffing to sandwiches for lunches or easy dinners, to your favorite meatloaf or meatballs, to a classic bread pudding dessert, these recipes bring bright smiles to everyone's faces.

It is always hard to feel different from other people, and being limited in the foods you can eat makes you stand out from the crowd. Now you can bring your own homemade bread with you to restaurants and enjoy it along with everyone else. The simple act of adding croutons to a salad may seem like a small thing until you no longer are able to. The breaded chicken cutlets that were once off-limits are back on your menu. Crunchy and satisfying grilled cheese sandwiches and panini are once again an option for quick dinners on busy weeknights. Being able to start your day with a decadent pile of French toast is not only possible but also a terrific way to use up bread that is a little stale. And your favorite Italian bruschetta crostini can be piled high with fresh tomatoes and basil leaves.

Now many of the foods that you grew up eating are safe again by using these breads instead of wheat breads. And being able to serve delicious gluten-free breads to people who can have wheat is a bonus.

HOMEMADE PLAIN
DRY BREAD CRUMBS

MAKES ABOUT 4 CUPS (460 G OR 16.2 OZ) • DAIRY FREE

Bread crumbs are the foundation for many of our favorite dishes and one of the best ways to use up leftover or stale bread. Save slices in the freezer until you have enough for a batch of bread crumbs or make a loaf just for crumbs.

1 loaf neutral-flavored gluten-free bread, such as Simple Sandwich Bread (page 38), Tender Buttermilk Bread (page 42), or Golden Millet Bread (page 68)

1 teaspoon kosher or fine sea salt, optional

1. Preheat the oven to 225°F (107°C).

2. Cut the loaf into nine or ten slices, then cut the slices in halves or quarters. Place the bread in a single layer on a baking sheet and bake until thoroughly dried out and toasty, flipping the slices over about halfway through baking. This can take 1 to 2½ hours, depending on the moisture in the bread and the heat of your oven. Remove the bread from the oven, transfer to a wire rack, and set aside to cool completely.

> **NOTE:** If you have leftover croutons, you can use them in place of the toasted bread slices. If they are frozen, thaw them and grind in the food processor as directed below.

3. Break the bread into chunks and place in the bowl of a food processor. Add the salt and pulse until the toasted pieces are processed to fine bread crumbs. Pour into a bowl. If you have any pieces that refuse to break down, remove them from the bowl and put them back in the processor. Pulse until they are finely ground and add to the rest of the crumbs. If you do not have a food processor, put the baked bread pieces into sturdy resealable plastic bags and use a rolling pin to pound and roll the bread into crumbs.

4. Store in one or more airtight resealable plastic bags or containers for several days in the refrigerator or up to 3 months in the freezer.

VARIATION

Italian-Style Dried Bread Crumbs

Makes about 4 cups (460 g or 16.2 oz)

Add 1 to 2 teaspoons dried Italian herb blend when you process the toasted bread to fine bread crumbs.

VARIATION

Fresh Bread Crumbs

If a recipe calls for fresh bread crumbs, use day-old bread that is partially dried out. Do not bake the bread in the oven. Tear the bread into pieces and pulse in a food processor until coarsely ground.

HOMEMADE CROUTONS

MAKES ABOUT 3 CUPS (680 G OR 24 OZ) • DAIRY-FREE OPTION

Croutons add a wonderful crunch and texture to salads and soups. They also make for a quick snack, or you can bake them a little longer and grind into bread crumbs. Use any bread you like or two different types for even more flavor. Customize them with any seasonings you like, such as garlic or onion powder, dried oregano, thyme, or rosemary.

1 loaf gluten-free bread (see headnote)

3 tablespoons (45 ml) olive oil or unsalted butter, melted

1 teaspoon kosher or fine sea salt

2 to 3 tablespoons dried herbs, optional

1. Preheat the oven to 250°F (120°C).

2. Trim the crusts from the loaf and then cut the loaf into ½-inch (1 cm) cubes. Store the crusts in the freezer; when you have enough, grind them into bread crumbs.

3. Place the cubes on a baking sheet, drizzle with the olive oil, and sprinkle with the salt and herbs, if using. Toss to evenly coat all the cubes. Spread out into a single layer.

4. Bake, tossing occasionally, until the croutons are toasty and nearly completely dried out. This can take 1½ to 2½ hours depending on the moisture in the bread. Taste one occasionally and take them out of the oven when they are crunchy nearly all the way through. You want them crisp but still soft enough to chew. If you will be using these for stuffing, bake them a little longer so they are firm enough to stand up to the liquid in the recipe. Set aside to cool completely.

5. Transfer to resealable plastic bags or airtight containers and store in the refrigerator for a few days or up to 3 months in the freezer. Thaw before using and recrisp in a low oven if necessary.

ITALIAN-FLAVORED CROUTONS

MAKES ABOUT 3 CUPS (680 G OR 24 OZ) • DAIRY-FREE OPTION

Add crunch and extra flavor to salads and steaming bowls of old-fashioned tomato soup. Or use these croutons for dipping in cheese fondue (don't bake them as long) and as a garnish for vichyssoise. You can also eat them as a snack instead of chips or popcorn.

1 loaf Pizza Pie Bread (page 156)

3 tablespoons (45 ml) olive oil or unsalted butter, melted, or a blend of the two

2 teaspoons dried oregano

1 teaspoon kosher or fine sea salt

Additional dried herbs, if desired

1. Preheat the oven to 250°F (120°C).

2. Trim the crusts from the loaf and then cut the loaf into ½-inch (1 cm) cubes. Store the crusts in the freezer; when you have enough, grind them into bread crumbs.

3. Place the cubes on a baking sheet, drizzle with the olive oil, and sprinkle with the oregano, salt, and herbs, if using. Toss to evenly coat all the cubes. Spread out in a single layer.

4. Bake, tossing occasionally, until toasty and nearly completely dried out. This can take 1½ to 2½ hours, depending on the moisture in the bread. Taste one occasionally and remove them from the oven when they are crunchy nearly all the way through. You want them crisp but still soft enough to chew. If you will be using these for stuffing, bake them longer so they are firm enough to stand up to the liquid in the recipe. Set aside to cool completely.

5. Transfer to resealable plastic bags or air-tight containers and store in the refrigerator for a few days or up to 3 months in the freezer. Thaw before using and recrisp in a low oven if necessary.

STUFFING OR DRESSING FOR POULTRY OR PORK

MAKES ABOUT 10 SERVINGS

Thanksgiving just isn't the same without stuffing. Now with the gluten-free breads in this book, you can make your own croutons several weeks in advance, store them in the freezer, and use them to make this side dish full of all the flavors you love. The "Thanksgiving" Sandwich Bread (page 52) is a natural choice for holiday meals. You can use a single type of bread or combine a variety for different flavors and textures. Maybe make it with half savory cornbread croutons (page 136, 138, or 140—your choice). It adds a lot of interest, and your guests will have fun guessing what kinds of breads you used. Whatever croutons you choose, make sure they are completely dried and very crunchy.

3 cups (680 g or 24 oz) croutons (see page 342) made from California Brown Bread (page 82)

3 cups (680 g or 24 oz) croutons (see page 342) made from Tender Buttermilk Bread (page 42), "Thanksgiving" Sandwich Bread (page 52), or other mild-flavored bread

2 tablespoons (30 ml) olive oil

4 tablespoons (56 g/2 oz or ½ stick) unsalted butter, melted

1 large onion, finely chopped

4 celery ribs, finely chopped

1 tablespoon dried sage

1 teaspoon dried thyme

½ teaspoon garlic powder

Kosher or sea salt, to taste

Freshly ground black pepper, to taste

2 to 3 cups (480 to 720 ml) Turkey Stock (page 346) or canned chicken broth

1 cup (110 g or 4 oz) chopped pecans, optional

1 cup (145 g or 5oz) dried cranberries, optional

2 tart apples, peeled, cored and finely chopped, optional

NOTE: If you want to make a vegetarian version, use vegetable stock.

1. Preheat the oven to 350°F (180°C). Butter an 8-cup casserole dish.

2. Put the croutons in a very large mixing bowl.

3. Heat the oil and butter in a skillet over medium-high heat. Add the onion and celery and cook, stirring often, until softened, about 4 minutes. Transfer to the bowl with the croutons. Sprinkle the herbs and seasonings over the top and toss thoroughly to combine. Pour in the stock and toss so that all the bread is moistened. Stir in the nuts, cranberries, and apples (if using). Taste and adjust the seasonings if needed.

4. Transfer to the casserole dish, cover with aluminum foil, and bake for 30 minutes. Remove the foil and continue baking until all of the ingredients are hot, the top is crispy, and the flavors have blended, 15 to 20 minutes.

5. The dressing can be assembled and baked up to 2 days in advance and cooled. Cover and store in the refrigerator, then uncover and reheat in the oven (not the microwave) until warmed thoroughly.

STUFFING VS. DRESSING

Stuffing is cooked inside the cavity of the bird; dressing is cooked outside. Did you know that stuffing the bird draws out the moisture and makes for a drier turkey or chicken? And when the stuffing is inside the bird, the meat is usually overdone before the stuffing reaches a high enough temperature (165°F/74°C) to be safe to eat. By using homemade stock as the liquid in the dressing, you get all the flavor of cooking it inside the bird without the safety issues and can serve a tender and moist bird every time.

TURKEY STOCK

MAKES ABOUT 6 QUARTS (6 LITERS)

Use this stock to flavor stuffing and dressing, to make gravy, and as the base for a wonderful soup made with the carcass after dinner is over. Don't worry about pulling the leaves off the thyme sprigs; you can add them whole and fish out the stems when it is done cooking.

Preheat the oven to 375°F (190°C).

Pour ¼ cup (60 ml) olive or vegetable oil into the bottom of a large roasting pan. Add 10 pounds (4.5 kg) turkey parts (backs, necks, wings, and legs), placing them skin side down. Roast uncovered until deep brown, 1 to 2 hours. Add a little water to the pan if the drippings start to get too dark. Using tongs, transfer the turkey parts to a 12-quart (12 liter) soup pot.

Add a little water to the roasting pan and scrape the bottom to loosen the browned bits, which are full of flavor. If they are being stubborn, add a little more water and bring to a boil on the stove top. Pour the pan drippings into a container, cover, and store in the refrigerator to use to make your gravy. Do not clean the pot.

Add 3 large onions, quartered; 4 large shallots, quartered (no need to peel the onions or shallots); 4 large carrots, chunked; and 4 large celery ribs, chunked; to the soup pot. Pour in 8 quarts (8 liters) water. Season with 2 to 3 teaspoons kosher salt, 10 to 15 black peppercorns, and 6 to 8 thyme sprigs. Bring the water to a boil over medium-high heat, reduce the heat to low, partially cover, and simmer until the stock is richly flavored, 2 to 3 hours. Taste and adjust the seasonings.

Remove the bones and meat and discard. Strain the stock through a fine-mesh sieve into a large bowl and cool to room temperature. Cover and refrigerate. When the stock is cold, skim the fat that solidifies on the top and add it to the reserved pan drippings to use for the gravy.

This stock can be refrigerated for 3 days or frozen for up to 3 months.

CROSTINI

MAKES ABOUT 40 (1 X 2-INCH/2.5 X 5 CM) TOASTS • DAIRY FREE

Crostini are toasted bread pieces often used as a base for any number of toppings. Though French Baguettes (page 119) are traditional, you can use any bread to make crostini—we suggest Italian Ciabatta (page 114) or a focaccia (pages 190 and 212–224). Use them with dips; sprinkle with cheese and melt under the broiler; or top with seasoned tomatoes, onions, and basil for the classic Italian bruschetta. Or how about rye topped with some smoked salmon, a little sour cream, and a sprinkling of onions? Keep some crostini in your freezer for simple appetizers or party hors d'oeuvres in a snap.

10 slices day-old gluten-free bread (any savory flavor you like)

2 tablespoons (30 ml) olive oil

Kosher or fine sea salt

1. Preheat the oven to 250°F (190°C). Lightly oil a baking sheet.

2. Cut the crusts off the bread slices; save in the freezer to make bread crumbs. Cut each slice into four strips, then crosswise to make rectangles, or use a small round cookie cutter for circles. Add the scraps to the crusts in the freezer.

3. Place the bread pieces on the oiled baking sheet. Brush each piece lightly with olive oil and sprinkle with salt.

4. Bake until the crostini are lightly golden and most of the moisture has evaporated, 45 minutes to 1 hour. Flip them to cook the second side and bake just until crispy and golden, about 15 minutes longer. Bite into one to see if they have reached the crispness you are looking for or if you want to bake them longer.

5. Transfer to a wire rack to cool (this lets the steam escape and keeps them crispy). When thoroughly cool, place in a resealable plastic bag and store at room temperature for up to 2 days. Refrigerate or freeze for longer storage.

FRESH TOMATO BRUSCHETTA WITH FETA CHEESE

MAKES 15 TO 20 PIECES

These crunchy pieces of bread topped with marinated tomatoes and shallots could be the perfect summer food. Use homegrown tomatoes if you have them or ripe cherry or plum tomatoes from the farmers' market. A little feta cheese adds richness and a delightful saltiness that balances the acidic marinade. If you double the amount of dressing and tomatoes, cover, and refrigerate, and you'll have plenty left over to toss with lettuce the following day for a light lunch.

TOMATOES

2 tablespoons (30 ml) olive oil

2 teaspoons balsamic vinegar

1 teaspoon minced shallot

¼ teaspoon minced garlic

Pinch of granulated cane sugar

Kosher or fine sea salt, to taste

Freshly ground black pepper, to taste

1 cup (180 g or 6.3 oz) finely chopped fresh tomatoes

¼ cup (10 g or 0.4 oz) loosely packed torn basil leaves

BRUSCHETTA

15 to 20 Crostini (page 347)

Crumbled feta cheese

1 or 2 basil sprigs, for garnish

1. Whisk the oil, vinegar, shallots, garlic, sugar, salt, and pepper together in a medium bowl. Add the tomatoes and 3 tablespoons of the basil, tossing to evenly coat everything. Set aside to marinate for 1 to 2 hours.

2. Line up the crostini on a serving platter. Using a slotted spoon, scoop about 1 tablespoon of tomatoes onto each crostini, enough to cover the surface. Top with a few crumbles of feta and sprinkle with the remaining 1 tablespoon basil. Add a sprig or two of basil to the platter and serve.

EVERYTHING'S BIGGER IN TEXAS TOAST

MAKES 4 SLICES

This bread, so big it is nearly its own food group, is a much more indulgent form of garlic bread. Made with slices of bread that are at least 1½ inches (4 cm) thick, it can fill you up before your entrée arrives if you're not careful.

4 slices (1½-inch/4 cm thick) white bread, such as Simple Sandwich Bread (page 38), Tender Buttermilk Bread (page 42), or Sorghum-Oat Buttermilk Bread (page 60)

4 tablespoons (56 g/2 oz or ½ stick) unsalted butter, at room temperature

2 teaspoons minced fresh parsley

½ teaspoon freshly minced garlic

¼ teaspoon kosher salt

Freshly grated Parmesan cheese

1. Preheat the broiler.

2. Lay the bread slices on a baking sheet.

3. Beat the butter, parsley, garlic, and salt together in a small bowl. Smear the garlic butter on both sides of the bread slices. Sprinkle the tops with a little Parmesan.

4. Broil until the top is lightly toasted and crunchy, 1 to 3 minutes. Watch carefully because they can burn easily. Use tongs to turn the bread over, sprinkle the second side with more Parmesan, and broil until golden brown, 1 to 3 minutes longer. Serve while warm.

LEMON-THYME CHICKEN SALAD SANDWICHES

MAKES 4 SANDWICHES • DAIRY FREE

There is nothing better than the counterpoint of sweet, crisp red grapes and savory, creamy chicken that you find in this salad. Freshly squeezed lemon juice lightly perfumes the mayonnaise and complements the thyme, making this perfect for hot summer days. You can use poached, barbecued, roasted, or sautéed chicken, freshly made or left over—even a rotisserie chicken from the market. Just make sure the seasoning used on the chickens is gluten free.

SALAD

3 cups (420 g or 14.8 oz) chopped cooked chicken

1 cup (150 g or 5.3 oz) red or green seedless grapes, halved or quartered, or ⅓ cup (50 g or 1.8 oz) dried cranberries, plumped in warm water

⅔ cup (80 g or 2.8 oz) diced celery

¼ cup (40 g or 1.4 oz) minced red onion

1 teaspoon capers, drained and minced

½ teaspoon dried thyme or 1 teaspoon fresh thyme leaves

DRESSING

½ cup (115 g or 4 oz) light or regular mayonnaise

2 teaspoons freshly squeezed lemon juice, or more to taste

½ teaspoon kosher or fine sea salt

½ teaspoon gluten-free lemon pepper

SANDWICHES

8 slices gluten-free bread, such as Lemon-Thyme Bread (page 144), Tender Buttermilk Bread (page 42), or Almost Wheat Sandwich Bread (page 56)

4 lettuce leaves

1. Put the chicken in a large mixing bowl. Add the grapes, celery, onion, capers, and thyme. Toss well.

2. Whisk the dressing ingredients together in a small bowl. Taste and adjust the seasonings.

3. Add half of the dressing to the chicken, tossing until all the ingredients are evenly coated. Add more dressing if desired. Leftover dressing can be covered and stored in the refrigerator.

4. Set out the bread slices in sets of two. Lay a lettuce leaf on half of them, add a scoop of the salad, and top with the second slice of bread.

GRILLED HAM AND CHEESE SANDWICHES

MAKES 4 SANDWICHES

On cold and blustery days, there is no better combination than a grilled cheese sandwich and a steaming bowl of tomato soup. Adding ham to the sandwich boosts the amount of protein, keeping us feeling fuller longer. Cheese slices on both sides of the ham helps the sandwiches hold together when flipping and makes them doubly delicious. Serve these at lunch or dinner and bring back happy childhood memories with every bite.

Butter, at room temperature

8 slices Simple Sandwich Bread (page 38), Tender Buttermilk Bread (page 42), or your favorite gluten-free bread

8 thin slices cheddar cheese

8 thin slices boiled or baked ham

1. Lightly spread butter on one side of each slice of bread. Press the buttered sides of two pieces together, creating 4 stacks. Cover the top of each stack with 1 slice of cheese, add 2 slices of ham to each stack, then cover the ham with 1 more slice of cheese.

2. Heat a griddle or very large skillet over medium-high heat. Pick up one of the sandwiches, leaving the bottom piece of bread on the board. Set the sandwich on the griddle and top with the other slice of bread, buttered side up. Repeat with the remaining sandwiches.

3. Cook until the cheese has started to melt and the bread is golden brown, about 2 minutes. Use a spatula to flip the sandwiches. Cook on the second side until the cheese is melted and the bread is golden brown, about 2 minutes. Transfer the sandwiches to a cutting board, cut each in half, and serve hot.

CHEESY GRILLED STEAK SANDWICHES

MAKES 6 SANDWICHES

This is the recipe you want when you have a hungry crowd to feed. Gluten-free hamburger or hot dog buns (page 92) stuffed with juicy marinated steak and gooey cheese will be sure to bring smiles to everyone's face. You can also use Italian Ciabatta (page 114) or Chewy Focaccia (page 212). Grill the meat to order, or prepare in advance and refrigerate until an hour before serving. Then slice and serve either at room temperature or gently reheated.

MARINADE

½ cup (120 ml) olive oil

¼ cup (60 ml) freshly squeezed lemon juice

3 tablespoons (45 ml) steak sauce (A.1. is gluten free)

3 tablespoons (45 ml) Worcestershire sauce (Lea & Perrins is gluten free)

2 tablespoons (22 g or 0.8 oz) honey mustard

1 tablespoon minced garlic

1 tablespoon dried oregano

1 tablespoon dried thyme

1 teaspoon dried rosemary

1 to 3 teaspoons chipotle powder, to taste

STEAK

1 (2- to 3-pound/905 to 1360 g) Chateaubriand or London broil, about 2 inches (5 cm) thick

SANDWICHES

6 hamburger or hot dog buns (page 92), split

Melted unsalted butter or olive oil, optional

Horseradish Mayonnaise (see opposite), optional

Thin (⅛ to ¼ inch/3 to 6 mm thick) slices provolone, Monterey jack, pepper jack (for more heat), Muenster, or other favorite cheese

Sliced tomatoes, optional

1. In a medium bowl, whisk together all of the marinade ingredients and pour into a large resealable plastic bag. Add the beef to the bag, press out the air, and seal shut. Flip the bag a few times to coat all surfaces of the meat. Lay flat on a small baking sheet and refrigerate for several hours or up to 2 days, flipping occasionally.

2. Preheat a gas grill for 15 minutes on high or build a hot charcoal fire.

3. Remove the meat from the marinade and place on a baking sheet lined with paper towels. Use extra paper towels to pat the entire steak dry on all sides. Discard the marinade.

4. Place the meat on the grill over direct heat. Reduce the heat to medium-high and grill until you have nice grill marks and an instant-read thermometer inserted through the side of the steak registers 130°F to 135°F (54°C to 57°C) for medium-rare, 4 to 5 minutes per side. If the meat sticks to the grill when you try to flip it, let it cook for a minute or two longer—it will release easily when it is ready to flip.

5. Transfer the beef to a clean baking sheet, tent loosely with aluminum foil, and let rest for about 15 minutes. This gives the meat time to gently finish cooking with the residual heat (see page 363), allowing the juices to redistribute throughout the roast. Leave the grill on medium heat.

6. Split the buns in half horizontally, brush with melted butter or olive oil, if desired, and place them cut side down on the hot grill (use foil if needed). Reduce the heat to medium-low and grill until lightly toasted, with some grill marks.

7. Transfer the beef to a cutting board and slice thinly on the diagonal against the grain.

8. Brush the buns with horseradish mayonnaise, if desired. Place several slices of beef on the bottom half of each roll, overlapping them slightly. Top with cheese and place back on the grill, over one of the cooler burners or on the rack above the grates for gentle heat. Close the grill and heat until the cheese melts.

9. Use a spatula to transfer the hot sandwiches to dinner plates. Add some tomatoes if you like and serve immediately.

HORSERADISH MAYONNAISE

MAKES ABOUT ¾ CUP (175 G OR 6 OZ ML)

Whisk together ½ cup (115 g or 4 oz) mayonnaise, ¼ cup (60 g or 2 oz) prepared horseradish, and ¼ teaspoon garlic powder. You can use it right away or store it, covered, in the refrigerator for up to 4 days.

SPANISH CHICKEN TORTAS

MAKES 2 SANDWICHES • DAIRY FREE

Spanish tortas are a Latin version of panini—pressed and grilled sandwiches. In this sandwich, a delicious blend of herbs and spices is used in multiple ways, boosting its flavor and adding complexity to what could be a boring chicken sandwich. You can use the same technique with turkey or pork. Plan in advance for this torta—you should have the seasoning blend on hand so you can sprinkle it on the focaccia before baking.

SEASONING BLEND

1 tablespoon ancho chilli powder

1 teaspoon sweet paprika

½ teaspoon dried oregano

½ teaspoon ground cumin

½ teaspoon onion powder

¼ teaspoon garlic powder

¼ teaspoon chipotle powder, or to taste

¼ teaspoon ground turmeric, optional

¼ teaspoon kosher or fine sea salt

CHICKEN

1 (7- to 9-ounce/200 to 255 g) boneless, skinless chicken breast

Kosher or fine sea salt

Freshly ground black pepper

2 teaspoons olive oil

TORTAS

1 recipe Italian Herb Focaccia (page 216), sprinkled liberally with the seasoning blend and kosher salt before baking

2 tablespoons (28 g or 1 oz) mayonnaise

1 tomato, sliced

1 avocado, sliced

Kosher salt

Freshly ground black pepper

½ small red onion, thinly sliced

Chopped fresh cilantro leaves, optional

2 teaspoons olive oil

½ lime, sliced

1. Stir all the ingredients for the seasoning blend together in a small bowl. Reserve 1 tablespoon for the chicken and the torta. Use some of the rest to season the focaccia before baking. Store the remainder in an airtight container in a dark cupboard.

2. Pat the chicken dry and season with salt, pepper, and 1½ teaspoons seasoning blend, rubbing it all over the surface.

3. Heat the oil in a nonstick skillet over medium-high heat. Add the chicken and cook until an instant-read thermometer registers 160°F (71°C) in the center, 4 to 6 minutes per side. Transfer the chicken to a cutting board to rest. Wipe out the pan and leave it on the stove, off the heat. Have ready a very heavy pot (enameled cast iron is perfect) just big enough to sit inside the skillet.

4. When the chicken is cool enough to handle, cut it into thin slices.

5. Cut two 4-inch (10 cm) pieces from the focaccia; reserve the rest of the bread for another meal. Cut the focaccia in half horizontally.

6. Whisk the mayonnaise with the reserved 1½ teaspoons seasoning blend in a small bowl. Spread the mayonnaise on the cut sides of the focaccia. Divide the chicken between the bottom halves. Top with some tomato slices, avocado slices, a pinch or two of kosher salt and a little black pepper, a few onion slices, and some cilantro, if desired. Place the top bread halves on the fillings.

7. Heat the oil in the skillet you used to cook the chicken over medium heat. Set the filled tortas in the hot pan and set the heavy skillet over the top. Cook until the bottom is toasted and browned. Flip the tortas, top with the heavy skillet again, and cook until the second side is toasted and browned, 3 to 5 minutes.

8. Cut the tortas in half diagonally and serve immediately, garnished with lime slices.

TURKEY AND POMEGRANATE-CRANBERRY PANINI

MAKES 2 SANDWICHES

When you don't have enough leftovers to recreate a meal on the plate, a sandwich is a great alternative. Leftover sliced poultry and cranberry sauce with some fresh spinach or arugula on great bread grilled in a panini press, skillet, or even a waffle maker will let you enjoy the wonderful holiday flavors all over again.

8 slices turkey or chicken

4 slices Almost Wheat Sandwich Bread (page 56)

½ cup (160 g or 5.6 oz) Pomegranate-Cranberry Relish (see opposite)

2 slices Provolone cheese

1 cup (20 g or 0.7 oz) baby spinach or baby arugula, rinsed and patted dry

1 tablespoon red pepper flakes, to taste

1. Coat a panini press or skillet with nonstick cooking spray and place over medium heat.

2. To assemble the sandwiches, divide the turkey between 2 slices of bread, spread each with ¼ cup of the relish, and top each with a slice of cheese, half of the greens, half of the red pepper flakes (if using), and the remaining bread slice.

3. Transfer the sandwiches to the panini press and close the lid. Grill until the cheese is melted and the bread is toasted, 8 to 10 minutes. If using a skillet, set a cast-iron skillet on top of the sandwiches to weight them and flip after 5 minutes of cooking.

4. Cut the panini in half and serve hot.

POMEGRANATE-CRANBERRY RELISH

MAKES ABOUT 2 CUPS (640 G OR 22.5 OZ)

Love cranberry sauce? Want to try a new flavor combination? The combination of dried cherries, fresh cranberries, and ginger creates a sweet-tart flavor that will quickly become the new standard. Pomegranate seeds add a layer of crunch to the final relish, which is great with roast turkey or chicken and as a sandwich spread.

Set the bread pan on the counter and insert the beater paddle(s). Add 12 ounces (340 g) fresh cranberries, ½ cup (75 g or 2.6 oz) dried cherries, 1 teaspoon ground ginger, and ¼ teaspoon ground allspice to the bread pan.

Bring 1 cup (240 ml) water, 1 cup (200 g or 7.1 oz) granulated cane sugar, and ⅛ teaspoon kosher salt to a boil in a small saucepan over medium heat. Stir to dissolve the sugar and pour into the bread pan.

Place the bread pan in the machine, settle it in the center, and lock it in place. Close the lid and select:

Jam cycle
Start

When the cycle is done, remove the pan from the machine. Let it cool for 10 minutes, then stir in 1 cup (180 g or 6 oz) pomegranate seeds. Cool completely before transferring to an airtight container. Store in the refrigerator for up to 1 week.

RIBOLLITA
(TUSCAN BREAD SOUP)

SERVES 4 ◆ DAIRY-FREE OPTION

On cool autumn days or in the middle of winter, there is nothing more warming and comforting than a bowl of hearty soup, especially if you enjoy it while sitting next to a roaring fire. Peasant soups like this ribollita are packed with healthy vegetables, inexpensive, easy to make, and a great way to use up stale bread. You just throw everything into a pot and let it cook. It will fill the house with wonderful aromas that will have your kids happy to come in from playing. When you have end slices or a little bit of a loaf left, put them in a resealable plastic bag and freeze them. When you have enough to make a pot of soup, pull it out and thaw overnight in the refrigerator.

1¾ cups (10 oz or 285 g) dried cannellini or other small white beans

2 tablespoons (30 ml) olive oil, plus more for serving

2 medium onions, sliced

2 carrots, cut into chunks

2 celery ribs, cut into chunks

2 russet potatoes, peeled and coarsely chopped

½ head cabbage, cored and cut into chunks

2 zucchini, trimmed and cut into chunks

2 bunches Swiss chard, tough stems discarded and leaves chopped

2 plum tomatoes, peeled, cored and cut into chunks

1 tablespoon dried oregano

Kosher or fine sea salt

Freshly ground black pepper

4 cups (950 ml) vegetable broth

10 ounces (283 g or ⅓ loaf) very stale bread, such as Italian Ciabatta (page 114) or French Baguette (page 119), cut into bite-size cubes

Grated Parmesan cheese, for serving, optional

Chopped fresh basil, for garnish

MAKE YOUR BREAD STALE

If you don't have any stale bread on hand, you can use a fresh loaf. Slice or cut it into cubes, place on a baking sheet, and bake in a low oven, about 250°F (120°C), until dry and firm but not crunchy, 1½ to 2½ hours. Don't worry if a few pieces get over-toasted. They will be soaking in the soup and absorbing its liquid.

1. Carefully sort through the beans, discarding any tiny pebbles or stones you find and any beans that are discolored or soft. Rinse well under cold water. Put the beans in a large saucepan and cover with cool water by at least 2 inches. Bring to a boil over high heat, reduce the heat to low, and simmer for 1 hour. Drain the beans, return to the pan, and cover with 2 quarts fresh water. Bring to a simmer and cook over low heat until the beans are tender but not mushy, 1½ to 2½ hours. Drain, reserving the cooking water.

2. Heat the oil in a large saucepan or stockpot over medium-high heat. Add the onions and cook, stirring often, until they have softened, about 3 minutes. Add the carrots and celery and cook for another 3 minutes, stirring often, then add the potatoes, cabbage, zucchini, Swiss chard, and tomatoes. Reduce the heat to medium and cook, stirring often, until all the vegetables have softened, about 10 minutes. Add the oregano and a little salt and pepper. Add half of the beans and 1 cup of the reserved cooking water.

3. Transfer the remaining beans to a blender with ½ cup of the cooking water. Puree until smooth, adding more cooking water as needed. Pour the pureed beans into the pot. Add the vegetable broth and stir. Add a pinch of salt and some fresh pepper, reduce the heat to low, and simmer, covered with the lid ajar to allow steam to escape, stirring occasionally, for 30 minutes.

4. Increase the heat to high, add the bread to the pot, and bring to a boil. Cook at a low boil for 10 minutes to break down the bread and thicken the soup. Taste and adjust the seasonings. Remove from the heat and let rest for 15 to 20 minutes.

5. Ladle the soup into serving bowls. Drizzle with a little olive oil, sprinkle with Parmesan if desired, and garnish with fresh basil. Serve, passing additional cheese at the table if desired.

PASSPORT TO FRANCE

Turn this into French onion soup! Set four oven-safe soup bowls on a rimmed baking sheet lined with a silicone baking mat (to help keep the bowls from sliding around). Fill the bowls almost to the top with hot soup. Set a round of toasted bread on the top of each serving and add a large handful of shredded cheese (a blend of mozzarella, Monterey jack, and Emmentaler is nice). Place under the broiler. Broil until the cheese is melted, bubbling, and starting to brown. Let the soup cool for a couple of minutes and then serve.

ARANCINI (CHEESY RISOTTO BALLS)

MAKES ABOUT 3 DOZEN

If you are looking for an appetizer to serve before an Italian-themed dinner party, these arancini are the perfect choice. Warm and crunchy, with a surprising melted cheese center, these breaded rice balls are sure to please everyone and set the mood for a wonderful evening. The next time you are preparing risotto for dinner, make twice as much and plan on making arancini for a wonderful dinner the following night.

2 cups (230 g or 8.1 oz) Homemade Plain Dry Bread Crumbs (page 340)

2 tablespoons minced fresh Italian parsley

2 teaspoons minced fresh basil, plus additional for garnish

1½ teaspoons dried oregano

1 teaspoon kosher or fine sea salt

½ teaspoon freshly ground black pepper

2 large eggs

1 recipe Creamy Risotto (see opposite), chilled overnight

8 ounces (225 g) fresh buffalo mozzarella, drained and cut into ¼-inch (6 mm) cubes

Vegetable oil (peanut, rice bran, or other oil with a high smoke point), for frying

Warmed Pizza Sauce (page 203), for serving

1. Combine the bread crumbs, parsley, basil, oregano, salt, and pepper in a shallow bowl. Stir until evenly blended. Beat the eggs in another shallow bowl and set beside the bread crumbs. Line a baking sheet with parchment paper and set it next to the bowls.

2. Wet your hands and scoop 1 tablespoon of risotto. Shape it into a flat disk in the palm of your hand. Place a mozzarella cube in the center and gently press the rice around the cheese, forming a ball. Roll it gently between your palms to make sure all the cheese is covered. Set it on the lined baking sheet and repeat until all the mozzarella cubes and risotto are used up.

3. Roll the rice balls in the beaten eggs and then in the bread crumb mixture, pressing gently to adhere the crumbs to the rice. Place back on the baking sheet.

4. Line another baking sheet with paper towels and set it next to the stove. Pour 2 inches (5 cm) of oil into a large Dutch oven. Turn the heat to medium-high. Use a candy or instant-read thermometer to monitor the temperature of the oil. When the oil reaches 350°F (180°C), carefully add 6 to 10 rice balls at a time, making sure there is plenty of room in the pot so they can move around easily and cook evenly. Keep the arancini moving constantly, turning them with a slotted spoon, until they are golden brown on all sides, 3 to 4 minutes. When done, transfer them to the lined baking sheet. Wait for the oil to return to 350°F (180°C) before frying the next batch. Continue until all the arancini are fried. You can keep the cooked arancini warm in a low oven.

5. Place the fried arancini on a platter. Garnish with chopped basil. Serve with warmed pizza sauce for dipping.

CREAMY RISOTTO

MAKES 4 SERVINGS

Bring 4 cups (1 liter) chicken stock to a simmer. Keep warm.

Heat 1 tablespoon unsalted butter and 2 tablespoons (30 ml) olive oil in a 10-inch (25 cm) nonstick sauté pan with 2-inch (5 cm) sides over medium-high heat. Add 1 minced shallot and 2 thinly sliced scallions and sauté until they have softened, 2 to 3 minutes. Add 1½ cups (150 g or 5.3 oz) Arborio rice and sauté, stirring, until all the grains are coated with the oil and lightly toasted, about 1 minute. Reduce the heat to medium, add ¾ cup (180 ml) dry white wine or dry vermouth, and cook, stirring occasionally, until the wine is absorbed.

Add a ladle of stock to the rice and cook, stirring, until the stock is mostly absorbed. To check, scrape a spoon across the bottom of the pan; there should be a channel, with the bottom of the pan visible. Continue adding stock, a ladle at a time, stirring frequently, until the rice is creamy and al dente; you may not need all the stock. This will take about 18 minutes. Taste the rice occasionally to judge doneness.

Whisk in ¼ cup (25 g or 1 oz) grated Parmesan cheese. Taste and adjust the seasoning with salt and pepper.

The risotto will thicken as it stands. Keep extra warm stock on the stove to stir in just before serving for the best consistency.

Spoon the risotto into warmed dishes, sprinkling the top with chopped chives. Serve immediately.

If you are making this for Arancini (page 360), spread the cooked risotto out on a baking sheet and let it cool a bit, then cover with plastic wrap and refrigerate overnight.

ITALIAN MEATBALLS

SERVES 5 TO 6 • *DAIRY-FREE OPTION*

Serve these meatballs with pasta for a traditional Italian-American main course or on their own with a little sauce as a first course. Or put them in a chafing dish with marinara or Pizza Sauce (page 203) as an hors d'oeuvre at your next party. Be sure to have a bowl of grated Parmesan cheese for your guests to sprinkle over the top. And on game day, everyone loves meatball sandwiches dripping with sauce.

¼ cup (30 g or 1.1 oz) Homemade Plain Dry Bread Crumbs (page 340)

3 tablespoons (45 ml) milk (regular or nondairy, such as unsweetened soy or almond milk)

1 large egg

¼ cup (40 g or 1.4 oz) grated onion

3 tablespoons (19 g or 0.7 oz) grated Parmesan cheese (or nondairy cheese)

1 teaspoon Worcestershire sauce (Lea & Perrins brand is gluten free)

1 tablespoon dried Italian herb blend

1 teaspoon dried oregano

½ teaspoon dry mustard

½ teaspoon kosher or fine sea salt

¼ teaspoon freshly ground black pepper

¼ teaspoon garlic powder

1 pound (455 g) ground beef (80% lean), ground pork, ground dark turkey, or a combination

1. Stir the bread crumbs and milk together in a small bowl. Set aside to soak.

2. Set an oven rack in the center of the oven and preheat to 400°F (200°F). Line a rimmed baking sheet with parchment paper.

3. Beat the egg in a large mixing bowl. Add the onion, Parmesan, Worcestershire, Italian herb blend, oregano, mustard, salt, pepper, and garlic powder. Whisk to combine. Add the ground meat and soaked bread crumbs. Use your hands to mix everything together. Roll the mixture into balls the size of ping-pong balls, about 2 tablespoons per meatball. Do not compress them too much, just enough to hold together. Set the meatballs on the lined baking sheet.

4. Bake until an instant-read thermometer registers 165°F (74°C) when inserted in the center, 20 to 30 minutes. Less fatty meats will cook faster and can easily dry out, so watch them carefully and pull them out of the oven at about 162°F (72°C). Residual heat will finish the cooking. Each oven is different, so go by the internal temperature more than the timing.

5. The meatballs can be made ahead of time. Let the cooked meatballs cool completely on the baking sheet. Store, covered, in the refrigerator. To freeze, slip the cooled meatballs into the freezer for at least an hour. Then transfer to a resealable plastic bag and freeze for up to 2 months. Place frozen meatballs in a pot of simmering sauce to thaw, or bake for 15 minutes to reheat.

RESIDUAL HEAT

Because of carryover or residual heat, you can pull proteins off the heat before they have reached their final temperature. As meat rests, it will continue to cook, and the internal temperature will rise anywhere from 5 to 10 degrees.

OLD-FASHIONED MEATLOAF

There is something so comforting about foods from our childhood. Made with turkey and plenty of vegetables, this meatloaf is a healthier version of a comfort food classic. And it's packed with flavor.

MEATLOAF

3 tablespoons (45 ml) olive oil

½ large onion, finely chopped

3 celery ribs, finely chopped

½ red bell pepper, finely chopped

¼ teaspoon dried rosemary

1 pound (455 g) ground dark turkey, beef, or pork, or a combination

⅓ cup (40 g or 1.4 oz) Homemade Plain Dry Bread Crumbs (page 340)

½ teaspoon onion powder

¼ teaspoon garlic powder

Kosher or fine sea salt

Freshly ground black pepper

1 large egg, beaten

GLAZE

½ cup (120 g or 4.2 oz) ketchup

1 tablespoon packed brown sugar

1 teaspoon prepared mustard (yellow, Dijon, or spicy brown)

½ teaspoon chipotle powder, optional

1. Heat the olive oil in a 10-inch (25 cm) nonstick skillet over medium-high heat. Add the onion, celery, and bell pepper. Cook, stirring often, for 2 to 3 minutes. Add the rosemary and continue cooking until the vegetables have wilted and are just beginning to brown slightly, 4 to 6 minutes. Set aside to cool.

2. Set a rack in the center of the oven and preheat to 350°F (180°C).

3. Put the ground meat in a large mixing bowl and add the bread crumbs, onion and garlic powders, salt, and pepper. Use your hands to combine the ingredients. Add the cooled vegetables and the beaten egg. Mix until all the ingredients are evenly distributed.

4. Transfer the mixture to a rimmed baking sheet and press into a mounded oval shape. Not using a loaf pan gives you a lot more surface area for the glaze and thus a crispier crust.

5. Whisk the glaze ingredients together in a small bowl. Brush half of the glaze over the top and sides of the meatloaf.

6. Bake the meatloaf for 30 minutes. Rotate the baking sheet and brush the meatloaf with the remaining glaze. Continue baking until an instant-read thermometer inserted in the center registers 163°F to 165°F (73°C to 74°C), 15 to 20 minutes.

7. Let rest for about 10 minutes so the slices hold together better. Cut into thick slices and serve while hot.

FOOD SAFETY NOTE

Solid pieces of meat have bacteria only on the outside, which is killed at 140°F (60°C), or when the exterior is browned. When meat is cut up and ground, the bacteria gets dispersed all the way through, requiring a higher finished temperature. The center of meatloaf, meatballs, hamburgers, and other dishes using ground beef needs to register 165°F (74°C) in order to be safe to eat.

SAUSAGE STRATA
(SAVORY BREAD PUDDING)

<u>SERVES 8 TO 10</u>

Strata is a fancy name for a savory bread pudding. Bread cubes are soaked in an egg mixture until softened and then baked until golden. Crispy on top and creamy in the center, it is the perfect way to start any day. It's great when you're cooking for a crowd because you can assemble it in advance and concentrate on the rest of the meal while it bakes. Any fairly neutral-flavored bread will work, but the Pizza Pie Bread (page 156) would also be a fun choice, adding an Italian flavor profile that you could enhance with extra oregano and basil. Gluten-free breads are delicate, so pay attention to the soaking times to avoid making a goopy mess. If all you can find are sausage links, remove the meat from the casings before cooking.

8 slices day-old bread, such as Simple Sandwich Bread (page 38), Sourdough Sandwich Bread (page 180), Golden Millet Bread (page 68), Pizza Pie Bread (page 156), or Brioche Hamburger and Hot Dog Buns (page 92)

1 pound (455 g) bulk pork, chicken, or turkey sausage

8 large eggs

1 cup (240 ml) whole milk

1 cup (120 g or 4.2 oz) grated mild cheese, such as cheddar, Colby, Monterey Jack, Havarti, or a blend of your choice

2 tablespoons (28 g or 1 oz/¼ stick) cold unsalted butter, cut into small cubes

3 scallions, trimmed and chopped, plus extra for garnish

½ red bell pepper, finely chopped

½ teaspoon kosher or fine sea salt

½ teaspoon freshly ground black pepper

1. Preheat the oven to 350°F (180°C). Butter a 9 x 13-inch (23 x 33 cm) baking dish.

2. Trim the crusts from the loaf and then cut the bread into ½-inch (1 cm) cubes. Store the crusts in the freezer, and when you have enough, grind into bread crumbs or use in Ribollita (page 358). Spread out on a baking sheet and bake, shaking the pan occasionally, until the cubes are lightly toasted, about 15 minutes. Set aside to cool.

3. Cook the sausage in a large skillet over medium heat until browned, breaking up clumps as they form. Use a slotted spoon to transfer the sausage to a paper towel-lined plate. Pat with additional paper towels until the excess grease has been absorbed. Set aside to cool.

4. Whisk the eggs in a very large mixing bowl. Stir in the remaining ingredients, including the sausage and bread cubes; blend well. Pour into the baking dish and set aside for 15 minutes to allow the bread to absorb some of the liquid.

5. Lower the oven temperature to 325°F (170°C).

6. Bake until the strata has puffed up and is firm in the center, about 1 hour.

7. Let the strata rest for about 15 minutes, then cut into squares, sprinkle with the extra chopped scallions, and serve.

EASY ROMESCO SAUCE

MAKES ABOUT 2 CUPS (480 ML) ◆ DAIRY FREE

This sauce—made from almonds, red peppers, and bread—was first created in Tarragona, Spain. Originally, it was made by Spanish fishermen to eat with their meals, and it will make you feel as if you have traveled to the coast of Spain. Spread some on your toast for the perfect open-faced sandwich—top with a poached egg, crispy bacon, and some sliced avocado for breakfast or brunch.

2 slices Almost Wheat Sandwich Bread (page 56) or any neutral-flavored bread

½ cup (55 g or 1.9 oz) slivered almonds

2 garlic cloves, peeled

7 ounces (198 g) jarred roasted red peppers, drained

⅔ cup (160 ml) olive oil

2 tablespoons (30 ml) sherry vinegar

1 teaspoon kosher salt

½ teaspoon smoked paprika, optional

Kosher or fine sea salt

Freshly ground black pepper

1. Preheat the oven to 400°F (200°C).

2. Spread out the bread slices, almonds, and garlic cloves on a rimmed baking sheet. Bake until lightly toasted, 8 to 10 minutes.

3. Transfer the bread, almonds, and garlic to a food processor. Add the remaining ingredients and pulse until smooth. If needed, add 1 to 2 tablespoons (15 to 30 ml) water to thin the sauce. Taste and adjust the seasonings.

4. Transfer the sauce to an airtight container and store in the refrigerator for up to 1 week.

BREAKFAST EGGS IN A NEST

SERVES 2

There is something so cheery when you sit down to breakfast and see a smiling face on your plate, looking back at you. The concept is simple—cut a hole in a piece of toast and cook an egg in the center. It's all the same ingredients as usual but presented in a fun way that makes any day bright and sunny.

4 slices bread, such as Simple Sandwich Bread (page 38), Tender Buttermilk Bread (page 42), or Easy Sorghum Sandwich Bread (page 58)

1 tablespoon unsalted butter

4 large eggs

Kosher or sea salt and freshly ground black pepper to taste

1. Set the slices of bread on a cutting board and use a 3-inch cookie cutter to cut a circle out of the center of each slice.

2. Place a griddle over medium heat and rub the butter over the surface. Place the 4 slices of bread on the griddle, creating a square, and place the four circles outside the square. Break an egg into the hole of each piece of bread. Sprinkle with salt and pepper to taste. When the egg is cooked about halfway through and set on the bottom, use a spatula to flip the circles and each piece of bread. Finish cooking the eggs, about 1 minute.

3. Flip upright and transfer to warmed dinner plates. Serve hot.

FRENCH TOAST WITH BLUEBERRY MAPLE SYRUP

SERVES 6 TO 8

French toast is always a popular breakfast dish, and when served with this blueberry maple syrup, it is extra special. The blueberries add a touch of tartness that balances the sweetness of the syrup. If you want to make this look fancy, add a dollop of sweetened whipped cream and scatter a few fresh blueberries over the top.

10 large eggs

1½ cups (360 ml) half-and-half or whole milk

1 teaspoon pure vanilla extract

Vegetable oil

1 loaf bread, such as Brioche Loaf (page 48), Buttery Challah (page 116), Tender Buttermilk Bread (page 42), or Portuguese Sweet Bread (page 166), sliced about ½-inch (1 cm) thick

Blueberry Maple Syrup (see opposite), for serving

1. Preheat the oven to 225°F (107°C).

2. Whisk the eggs, half-and-half, and vanilla together in a large bowl. Transfer to a 9 x 13-inch (23 x 33 cm) casserole and set next to the stove.

3. Heat a griddle over medium-high heat and brush the surface with about 2 tablespoons of vegetable oil.

4. Working in batches, dip the bread slices into the egg mixture, letting them sit for about 15 seconds on each side. Place the dipped bread slices on the griddle and cook until browned and cooked through, 2 to 3 minutes per side. Transfer to a baking sheet and keep warm in the oven while you cook the rest of the French toast.

5. Serve hot with the Blueberry Maple Syrup.

BLUEBERRY MAPLE SYRUP

MAKES ABOUT 2¼ CUPS (600 ML)

Combine 1½ cups (360 ml) pure maple syrup and 1 to 2 cups (150 to 300 g) rinsed frozen blueberries in a small saucepan over medium-low heat. Cook, pressing down lightly on the berries to release some of their juices and stirring occasionally, until the syrup is warm and the flavors have blended, about 3 minutes. Add a little lemon juice if desired to cut the sweetness.

When you are ready to serve, transfer some of the syrup to a warmed pitcher. Place the pitcher on a small plate to catch any drips and serve with your choice of French toast, pancakes, or waffles.

Store any leftover syrup in a sealed jar in the refrigerator for up to 1 week.

NOTE: If using fresh blueberries instead of frozen, add 2 cups of fresh berries to the syrup and cook for about 5 minutes. Then smash to release the juices.

HAWAIIAN BREAD PUDDING

SERVES 8

This bread pudding, served with chunks of caramelized pineapple and a coconut crème anglaise, is the perfect way to highlight our Sweet Hawaiian Bread. This is definitely a special occasion treat, so serve it when you have a large group coming to dinner. That way you won't be tempted to eat the entire pan yourself.

BREAD PUDDING

1 loaf slightly stale Sweet Hawaiian Bread (page 164)

3 large eggs

1½ cups (300 g or 10.6 oz) granulated cane sugar

3½ to 4 cups (830 to 950 ml) whole milk

2 tablespoons (30 ml) pure vanilla extract

COCONUT CRÈME ANGLAISE

1 cup (240 ml) whole milk

⅓ cup (80 ml) heavy cream or half-and-half

2 teaspoons pure vanilla extract

6 tablespoons (75 g or 2.6 oz) granulated cane sugar

4 large egg yolks, at room temperature

4 to 6 drops coconut flavoring

2 tablespoons (30 ml) dark rum, optional

FOR SERVING

Caramelized Pineapple Chunks (see opposite)

Fresh mint sprigs

1. Set a rack in the center of the oven and preheat to 350°F (180°C). Butter a 9 x 13-inch (23 x 33 cm) baking dish. Place a wire strainer over a bowl and set aside.

2. Cut the bread into large cubes. The bread should have a tender crust, but if your machine bakes hotter and the crust is dark, cut it off and then cube the bread. Freeze the crusts for later use.

3. Whisk the eggs, sugar, milk, and vanilla together in a large bowl until the sugar is dissolved. Add the bread cubes and mix well. Let sit for 10 minutes.

4. Scoop the bread mixture into the baking dish. Cover with aluminum foil and bake for 1 hour, rotating the dish after about 30 minutes. Remove the foil, return to the oven, and continue to bake until the top is

golden brown and the center is fully set, about 15 minutes. Set on a wire rack to cool.

5. While the bread pudding is baking, make the coconut crème anglaise. Bring the milk and cream to a simmer in a small saucepan over medium-low heat. Stir regularly so the cream doesn't stick to the bottom of the pan. Stir in the vanilla.

6. While the cream is heating, whisk the sugar and egg yolks together in a medium bowl until light and fluffy.

7. When the cream mixture comes to a simmer, remove it from the heat and stir in the coconut flavoring and rum (if using). Whisking constantly, slowly ladle half of the hot cream mixture into the eggs to temper them. While whisking briskly, pour the tempered eggs back into the saucepan.

8. Place the saucepan back over medium heat and cook, stirring constantly, until the sauce thickens and coats the back of a spoon. Pour the sauce through the wire strainer into the bowl. Use a flexible spatula to gently push the sauce through and don't forget to scrape the bottom of the strainer to get every drop. Discard any solids.

9. The sauce can be served warm, at room temperature, or slightly chilled. If serving cool, place the bowl with the crème anglaise in a shallow bowl of ice water to chill it quickly, stirring as it cools. Store, covered, in the refrigerator, for up to 3 days.

10. Scoop the warm bread pudding into serving bowls. Drizzle a little of the crème anglaise over the top and add a few pieces of caramelized pineapple. Garnish with a sprig of mint and serve.

CARAMELIZED PINEAPPLE CHUNKS

MAKES ABOUT 2 CUPS (600 G/21 OZ)

Drain 2 (20-ounce/567 g) cans of pineapple chunks packed in pineapple juice (*not* syrup) in a strainer set over a bowl. Reserve the juice.

Transfer the pineapple to a 12-inch (30 cm) skillet and sprinkle with 1 cup firmly packed (225 g or 7.9 oz) brown sugar and 1 tablespoon (15 ml) of the reserved pineapple juice. Set the skillet over medium-high heat and cook, stirring regularly, until the sugar has caramelized and the liquid has almost completely evaporated, 10 to 20 minutes. The larger the skillet, the faster this will reduce. The pineapple will soften and take on a lovely golden color.

Remove from the heat. Add more of the juice if desired. Serve warm, as the sauce will thicken as it cools. Store any leftovers, covered, in the refrigerator for up to 1 week.

BLUEBERRY BREAD PUDDING WITH CRÈME ANGLAISE

SERVES 8

When we saw Chef Dennis Littley's photo of his beautiful blueberry bread pudding, we knew it would be the perfect way to showcase our Portuguese Sweet Bread, and he graciously allowed us to adapt his recipe. The subtle sweetness of the bread is a lovely counterpoint to the slight tartness of the berries.

BREAD PUDDING

1 loaf slightly stale Portuguese Sweet Bread (page 166)

3 large eggs

1½ cups (300 g or 10.6 oz) granulated cane sugar

3½ to 4 cups (830 to 950 ml) whole milk

2 tablespoons (30 ml) pure vanilla extract

1 teaspoon ground cinnamon

2 cups (290 g) fresh blueberries, picked over and rinsed

4 tablespoons (56 g or 2 oz/½ stick) unsalted butter, melted, optional

CRÈME ANGLAISE

1 cup (240 ml) whole milk

⅓ cup (80 ml) heavy cream or half-and-half

1 teaspoon pure vanilla extract

6 tablespoons (75 g or 2.6 oz) granulated cane sugar

4 large egg yolks, at room temperature

1. Set a rack in the center of the oven and preheat the oven to 350°F (180°C). Butter a 9 x 13-inch (23 x 33 cm) baking dish. Place a wire strainer over a bowl and set next to the stove.

2. Cut the bread into large cubes. The bread should have a tender crust, but if your machine bakes hotter and the crust is dark, cut it off and then cube the bread. Freeze the crusts for later use.

3. Whisk the eggs, sugar, milk, vanilla, and cinnamon together in a large mixing bowl until the sugar is dissolved. Add the bread cubes to the bowl and mix well. Let sit for about 10 minutes. Fold the blueberries into the mixture, distributing them evenly.

4. Transfer the bread mixture to the baking dish. Brush the melted butter over the top. Cover the pan with aluminum foil and bake for 1 hour. Remove the foil. If the butter has pooled in any areas, brush it over the top of the pudding, helping to promote browning. Return to the oven and continue to bake until the center is fully set and the top is beautifully browned, about 15 minutes. Set on a wire rack to cool to lukewarm.

5. For the crème anglaise, bring the milk and half-and-half to a simmer in a small saucepan set over medium-low heat. Stir regularly so the cream doesn't stick to the bottom of the pan. Stir in the vanilla.

6. Meanwhile, whisk the sugar and egg yolks together in a mixing bowl until light and fluffy.

7. When the milk mixture comes to a simmer, remove it from the heat. Whisking constantly, slowly ladle half of the hot milk mixture into the eggs to temper them. While whisking briskly, pour the tempered eggs back into the saucepan.

8. Place the saucepan back over medium heat and cook, stirring constantly, until the sauce thickens and coats the back of a spoon. Pour the sauce through the wire strainer into the bowl. Use a flexible spatula to gently push the sauce through and don't forget to scrape the bottom of the strainer to get every drop. Discard any solids.

9. The sauce can be served warm, at room temperature, or slightly chilled. If serving cool, place the bowl with the crème anglaise in a shallow bowl of ice water to cool it down quickly, stirring as it cools. Store, covered, in the refrigerator, for up to 3 days.

10. Serve squares of the pudding warm with the crème anglaise.

Resources

SHOPPING GUIDE

Amazon	A great source for nearly all the equipment and ingredients you will use regularly.	amazon.com
Amphora Nueva	Tunisian baklouti oil, for a pop of spice and flavor; use sparingly at first, adding more as desired.	amphoranueva.com
Anti-Grain	Butternut squash flour, sweet potato flour, and apple flour.	anti-grain.com
Arianna Trading Company	Products imported from Greece, including the olive oil used in developing the recipes for this book.	ariannatradingcompany.com
Authentic Foods	The best superfine-grind gluten-free flours available, made and packaged in a dedicated gluten-free facility. Their Multi-Blend Flour can be used as an alternative for the flour blends in the book. *Note:* This blend contains xanthan gum, so reduce the xanthan in our recipes by half.	authenticfoods.com
Baking Steel	The Baking Steel is the perfect way to get crispy pizza crusts in your oven without worrying about breakage.	bakingsteel.com
Bell Plantation	PB2 powdered peanut butter in regular and chocolate flavor.	bellplantation.com
Bob's Red Mill	Gluten-free flours and ingredients made and packaged in a dedicated gluten-free facility. Their 1-to-1 Baking Flour can be used as an alternative for the flour blends in the book. *Note:* This blend contains xanthan gum, so reduce the xanthan in our recipes by half.	bobsredmill.com
Cabot	Cheddar cheese powder, as well as many delicious cheeses.	cabotcheese.coop
Cambro	Containers to hold flour blends; food-safe with tight-fitting lids for years of use.	cambro.com
Cultures for Health	Brown rice sourdough starter, one of the few gluten-free starters on the market.	culturesforhealth.com
Edison Grainery	Organic quinoa bran, an excellent source of natural fiber, similar in texture to millet and teff flours.	edisongrainery.com
Enjoy Life	Nondairy, gluten-free, vegan chocolate chips and chunks.	enjoylifefoods.com
Gourmet Garden	Herb and spice pastes and lightly dried herbs that taste like fresh!	gourmetgarden.com/en-us
JB Prince	Long-handled kitchen tweezers.	jbprince.com
King Arthur Flour	Gluten-free flours and baking equipment. Their Gluten-Free All-Purpose Baking Mix can be used as a substitute for the flour blends in the book.	kingarthurflour.com
LorAnn	Oils and flavorings for baked goods, candy making, and ice cream making. Their products are extremely high quality and will give you the flavor you are looking for without an aftertaste.	lorannoils.com
Mountain Rose Herbs	Organic herbs and seasonings with reduced bulk rates.	mountainroseherbs.com

Namaste Foods for Everyone	A wide variety of gluten-free baking mixes and an excellent gluten-free all-purpose flour blend called Perfect Flour Blend.	namastefoods.com
Nutiva	Coconut flour and other gluten-free products.	nutiva.com
Penzey's	Nearly all the herbs and spices a cook and baker needs; available in individual sizes, or save money by buying in bulk.	penzeys.com
Spice Ace	Offers more than 400 spices, herbs, salts, chillies, and other seasonings.	spiceace.com
Sur la Table	All types of kitchen tools, bakeware, pizza stones, baking steels, dockers, and more.	surlatable.com
The Kosher Cook	Silicone challah molds.	thekoshercook.com
The Spice House	Excellent resource for less common herbs, spices, and seasonings such as tomato powder and chai powder.	thespicehouse.com
ThermoWorks	Instant-read thermometers and timers, such as their Thermapen and the TimeStick Trio timer.	thermoworks.com
USA Pan	Biscotti pans for ciabatta, specialized hot dog bun pans, muffin pans, and much more.	usapans.com
Vance's Foods	DariFree is a gluten-free, casein-free, fat-free, potato-based milk powder substitute. Suitable for a variety of dietary restrictions.	vancesfoods.com
Whole Spice	A huge selection of freshly ground spices, herbs, and blends, including organic varieties. We get our caraway powder here.	wholespice.com

MORE HELP WITH HIGH-ALTITUDE BAKING

- Go to the Colorado State University Extension website (extension.colostate.edu) and search "high altitude food preparation p41."

  You can purchase either of the following publications from the CSU Extension online store: csuextstore.com.

- *A Complete Guide to High Altitude Baking*: Detailed information and 200 delicious recipes. You will have to adjust these recipes for gluten-free baking; use our flour blends in place of the wheat flours called for (120 g per cup of regular flour) and make more adjustments as needed.

- *Wheat, Gluten, Egg, and Milk-Free Recipes at High Altitudes and Sea Level*: A great resource for people with multiple dietary restrictions, this book contains 43 recipes designed specifically for high-altitude baking. You can use these recipes as a guide for adapting other favorites.

About the Authors

JANE BONACCI is a freelance food and travel writer, recipe developer, editor, and event manager. She grew up at her grandmother and mother's sides, watching as each recipe was made, learning by example and with gentle supervision, mastering the traditional recipes of her family's heritage. Being diagnosed with gluten intolerance opened new horizons as she explored different techniques and ingredients to create recipes everyone can safely eat and enjoy. On her website *The Heritage Cook*, Jane shares her memories, experiences, and guidance, enticing people to get back in the kitchen and helping them become as ardent about cooking and baking as she is. Her goal is to help families return to the custom of sharing meals together with the hope that culinary traditions continue to be passed from one generation to the next.

SHANNON KINSELLA graduated with honors from the Cooking and Hospitality Institute of Chicago's Le Cordon Bleu College of Culinary Arts and has an associate's degree in Culinary Arts and Italian Culinary Exploration from Etoile Academy in Venice. Influenced by world cuisines—most notably French, Italian, and Mexican—Shannon has traveled extensively and lived in the French countryside. She also worked behind the scenes as Kitchen Director for over 100 episodes of chef Rick Bayless's television cooking show "Mexico: One Plate at a Time." Her areas of expertise include research and development, recipe testing and writing, demonstrations, trade show representation, teaching, food styling, culinary tours, and project management for several corporate clients including Kraft Kitchens, Sara Lee, The Pampered Chef, the National Cattlemen's Beef Association, the National Pork Board, Sur La Table, Riba Foods, ConAgra Foods, *Cooking Light* magazine, and Frontera Foods. An active member of the International Association of Culinary Professionals (IACP) since 2001, Shannon was on the host committee for the 2007 Chicago IACP. The current program chair for the board of the Chicago chapter of Les Dames d'Escoffier, Shannon also volunteers for various arts organizations, Girl Scouts, and Chicago-area schools.

Acknowledgments

This book would not have been possible without the generosity of some special people. Thank you to Steve at Authentic Foods for sharing not only his incredible products but also his personal experience as we figured out the right formula for the base flour blends and surmounted the challenges of creating beautiful loaves of bread in a wide variety of bread machines.

The generous donations and support from Arianna Trading, Authentic Foods, and California Olive Ranch helped us develop these recipes. We are forever grateful to our recipe testers for their invaluable feedback in helping to hone our recipes and make this book a reality.

FROM JANE BONACCI

It takes a village…and I am blessed with incredible family and friends. Thank you for your unflagging support, your compassion, and for always making me laugh. Know that you are loved and appreciated. My admiration knows no bounds for Katrina, our most prolific tester. You are a true blessing. Thanks to Dr. Jean Layton for helping me understand the nuances of sourdough baking. Thank you to Amy Atherton for her guidance in making dairy-free adjustments, as well as her never-ending positivity, and Kate McDermott, who shared invaluable support and insight. My greatest thanks go to my loving husband James, who always gave me his honest opinion, washed dishes after hours of testing, and never let me forget how much he believes in me.

FROM SHANNON KINSELLA

My first inspiration was my grandmother Catherine Riley, who exemplified the meaning of master baker. She loved baking, but it was also necessary to feed her family of 14. My Dad taught me that I could be anything I wanted. Without his love of travel and adventure, I would not have lived in France during a formative time in my life. He believed that when in Rome, or in this case France, we should embrace the culture and the food—and I have never looked back. My French boyfriend taught me to make *pissaladier* (caramelized onion pizza with olives), and my love of making homemade pizza dough was born. France's baked goods continue to inspire me to make gluten-free versions that will even delight wheat lovers. My brothers (you know who you are) have influenced my culinary journey and been wonderful cheerleaders and tasters. Thanks to my sister Meghan and her family, who allow me to take over their kitchen no matter the project, and who indulge me every time I turn up on their doorstop with my dietary parameters. Thank you to my amazing circle of friends, The Ashepoo Council and Bookworms to name a few, who have supported and encouraged me. The culinary community, which embraced me through IACP and Les Dames, has taught me so much—especially Jean Marie Brownson, an amazing boss, mentor, and friend. Last, but not least, thank you to my favorite dish washer for the past 29 years: my husband Gene. He will eat, haul, and most importantly clean up any mess I create.

Index